PYTHON

PYTHON

An Introduction to Programming

James R. Parker
University of Calgary

MERCURY LEARNING AND INFORMATION
Dulles, Virginia
Boston, Massachusetts
New Delhi

Publisher: David Pallai

Mercury Learning and Information
22841 Quicksilver Drive
Dulles, VA 20166
info@merclearning.com
www.merclearning.com
(800) 232-0223

James R. Parker. *PYTHON: An Introduction to Programming.*
ISBN: 978-1-9445346-5-3

The publisher recognizes and respects all marks used by companies, manufacturers, and developers as a means to distinguish their products. All brand names and product names mentioned in this book are trademarks or service marks of their respective companies. Any omission or misuse (of any kind) of service marks or trademarks, etc. is not an attempt to infringe on the property of others.

Library of Congress Control Number: 2016915244

161718321   Printed in the United States of America
This book is printed on acid-free paper.

Our titles are available for adoption, license, or bulk purchase by institutions, corporations, etc. For additional information, please contact the Customer Service Dept. at 800-232-0223 (toll free). Digital versions of our titles are available at: www.authorcloudware.com and other e-vendors. All companion files are available by writing to the publisher at info@merclearning.com.

The sole obligation of Mercury Learning and Information to the purchaser is to replace the book and/or disc, based on defective materials or faulty workmanship, but not based on the operation or functionality of the product.

Contents

Preface

This book is intended to teach introductory programming. Material is included for the introductory computer science course, but also for students and readers in science and other disciplines. I firmly believe that programming is an essential skill for all professionals and especially academics in the 21st century and have emphasized that in the content discussed in the book.

The book uses a "just-in-time" approach, meaning that I try to present new information just before or just after the reader needs it. As a result, there are numerous examples, carefully selected to fit into their proper places in the text. Not too soon, and not too late.

I believe in object-oriented programming. My master's thesis in the late 1970s was on that subject, cut my teeth on *Simula*, was there when C++ was created, and knew the creator of Java. I do not believe that object-oriented programming is the only solution, though, and realized early that good objects can only be devised by someone who can already program. I am therefore not an "objects first" instructor, but a "whatever works best" instructor.

Many of the examples involve computer games and game development. As we know, the majority of undergraduate students play games. They understand them better than, say, accounting or inventory systems, which have been the typical early assignments. I believe in presenting students assignments that are interesting.

I don't think that catering to any particular language form in an introductory text serves the student or the language. The student, if sensible, will learn other languages. Bringing Python idioms into play *too* soon may interfere with the generality of the ideas being presented and will not assist the student when learning Java, C++, or Ruby.

This book introduces a multimedia code module *Glib* that can assist the programmer with graphics, animation, sound, interaction, and video. Glib is included on the companion disc or can be downloaded from the book's web site. The basic library, *static Glib*, needs nothing but a standard 3.4 or better installation of Python. It uses *tkinter* as a basis, which is distributed with the language. The expanded library uses *pygame*, and that is easily downloaded and installed. The extended *Glib*, called *dynamic Glib*, allows exactly the same interface as does *static Glib*, but extends it to also include sound, interface, and video. Thus, if *static Glib* compiles and runs a program, then *dynamic Glib* should too.

There is a wiki concerning the book at *https://sites.google.com/site/python-parker/* and I am happy to receive comments, code fixes, extensions, extra teaching material, and general suggestions. I see a good textbook as a community, and encourage everyone – especially first year students, the target audience of this book - to send me their experiences and ideas.

Software (any computer program) is ubiquitous. Cars, phones, refrigerators, television, (and almost everything in our society) are computerized. Decisions made about how a program is to be built tend to survive, and even after many modifications, they can affect how people use that device or system. Creating efficient software helps in achieving a productive and happy civilization.

Python is a great language for beginning programmers. It is easy to write the first programs, because the conceptual overhead is small. That is, there's no need to understand what "void" or "public" means at the outset. Python does many things for a programmer. Do you want something sorted? It's a part of the language. Lists and hash tables (dictionaries) are a part of the language. You can write classes, but do not have to, so it can be taught *objects first* or not. The required indentation means that it is much harder to place code incorrectly in loops or if statements. There are hundreds of reasons why Python is a great idea.

And it is *free*. This book was written using version 3.4, and with the *PyCharm* API. The modules used that require download are few, but include *PyGame* and *tweepy*. All free.

Overview of Chapters

Here's a brief outline of the book. It can be used to teach computer science majors or science students who wish to have a competency in programming.

Chapter 0: Historical and technological material on computers. Binary numbers, the fetch-excute cycle. This chapter can be skipped in some syllabi.

Chapter 1: Problem solving with a computer; breaking a problem down so it can be solved. The Python system. Some simple programs involving games that introduce variables, expressions, print, types, and the **if** statement.

Chapter 2: Repetition in programming: **while** and **for** statements. Random numbers. Counting loops, nested loops. *Drawing a histogram.* Exceptions (**try-except**).

Chapter 3: Strings and string operations. Tuples, their definition and use. Lists and list comprehension. Editing, slices. The *bytes* type. And set types. Example: the game of *craps*.

Chapter 4: Functions: modular programming. Defining a function, calling a function. Parameters, including default parameters, and scope. Return values. Recursion. *The Game of Sticks.* Variable parameter lists, assigning a function to a variable. Find the maximum of a mathematical function. Modules. *Game of Nim.*

Chapter 5: Files. What is a file and how are files represented. Properties of files. File exceptions. Input, output, append, **open**, **close**. Comma separated value (CSV) files. Game of *Jeopardy.* The **with** statement.

Chapter 6: Classes and object orientation. What is an object and what is a class? Types and classes. Python class structure. Creating instances, __init__ and **self**. Encapsulation. Examples: *deck of playing cards*; a *bouncing ball*; *Cat-a-pult*. Designing with classes. Subclasses and inheritance. Video game objects. Duck typing.

Chapter 7: Graphics. The *Glib* module. Drawing window; color representation, pixels. Drawing lines, curves, and polygons. Filling. Drawing text. Example: *Histogram*, *Pie chart*. Images and image display, getting and setting pixels. *Thresholding.* Generative art.

Chapter 8: Data and information. Python dictionaries. *Latin to English translator.* Arrays, formatted text, formatted input/output. *Meteorite landing* *data*. Non-text files and the *struct* module. *High score file* example. Random access. Image and sound file types.

Chapter 9: Digital media: dynamic *Glib* module. Using the mouse and the keyboard. Animation. *Space shuttle control console* example. Transparent colors. Sound: playing sound files, volume, pause. Video: play and position a video, accessing frames and pixels in a video.

Chapter 10: Basic algorithms in computer science. Sorting (selection, merge) and searching (linear, binary). Timing code execution. Generating random numbers; cryptography; data compression (including Huffman codes and RLE); hashing.

Chapter 11: Programming for Science. Roots of equations; differentiation and integration. Optimization (minimum and maximum) and curve fitting (regression). Evolutionary algorithms. Longest common subsequence, or edit distance.

Chapter 12: Writing **good** code. A walk through two major projects: a word processor written as procedural code and a *breakout* game written as object oriented code. A collection of effective rules for writing good code.

Chapter 13: Dealing with real world interfaces, which tend to defined for you. Examples are Email (send and receive), FTP, inter-process communication (client-server), Twitter, calling other languages like C++.

Chapter 14: A reference for both versions of Glib.

Chapter Coverage for Different Majors

A **computer science** introduction could use most chapters, depending on the background of the students, but Chapters 0, 7, 9, and / or 11 could be omitted.

An **introduction to programming for science** could omit chapters 0, 10, 12.

Chapter 13 is always optional, but is interesting as it explains how social media software works under the interface.

Basic **introduction to programming for non-science** should include Chapters 0, 1, 2, 3, 4, 5, and 7.

Companion Files (*Disc included in physical book or files available for downloading*)

The companion files contain useful material for each chapter:

- Selected exercises are solved, including working code when that is a part of the solution.

- All significant programming examples are provided as Python code files(over 100), that can be compiled and executed, and that can be modified as exercises or class projects. This includes sample data files when appropriate.

- An important aspect of this book is the use of a *graphics library* named Glib. Source code for this module is provided on the disc and online. There are two versions: one that works with the built-in module tkinter which allows graphics, and a second that extends the previous module using *pyGame* and allows videos, interaction, and sound.

- All figures are available as images, in full color.

Instructor Ancillaries

- Solutions to almost all of the programming exercises given in the text.

- MS PowerPoint *lectures* provided for an entire semester (35 files) including some new examples and short videos.

- Likely the most important aspect of this book, aside from the very practical viewpoint, is the provision of the Glib *graphics and multimedia library*. This comes in two versions: a universal version that handles basic graphics and that can execute without any extra installation step; and the full multimedia extension that handles sound, video, and interaction, but that requires that *pyGame* be installed, which is a simple process.

- All of the Python code that appears in the books has been executed, and all complete programs are provided as .py files. Some of the numerous programming examples (over 100) that are explored in the book and for which working code is included:

  o An interactive breakout game

  o A text formatting system

o   Plotting histograms and pie charts

o   Reading Twitter feeds

o   Play Jeopardy Using a CSV Data Set

o   Sending and receiving Email

o   A simple Latin to English translator

o   Rock-Paper-Scissors

- Hundreds of answered multiple choice quiz and examination questions in MS Word files that can be edited and used in various ways.

Dedicated Web Site

An online community has been started at *https://sites.google.com/site/python-parker/* for comments, new exam questions and exercises, extra code, and as a place to report problems.

Please consider contributing material to the on-line community, and do have fun. If you don't, then you're doing it wrong.

J. Parker
October 2016

MODERN
COMPUTERS

■ ■ ■ ■ ■

In this chapter

Humans are tool makers and tool users. This is not unique in the animal kingdom, but the facility that humans have with tools and the variety of applications we have for them does make us unique. Starting with mechanical tools (*machines*) like levers and wheels that could lighten the physical effort of everyday life, more and more complex and specific devices have been created to assist with all facets of our lives. This was extended in the twentieth century to assisting with mental efforts, specifically calculation.

Computers are devices that humans have built in order to facilitate complex calculations. Early computers were used to do some of the computations needed to design the first nuclear bombs, but now computers seem to be everywhere, even embedded within cars and kitchen appliances, and even within our own bodies. The success of these devices in such a wide range of application areas is a result of their ability to be *programmed*—that is, the device itself is only a potential when first built and has no specific function. It is designed to be configured to do any task that requires calculations, and the configuring process is what we call programming.

To some extent this has taken the place of a lot of other tool development that used to be done by engineers. When designing a complex machine like an automobile, for example, there used to be a lot of mechanical work involved. The careful timing of the current to the spark plug was accomplished by rotating shafts with sensors, and resulted in the firing of each cylinder at the correct moment. The air to gasoline mixture fed into the engine was controlled by tubes and cables and springs. Now all of these things and many more are done using computers that sense electric and magnetic events, do calculations, and send electrical control signals to actuators in the engine. The same computer can be used to control a refrigerator, make telephone calls on a cellular phone, change channels on a television, and wake you up in the morning. It is the flexibility of the computer that has led to them becoming a dominant technology in human society, and the flexibility comes largely from their ability to be programmed.

0.1 CALCULATIONS BY MACHINE

People have been calculating things for thousands of years, and have always had mechanical aids to help.

When someone programs a computer, they are really communicating with it. It is a very imperative and precise communication to be sure. Imperative because the computer has no choice; it is being told what to do, and will do exactly that. Precise because a computer does not apply any interpretation to what it is being told. Human languages are vague and subject to interpretation and ambiguity. There are sentences that are legal in terms of syntax that have no real meaning: "Which is faster, to Boston or by bus?" is a legal sentence in English that has no meaning. Such things are not possible in a computer language. Also, computers do not *think* and so can't evaluate a command that would amount to "expose the patient to a fatal dose of radiation" with any skepticism. As a result, we, as programmers, must be careful and precise in what we instruct the machine to do.

When humans communicate with each other we use a language. Similarly, humans use languages to communicate with computers; it is easy for us. Such languages are artificial (humans invented them for this purpose, all at once), terse (there are few if any modifiers, no way to express emotions or graduations of any feeling), precise (each item in the language means one thing), and written (we do not speak to the computer in a programming language. Not yet, perhaps never).

Computer languages operate at a high level, and do not represent the way the computer actually works. For the purposes of learning to program there are a few fundamental things that need to be known about computers. It's not required to know how they operate electronically, but there are basic principles that should be understood in order to put the process of using computers in practical contexts.

0.2 HOW COMPUTERS WORK AND WHY WE MADE THEM

The reason people use computers is different depending on the point in history in which one looks, but the military always seems to be involved. There have been many calculating devices built and used throughout history, but the first one that would have been *programmable* was designed by Charles Babbage. The military, as well as the mathematicians of the day, were interested in more accurate mathematical tables, such as those for logarithms. At the time these were calculated by hand, but the idea that a machine could be built to compute more digits of accuracy was appealing. This would have been a mechanical device of gears and shafts, but it was not completed due to budget and contracting issues.

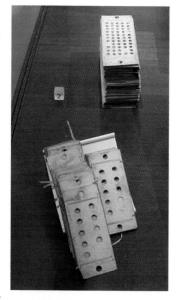

Babbage continued his work in design and created, on paper, a programmable mechanical device called the *analytical engine* in 1837. What does *programmable* mean? A calculation device is manipulated by the operator to perform a sequence of operations: add this to that, then subtract this and divide by something else. On a modern calculator

Figure 0.1
Punched cards for the analytical engine.

Figure 0.2
A portion of Babbage's analytical engine.

this would be done using a sequence of key presses, but on older devices it may involve moving beads along wires or rotating gears along shafts. Now imagine that the sequence of key presses can be encoded on some other media: a set of cams, or plugs into sockets, or holes punched into cards. This is a *program*.

Such a set of punched cards or cams would be similar to a set of instructions written in English and given to some human to calculate, but would instead be coded in a form (language) that the computing device could use immediately. The directions on the cards could be changed so that something new could be computed as needed. The difference engine would only find logarithms and trigonometric functions, but a device that could be programmed in this way could, in theory, calculate anything. The analytical engine was programmed by punching holes in stiff cards, an idea that was derived from the Jacquard loom of the day. The location of holes would indicate either an operation (e.g., add, subtract, etc.) or data (a number). A sequence of such cards would be executed one at a time and yield a value at the end.

Although the analytical engine was never completed, a program was written for it, but not by him. The world's first programmer may have been a woman, Augusta Ada King, Countess of Lovelace. She worked with Babbage for a few years and wrote a program to compute *Bernoulli numbers*. This is the first algorithm ever designed for a computer and is often claimed to be the first computer program ever written, although it was never executed.

The very concept of *programmability* is a more important development than is the development of the difference or analytical engines. The idea that a machine can be made to do different things depending on a user-defined set of instructions is the very basis of all modern computers, while the use of mechanical calculation has become obsolete; it is too slow, expensive, and cumbersome. This is where it began, though, and the programming concept is the same today.

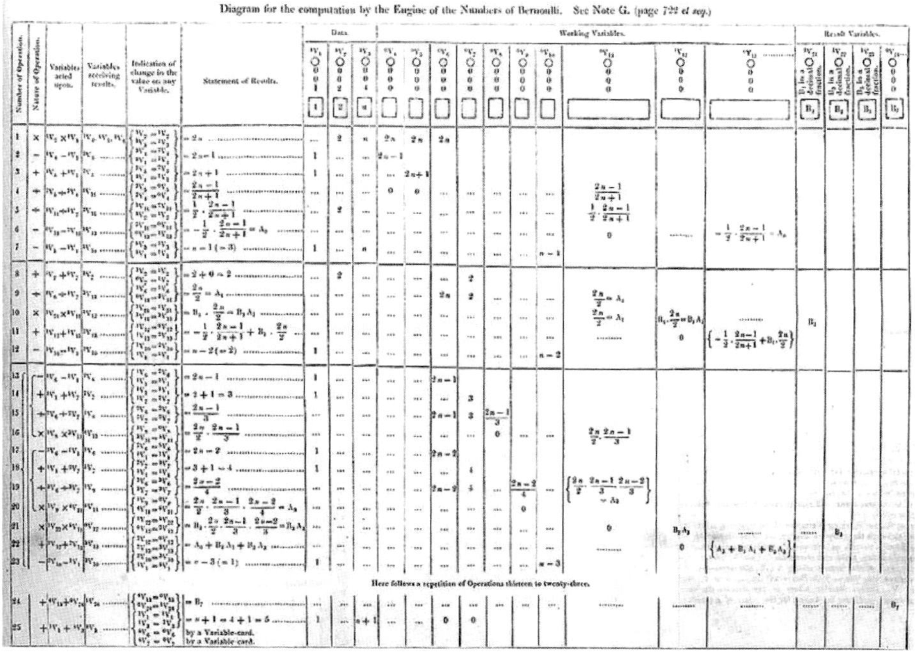

Figure 0.3
Possibly the word's first program: to calculate Bernoulli numbers on the analytical engine.

During World War II computers made the leap to being electrical. Work on breaking codes and building the atomic bomb required large amounts of computing. Initially some of this was provided by rooms full of humans operating mechanical calculators, but they could not keep up with the demand, so electronic computers were designed and built. The first was Colossus, designed and built by Tommy Flowers in 1943. It was created to help break German military codes, and an updated version (Mark II) was built in 1944.

Figure 0.4
The Colossus computer breaking a code during World War II with the help of Dorothy Du Boisson (left) and Elsie Booker.

In the United States there was a need for computational power in Los Alamos when the first nuclear weapons were being built. Electro-mechanical calculators were replaced by IBM punched-card calculators, originally designed for accounting, and these were a little faster than the humans running calculators, but could run twenty-four hours a day and made fewer errors. This computer was programmed by plugging wires into sockets to create new connections between components.

0.2.1 Numbers

The electronic computers described so far, and those of the 1940s generally, had almost no storage for numbers. Input was through devices like cards, and they could have numbers on them. They could be transferred to the computation unit, then moved ahead or back, and perhaps read again. Memory was a primitive thing, and various methods were devised to store just a few digits. A significant advance came when engineers decided to use *binary numbers*. This will require some explanation.

Electronic devices use current and voltage to represent information, such as sounds or pictures (radio and television). One of the simplest devices is a switch, which can open and close a circuit and turn things like lights on and off. Electricity needs a complete circuit or route from the *source* of electrons, the negative pole of a battery perhaps, to the *sink*, which could be the positive pole. Electrons, which is what electricity is, in a simple sense, flow from the negative to the positive poles of a battery. Electricity can be made to do work by putting devices in the way of the flow of electrons. Putting a lamp in the circuit can cause the lamp to light up, for example.

A switch makes a break in the circuit, which stops the electrons from flowing; they cannot jump the gap. This causes the lamp to go dark. This seems obvious to anyone with electric lights in their house, but what may not be so obvious is that this creates two states of the circuit, *on* and

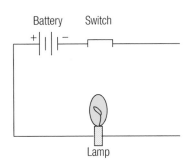

Figure 0.5
The switch is closed and the current is flowing, turning the lamp on. This is a "1."

off. These states can be assigned numbers. Off could be 0, for example, and on could be 1. This is how most computers represent numbers: as on/off or 1/0 states. To be more clear about this way of representing numbers, consider the usual way, which is called positional numbering.

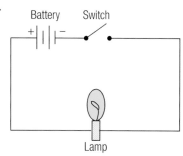

Battery   Switch

Lamp

Figure 0.6
The switch is off (open) and the lamp is off, indicating a "0."

Most human societies now use a system that uses ten digits: 0, 1, 2, 3, 4, 5, 6, 7, 8, and 9. The number 123 is a combination of digits and powers of ten. It is a shorthand notation for 100 + 20 + 3, or $1 \times 10^2 + 2*10^1 + 3*10^0$. Each digit is multiplied by a power of ten and summed to get the value of the number. Anyone who has been to school accepts this and does not think about it, but really the value used as the basis of the system, ten, is not magical. It simply happens to be the number of digits humans have on their hands. Any base would work almost as well.

Example: Base

Numbers that use 4 as a base can only have the digits 0,1,2, and 3. Each position in the number represents a power of 4. Thus the number 123 is, in base 4, $1 \times 4^2 + 2*4^1 + 3*4^0$, which is $1 \times 16 + 2*4 + 3 = 16 + 8 + 3 = 27$ in traditional base 10 representation.

This could get confusing, what with various bases and such, so numbers will be considered to be in base 10 unless specific by a suffix. 123_4 is 123 in base 4, whereas 123_8 is 123 in base 8, and so on.

Binary numbers can have digits that are 1 or 0. The numbers are in base 2, and can therefore only have the digits 0 and 1. These numbers can be represented by the on/off state of a switch or *transistor*, which is an electronic switch, which is why they are used in electronic computers. Modern computers represent all data as binary numbers because it is easy to represent those numbers in electronic form; a voltage is arbitrarily assigned to "0" and to "1." When a device detects a particular voltage, it can then be converted into a digit, and vice versa. If 2 volts is assigned to a 0 and 5 volts is assigned to a 1, then the following circuit could signal a 0 or 1 depending on what switch was selected:

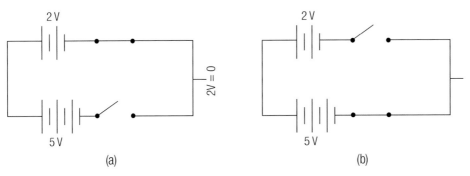

Figure 0.7
(a) A configuration giving a 2-volt value, or a zero.
(b) A configuration giving a 5-volt value, or a one.

Convert Binary Numbers to Decimal

Consider the binary number 110112. It can be converted in base 10 by multiplying each digit by its corresponding power of two and then summing the results.

Digit	1	1	0	1	1
Position	4	3	2	1	0
Power of 2	$2^4 = 16$	$2^3 = 8$	$2^2 = 4$	$2^1 = 2$	$2^0 = 1$
Digit*power	16	8	0	2	1
Sum is $16 + 8 + 2 + 1 = 27_{10}$					

Some observations:

- Terminology: A digit in a binary number is called a *bit* (for **b**inary dig**it**)
- Any even number has 0 as the low digit, which means that odd numbers have 1 as the low digit.
- Any exact power of two, such as 16, 32, 64, and so on, will have exactly one digit that is a 1, and all others will be 0.
- Terminology: A binary digit or bit that is 1 is said to be *set*. A bit that is 0 is said to be *clear*.

Convert Decimal Numbers to Binary

Going from base 10 to base 2 is more complicated than the reverse. There are a few ways to do the calculation, but here's one that many people find easy to understand. If the lowest digit (rightmost) is 1 then the number is odd, and otherwise it is even. If the number 73_{10} is to be converted into binary the rightmost digit will be 1, because the number is odd.

The next step is to divide the number by 2, eliminating the rightmost binary digit, the one that was just identified, from the number. $73_{10} / 2_{10} = 36_{10}$, and there can be no fractional part, so any such part is to be discarded. Now the problem is to convert 36_{10} to binary and then append the part already converted to that. Is 36_{10} even or odd? It is even, so the next digit is 0. The final two digits of 73_{10} in binary are 01.

The process is repeated:

Divide 36 by 2 to get 18, which is even, so the next digit is 0.

Divide 18 by 2 to get 9, which is odd, so the next digit is 1.

Divide 9 by 2 to get 4, which is even, so the next digit is 0.

Divide 4 by 2 to get 2, which is even, so the next digit is 0.

Divide 2 by 2 to get 1, which is odd, so the next digit is 1.

Divide 1 by 2 to get 0. When the number becomes 0, the process is complete.

The conversion process gives the binary numbers in reverse order (right to left) so the result is that $73_{10} = 1001001_2$.

Is this correct? Convert this binary number into decimal again:

$$1001001_2 = 1 \times 2^0 + 1*2^3 + 1*2^6 = 1 + 8 + 64 = 73_{10}.$$

A summary of the process for converting x into binary is:

```
Start at digit n=0 (rightmost)
repeat
    If x is even, the current digit n is 0, otherwise it is 1
    Divide x by 2
    Add 1 to n
    If x is zero, then end the repetition
```

Arithmetic in Binary

Computers do all operations on data as binary numbers, so when two numbers are added, for example, the calculation is performed in base 2. It turns out that base 2 is easier than base 10 for some things, and adding is one of those things. It's done in the same way as in base 10 but there are only 2 digits, and twos are carried instead of tens. For example: add 01011_2 to 01110_2:

$$
\begin{array}{ccccc}
0 & 1 & 0 & 1 & 1_2 \\
0 & 1 & 1 & 1 & 0_2 \\
\end{array}
$$

Starting the sum on the right as usual, there is a 0 added to a 1 and the sum is 1, just as in base 10.

$$
\begin{array}{ccccc}
0 & 1 & 0 & 1 & 1_2 \\
0 & 1 & 1 & 1 & 0_2 \\
\hline
 & & & & 1_2 \\
\end{array}
$$

The next column in the sum contains two 1s. $1 + 1$ is two, but in binary that is represented as 10_2. So, the result of $1 + 1$ is 0 with a carry of 1:

$$
\begin{array}{ccccc}
 & 1 & & & \\
0 & 1 & 0 & 1 & 1_2 \\
0 & 1 & 1 & 1 & 0_2 \\
\hline
 & & & 0 & 1_2 \\
\end{array}
$$

The next column has $1 + 0$, but there is a carry of 1 so it is $1 + 0 + 1$. That's 0 with a 1 carry again:

$$
\begin{array}{ccccc}
 & 1 & & & \\
0 & 1 & 0 & 1 & 1_2 \\
0 & 1 & 1 & 1 & 0_2 \\
\hline
 & & 0 & 0 & 1_2 \\
\end{array}
$$

Now the column is $1 + 1$ with a 1 carry, or $1 + 1 + 1$. This is 1 with a carry of 1:

$$
\begin{array}{ccccc}
 & 1 & & & \\
0 & 1 & 0 & 1 & 1_2 \\
0 & 1 & 1 & 1 & 0_2 \\
\hline
 & 1 & 0 & 0 & 1_2 \\
\end{array}
$$

Finally, the leading digits are $0 + 0$ with a carry of 1, or $0 + 0 + 1$. The answer is 11001_2. Is this correct? Well, 01011_2 is 11_{10} and 01110_2 is 14_2, and $11_{10} + 14_{10} = 25_{10}$. The answer 11001_2 is, in fact, 25_{10} (confirm this!) so it all works out.

Binary numbers can be subjected to the same operations as any other form of number (i.e., multiplication, subtraction, division). In addition, these operations can be performed by electronic circuits operating on voltages that represent the digits 1 and 0.

0.2.2 Memory

Adding memory to computers was another huge step forward. A computer memory must hold steady a collection of voltages that represent digits, and the digits are collected into sets, each of which is a number. A switch can hold a binary digit, but switches are activated by people. Computer memory must store and recall (retrieve) numbers when they are required by a calculation without human intervention.

The first memories were rather odd things: *acoustic delay lines* store numbers as a sound passing through mercury in a tube. The speed of sound allows a small number of digits, around 500, to be stored in transit from a speaker on one end to a receiver on the other. A phosphor screen can be built that is activated by an electric pulse and draws a bright spot on a screen that needs no power to maintain it. Numbers can be saved as bright and dark spots (1 and 0) and retrieved using light sensitive devices.

Other devices were used in the early years, such as relays and vacuum tubes, but in 1947 the magnetic core memory was patented, in which bits were stored as magnetic fields in small donut-shaped elements. This kind of memory was faster and more reliable than anything used before, and even held the data in memory without power being applied, a handy thing in a power failure. It was also expensive, of course.

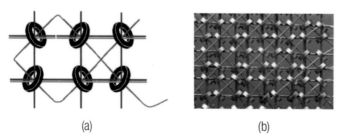

(a)   (b)

Figure 0.8
(a) A diagram of core memory showing six bits.
(b) Actual core memory magnified to show the individual bits.

This kind of memory is almost never used anymore, but its legacy remains in terminology: memory is still frequently referred to as *core*, and a *core dump* is still what many people call a listing of the contents of a computer memory.

Current computers use transistors to store bits and solid state memories that can hold billions of bits (*Gigabits*), but the way they are used in the computer is still the same as it was. Bits are collected into groups of 8 (a *byte*) and then groups of multiple bytes to for a *word*. Words are collected into a linear sequence, each numbered starting at 0. These numbers are called *addresses*, and each word, and sometimes each byte, can be accessed by specifying the address of the data that is wanted. Acquiring the data element at a particular location is called a *fetch*, and placing a number into a particular location is a *store*. A computer program to add two numbers might be specified as:

Fetch the number at location 21

Fetch the number at location 433

Add those two numbers

Store the result in location 22

This may seem like a verbose way to add two numbers, but remember that this can be accomplished in a tiny fraction of a second.

Memory is often presented to beginning programmers as a collection of mailboxes. The address is a number identifying the mailbox, which also contains a number. There is some special memory in the computer that has no specific address, and is referred to in various ways. When a fetch is performed, there is a question concerning where the value that was fetched goes. It can go to another memory location, which is a *move* operation, or it can go into one of these special locations, called *registers*.

A computer can have many registers or very few, but they are very fast memory units that are used to keep intermediate results of computations.

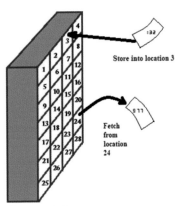

Figure 0.9
Memory as a set of cubbyholes or mailboxes, each with a unique address.

The simple program above would normally have to be modified to give registers that are involved in the operations:

Fetch the number at location 21 into register R0

Fetch the number at location 433 into register R1

Add R1 and R0 and put the result into R3

Store R3 (the result) in location 22

This is still verbose, but more correct.

0.2.3 Stored Programs

The final critical step in creating the modern computer occurred in 1936 with Alan Turing's theoretical paper on the subject, but an actual computer to employ the concept was not built until 1948 when the Manchester Small-Scale Experimental Machine ran what is considered to be the first stored program. It has been the basic method by which computers operate ever since.

The idea is to store a computer program in memory locations instead of on cards or in some other way. Programs and data now coexist in memory, and this also means that computer programs have to be encoded as numbers; *everything* in a computer is a number. There are many different ways to do this, and many possible different instruction sets that have been implemented and various different configurations of registers, memory, and instructions. The computer hardware always does the same basic thing: first it fetches the next instruction to be executed, and then it decodes it and executes it. Executing an instruction could involve more accesses to memory or registers.

This repeated fetch then execute process is called, not surprisingly, the *fetch-execute cycle*, and is at the heart of all computers. The location or address of the next instruction resides in a register called the *program counter*, and this register is incremented every time an

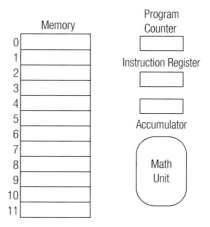

Figure 0.10

The simple fictional computer used to explain stored programs.

instruction is executed, meaning that instructions will be placed in consecutive memory locations and will be fetched and executed naturally in that order. Sometimes the instruction is fetched into a special register too, called the *instruction register*, so that it can be examined quickly for important components like data values or addresses. Finally, a computer will need at least one register to store data; this will be called the *accumulator*, because that's usually what such a register is called.

The stored program concept is actually pretty difficult to grasp, so a detailed example is in order. Imagine a computer that has 12 bit words as memory locations and that possesses the registers described above. This is a fictional machine, but it turns out to have some of the properties of an old computer from the 1960s called the PDP-8.

To demonstrate the execution of a program on a stored program computer a very simple program will be used: add 21 and 433, placing the answer in location 11. As an initial assumption, assume that the value 21 is in location 9 and 433 is in location 10. The program itself will reside in consecutive memory locations beginning at address 0.

The program should be described in English first. Note that it is very much like the previous two examples, but in this case there is only one register to put data into, the accumulator. The program could perhaps look like this:

Fetch the contents of memory location 9 into the accumulator

Add the contents of memory location 10 to the accumulator

Store the contents of the accumulator into memory location 11

The program is now complete, and the result 21 + 433 should be found in location 11. Computer programs are normally expressed in terms that the computer can immediately use, normally as fairly terse and precise commands. The next stage in the development of this program is to use a symbolic form of the actual instructions that the computer will use.

The first step is to move the contents of location 9 to the accumulator. The instruction that does this kind of thing is called *Load Accumulator*, shorted as the mnemonic LDA. The instruction would be in location 0:

```
0: LDA 9   # Load accumulator with location 9
```

The text following the "#" character is ignored by the computer, and is really a comment to remind the programmer what is happening. The next instruction is to add the contents of location 10 to the accumulator; the instruction is ADD and it is placed in address 1:

```
1: ADD 10  # Add contents of address
10 to the accumulator
```

Finally, the result, current in the accumulator register, will be saved into the memory location at address 11. This is a Store instruction:

```
2: STO 11  # Answer into location 11
```

The program is complete. There is a Halt instruction:

```
3: HLT    # End of program
```

Figure 0.11

An actual PDP-8 computer. Programs could be entered as binary numbers, using the switches on the front console. This was the smallest computer in its day.

http://www.vandermark.ch/ pdp8/index.php?n=PDP8. Emulator

If this program starts executing at address 0, and if the correct data is in the correct locations, then the result 454 should end up in location 11. But these instructions are not yet in a form the computer can use. They are characters, text that a human can read. In a stored program computer these instructions must be encoded as numbers, and those numbers must agree with the ones the computer was built to implement.

An instruction must be a binary number, so all of the possible instructions have numeric codes. An instruction can also contain a memory address; the LDA instruction specifies a memory location from which to load the accumulator. Both the instruction code and the address have to be placed into one computer word. The designers of the computer decide how that will be done, and the programmers have to live with the result.

This computer has 12 bit words. Imagine that the upper 3 bits indicate what the instruction is. That is, a typical instruction is formatted like this:

Figure 0.12
The format of a binary instruction

There are 9 bits at the lower (right) end of the instruction for an address, and 3 at the top end for the code that represents the instruction. The code for LDA is 3; the code for ADD is 5 and the code for STO is 6. HLT on most computers that have such an instruction is code 0. Here is what the program looks like as numbers:

Code 3 Address 9

Code 5 Address 10

Code 6 Address 11

Code 0 Address 0

These have to be made into binary numbers to be stored in memory, but that's pretty easy. For the LDA instruction the code 3_{10} is 011_2 and the address is $9_{10} = 000001001_2$, so the instruction as a binary number is $011\ 000001001_2$, where the space between the code and the address is only present to make it obvious to a person reading it.

The ADD instruction has code 5_{10}, which is 101_2, and the address is 10, which in binary is 0001010_2. The instruction is $101\ 000001010_2$.

The STO instruction has code 6, which is 110_2, and the address is 11, which is 001011_2. The instruction is $110\ 000001011_2$.

The HLT instruction is code 0, or in 12 bit binary $000\ 000000000_2$.

The codes are made up by the designers of the computer. When memory is set up to contain this program here's what it looks like:

Memory

0	011000001001
1	101000001010
2	110000001011
3	000000000000
4	000000000000
5	000000000000
6	000000000000
7	000000000000
8	000000000000
9	000000010101
10	000110110001
11	000000000000

Figure 0.13
The simple example program as it looks in memory.

This is how memory looks when the program begins. The act of setting up the memory like this so that the program can execute is called *loading*. The binary numbers in memory locations 9 and 10 are 21 and 433 respectively (check this!), which are the numbers to be summed.

Of course there are more instructions than these in a useful computer. There is not always a subtract instruction, but subtraction can be done by making a number negative and then adding, so there is often a NEGate instruction. Setting the accumulator to zero is a common thing to do, so there is a CLA (Clear Accumulator) instruction; and there are many more.

The fetch-execute cycle involves fetching the memory location addressed by the program counter into the instruction register, incrementing the program counter, and then executing the instruction. Execution involves figuring out what instruction is represented by the code and then sending the address or data through the correct electronic circuits, a process beyond anything this chapter will address.

A very important instruction that this program does not use is a *branch*. The instruction BRA 0 will cause the next instruction to be executed starting at memory location 0. This allows a program to skip over some instructions or to repeat some many times. A conditional branch will change the current instruction if a certain condition is true. An example would be Branch if Accumulator is Zero (BAZ), which will only perform a branch if, as the instruction indicates, there is a value of zero in the accumulator. The combination of arithmetic and control instructions makes it possible for a programmer to describe a calculation to be performed very precisely.

0.3 COMPUTER SYSTEMS ARE BUILT IN LAYERS

Entering a program as binary numbers using switches is a very tedious, time-consuming process. Lacking a disk drive, the early computers depended on other kinds of storage: punched cards again, or paper tape. It should be understood that because there was no permanent storage, booting one of these machines often meant toggling a small "boot loader" program, then reading a paper tape. Now the computer would respond sensibly to its peripheral devices, like a printer or card reader. The paper tape contained a primitive "operating system" that would control the few devices available. That's what operating systems do: allocate resources and control devices.

The boot loader (bootstrap program) is the lowest layer of software. It was provided by the computer manufacturer, but has to be entered by the user. The paper tape system was the second layer, and the user did not have to write this program. Gradually more and more layers were written so as to provide the user with a high level of abstraction rather than having to understand the entire machine. After all, physicists and engineers have other things to do rather than tend to the computer.

When disk drives became available, the operating system would be stored on them, and a bootstrap loader would be saved in a special section of memory that could not be erased (read only memory) so that when the computer was turned on it would run the loader, which would load the operating system. Very convenient, and it is essentially what happens today on Windows.

This operating system on the disk drive is a third layer of software. It provides basic hardware allocation functionality and also gives the user access to some programs to use for printing and saving things on disk—a *file system*.

0.3.1 Assemblers and Compilers

Programming a computer could still be a daunting task if done in binary, so the first thing that was provided was an *assembler*. This was a program that would permit a programmer to enter a text program that could be converted into a binary executable. It would allow memory locations to be named instead of using an absolute number as an address, and would convert text operation codes and addresses into binary programs. The addition program from the previous section could be written in assembler as:

```
        LDA Data1
        ADD Data2
        STO Res
        HLT
Data1:  21
Data2:  433:
Res:    0
```

Usually one line of text in an assembler corresponds to a single instruction or memory location. It's the same program but is easier for a programmer to understand because of the named memory locations and mnemonic instruction names.

It is much harder to describe *how* a compiler works, but relatively easy to explain *what* it does. A compiler translates high level language statements into assembler, which in turn converts it into binary code. Compilers translate statements like:

```
A = 21
B = 433
C = A+B
```

into executable code. It is a very complex process, but essentially it allows the programmer to declare that certain names represent integers, that values are to be assigned, and that arithmetic can be done. There are also more complex statements like conditional execution of code and function calls with parameters, as will be seen in later chapters.

Compilers also implement input and output from the user (reading from a keyboard and writing to the video screen), sophisticated data types, and mathematical functions. An *interpreter*, which is what the language Python is, does a part of the compilation process but does not produce executable code. Instead, it simulates the execution of the code, doing most of the work in software. The Java language does a similar thing in many cases.

The programs that someone writes (software) create another layer for someone to use. An example might be a database management system that gives a user access to a computer that can query data for certain kinds of values. A graphics system gives a programmer access to a set of operations that can draw pictures.

0.3.2 Graphical User Interfaces (GUIs)

Most computers now interface with their owners through a keyboard, one of the first devices to be interfaced to a computer; a mouse, the first device to permit 2D navigation on a screen; and windows, a graphical construction that allows many independent connections to a computer to share a single video screen. GUIs are popular because they improve the user's perception of what is happening on a computer. Previous computer interfaces were completely text based, so if something was going wrong in a place where the user was not looking, then it would probably not be noticed.

On the other hand, GUIs are more difficult to program. Just opening a new window in a Microsoft-based operating system can require scores of lines of C++ code that would take a great deal of time to understand. Naturally, it is the job of a programmer to be able to do this, but it means that the average user could not create their own software that manipulated the interface in any reasonable way. So, what is a window, and what's involved in a GUI?

A window, in the operating system sense, is a rectangle on the computer screen within which an exchange of information takes place between the user and the system. The rectangle can generally be resized, removed from the screen temporarily (minimized), moved, and closed. It can be thought of as a virtual computer terminal in that each one can do what the entire video screen was needed to do in early systems. When the window is active, a user can type information to be received by the program controlling it, and can manipulate graphical objects within the window using a mouse or, more recently, by using their fingers on a touch screen. Without a mouse or something like it, a window-based system is pretty much crippled, so the two are almost always used together.

Figure 0.14
The first computer mouse. *https://commons.wikimedia.org/wiki/File:Telefunken_Rollkugel_RKS_100-86.jpg*

Figure 0.15
Englebart's computer mouse.

The mouse is a variation on the tracker ball, and it is agreed that the German engineering company *Telefunken* devised a working version and was the first to sell it. A mouse is linked through software to a cursor on the screen, and left-right motions of the mouse cause left-right motions of the cursor; forward and backward motions of the mouse cause the cursor to move up and down the screen. When the cursor is inside of a window, then that window is active. A mouse has buttons, and pressing a mouse button activates whatever software object is related to the cursor position on the screen. This describes things that are obvious to anyone used to computers built since the 1980s.

Widgets

A widget is a graphical object drawn in a window or otherwise on a computer screen that can be selected and/or operated using the mouse and mouse buttons.

It is connected to a software element that will be sent a control signal or numerical parameter by virtue of the widget being manipulated. That's a pretty formal description, but a widget is exemplified by the *button*, a very commonly used widget on web pages and interfaces. Buttons can be used to display information as well as to control a program. Some popular widgets are:

Button: When the mouse cursor is within the boundaries of the button on the screen, the button is said to be activated. Pressing a mouse button when the button widget is activated will cause the software connected to the button to perform its function.

Figure 0.16
Button.

Radio Button: A set of two or more buttons used to select from a set of discrete options. Only one of the buttons can be selected at a time, mean that the options are mutually exclusive.

Figure 0.17
Radio button.

Check Box: A way to select a set of options from a larger set. This widget consists of a collection of boxes or buttons that can be chosen by clicking on them. When chosen, they indicate that fact by using a graphical change, sometimes a check mark but sometimes a color or other visual effect.

Figure 0.18
Check box.

Slider: A horizontal or vertical control with a selection tool that can be slid along the control. The relative position of the control dictates the value that the widget provides. This value is often displayed in a text box, and the range is also commonly displayed.

Figure 0.19
Slider.

Drop-down List: A box containing text that displays a complete set of options that can be displayed when the mouse button is clicked within it. Then any one of the options can be selected using the mouse and the mouse button.

Icon: An icon is a small graphical representation (pictogram) that represents the function of a program or file. When selected, the program will execute or the file will be opened.

Figure 0.20
Drop-down list.

Figure 0.21
Icon.

There are many other widgets and variations on the ones shown here. There are two basic principles at play:

1. The widget represents an activity using a commonly understood symbol, and performs that activity, or one related to the symbol, when selected using the mouse. This is a graphical and tactile operation that replaces the typing of a command in previous computer systems.

2. The software that implements the widget is a *module*, a piece of software that can be reused and reconfigured for various circumstances. A button can be quickly created to perform any number of tasks because the program that implements it is designed for that degree of flexibility.

0.4 COMPUTER NETWORKS

Schools, offices, and some homes are equipped with computer *networks*, which are wires that connect computers together and software and special hardware that allows the computers to communicate with each other. This allows people to send information to each other through their computers; a lot of work is done in a computer readable form in any case, and it is convenient to allow computers to share information. But how does this really work?

Computers use electricity to perform calculations on binary numbers. Arbitrary voltages have been selected to represent 0 and 1, and so long as everyone agrees on that representation, those voltages can be sent along a wire no matter how long and still be numbers at the receiving end. As long as two computers are being connected this works fine, but if two wires are needed to connect any two computers then six are needed to fully connect three computers to each other and twelve to connect four computers. A room with thirty networked computers would be full of wires (870 to each computer)! There must be a better way.

Hawaii has an unusual problem when it comes to computer network communication. It is a collection of islands. Linking them by cables is an expensive proposition. In the early 1970s the folks at the University of Hawaii had a good idea—to link the computers using radio. Radio transmission is really similar to wire transmission in many practical ways, and allocating 35 radio frequencies to connect one computer on each island to all of the others would have been possible, but their idea was better. They used a single radio link for all computers. When a computer wanted to send information along the network, it would listen to see if another computer was already doing so. If so, it would wait. If not, it would begin to send data to *all* of the other computers and would include in the transmission a code for which computer was supposed to receive it. All could hear it, but all would know which computer was the correct destination so the others would ignore it. This system was called *Alohanet*.

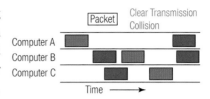

Figure 0.22
Packets transmitted on a network. Red ones are collisions.

There is a problem with this scheme. Two or more computers could try to send at almost the same time, having noted that no other computer was sending when they checked. This is called a *collision*, and is relatively easy to detect; the data received is nonsense. When that happens each computer waits for a random time, checks again, and tries again to send the data. An analogy would be a meeting where many people are trying to speak at once.

Obviously the busier the network is the more likely a collision will be, and the retransmissions will make things worse. Still, this scheme works very well and is functioning today in the form of the most common networking system in earth—*Ethernet*.

Ethernet is essentially Alohanet along a wire. It means that each computer has one connection to it, rather than connections to each of the possible destinations, and collisions are possible. There is another consideration that makes this scheme work better, and that it is use of *packets*. Information along these networks is sent in fixed-size packages of a few thousand bytes. In this way, the time needed to send a packet should be more or less constant, and it's more efficient than sending a bit or a byte at a time.

Each packet contains a set of data bytes intended for another computer, so within that packet should be some information about the destination, the sender, and other important stuff. For instance, if a data file is bigger than a packet, then it has to be split up into parts to be sent. Thus, a part of the packet is a sequence number indicating which packet it is (e.g., number 3 of 5). If a particular packet never gets received for some reason, then the missing one is known, and the receiver can ask the sender for that packet to be resent. There are also codes than can be used to determine whether an error has occurred.

0.4.1 Internet

The Internet is a computer network designed to communicate reliably over long distances. It was originally created to be a reliable communications system that could survive a nuclear attack, and was funded by the military. It is distributed, in that data can be sent from one computer to another in a chain until it reaches its destination.

Imagine a collection of a few dozen computers, and that each one is connected to multiple others, but not directly to all others. Computer A wishes to send a message to computer B, and does so using a packet that includes the destination. Computer A sends the message to all computers that it is connected to. Each of those computers sends it to all of the computers that they are connected to, and so on until the destination is reached. All of the computers will receive every message, which is pretty inefficient, but so long as there exists some path from A to B the message will be delivered.

It would be hard to tell when to stop sending a message in this scheme. Another way to do it is to have a table in each computer saying which computers in the network are connected to which others. A message can be sent to a computer known to be a short path to the destination, one computer at a time, and in this case not all computers see the message, only the ones along the route do. A new computer added to the network must send a special message to all of the others telling them which of the existing computers it is directly connected to, and this message will propagate to all machines, allowing them to update their map. This is essentially the scheme used today.

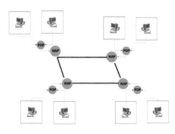

Figure 0.23
The organization of the internet.

The Internet has a hierarchy of communication links and processors. First, all computers on the Internet have a unique IP (*Internet Protocol*) address through which they are reached. Because there are a lot of computers in the world, an IP address is a large number. An example would be 172.16.254.1 (obtained from Wikipedia). When a computer in, say, Portland wants to send a message to, for example, London, the Portland computer composes a packet that contains the message, its address, and the recipient's address in London. This message is sent along the connection to its Internet service provider, which is a local computer, at a relative low speed, 10 megabits per second perhaps. The service provider operates a collection of computers designed to handle network traffic. This is called a *Point of Presence* (POP) and collects messages from a local area and concentrates them for transmission further down the line.

Multiple POP sites connect to a Network Access Point (NAP) using much faster connections than users have to connect with the POP. The NAP concentrates even more users, and provides a layer of addressing that can be used to send the data to the destination. The NAP for the Portland user would have the message delivered to a relatively local NAP, which would send it to the next NAP along a path to the destination in London using an exceptionally fast (high bandwidth) data connection. The London NAP would send the message to the appropriate local POP, which would in turn send it to the correct user.

An important consideration is that the message can be read by any POP nor NAP server along the route. Data sent along the Internet is public unless it is properly encrypted by the users.

0.4.2 World Wide Web

The World Wide Web, or simply the *Web*, is in fact a layer of software above the Internet protocols. It is a way to access files and data remotely through a visual interface provided by a program that runs on the user's computer, a *browser.* When someone accesses a web page, a file that describes that page is downloaded to the user and displayed. That file is text in a particular format, and the file name usually ends in ".html" or ".htm." The file holds a description of how to display the page: what text to display, where images can be found that are part of the page, how the page is formatted, and where other connected pages (links) are found on the Internet. Once the file is downloaded, all of the hard work concerned with the display of the file, such as playing sounds and videos and drawing graphics and text, is done by the local (receiving) computer.

The Web is the basis for most of the modern advances in social networking and public data access. The Internet provides the underlying network communications facility while the Web uses that to fetch and display information requested by the user in a visual and auditory fashion. Podcasts, blogs, and wikis are simple extensions of the basic functionality.

The Web demands the ability for a user in Portland to request a file from a user in London and to have that file delivered and made into a graphical display, all with a single click of a mouse button. Web pages are files that reside on a computer that has an IP address, but the IP address is often hidden by a symbolic name called the Universal Resource Locator (URL). Almost everyone has seen one of these: "*http://www.facebook.com*" is one example. Web pages each have a unique path or address based on a URL. It is a pretty amazing fact that anyone can create a new web page that uses its very own unambiguous URL at any time, and that most of the world would be able to view it.

The Web is an example of what programmers call a *client-server* system. The client is where the person requesting the web page lives, and is making a request. The server is where the web page itself lives, and it satisfies the request. Other examples of such systems would be online computer games, Email, *Skype*, and *Second Life*.

0.5 REPRESENTATION

When applying a computer to a task or writing a program to deal with a type of data that seems to be non-numeric, the issue of how to represent the data on the computer will invariably arise. Everything stored and manipulated on a computer has to be a number. What if the data is not numeric?

A fundamental example of this is character data. When a user types at the computer keyboard, what actually happens? Each key, and some key combinations (e.g., shift key and "1" held down at the same time), when pressed will result in electrical signals being sent along a set of wires that connect to an input device on the computer, a USB port perhaps. While knowing the details of USB and the keyboard hardware is beyond the scope of this book, it is easy to understand that pressing a key can result in an identifiable combination of wires being given a voltage. This is in fact a representation of the character, and one that underlies the one that will be used on the computer itself. As described previously, voltages can be used to represent binary numbers.

The representation of characters on a computer amounts to an assignment of a number to each possible character. This assignment could be arbitrary, and for some data it is. The value of the letter "a" could be 1, "b" could be 12, and "c" could be 6. This would work, but it would be a poor representation because characters are not in an arbitrary order. The letter "b" should be between "a" and "c" in value because it is positioned there in the data set, the set of characters. In any case, when creating a numeric representation, the first rule is:

1. If there are a relatively small number of individual data items, assign them consecutive values starting at 0. If there is a practical reason to start at some other number, then do so.

   The second rule considers the existing ordering of the elements:

2. In cases where data items are assigned consecutive values, assign them in a manner that maintains any predefined *order* of the elements.

   This means that in a definition of characters, the letters "a," "b," and "c" should appear in that order.

3. In cases where data items are assigned consecutive values, assign them in a manner that maintains any preexisting *distance* between the elements.

   This means that the letters "a," "b," and "c" would be adjacent to each other in the numeric representation because they are next to each other in the alphabet. It also means that character classes will stay together; the uppercase letters will be consecutive, the digits will also have consecutive codes so that the code for "0" will be adjacent to and smaller than the code for "1", and so on. This set of three rules actually creates a pretty good mapping of characters to numbers. However, there are more rules for making representations.

4. In cases where data items are assigned consecutive values, assign them in a manner that simplifies the operations that are likely to be performed on the data.

   In the present example of character data, there are relatively few places where this rule would be invoked, but one would be when comparing characters to each other. A character "A" is usually thought to come before "a," so this means that all of the uppercase letters will come before all lowercase ones, in a numerical sense. Similarly, "0" comes before "A," so all digits come before all letters in the representation. A space would come before (i.e., have a smaller value than) any character that prints.

   One of the most common character representations, named the *American Standard Code for Information Interchange* or *ASCII*, has all of these properties and a few others. The standard ASCII character set lists

128 characters with numerical codes from 0 to 127. In the table below, each character is listed with the code that represents it. They appear in numerical order. The characters in orange are telecommunications characters that are never used by a typical computer user; green characters are non-printing characters that are used for formatting text on a page; letters and numbers for English are red; special characters like punctuation are blue. The space character is in some sense unique, and is black.

Code	Char	Code	Char	Code	Char	Code	Char	Code	Char	Code	Char	Code	Char	Code	Char
0	NUL	16	DLE	32	Space	48	0	64	@	80	P	96	`	112	p
1	SOH	17	DC1	33	!	49	1	65	A	81	Q	97	A	113	q
2	STX	18	DC2	34	"	50	2	66	B	82	R	98	B	114	r
3	ETX	19	DC3	35	#	51	3	67	C	83	S	99	C	115	s
4	EOT	20	DC4	36	$	52	4	68	D	84	T	100	D	116	t
5	ENQ	21	NAK	37	%	53	5	69	E	85	U	101	E	117	u
6	ACK	22	SYN	38	&	54	6	70	F	86	V	102	F	118	v
7	BEL	23	ETB	39	'	55	7	71	G	87	W	103	G	119	w
8	BS	24	CAN	40	(	56	8	72	H	88	X	104	H	120	x
9	TAB	25	EM	41	)	57	9	73	I	89	Y	105	I	121	y
10	LF	26	SUB	42	*	58	:	74	J	90	Z	106	J	122	z
11	VT	27	ESC	43	+	59	;	75	K	91	[	107	K	123	{
12	FF	28	FS	44	,	60	<	76	L	92	\	108	L	124		
13	CR	29	GS	45	-	61	=	77	M	93	]	109	M	125	}
14	SO	30	RS	46	.	63	>	78	N	94	^	110	N	126	~
15	SI	31	US	47	/	63	?	79	O	95	_	111	O	127	DEL

Further on the subject of representation, if there are a very large number of possible data values, then enumerating them would seem unreasonable. There are usually other ways to attack that sort of problem.

5. If the data can be broken up into enumerable parts, then try to do that.

Dates can be an example of this kind of data. There are too many dates to store as discrete values, as there is no actual day 0 and there is no practical final day in the general case. However, a common way to state a date is to give a year, a month, and a day. This is awkward from a computer perspective because of the variable number of days in each month, but works pretty well for humans. Each component is enumerable, so a possible representation for a date would be as three numbers: year, month, day; it would be YYYYMMDD, where YYYY is a four-digit year, MM is a number between 0 (January) and 11 (December), and DD is a number between 0 and 30, which is the day of the month.

This representation should keep the dates in the correct sequence, so Dec 9, 1957 (19571108) will come after Aug 24, 1955 (19550723). However, another common operation on dates is to find the number of days between two specified dates. This is difficult, and the only representation that would simplify it would be to start counting days at a zero point. If that zero point were Jan 1, 1900, then the representation for the date Oct 31, 2017 would be 43037. The number of days between two dates would be found by subtraction. However, printing the date in a form for humans to read is difficult. When selecting a representation, the most common operations on the data should be the easiest ones to perform.

Another example of this sort or representation is *color*, which will be discussed in detail in a later chapter.

6. When the data is part of a continuous stream of real values, then it may be possible to *sample* them and/or *quantize* them.

Sampling means to represent a sequence by using a subset of the values. Imagine a set of numbers coming from a seismometer. The number sequence represents measurements of the motion of the ground captured continuously by a mechanical device. It is normally OK to ignore some of these values, knowing that between a value of 5.1 (whatever that means) and a value of 6.3, the numbers would have taken on all possible values between those two; that's what continuous means.

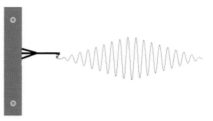

Figure 0.24
A continuous set of data has a measurable value between any other two.

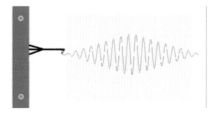

So instead of capturing an infinite number of values, which is not possible, why not capture a value every second, or tenth of a second, or at whatever interval makes sense for the data concerned. Some data will be lost. The important thing is not to lose anything valuable.

Figure 0.25
Sampling means picking an interval and only keeping the data values at those locations. The vertical lines here are sampling positions.

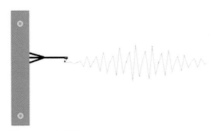

Figure 0.26

The resulting signal is not as smooth as the original (lower resolution).

The same thing can be done spatially. If someone is building a road, then it must be surveyed. A set of height values for points along the area to be occupied by the road is collected so that a model of the 3D region can be built. But between any two points that can be sampled there is another point that could be sampled, on to infinity. Again, a decision is made to limit the number of samples so that the measurements are made every few yards. This limits the accuracy, but not in a practical way. The height at some specific point may not have been measured, but it can be estimated from the numbers around it.

The distance between two sample points is referred to casually as the *resolution*. In spatial sampling it will be expressed in distance units and says something about the smallest thing that can be precisely known. In time sampling it is expressed in seconds.

Quantization means how accurately each measurement is known. In high school science, numbers that are measurements are given to some number of significant figures. Measuring a weight as 110.9881 pounds would seem impossibly accurate, and 111 would be a more reasonable number. Quantization in computer terms would be *restricting the number of bits used to represent the value*. Something that is stored as an 8-bit number can have 256 distinct values, for example. If the world's tallest person is under 8 feet tall, then using 8 bits to represent height would mean that 8 feet would be broken up into 256 parts, which is 0.375 inches; that is, 8 feet x 12 inches/foot = 96 inches, and dividing this in to 256 parts = 0.375. The smallest difference in height that could be expressed would be this value, a little over a third of an inch.

Quantization is reflected in the representation as a possible error in each value. The greater the number of bits per sample the more accurately each one is represented. The use of sampling and quantization is very common, and is used when saving sounds (MP3), images (JPEG), and videos (AVI).

There are other possible options for creating a representation for data, but the six basic ideas here will work most of the time, alone or in combination.

A programmer will spend most of his or her time living with the consequences of the representations they chose for their data. A poor choice will result in more complex code, which generates more errors and less overall satisfaction with the result. Spending a little extra time at the beginning analyzing the possibilities can save a lot of effort later.

0.6 SUMMARY

Computers are devices that humans have built in order to facilitate complex calculations and are tools for rapidly and accurately manipulating numbers. When humans communicate with each other, we use a language. Similarly, humans use languages to communicate with computers. A computer program can be thought of as a sequence of operations that a computer can perform in order to accomplish a calculation. The key is that it must be expressed in terms that the computer can do.

Early computers were mechanical, using gears to represent numbers. Electronic computers usually use two electrical states or voltages to represent numbers, and those numbers are in binary or base 2 form. Electronic computers have memories that can store numbers, and everything stored in memory must be in numeric form. That includes the instructions that the computer can execute.

Computers have been around long enough to provide many layers of computer programs that can assist in their effective use: graphical user interfaces, assemblers, compilers for programming languages, web browsers, and accounting packages each provide a user with a different view of a computer and a different way to use it. Computers can exchange data between each other using wires over short distances (computer network) and long ones (Internet). The World Wide Web sits atop the Internet and provides an easy and effective way for computers all over the world to exchange information in any form.

Everything stored and manipulated on a computer has to be a number. What if the data is not numeric? In that case a numeric representation has to be devised that effectively characterizes the information while permitting its efficient manipulation.

Exercises

1. Convert the following binary numbers into decimal:
   a) 0100000
   b) 0000100
   c) 0000111
   d) 0101010
   e) 0110100101
   f) 0111111
   g) 110110110

2. Convert the following decimal numbers into binary:
   a) 10
   b) 100
   c) 64
   d) 128
   e) 254
   f) 5
   g) 999

3. Core memory would not erase itself when its power source was removed. Give reasons why this is a valuable property.

   _____

   _____

   _____

4. Specify a device that is used for:
   a) Output only
   b) Input only
   c) Both input and output

5. Ada Countess of Lovelace is generally considered to be the first programmer, but some contrary information has come to light recently. Search the literature for two articles on each side of the argument and formulate a conclusion. Was she?

6. What is the difference between a compiler and an interpreter? Give an example of each.

7. Identify a GUI widget that was not discussed in this chapter. Sketch its appearance and describe its operation. Give an example of a situation where it might be used.

8. Give the ASCII codes for the following characters:
   a) 'P'
   b) ';'
   c) 'r'
   d) ','
   e) '='

9. What is the value of the ASCII code for the character "1" minus the code for the character "0"? What is "2"-"0"? What does this say about converting from the character form of a number into its numeric value in general?

10. Consider the imaginary computer devised in this chapter. It has a memory in which each location has 12 binary digits (bits) to store a number. In one of the memory locations the value 101000000000 is seen. What is this? Is it an instruction, a number, a character, an address, or something else? How can this be determined?

Notes and Other Resources

1. L. Carlitz. (1968). **Bernoulli numbers**, *Fibonacci Quarterly*, 6, 71–85.

2. Digital Equipment Corporation. (1972). **Introduction to Programming**, PDP-8 handbook series, online version *http://www.mirrorservice.org/sites/ www.bitsavers.org/pdf/dec/pdp8/handbooks/IntroToProgramming1969.pdf*

3. James Essinger. (2004). **Jacquard's Web**, Oxford University Press, Oxford, ISBN 978-0-19-280578-2.

4. Tony Sale. **The Colossus Computer 1943–1996: How It Helped to Break the German Lorenz Cipher in WWII**, M.&M. Baldwin, Kidderminster, 2004, ISBN 0-947712-36-4.

5. Stephen Stephenson. (2013). **Ancient Computers, Part I - Rediscovery, 2nd Edition**, ISBN 1-4909-6437-1.

6. A. M. Turing. (1936). **On Computable Numbers, with an Application to the Entscheidungsproblem.**

7. Michael R. Williams. (1998). **The "Last Word" on Charles Babbage,** *IEEE Annals of the History of Computing, 20*(4), 10–4, doi:10.1109/85.728225

8. Javier Yanes. (2015). **Ada Lovelace: Original and Visionary, but No Programmer,** OpenMind, December 9, 2015, *https://www.bbvaopenmind. com/en/ada-lovelace-original-and-visionary-but-no-programmer/*

## CHAPTER 1

COMPUTERS AND
PROGRAMMING

In this chapter

The vast majority of computers that most people encounter are referred to as *digital* computers. This refers to the fact that the computer works on numbers. Other kinds of computers do exist but are not as common; *analog* computers operate in a number of other ways, but are usually electrical—they manipulate electrical voltages and currents—or mechanical—they use gears and shafts to calculate a mechanical response.

The fact that any problem must be expressed in numerical form has presented a problem to some potential programmers. *I'm not good at math* is a common complaint, and the belief that computer programming requires a knowledge of advanced mathematics is used as a reason to not study programming. In fact, the kind of math commonly needed would more properly be called arithmetic, not math.

In order for a problem to be solved using a computer, the problem must be expressed in a way that manipulates numbers, and the data involved must be numeric. This is often accomplished by some kind of encoding of the data. It is so common that the process is invisible on modern computers. Most data have a variety of encodings that have been used for years and are taken for granted: images in JPEG format or sounds in MP3 are examples of commonly used encoding of data into numbers.

What can computers do with numbers? Addition, subtraction, multiplication, and division are the basic operations, but computers can compare the value of numbers too.

1.1 SOLVING A PROBLEM USING A COMPUTER

The process begins with a problem to be solved, and the first step is to state the problem as clearly as possible. This first step is critically important because unless the problem is completely understood, its solution on a computer is impossible. Then the problem is analyzed to determine methods by which it may be solved. As computers can only directly manipulate numbers, it is common for solutions discussed at this stage to be numerical or mathematical and for them to involve deciding upon representations for the data that will facilitate solving the problem. Then a sketch of the solution, perhaps on paper in a human language and math, is created. This is translated into computer language and then typed into computer form using a keyboard. The resulting text file is called a *script, source code*, or more commonly the *computer program*. A program called a **compiler** takes this program and converts it into a form that can be executed on the computer. Basically, all programs are converted into a set of numbers called machine code, which the computer can execute.

We are going to learn a language called *Python*. It was developed as a general purpose programming language and is a good language for teaching because it makes a lot of things easy. Quite a few applications are built using Python; for example: the games *Eve Online* and *Civilization IV*, *BitTorrent*, and *Dropbox* to name only a few. It is a bit like a lot of other languages in use these days in terms of structure (syntax) but has some simplifying ideas that will be discussed in later chapters.

In order to use a programming language, there are some basic concepts and structures that need to be understood at a basic level. Some of these concepts will be introduced in this chapter, and the rest of the book will teach you to program by example; in all cases, coding examples will be introduced by stating a problem to be solved. The problems to be solved in this chapter include: a simple *guess-a-number* game and the game of *rock-paper-scissors*. These problems will be the motivation for learning more about either the Python language itself or about methods of solving problems. Any computer programs in this book will execute on a computer running any major operating system once the free Python language download has been installed.

1.2 EXECUTING PYTHON

Figure 1.1
Running the Python GUI.

Installing Python is not too difficult, and involves downloading the installer, running it, and perhaps configuring a few specific details. This process can be found on the net. Once installed there are a few variations that can be used with it, the simplest probably being the *Python Graphical User Interface* or *GUI*. If running Python on a Windows PC, look at the Start menu for Python and click; a link named "IDLE (Python GUI)" will be seen, as shown in Figure 1.1. Click on this and the user interface will open. Click the mouse in the GUI window so that you can start typing characters there.

Python can be run interactively in the GUI window. The characters ">>>" are called a *prompt*, and indicate that Python is waiting for something to be typed at the keyboard. Anything typed here will be presumed to be a Python program, or at least part of one. As a demonstration, type "1" followed by "Enter." Python responds by printing "1." Why? When "1" was typed it was a Python expression, something to be evaluated. The value of "1" is simply "1," so that was the answer Python computed.

Now type "1+1." Python responds with "2." Python inputs what the user/programmer types, evaluates it as a mathematical (in Python form) expression, and prints the answer. This is not really programming yet, because a basic two-dollar calculator can do this, but it is certainly a start.

IDLE is good for many things, but eventually a more sophisticated environment will be needed, one that can indent automatically, detect some kinds of errors, and allow programs to be run and debugged and saved as *projects*. This kind of system is called an integrated development environment, or IDE. There are many of these available for Python, some costing quite a lot and some freely downloadable. The code in this book has been compiled and tested using one called *PyCharm*, but most IDEs out there would be fine, and it is largely a matter of personal preference. Basic PyCharm is free, and it has a bigger brother that costs a small amount.

An advantage of an IDE is that it is easy to type in a whole program, run it, find the errors, fix them, and run it again. This process is repeated until the program works as desired. Multiple parts of a large program can be saved as separate files and collected together by the IDE, and they can be worked on individually and tested together. And a good IDE uses color to indicate syntax features that Python understands and can show some kinds of error while the code is being entered.

To begin programming it must be understood that a language has a *syntax* or structure, and that for computer languages this structure cannot be varied. The computer will always be the arbiter of what is correct, and if any program has a syntax error in it or produces erroneous results, then it is the program and not the computer that is at fault.

Next, one should appreciate that the syntax is arbitrary. It was designed by a human with attitudes and biases and new ideas, and while the syntax might sometimes be ugly and hard to recall, it is what it is. Parts of it might not be understood at first, but after a while and after reading and executing the first programs in this book, most of it will make sense.

A program, just like any sentence or paragraph in English, consists of symbols, and order matters. Some symbols are special characters with a defined meaning. For example, "+" usually means *add*, and "-" usually means *subtract*. Some symbols are words. Words defined by the language, like *if*, *while*, and *true*, cannot also be defined by a programmer—they mean what the language says they mean, and are called *reserved words*. Some names have a definition given by the system but can be reused by a programmer as needed. These are called *predefined names* or *system variables*. However, some words can be defined by the programmer, and are the names for things the programmer wants to use in the program: *variables* and *functions* are examples.

1.3 GUESS A NUMBER

Games that involve guessing are common, and are sometimes used to resolve minor conflicts such as who gets the next piece of cake or who gets the first kick at a football. It's also sometimes a way to occupy time, and can simply be fun. How can we write a program to have the user guess a number that the program has chosen?

There are many variations on this simple game. In one the number is to be guessed precisely. One person (the *chooser*) has selected a number, an integer, in a specified range. "Pick a number between one and ten" would be a typical problem. The other person, the guesser, must choose a number in that range. If they select the correct number, then the guesser wins. This is a boring game and is biased in favor of the chooser.

A more interesting variation would be to start with one guess and have the chooser then say whether the target number is greater than or less than the guessed number. The guesser then guesses again, and the process continues until the number is guessed correctly. The roles of guesser and chooser can now switch and the game starts again. The best guesser is the one who uses the fewest guesses.

A third alternative is to have multiple guessers. All guessers make their selection and the one who has chosen a number nearest the correct number is the winner. This is the best game for solving disputes, because it involves one guess from each person. Ties are possible, in which case the game can be played again.

1.4 ROCK-PAPER-SCISSORS

Although this game is used by children to settle disputes and make random decisions such as "who goes first," it has been taken more seriously by adults. There are actually competitions where money is at stake. A televised contest in Las Vegas had a prize of $50,000. This game is not as trivial as it once was.

In this game each of two players selects one item from the list [rock, paper, scissors] in secret, and then both display their choice simultaneously. If both players selected the same item, then they try again. Otherwise, rock beats scissors, scissors beats paper, and paper beats rock. This contest can be repeated for a "best out of N" competition.

Both of these games form the first problem set, and serve as the motivation for learning the elements of the Python language.

1.5 SOLVING THE *GUESS A NUMBER* PROBLEM

The simple version of the guessing program has two versions, depending on who is guessing. The computer should pick the number and the human user should guess, because the other way around can use some complex programming. In that case here's what has to happen:

1. The computer selects a number.
2. The computer asks the player to guess.
3. The player types a number on the keyboard and the computer reads it in.

4. The computer compares the input number against the one that it selected, and if the two agree, then the player wins. Otherwise the computer wins.

The Python features needed to do this include: printing a message, reading in a number, having a place to store a number (a variable), having a way to select a number, and having a way to compare the two numbers and act differently depending on the result.

The second version requires the above, plus a way to repeat the process in cases when the guess is wrong and until it is correct. In this case the method becomes:

1. The computer selects a number.
2. The computer asks the player to guess.
3. The player types a number on the keyboard and the computer reads it in.
4. The computer compares the input number against the one that it selected, and if the two agree, then the player has guessed correctly. Exit to Step 7.
5. The computer determines whether the guess is higher or lower than the actual number and prints an appropriate message.
6. Repeat from Step 2.
7. Game over.

The repetition mechanism is the only new aspect to this solution, but it is an essential component of Python and every other programming language.

1.6 SOLVING THE *ROCK-PAPER-SCISSORS* PROBLEM

The solution to this problem has no new requirements, but re-enforces the language features of the previous solutions. One solution to this problem is:

1. Select a random choice form the three items rock, paper, or scissors. Save this choice in a variable named **choice**
2. Ask the player for their choice. Use an integer value, where 1 = rock, 2 = paper, and 3 = scissors
3. Read the player's selection into a variable named **player**
4. If **player** is equal to **choice**

5. Print the message "Tie. We'll try again."

6. Repeat from Step 1

7. If **player** is equal to rock

8. If **choice** is equal to scissors, go to Step 17

9. Else go to Step 18

10. If **player** is equal to paper

11. If **choice** is equal to scissors, go to Step 17

12. Else go to Step 18

13. If **player** is equal to scissors

14. If **choice** is equal to rock, go to Step 17

15. Else go to Step 18

16. Print error message and terminate

17. Print "Computer wins" and terminate

18. Print "You win" and terminate

For each player selection, one of the alternate items will beat it and one will lose to it. Each choice is checked and the win/lose decision is made based on the known outcomes.

The solutions to both problems require similar language elements: a way to store a value (a *variable*), a way to execute specific parts of the program depending on the value of a variable or expression (an *if* statement), a way to read a value from the keyboard, a way to print a message on the screen, and a way to execute code repeatedly (a *loop*).

1.6.1 Variables and Values – Experimenting with the Graphical User Interface

A *variable* is a name that the programmer can define to represent some value, a number or a text string generally. It represents the place where the computer stores that value; it is a symbol in text form, something humans like, representing a value. Everything that a computer does is ultimately done with numbers, so the location of any thing is a number that represents the place in computer memory where that thing is stored. It's like offices in a building. Each office has a number (its address) and usually has a name too (the occupant or business found there).

Additionally, the office has contents, and those contents are often described by the name given. In Figure 1.2 a collection of offices in a specific building can be seen. In this metaphor the office number corresponds to the address, and the name (variable name), being more human friendly, is how it is often referred to by a person (programmer). In all cases, though, it is the contents of the office (location) that are important. The number and name are ways to access it. So, someone might say *"Bring me the Python manual from the Server Room"* or *"Bring me the Python manual from 607"* and both would be the same thing. The contents of location 607 would be the Python manual. Now someone could say *"Put this Python manual in the Digital Media Lab,"* which would change the contents of location 611. In actual Python the act of retrieving a value from a location does not change the contents of that location, but instead makes a copy, but the basic metaphor is sound.

Not all strings or characters can be variable names. A variable cannot begin with a digit, for example, or with most non-alphabetic characters like "&" or "!," although in some cases beginning with "_" is acceptable. A variable name can contain upper- or lowercase letters, digits, and "_". Uppercase and lowercase are distinct, so the variables **Hello** and **hello** are different.

Figure 1.2
Variables are names that represent addresses, like offices in a building. The name is used in programming to represent the value found inside. These door signs are from the author's workplace.

So a variable can change values but, unlike a real office, a simple variable can hold only one value at a time. The name chosen does not have to be significant. Programs often have variables named **i** or **x**. However, it is a good idea to select names that represent the kind of value that the variable it to contain so as to communicate that meaning to another person, a programmer probably. For example, the value 3.1415926 should be stored in a variable named **pi**, because that's the name everyone else gives to this value.

In the GUI type **pi = 3.1415926**. Python responds with a prompt, which indicates that it is content with this statement, and that it has no value to print. If you now type **pi**, the response will be **3.1415926**; the variable named **pi** that was just created now has a value.

In the syntax of Python, the name **pi** is a variable, the number **3.1415926** is a constant, but is also an *expression*, and the symbol = means *assign to*. In the precise domain of computer language, **pi = 3.1415926** is an *assignment statement* and gives the variable named **pi** the specified value.

Continuing with this example, define a new variable named **radius** to be 10.0 using an assignment statement **radius = 10.0**. If you type **radius** and "enter," Python responds with **10.0**. Finally, we know that the circumference of a circle is **2pr** in math terms, or *2 times pi times the radius* in English. Type **2*pi*radius** into the Python GUI, and it responds with **62.831852**, which is the correct answer. Now type **circumference = 2*pi*radius**, and Python assigns the value of the computation to the variable **circumference**.

Python defines a variable when it is given a value for the first time. The type of the variable is defined at that moment too; that is, if a number is assigned to a name, then that name is expected to represent a number from then on. If a string is assigned to a name, then that name will be expected to be a string from then on. Trying to use a variable before it has been given a value and a type is an error. Attempting the calculation:

$$\text{area = side*side}$$

is not allowed unless there is a variable named **side** already defined at this point. The following is OK because it defines **side** first, and then in turn is used to define **area**:

$$\text{side = 12.0}$$
$$\text{area = side*side}$$

The two lines above are called *statements* in a programming language, and in Python a statement usually ends at the end of the line (the "enter" key was pressed). This is a bit unusual in a computer language, and people who already know Java or C++ have some difficulty with this idea at first. In other computer languages statements are separated by semicolons, not by the end of the line. In fact, in most languages the indenting of lines in the program does not have any meaning except to the programmer. In Python that's not the case either, as will be seen shortly.

The expressions we use in assignments can be pretty complicated, but are really only things that we learned in high school. Add, subtract, multiply, and divide. Multiplication and division are performed before addition and subtraction, which is called a *precedence rule*, so 3*2+1 is 7, not 9; otherwise, *evaluation is done left to right*, so 6/3*2 is 4 (do the division first) as opposed to 1 (if the multiplication was done first). These are rules that should be familiar because it is how people are taught to do arithmetic. The symbol "**" means exponent *or to the power of*, so **2**3** is 2^3 which is 8, and this operator has a higher precedence (i.e., is done before) than the others. Parentheses can be used to specify the order of things. So, for example, **(2+3)**2** is 25, because the expression within the parenthesis is done first, then the exponent.

1.6.2 Exchanging Information with the Computer

When using most programming languages, it is necessary to design communication with the computer program. This goes two ways: the program will inform the user of things, such as the circumference of a circle given a specific radius, and the user may want to tell the program certain things, like the value of the radius with which to compute the circumference. We communicate with a program using *text*, which is to say characters typed into a keyboard. When a computer is presenting results, that text is often in the form of human language, messages as sentences. "The circumference is 62.831852" could be such a message. The sentence is actually composed by a programmer and has a number or collection of numbers embedded within it.

Python allows a programmer to send a message to the screen, and hence to the user, using a **print** directive. This is the word **print** followed by a character string, which is often a set of characters in quotes. An example:

```
print ("The answer is yes.")
```

The parentheses are used to enclose everything that is to be printed; such a statement can print many strings if they are separated by commas. Numbers will be converted into strings for printing. So the following is correct:

```
print ("The circumference is ", 62.831852)
```

Figure 1.3
The Python GUI window showing the examples so far.

If a variable appears in the list following print, then the value of that variable will be printed, not the name of the variable. So:

```
print ("The circumference is ", circumference)
```

is also correct.

1.6.3 Example 1: Draw a Circle Using Characters

Assuming that it is desired to print a circle having a constant predefined radius, this can be done with a few print statements. The planning of the graphic itself (the circle) can be done using graph paper. Assuming that each character uses the same amount of space, a circle can be approximated using some skillfully placed "*" characters. Then print each row of characters using a print statement. A sample solution is:

```
print ("        ***         ")
print ("     *********       ")
print ("   *************     ")
print (" ***************     ")
print (" ***************     ")
print (" ***************     ")
print ("   *************     ")
print ("     *********       ")
print ("        ***         ")
```

1.6.4 Strings, Integers, and Real Numbers

Computer programs deal mainly with numbers. Integers, or whole numbers, and reals or floating point numbers, which represent fractions, are represented differently, and arithmetic works differently on the two types of numbers. A Python variable can hold either type, but if a variable contains an integer then it is treated as an integer, and if it's holding a floating point number then it is treated as one of those. What's the difference? First, there's a difference in how they are printed out. If we make the assignment **var = 1** and then print the value of **var**, it prints simply as 1. If we make the assignment **var = 1.0** and then print **var**, it prints as 1.0. In both cases **var** is a real or floating point number and will be treated as such. Numeric constants will be thought of as real numbers. However, a variable can be first one thing and then another. It will be the last thing it was assigned.

Arithmetic differs between integers and reals, but the only time that difference is really apparent is when doing division. Integers are always whole, non-fractional numbers. If we divide 3 by 2, both 3 and 2 are integers and so the division must result in an integer: the result is 1. This is because there is exactly a single 2 in 3, or if you like, 2 goes into 3 just once, with a remainder of 1. There is a specific operator for doing integer division: "//." So, 3//2 is equal to 1. The remainder part can't be handled and is discarded, but can be found separately using the "%" operator. For example, 8//5 is 1, and 8%5 is the remainder, 3. This explanation is an approximation to the truth, and one that can be cleared up later, but it works perfectly well for positive numbers.

Of course fractions work fine for real numbers, and will be printed as decimal fractions: 8.0/5.0 is 1.6, for example. What happens if we mix reals and integers? In those cases things get converted into real, but now things get more complicated, because order can matter a great deal. The expression 7//2*2.0 does the division 7//2 first, which is 3, and then multiplies that by 2.0, yielding the result 6.0; the result of 8/3*3.0 would be 5.333. Mixing integers and reals is not a good idea, but if done, the expressions should use parentheses to specify how the expression should be evaluated.

A real can be used in place of an integer in most places, but the result will be real. Thus, 2.0 * 3 = 6.0, not 6, and 6.0//2 is 3.0, not 3. There are some exceptions. To convert an integer to a real, there is a special operation named **float: float(3)** yields 3.0. Of course it's possible to simply multiply by 1.0 and the result will be float too. Converting float values to integers is more complicated, because of the fraction issue: what happens to the digits to the right of the decimal? The operation **int** will take a floating point value and throw away the fraction. The value of **int(3.5)** will be 3, as a result. It is normal in human calculations to round to the nearest integer, and the operation **round(3.5)** does that, resulting in 4.

1.6.5 Number Bases

In elementary school, perhaps grade 3 or 4, the idea of positional number systems is taught. The number 216 is a way to write the value of $6 + 1*10 + 2*100$. Not all civilizations use such a scheme; Roman numerals are not positional, for example. Still, most people are comfortable with the idea. What people are not as comfortable with is changing the number base away from 10. In Chapter 0, the binary system, or base 2, was discussed, but any base that is a power of 2 is of some interest, especially base 8 and base 16.

Humans use a base 10 scheme probably because we have 10 fingers. What it means is that we have a symbol for each of the 10 digits, 0 through 9, and each digit position to the left of the first digit is multiplied by the next power of 10. The number 216 is really $2*10^2 + 1*10^1 + 6*10^0$. The base is 10, and each digit represents a power of the base multiplied by a digit. What if the base is 8? In that case 216 is really $2*8^2 + 1*8^1 + 6$. If the arithmetic is carried out, this number turns out to be $128 + 8 + 6 = 142$.

If multiple number bases are used, it is common to give the base as a subscript. The number 216 in base 8 is written as 216_8. The default would be base 10. In base 8 there are only 8 digits, 0 through 7. The digits 8 and 9 cannot appear. In bases larger than 10 more symbols are needed. A common base to be used on computers is 16, or hexadecimal (hex for short). In a hex number 16 digits are needed, so the regular ones are used and then "A" represents 10, "B" is 11, "C" is 12, "D" is 13, "E" is 14, and "F" is 15. The hex number 12_{16} is $1*16 + 2$, or 18_{10}. The number $1A_{16}$ is $1*16 + 10 = 26_{10}$.

In Python numbers are given in decimal (base 10) by default. However, if a number constant begins with "0o" (zero followed by the letter "o") Python assumes it is base 8 (octal). The number **0o21**, for example, is $21_8 = 17_{10}$. A number that begins with "0x" is hexadecimal. **0x21** is $21_{16} = 33_{10}$. This applies only to integers.

There is a number base that is the most important, because it lies under all of the numbers on a computer. That would be base 2. All numbers on a modern digital computer are represented in base 2, or binary, in their internal representation. A binary number has only two digits, 0 and 1, and each represents a power of 2. Thus, 1101_2 is $1*2^3 + 1*2^2 + 0*2^1 + 1 = 8 + 4 + 1 = 13_{10}$. In Python a binary number begins with "0b," so the number **0b10101** represents 21_{10}.

These number bases are important for many reasons, but base 2 is fundamental, and bases 8 and 16 are important because they are powers of 2 and so convert very easily to binary but have fewer digits. One example of the use of hex is for colors. In Python they can represent a color, and on web pages they are certainly used that way. The number 0xFF0000 is the color red, for example, if used on a web page. But more of that later.

1.6.6 Example 2: Compute the Circumference of any Circle

When humans send information into a computer program, the text tends to be in the form of numbers. The Python code that was written to calculate the radius of a circle only did the calculation for a single radius: 10. That's not as useful as a program that computes the circumference of any circle, and that would mean allowing the user to tell the program what radius to use. This should be easy to do, because it is something that is needed frequently. Frequently needed things should always be easy. In the case of sending a number into a program in Python, the word **input** can be used within a program. For example:

```
radius = input ()
```

will accept a number from the keyboard, typed by the user, and will return it as a string of characters. This makes sense because the user typed it as a string of characters, but it can't be used in a calculation in this form. To convert it into the internal form of a number, we must specifically ask for this to be done:

```
radius = input()
radius = float(radius)
```

will read a string into **radius**, then convert it into a *floating point* (real) number and assign it to the variable **radius** again. This can be done all in one statement:

```
radius = float(input())
```

Now the variable radius can be used to calculate a circumference. This is a whole computer program that does a useful thing. If the value of **radius** was to be an integer, the code would read:

```
radius = int(input())
```

If the conversion to a number is not done, then Python will give an error message when the calculation is performed, like:

```
Traceback (most recent call last):
  File "<pyshell#13>", line 1, in <module>
      circumference = 2*pi*radius
  TypeError: can't multiply sequence by non-int of
  type 'float'
```

This is pretty uninformative to a beginning programmer. What is a *Traceback*? What's *pyshell*? There are clues as to what this means, though. The line of code at which the error occurs is given and the term *TypeError* is descriptive. This error means that something that can't be multiplied (a string) was used in an expression involving a multiplication. That thing is the variable **radius** in this instance because it was a text string and was not converted to a number.

Also note that **int(input())** can present problems when the input string is not in fact an integer. If it is a floating point number, this results in an error. The expression **int("3.14159")** could be interpreted as an attempt convert *pi* into an integer, and would have the value 3; in fact, it is an error. The function **int** was passed a string and the string contained a float, not an int. This is something of a quirk of Python. It is better to convert input numbers into floats.

1.6.7 Guess a Number Again

The simple version of the guessing program can now nearly be written in Python. Examining the method of solution, here's what can be coded so far; versions depend on who is guessing. The computer should pick the number and the human user should guess, because the other way around can involve some complex programming. In that case here's what has to happen:

1. The computer selects a number.
   ```
   choice = 7
   ```

2. The computer asks the player to guess.

```
print ("Please guess a number between 1 and 10: ")
```

3. The player types a number on the keyboard and the computer reads it in.

```
playerchoice = input()
```

4. The computer compares the input number against the one that it selected, and if the two agree, then the player wins. Otherwise the computer wins.

It is the final step that is still not possible with what is known. It is necessary in this program, as it is in most computer programs, to make a decision and to execute certain code (i.e., do specific things) conditionally based on the outcome of that decision. People do that sort of thing all of the time in real life. Examples include:

"If the light is red then stop, otherwise continue through the intersection."

"If all tellers are busy when you arrive at the bank, then stand in line and wait for the next one to become available."

"If you need bread or milk, then stop at the grocery store on the way home."

"If it rains, the picnic will be cancelled."

Notice that all of these examples use the word "if." This word indicates a standard *conditional sentence* in English. The condition in the first case is the phrase "if the light is red" (called in English the *protaxis* or *antecedent*) and the consequence to that is the phrase "then stop" (the *apodosis* or *consequent*). Terminology aside, the intent is clear to an English speaker: on the condition that or in the event that the light is red, then the necessary action is that the driver is to stop their car. The action is conditional on the antecedent, which in Python will be called an *expression* or, more precisely, a *logical expression*, which has the value True or False.

The structure or syntax of this sort of thing in Python would be:

```
if the light is red:
    stop
```

or more exactly:

```
if light == red:
    # execute whatever code makes the car stop
```

This is called an **if** statement, and is more profound with a more complex syntax than can be inferred from this example.

1.7 IF STATEMENTS

In Python an if statement begins with the word **if**, followed by an expression that evaluates to **True** or **False**, followed by a colon (:), then a series of statements that are executed if the expression is true. The names True and False are constants having the obvious meaning, and a variable that can take on these values is a *logical* or *Boolean* (named after the man who invented two state or logical algebra) variable. The expression is the only tricky part. It can be a constant like **True**, or a variable that has a **True** or **False** value, or a *relational expression* (one that compares two things) or a logical combination of any of these—anything that has a result that is true or false.

```
if True:          # Constant
if flag:          # Logical variable
if a < b:         # relational expression
if a<b and c>d:   # logical combination
```

A logical expression can be any arithmetic expressions being compared using any of the following operators:

<	Less than
>	Greater than
<=	Less than or equal to
>=	Greater than or equal to
==	Equal to
!=	Not equal to

Logical combinations can be:

```
and    EG:    a==b and b==c
or     EG:    a==b or a==c
not    EG:    not (a == b)        # same as !=
```

The syntax is simple and yet allows a huge number of combinations. For example:

```
if p == q and not p == z and not z == p:
if pi**2 < 12:
if (a**b)**(c-d)/3 <= z**3:
```

The *consequent*, or the actions to be taken if the logical expression is true, follows the colon on the following lines. The next statement is indented more than the **if**, and all statements that follow immediately that have the same indentation

if   a<b   :

| The key word, known by Python, that indicates this is an IF statement. | An expression that evaluates to **True** or **False** | The colon indicates the end of the first part of the statement. Think of it as meaning **THEN**, as in **IF expression THEN** |

Figure 1.4
Syntax of an IF statement.

are a part of the consequent and are executed if the condition is true, otherwise none of them are. As an example, consider:

```
if a < b:
    a = a + 1
    b = b - 1
c = a - b
```

In this case the two statements following the ":" are indented by 4 more spaces than is the **if**. This tells Python that they are both a part of the **if** statement, and that if the value of **a** is smaller than the value of **b**, then both of those statements will be executed. Python calls such a group of statements a *suite*. The assignment to the variable c is indented to the same level as the **if**, so it will be executed in any case and is not conditional.

The use of indentation to connect statements into groups is unusual in programming languages. Most languages in use pretty much ignore spaces and line breaks altogether, and use a statement separator such as a semicolon to demark statements. So, in the Java language the above code would look like this:

```
if (a<b) {
   a = a + 1;
   b = b - 1;
}
c = a - b;
```

The braces { ... } enclose the suite, which would probably be called a *block* in Java or C++. Notice that this code is also indented, but in Java this means nothing to the computer. Indentation is used for clarity, so that someone reading the code later can see more clearly what is happening.

Semicolons are used in Python too, but much more rarely. If it is desired to place more than one statement on a single line, then semicolons can be used to separate them. The Python **if** statement under consideration here could be written as:

```
if a < b:
```

```
a = a + 1;
b = b -1
c = a - b
```

This is harder to comprehend quickly and is therefore less desirable. There are too many symbols all grouped together. A program that is easy to read is also easier to modify and maintain. Code is written for computers to execute, but it is also for humans to read.

There are some special assignment operators that can be used for incrementing and decrementing variables. In the above code the statement **a = a + 1** could be written as **a += 1**, and **b = b − 1** can be written as **b -= 1**. There is no real advantage to doing this, but other languages permit it so Python adopted it too. There is another syntax that can be used to simplify certain code in languages like Java and C, and that is the increment operator "++" and the decrement operator "—." Python does not have these. However, an effect of the way that Python deals with variables and expressions is that "++x" is legal; so is "++++x." The value is simply **x**. The expression "x++" is not correct.

1.7.1 Else

An **if** statement is a two-way or *binary* decision. If the expression is true, then the indicated statements are executed. If it is not true, then it is possible to execute a distinct set of statements. This is needed for the *pick a number* program. In one case the computer wins, and in the other the human wins. An *else* clause is what will allow this.

The *else* is not really a statement on its own, because it has to be preceded by an **if**, so it's part of the **if** statement. It marks the part of the statement that is executed only when the condition in the **if** statement is false. It consists of the word else followed by a colon, followed by a suite (sequence of indented statements). So a trivial example is:

```
if True:
    print ("The condition was true")
else:
    print ("the condition was false")
```

The **else** as a clause is not required to accomplish any specific programming goals, and it can be implemented using another **if**. The code:

```
if a < b:
   print ("a < b")
else:
   print ("a >= b")
```

could also be written as:

```
if a < b:
   print ("a < b")
if  not (a<b):
   print ("a >= b")
```

The **else** is *expressive, efficient,* and *syntactically convenient.* It is expressive because it represents a way that humans actually communicate. The word *else* means pretty much the same thing in Python as it does in English. It is efficient because it avoids evaluating the same expression twice, which costs something in terms of execution speed. And it is syntactically convenient because it expresses an important element of the language in fewer symbols than when two **if**s are used.

The final Python code for the simple solution of the guess a number program can now be written. It is:

```
choice = 7
print ("Please guess a number between 1 and 10: ")
playerchoice = int(input())
if choice == playerchoice:
    print ("You win!")
else:
    print ("Sorry, You lose.")
```

1.8 DOCUMENTATION

There are some problems with this program, but is does work. A large problem is that it always chooses the same number every time it is executed (that number being 7). This will be fixed later on. A less critical problem is that it is *undocumented*; that is, there are no instructions to a player concerning how to use the program and there is no description of how the program works that another programmer might use if modifying this code. This can be fixed by providing *internal* and *external* documentation.

External documentation is like a manual for the user. Most programs have such a thing, and even though this program is quite simple, some degree of documentation can be provided. In fact, it is brief enough that it could be printed whenever the program starts to run. For example:

```
print ("Pick-a-number is a simple guessing game. The")
print ("computer will select a number between 1 and 10").
print ("and you are expected to guess what it is.")
print ("When the program displays 'Please guess")
print ("a number between 1 and 10: ' you type in")
print ("your guess followed by the <enter> key. Your ")
print ("guess must be an integer in the range 1 to 10.")
print ("The computer will tell you if you win or lose.)
```

For many more sophisticated programs, such as *PowerPoint* for example, the documentation is many pages and forms a small book. It would be distributed as a booklet along with the software or provided as a web site.

Internal documentation is intended for programmers who have access to the source code of the program. It can take the form of written documents too, but is commonly a set of comments that appears along with the code itself. High-level languages like Python allow the programmer to add human language text to the code that will be completely ignored by the computer but that can be read by anyone looking at the code. These comments describe the action of the program, the meaning of the variables, details of computational methods used, and many other items of interest.

In Python a comment begins with the character "#" and ends at the end of the line.

There are no rules for what can appear typed in a comment, but there are some guidelines developed through years of programming practice. A comment should not simply repeat what appears in the code; a comment should shed some light on an aspect of the program that might not be clear to everyone looking at it, and it should be written in plain language. As an example, here is the *guess-a-number* program with comments included:

```
# This program selects a number between 1 and
# 10 and allows a user (player) to guess what
# it is.
choice = 7   # The number selected by the computer

# Prompt the user, indicating what is expected
print ("Please guess a number between 1 and 10: ")
```

```
# Read the player's input from the keyboard
playerchoice = int(input()) # convert from string

# Print the outcome of the game.
if choice == playerchoice:  # Is the player's guess
    print ("You win!")      # correct? Player wins!
else:                       # Otherwise the computer wins
    print ("Sorry, You lose.")
```

All programs should be documented, not after the fact but as they are being written. Why? Because relatively few programs are written all in one sitting. The comments in the code serve as reminders to the programmer about what the variables represent and why particular code segments read the way they do. It also indicates the current state of thinking about the design of the code. When the program is looked at again at the beginning of a new working (or school) day, the comments can be essential in resuming the work.

There is also something called a *docstring* that seems to do the same things as a comment, but covers multiple lines and is not really a comment. A *docstring* begins and ends with a triple quote:

```
print ("This code will execute")
"""
print ("This code is within a docstring")
"""
```

A *docstring* is actually a string, not a comment, but behaves like a comment and can be used in that way. It can be especially useful for temporarily commenting out small sections of code while trying to find out where errors are. There are also programs that will collect the *docstrings* into a separate document that can be used as a description of the program. For that reason their intended use is to allow the programmer to explain the purpose of certain sections of code.

1.9 ROCK-PAPER-SCISSORS AGAIN

With what is now known about Python, it is time to look at the rock-paper-scissors problem and see if it can be coded. It takes more steps, but it is really no more complicated than the guess-a-number program. The code is the same.

1. Select a choice from the three items rock, paper, or scissors. Save this choice in a variable named **choice**.

A representation for the three items was when the solution was first described, where each choice was an integer. However, **input** reads strings, so it should be possible to avoid the conversion to numbers and use the strings directly.

```
choice = "paper"  # Computer chooses paper.
```

2. Ask the player for their choice.

   Print as prompt message.

```
print ("Rock-paper-scissors: type in your choice:    ")
```

3. Read the player's selection into a variable named **player**.

   Use **input** as we did before, but this time read a string and keep it that way. The player must type one of "rock," "paper," or "scissors," or else an error will be reported.

```
player = input ()
```

4. If **player** is equal to **choice**:

5. Print the message "Tie. We'll try again."

   Strings can be compared against each other for equality, so this step is quite simple:

```
if player == choice:
   print ("Game is a tie. Please try again.")
```

6. If **player** is equal to rock

7. If **choice** is equal to scissors, go to Step 17

   The will be no "go to Step 17," but that step simply says that the player wins. Just print that message here.

```
if player == "rock":
   if choice == "scissors":
      print ("Congratulations. You win.")
   else:
      print ("Sorry - computer wins.")
```

8. If **player** is equal to paper

9. If **choice** is equal to scissors, go to Step 17

```
if player == "paper":
   if choice == "scissors":
       print ("Sorry - computer wins.")
   else:
       print ("Congratulations. You win.")
```

10. If **player** is equal to scissors

11. If **choice** is equal to rock, go to Step 17

```
if player == "scissors":
    if choice == "rock":
        print ("Sorry - computer wins.")
    else:
        print ("Congratulations. You win.")
```

This code illustrates a new concept, if not a new language feature. It has **if** statements that are nested one within the other. Again, it's not necessary to do this because non-nested statements can implement the same decision. For example:

Nested **IFs**

```
if player == "scissors":
    if choice == "rock":
        print ("Computer wins.")
    else:
        print ("You win.")
```

Non-nested **IFs**

```
if player == "scissors and
             choice == "rock"
    print ("Computer wins")
if player == "scissors" and
             choice != "rock"
    print ("You win")
```

Nested if statements seem more expressive, and communicate the flow of the program better to a human programmer than does the non-nested code.

There is another Python language element that can be used here. Looking at the code, there is no indication when the user makes an error. For example, if the user enters "ROCK" (i.e., uppercase), then it will not match any of the choices, and the program will not indicate this. In fact, it won't print anything at all. What is really wanted is a sequence of **if-else-if-else** statements such as:

```
if player == "scissors":
    if choice == "rock":
else:
    if player == "rock":
        if choice == paper:
    else:
        if player == "scissors":
## and so on …
```

Python has a special feature that implements this nesting of **if** and **else**: the **elif**. The **elif** construct combines an **else** and an **if**, and this reduces the amount of indenting that has to be done. The following code snippets do the same thing:

```
if a<b:                              if a<b:
```

```
    print ("a<b")                    print ("a<b")
elif a>b:                        else:
    print ("a>b")                    if (a>b):
else:                                    print ("a>b")
    print ("a=b")                    else:
                                         print ("a=b")
```

If too many nested if-else statements exist, then the indenting gets to be too much, whereas the **elif** allows the same indent level and has the same meaning. In some programs this is essential, and in general is easy to read. Using the **elif** statement the program for the *rock-paper-scissors* problem looks like this:

```
choice = "paper"   # Computer chooses paper.
print ("Rock-paper-scissors: type in your choice:    ")
player = input ()
if player == choice:
    print ("Game is a tie. Please try again.")
if player == "rock":
if choice == "scissors":
    print ("Congratulations. You win.")
else:
        print ("Sorry - computer wins.")
elif player == "paper":
if choice == "scissors":
    print ("Sorry - computer wins.")
else:
    print ("Congratulations. You win.")
elif player == "scissors":
if choice == "rock":
    print ("Sorry - computer wins.")
else:
    print ("Congratulations. You win.")
else:
    print ("Error: Select one of: rock, paper, scissors")
```

Now all of the possible outcomes are handled by the code.

1.10 TYPES ARE DYNAMIC (ADVANCED)

To programmers who only program using Python, it would seem odd that a particular variable could have only one type and that it would have to be initially defined to have that type, but it is true. In Python the type associated with a variable can change. For example, consider the statements:

```
x = 10              # X is an integer
x = x*0.1           # X is floating point now
x = (x*10 == 10)    # X is Boolean
```

Some find this perfectly logical, and others find it confusing. The fact is that so long as the variable is used according to its current type, all will be well.

It is also true that even apparently simple Python types can be quite complex in terms of their implementation. The point is that the programmer rarely needs to know about the underlying details of types like *integers*. In many programming languages an integer is simply a one or two-word number, and the languages build operations like "+" from the instruction set of the computer. If, for example, a one-word integer A is added to another one B, it can be done using a single computer instruction like ADD A, B. This is very fast at execution time.

Python was designed to be convenient for the programmer, not fast. An integer is actually a complex object that has attributes and operations. This will become clearer as more Python examples are written and understood, but as a simple case think about the way that C++ represents an integer. It is a 32-bit (4 byte) memory location, which is a fixed size space in memory. The largest number that can be stored there is 2^{32}-1. Is that true in Python?

Here's a program that will answer that question, although it uses more advanced features:

```
for i in range (0,65):
 print (i, 2**i)
```

Even an especially long integer would be less than 65 bits. The fact is that this program runs successfully, and even rather quickly. Integers in Python have an arbitrarily large size. So calculating $2^{64} * 2^{64}$ is possible and results in 340282366 920938463463374607431768211456. This is very handy indeed from a programmer's perspective.

The type of a variable can be determined by the programmer as the program executes. The function **type()** will return the type of its parameter as a string, and can be printed or tested. So, the code:

```
z = 1
print (type(z))
```

```
z = 1.0
print(type(z))
```

will result in:

```
<class 'int'>
<class 'float'>
```

If one needed to know if **z** was a float at a particular moment, then:

```
if type(z) is float:
```

would do the trick. **Type(z)** does not return a string, it returns a *type*. The **print()** function recognizes that and prints a string, just as it does for **True** and **False**. So:

```
if type(z) == "<class 'float'>":
```

would be incorrect.

In future chapters this malleability of types will be further described, and practical methods for taking advantage of it in Python will be examined.

1.11 SUMMARY

A computer is a tool for rapidly and accurately manipulating numbers. It can perform tedious repetitive tasks accurately and quickly, but must be told what to do and follows its instructions very literally. A computer program is a set of instructions for performing a task using a computer, and Python is one language that can be used for this purpose. Python allows a programmer to define variables by simply using them, and associates a type with a variable based on what it is given. An **if** statement allows parts of a program to be executed when a certain condition becomes true, and it can have an **else** part that is executed when the condition is false. **If** statements can be nested, and sometimes the **elif** structure is a good way to express a set of nested conditional code.

In this chapter the main examples were two programs, one of which allowed a user to guess a number, while the other was the well-known game of *rock-paper-scissors.*

Exercises

In the following exercises some of the expressions may result in an error. If so, explain why the error occurs. When asked to write code it should be Python 3 code.

1. Evaluate the following expressions:

   a) `3*3/2`

   b) `3*3//2`

   c) `3*3%2`

   d) `(3*3)%2`

   e) `3**3/3`

   f) `(3+2)-(2-4)`

   g) `(3+2)/(2-4)`

2. If the statements:
   ```
   x = 3
   y = 9
   z = "2.4"
   ```

   have been executed then evaluate the following expressions. If an error occurs, state why:

   a) `x/y`

   b) `x//y`

   d) `x%y`

   e) `y/x*z`

   f) `float(x)/float(z)`

   g) `float(x)//float(z)`

   h) `int(x)//int(z)`

3. Given the variable definitions presented, evaluate the following expressions as being **True** or **False**.
   ```
   x = 12
   y = 14
   ```

   a) `x>3`

   b) `x >=12`

   c) `x<y`

d) `x<y and y>14`

e) `x<y or y>14`

f) `not (x == y)`

g) `not(x<y) and not(y>14)`

4. What will be printed by the following statements?

a) `print (int("23"))`

b)
```
if 3**2+4**2 == 5**2:
      print ("345")
  elif 3**2 < 4**2:
      print ("34")
  else:
      print ("5")
```

c)
```
if "toast" < "jam":
      print ("toast")
  else:
      print ("jam")
```

d)
```
if "12" < "5":
    print ("12")
  else:
    print ("5")
```

e)
```
a = 12.3
  b = 100
  c = 0
  if a < b: a = a + 1; b = b -1
  c = c - b
  print (a)
  print (c)
```

f)
```
a = 100
  b = 200
  c = 300
  ab = a<b
  cd = (c == a+b)
  if ab and cd:
        print ("AB and CD")
    elif ab:
        print ("AB")
    else:
        print ("Nope")
```

5. The United States measures temperature in Fahrenheit degrees, whereas Canada uses Celsius. A company is developing an app to convert between the two for people wanting to ski in Banff or Whistler. The formula to convert from Celsius degrees **C** to Fahrenheit degrees **F** is:

```
F = C*9/5 + 32
```

Write a program that will be the basis of this app: it will read a temperature in Celsius, convert it to Fahrenheit, and print the result.

6. The numerical values of coins have been arranged so that the *greedy algorithm* will result in the smallest number of coins when making change. This means that the largest valued coin is tried first, and as many of those coins are used as possible. Then the next smaller denomination coin is used, and so on until the pennies are dealt out. So for 84 cents in change, a 50-cent piece could be used (leaving 34 cents), then a 25-cent piece (leaving 9 cents), a 5 cent piece (leaving 4 cents), and 4 pennies. If no 50-cent piece was available, then 25-cent pieces would be used in its place: 3 quarters, followed by a nickel and four pennies. Write a program that reads a number between 1 and 99 that is an amount of change to be given and prints the coin values that would be used.

7. Three floating point variables **a, b**, and **c** have been read in from the console. Write a set of **if** statements that prints these in descending order.

8. If the value of 1.0/7.0 is printed, there are many numbers to the right of the decimal place. Devise a way to print only three places and write some Python code to test the idea.

9. Calculate an approximation to pi. There is an infinite series called the *Gregory-Leibniz* series that sums to pi. Of course it can never reach the exact value because there is no such thing, but it can compute as many digits as are desired. The series is:

$$\Pi = 4/1 - 4/3 + 4/5 - 4/7 + 4/9 - 4/11 \ldots.$$

Write a program that calculates the result of the first 15 terms of this series. How many digits of pi are correct? Add six more terms. How many digits are correct now?

10. Another series that can calculate pi is the *Nilakantha* series. It is a little more complicated to calculate, but gets close to pi much faster than does the *Gregory-Leibniz* series of Exercise 9. The *Nilakantha* series is:

$$\Pi = 3 + 4/(2*3*4) - 4/(4*5*6) + 4/(6*7*8) - 4/(8*9*10) \ldots$$

Calculate the first 15 terms of this series. How many digits of pi are correct?

Notes and Other Resources

Many teaching resources for Python exist, both in print and on the Internet.

Here is the development environment used to test the code for this book.

PyCharm. *https://www.jetbrains.com/pycharm/*

1. David Beazley and Brian K. Jones. **Python Cookbook, 3rd Edition: Recipes for Mastering Python 3**, *http://www.onlineprogrammingbooks.com/python-cookbook-third-edition/*

2. Cody Jackson. **Learning to Program Using Python**, *http://www.onlineprogrammingbooks.com/learning-program-using-python/*

3. Brad Miller. **Problem Solving with Algorithms and Data Structures Using Python**, *http://www.onlineprogrammingbooks.com/problem-solving-with-algorithms-and-data-structures/*

4. Harry Percival. **Test-Driven Development with Python**, *http://www.onlineprogrammingbooks.com/test-driven-development-with-python/*

5. Lennart Regebro. **Porting to Python 3: An In-Depth Guide**, *http://www.onlineprogrammingbooks.com/porting-to-python-3-an-in-depth-guide/*

6. Zed A. Shaw. **Learn Python the Hard Way**, *http://learnpythonthehardway.org/book/*

REPETITION

■ ■ ■ ■ ■

In this chapter

One of the things that makes computers attractive to humans is their ability to do tedious, repetitive tasks accurately and at high speed without getting bored. It is something they were designed to do. Humans have to do things repeatedly, and not all of them can be done for us by computers. Brushing our teeth, driving to work, cleaning the carpet—all are repeated actions, and many would be called chores. In programming terms some might be referred to as *loops*.

Consider a factory job on an assembly line. According to Henry Ford, one of the people principally connected with devising the assembly line concept, it is more efficient to have each worker do one job well and repeat it many times a day than to teach workers how to build entire things, in his case automobiles. Each worker does one relatively short job, and then the piece they are working on goes to the next station where the next person does their relatively short job. One such job could be the installation of the electronic ignition module bracket:

1. Acquire a bracket and place over attachment holes with wide end below the smaller end.
2. Place a two-inch bolt in the upper left bolt hole and screw in to two pounds of torque.
3. Place a four-inch bolt in the upper right bolt hole and screw in to two pounds of torque.
4. Place a two-inch bolt in the lower left bolt hole and screw in to two pounds of torque.
5. Place a ten-millimeter nut over the bolt at the lower right and tighten to ten pounds.
6. Re-tighten the bolts to ten pounds in the following order: upper left, upper right, lower left.

Before Step 1 above a new work piece (an engine, probably) is placed in front of the worker, and after Step 6 the piece is moved to the next station. So from the worker's perspective, *so long as* or *while* there is an engine at their station that needs a bracket, they repeat the steps. In a form that a computer might be able to understand this might be written as:

while there is an engine at their station that needs a bracket**:**

Acquire a bracket and place over attachment holes with wide end below the smaller end.

Place a two-inch bolt in the upper left bolt hole and screw in to two pounds of torque.

Place a four-inch bolt in the upper right bolt hole and screw in to two pounds of torque.

Place a two-inch bolt in the lower left bolt hole and screw in to two pounds of torque.

Place a ten-millimeter nut over the bolt at the lower right and tighten to ten pounds.

Re-tighten the bolts to ten pounds in the following order: upper left, upper right, lower left.

All of the actions that follow the **while** are indented to indicate that they are a part of the activities to be repeated, just as was done in a Python **if** statement to mark the things that were to be done if the condition was true. This example illustrates one of the Python repetition structures quite accurately: the **while** statement.

while	a<b	:
The key word, known by Python, that indicates that this is a **WHILE** statement.	An expression that evaluates to **True** or **False**	The colon indicates the end of the first part of the statement. Think of it as meaning **DO** as in **WHILE expression DO**

Figure 2.1
Essential syntax of the WHILE statement.

2.1 THE WHILE STATEMENT

When using this repetition statement, the condition is tested at the top or beginning of the loop. If upon that initial test the condition is true, then the body of the loop is executed; otherwise it is not, and the statement following the loop is executed. This means that it is possible that the code in the loop is not executed at all. The condition tested is the same kind of expression that is evaluated in an **if** statement: one that evaluates to **True** or **False**. It could be, and often is, a comparison between two numeric or string values, as it is in the example of Figure 2.1.

When the code in the body of the **while** statement has been executed, then the condition is tested again. If it is still true, then the body of the loop is executed again, otherwise the loop is exited and the statement following the loop is executed. There is an implication in this description that the body of the loop must change something that is used in the evaluation of the loop condition, otherwise the condition will always be the same and the loop will never terminate. So, here is an example of a loop that is entered and terminates:

```
a = 0
b = 0
while a < 10:
      a = a + 1
print (a)
```

The condition **a<10** is true at the outset because **a** has the value 0, so the code in the loop is executed. The lone statement in this loop increments **a**, so that after the first time the loop is executed, the value of **a** is 1. Now the condition is tested and, again, **a<10** so the loop executes again. In the final iteration of the loop, the value of **a** starts out as 9, is incremented and becomes 10. When the condition is tested it fails, because **a** is no longer less than 10 (it is equal) and so the loop ends. The statement following the loop is **print (a)** and the value printed is 10. This loop explicitly modifies one of the variables in the loop condition, and it is easy to see that the loop will end and what the value of **a** will be at that time.

Here is an example of a loop that is entered and does *not* terminate:

```
a = 0
b = 0
while b < 10:
        a = a + 1
print (a)
```

In this case the value of **b** is less than 10 at the outset, so the loop is entered. The body of the loop increments **a** as before, but does not change **b**. The loop condition does not depend on **a**, only on **b**, so when the loop condition is tested again the value of **b** is still 0, and the loop executes again. The value of **b** will always be 0 each time it is tested, so the loop condition will always be true and the loop will never end. The print statement will never be executed.

When this program is executed, the computer will seem to become unresponsive. As long as the loop is executing the program can do nothing else, and so the only indication that something is wrong is that nothing is happening. There are many reasons why a program can appear to be doing nothing: when waiting for the user to type some input, for instance, or when performing an especially difficult calculation. However, in this case, which is called an *infinite loop*, the only thing to do is to terminate the program and fix the loop.

Here is an example of a loop that is not entered:

```
a = 100
b = 0
while a < 10:
        a = a + 1
print (a)
```

The condition **a<10** is false at the outset because **a** has the value 100, so the code in the loop is not executed. The statement following the loop is executed next, which is the print statement, and the value printed is 100.

These loops are merely examples that illustrate the three possibilities for a **while** loop and do not calculate anything useful. The two examples from the previous chapter can make practical use of a while loop, and it would be useful to look at those again.

2.1.1 The Guess-A-Number Program Yet Again

The program as it was written in Chapter 1 is:

```
choice = 7
print ("Please guess a number between 1 and 10: ")
playerchoice = int(input())
if choice == playerchoice:
        print ("You win!")
else:
        print ("Sorry, You lose.")
```

The game would be better if it allowed the player to guess again, perhaps until a correct guess was achieved. A while loop could be used to accomplish this. Think about what the condition might be. The loop should end when the player guesses the answer. Another way to say this is that the loop should *continue* so long as the player has *not* guessed the answer. The condition is one for continuation of the loop, not termination, so the loop must be constructed in such a way that it continues when the condition is true. The loop will begin with this:

```
while choice != playerchoice:
```

At the beginning of the loop the variables **choice** and **playerchoice** must be defined. This means that before the while statement, there must be code that does this. The program now looks like this:

```
choice = 7
print ("Please guess a number between 1 and 10: ")
playerchoice = int(input())
while choice != playerchoice:
```

If the player has guessed incorrectly, then the body of the loop will execute. What should be done? One of the variables in the condition has to be changed, first of all, and the goal of the program must be kept in mind. In this case, because the player has guessed incorrectly, two things should happen. First, the player must be told that they are wrong and to make another guess. Next, the new guess must be read into the variable **playerchoice**, thus satisfying the rule that the loop condition must have an opportunity to become False. The program is now:

```
choice = 7
print ("Please guess a number between 1 and 10: ")
playerchoice = int(input())
while choice != playerchoice:
    print ("Sorry, not correct. Guess again: ")
    playerchoice = int(input())
```

When the player finally guesses the number the loop will exit; if the first guess is correct then the condition fails at the beginning, and this amounts to the same thing in this case. The last thing to do is to print a message to the player:

```
choice = 7
print ("Please guess a number between 1 and 10: ")
playerchoice = int(input())
while choice != playerchoice:
    print ("Sorry, not correct. Guess again: ")
    playerchoice = int(input())
print ("You have guessed correctly.")
```

Note that, as was true with the **if** statement and as is always true in Python, the indentation indicates which statements are a part of the loop (the *suite*) and which are outside.

2.1.2 Modifying the Game

A simple modification of the game involves telling the player whether their guess was too large or too small. This will help them shrink the possible range of values and thus guess the right answer more quickly. A modification to the body of the loop will accomplish this. If the value that the player guessed is smaller than the target, then a message to that effect is printed, and similarly if the player guesses a value larger than the target. The use of an **if** statement here would be appropriate, and that if statement would be nested inside of the **while** loop:

```
choice = 7
print ("Please guess a number between 1 and 10: ")
playerchoice = int(input())
while choice != playerchoice:
    if (playerchoice < choice):
        print ("Sorry, your guess was too small.
```

```
                        Guess again: ")
        else:
            print ("Sorry, your guess was too large.
                    Guess again.")
playerchoice = int(input())
print ("You have guessed correctly.")
```

This program illustrates a second level of indentation. The **if-else** are indented to indicate they are part of the **while** statement. The **print** statements are indented further, to show that they are also part of the **if** statement.

Doing some printing inside of the loop is useful because an infinite loop will be obvious. It will print a whole lot of stuff and never stop. It's not always practical to do that, so a degree of careful analysis should always be done to ensure that the loop can and will terminate.

2.2 ROCK-PAPER-SCISSORS YET AGAIN

This game really needs a loop, and the previous implementation was not complete. If there is a tie then the game has to be repeated, and a winner must be determined. This means that the loop in this case will be something like:

```
while there is no winner:
```

This happens only when the player and the computer select the same object, and in the original code was handled by the statements:

```
if player == choice:
    print ("Game is a tie. Please try again.")
```

The condition "no winner" becomes **player** == **choice**. The complete solution involves the **while** loop and another input from the user within the loop. Here is one possible answer:

```
choice = "paper"   # Computer chooses paper.
print ("Rock-paper-scissors: type in your choice:     ")
player = input ()

# --------- The new section of code --------------------
while player == choice:   # Repeat input until there is a
                          winner
    print ("Game is a tie. Please try again.")
```

```
player = input ()
# -------------------------------------------------------
if player == "rock":
    if choice == "scissors":
        print ("Congratulations. You win.")
    else:
        print ("Sorry - computer wins.")
elif player == "paper":
    if choice == "scissors":
        print ("Sorry - computer wins.")
    else:
        print ("Congratulations. You win.")
elif player == "scissors":
    if choice == "rock":
        print ("Sorry - computer wins.")
    else:
        print ("Congratulations. You win.")
else:
    print ("Error: Select one of: rock, paper, scissors")
```

The termination of the loop depends on the user's input and the value of the computer's choice, which could also (and should) change inside the loop. The probability of the loop continuing after one iteration is 1 in 3, and the probability that it will still be looping after N iterations is $(1/3)^N$, so there is a very small chance of the loop repeating more than 2 or 3 times.

2.2.1 Random Numbers

Most games depend on an element of unpredictability or chance. Those that do not might be more properly called *puzzles* (or *sports*—football and hockey ought to have a certain degree of skill involved). Given that computers do calculations, and that calculations should have the same result every time, how does one produce anything that is *random* using a computer? The answer is partly in how the term random is defined. The discussion involves some mathematics or at least some basic ideas in probability and statistics.

If integers in the range 1 through 10 inclusive are considered, what is the likelihood (chance, probability) that the number 5 will be selected at random? The answer is 1 in 10, or 0.1. This is true each time that question is asked. So if the number 5 has just been chosen and another number is to be chosen, what is the chance that it will be a 5? Same answer: 1 in 10. The principle is that the next choice does not depend on the previous one; it's a part of what makes them random.

Perhaps the wrong question was being asked. So, what is the likelihood that the number 5 will be selected twice in a row at random? The answer is 1 in 100, or 0.01. Why? Because it depends on the question asked. To get two in a row, the first one must be a 5 (1 in 10) and the second one must also be a 5 (also 1 in 10) so the resulting likelihood is 1 in 10*10 or 1 in 100. But each time a number is chosen, the number 5 has a 1 in 10 chance of being selected. A mathematical discussion of randomness depends on the asking the right question, and on probabilities. If some event is completely random, then it should have the same probability of happening as the other possible events, but events can be collected to form more complex events. Each card in a deck of playing cards should have the same probability of turning up, but if the question is "What's the chance of a flush," then the different ways that a flush can be comprised have to be taken into account. It can be a very complicated and interesting subject.

Numbers, in particular, are random only with respect to each other. Is the number "6" random? That's not really a good question. Is the sequence 87394 random? Perhaps a test could be devised to answer that. Is the sequence 66666 random? Most would say not, but it has the same probability of being generated at random as does 87354. To create good games and simulations, it is necessary to devise ways to generate a random number using a computer, and to test numbers to see if they are in fact random. Then it would be possible to simulate the flipping of a coin, or the rolling of a die.

What is the 100th digit of pi? It can be found easily. Are consecutive digits of pi effectively random? As it happens, the answer is not known, but it is a good question. What is 108763 divided by 98581? What is the remainder? Call the remainder x: what is 108763 divided by x? Are these numbers random? The search for a method for generating really good random numbers continues, but there are some pretty good methods (*See*: Chapter 10). In Python a random number created by a computer algorithm can be requested by using a built-in function.

A built-in function is like a mathematical function, and is provided by the language itself (and so is "built-in"). The language element **print** that has been used so much is really a built-in function. So are **int()** and **float()**. The functions *sine* and *square root* should be well understood by anyone who has graduated from high school, and are also built-in functions. Such functions belong to *modules* in Python and have to be specifically requested by the program so that they can be used. This means that the name of the module has to be known as well as the names of the built-in functions within it. The common mathematical functions are located within the module **math** and can be used by requesting the math module with the statement:

```
import math
```

Using a function in the math module involves using the name math followed by a period (".") followed by the name of the function. The "." opens the module so that the names within can be used, because there may be other built-in functions or even variables that have the same name. So, if the statements:

```
x = math.sqrt(64)
print (x)
```

are executed, the program will print the number 8, which is the square root of 64. The expression **sqrt(64)** is called a *function call*, and executes the code needed to calculate the square root of 64. The name **sqrt** is the name of the function, which is code provided by the Python language. This particular call will always return the value 8, because 8 is always the square root of 64. It is very much like the functions that are studied in grade school mathematics, such as **sine** and **cosine**. A module can be thought of as a bag of programs. Each bag contains a set of programs that do a particular class of things, like mathematics or drawing. By specifying the name of the module, access to all of the functions within is granted, and by specifying the specific name of a function, the code that we want is specifically made available.

By the way, the **import** statement should be at the very beginning of the program.

Now imagine that it is possible to have a function that produces a random number as a value. It is in the module named **random**, and the function could be called **random** too. For example:

```
import random
print ( random.random() )
```

Every time (well *almost* every time, because it *is* random, after all) the function is used it will give a different value, a random value. This value can be used to make games more realistic, because games have a random aspect.

This code prints the value 0.07229650795715237. Why? Because **random. random()** produces a random number between 0.0 and 1.0. This is the most common example of a random number function, and it is really very general. Increasing the range is done simply by multiplying by the maximum value desired; **random.random()*100** gives a random number between 0 and 100, for instance.

What if the problem is to simulate the roll of a die? The bag of code that is the **random** module contains other functions related to the generation of random numbers, and one of them is especially suited to this problem. A die roll would be implemented as:

```
random.randint (1, 6)
```

The **randint** function accepts two numbers, called parameters. The first is the lower limit of the range of random integers to be produced and the second is the upper limit. Specifying 1 as the lower limit and 6 as the upper, as in the example above, means that it will generate numbers between 1 and 6 inclusive, which is what would be expected from rolling a die. The result of rolling two dice would be a number between 2 and 12, found by **random.randint(2,12)**.

Flipping a coin is a two-level choice, and could be done with **random.randint(1,2)**. More completely:

```
if (random.randint(1,2) == 1):
    print ("Heads")
else:
    print ("Tails")
```

Going back again to the number guessing game, a random choice for the computer's number is now possible. Instead of the first line of code being:

```
choice = 7
```

it should now be:

```
choice = random.randint(1,10)
```

Every time the program executes, the program will select a new random number, as opposed to the choice always being 7.

The introduction of a random choice is a little more complicated for the rock-paper-scissors program because the variable holding the player's choice is a string. There are three possible choices, so to select one at random might look like this:

```
i = random.randint(1,3)
if i == 1:
    choice = "rock"
elif i == 2:
    choice = "paper"
else:
    choice = "scissors"
```

Many of the examples that will be developed will involve a game or puzzle of some kind, so the use of random numbers will be a consistent feature of the code shown.

2.3 COUNTING LOOPS

Features of programming languages are provided because the designers know they will be useful. The **while** loop is obviously useful, and is in fact the only kind of loop that is required in order to implement any program. However, loops that involve counting a certain number of iterations are pretty common, and adding syntax for this kind of thing would be certain to be valuable for a programmer. The idea is that sometimes a loop that executes, for example, ten times or a loop that iterated N times for some variable N would be wanted. In Python and many other languages, this is called a **for** loop.

In some languages a **for** loop involves a special syntax, but in Python it involves a new type (a class of types, really): a *tuple*. Here is an example of a **for** loop:

```
for i in (1,2,3,4,5):
    print i
```

This will print the numbers 1 2 3 4 5 each on a separate line. The variable **i** takes on each of the values in the collection provided in parentheses, and the loop executes once for each value of **i**. The collection (1,2,3,4,5) is called a *tuple*, and can contain any Python objects in any order. It's basically just a set of objects. The following are legal *tuples*:

```
(3,6, 9, 12)
(2.1, 3.5, 9.1, 0, 12)
("green", "yellow", "red")
("red", 3, 4.5, 2, "blue", i) #where i is a variable with a
                              value
```

The **for** loop has the loop control variable (in the case above it is **i**) take on each of the values in the tuple, in left to right order, and then executes the connected suite. The loop will therefore execute the same the number of times as there are elements in the tuple.

Sometimes it may be necessary to have the loop execute a great many times. If the loop was to execute a million times, it would be more than awkward to require a program to list a million integers in a tuple. Python provides a function to make this more convenient: **range()**. It returns a tuple that consists of all of the integers between the two parameters it is given, including the lower end point. So:

```
range (1,10)    is (1,2,3,4,5,6,7,8,9)
range (-1, 2)   is (-1, 0, 1)
range (-1, -3) is not a proper range.
range (1, 1000000) if the set of all integers from 1 to
                   9999999
```

Ranges involving strings are not allowed, although tuples having strings in them are certainly allowed. The original example for loop can now be written:

```
for i in range(1,6):
    print i
```

and the loop that is to execute a million times could be specified as:

```
for i in (0, 1000000):
    print i
```

This would print the integers from 0 to 999999. If **range()** is passed only a single argument, then the range is assumed to start at 0; this means that **range (0,10)** and **range (10)** are the same.

2.4 PRIME OR NON-PRIME

Here's a game that can illustrate the use of a **for** loop, and some other ideas as well. The computer presents the player with large numbers, one at a time. The player has to guess whether each number is *prime* or *non-prime*. A prime number does not have any divisors except 1 and itself; 3, 5, 11, and 17 are prime numbers. The game ends either when a specific number of guesses have been made, or when the player makes a specific number of mistakes.

for	**i**	**in**	**2,7,8**	**:**
The key word, known by Python, that indicates that this is a **for** statement.	A variable, the loop control variable, that will take on values in a given sequence	The key word **in**, which is basically a placeholder	A tuple (or other sequence type) that enumerates the values the variable will take	The colon indicates the end of the first part of the statement. Think of it as meaning **do**, as in **for i in (2,7,8) do**

Figure 2.2
The structure of a FOR statement.

A key problem to solve in this game is to determine when a number is prime. The computer must be able to determine whether the player is correct, and so for any given number there must be a way to figure out whether it is prime. Otherwise, the program for this game is not very complicated:

```
while game is not over:
    select a random integer k
    print k and ask the player if it is prime
    read the player's answer
    if player's answer is correct:
        print "You are right"
    else:
        print "You are wrong."
```

The mysterious portion of this program is the **if** statement that asks if the player's answer is correct. This really means that the program must determine whether or not the number K is prime and then see if the player agrees. How can it be determined that a number is prime? A prime number has no divisors, so if one can be found then the number is not prime. The *modulo* operator **%** can be used to tell if a division has a remainder: if k % n = 0 then the number n divides evenly into k, and k is not prime.

So to find out whether a number is prime, try dividing it by all numbers smaller than it, and if any of them have a zero remainder then the number is not prime. This is a job for a **for** loop. Here's a first draft:

```
isprime = True
for n in range (1, K):
    if k%n == 0:
        isprime = False
```

After the loop has completed, the variable **isprime** indicates whether K is prime or not. This seems pretty simple, if tedious. It does a lot of divisions. Too many, in fact, because it is not possible for any number larger than K/2 to divide evenly into K. So a slightly better program would be:

```
isprime = True                  # Is the number K prime?
for n in range (1, int(k/2))    # Divide K by all numbers < K/2
    if k%n == 0:                # If the remainder is 0 then n
        isprime = False         # divides evenly into K: not
                                # prime
# If isprime is still true here then the number is prime.
```

Next, this section of program should be incorporated into a complete program that plays the game. If the game is supposed to allow 10 guesses, then the first step is to repeat the whole thing 10 times:

```
import random
correct = 0                     # The number of correct guesses
for iteration in range(0, 10):  # 10 guesses
```

Now select a number at random. It should be large enough so that it is hard to see immediately if it is prime, although even numbers are a giveaway:

```
K = random.randint(10000, 1000000)   # Generate a new number
```

Next print a message to the user asking for their guess, and read it:

```
print ("Prime or Not: Is the number ",K," prime? (yes or
       no)")
answer = input()        # Read the user's choice
```

The user types in a string, "yes" or "no," as their response. The variable **isprime** that was used in the program that determines whether K is prime is logical, being **True** or **False**. It could be made into a string too so that it was the same as what the user typed, and then it could be compared directly against the user's input:

```
isprime = "yes"
```

Now comes the code for determining primality as coded above, except with **isprime** as a string:

```
isprime = True                  # Is the number K prime?
for n in range (1, int(k/2))    # Divide K by all numbers < K/2
    if k%n == 0:                # If the remainder is 0 then n
        isprime = "no"          # divides evenly into K: not prime
# If isprime is still true here then the number is prime.
```

At this point the variable **isprime** is either "yes" or "no," depending on whether K is actually prime. The user's guess is also "yes" or "no." If they are equal then the user guessed correctly.

```
if isprime==answer:
 print ("You are correct!")
    correct = correct + 1
 else:
    print ("You are incorrect.")
```

Finally, the outer loop is ended and the result is printed. The value of the variable **correct** is the number of correct guesses the user made, because it was incremented every time a correct answer was detected. The last statement is:

```
print ("You gave ",correct, " right answers out of 10.")
```

This program can be found on the CD in the directory "primegame."

2.4.1 Exiting from a Loop

A clever programmer would notice a pretty serious inefficiency with the prime number program. When it has been determined that the number is not prime, the loop continues to divide more numbers into **k** until **k/2** of them have been tried. If k= 999992 then it is known after the first iteration that the number if not prime; it is even, so it can't be prime. But the program continues to try nearly another half million numbers anyway. What is needed is a way to tell the program that the loop is over. There is a way to do this.

A loop can be exited using the **break** statement. It is simply the word **break** by itself. The correct way to use this in the program above would be:

```
for n in range (1, int(k/2)) # Divide K by all numbers < K/2
    if k%n == 0:                # If the remainder is 0 then n
        isprime = "no"     # divides evenly into K: not prime
        break
```

This loop terminates when the number **k** is known to be not prime. The statement following the loop will be executed next. This can save a lot of computer cycles, but does not make the program more correct—just faster.

A variation on this is the **continue** statement. This will result in the next iteration of the loop being started without executing any more statements in the current iteration. This avoids doing a lot of work in a loop after it is known it's not necessary. For example, doing some task for a bunch of names except for people named "Smith" could use a continue statement:

```
for name in ('Jones','Smith','Peters','Sinatra','Bohr',
             'Conrad'):
    print (name);
    if name == 'Smith':
        continue
# Now do a bunch of stuff …
```

Both the **break** and **continue** do the same thing in both **while** and **for** loops.

Modifying the loop variable will not change the number of iterations the loop will execute. In fact, it has no effect. This loop demonstrates that:

```
for i in range(0, 10):
    print ("Before ",i)
    i = i + 1000
    print ("After ",i)
```

It prints:

```
Before  0
After   1000
Before  1
After   1001
   .   .   .
```

and so on. It seems that the value of **i** changes after the assignment for the remainder of the loop and then is set to what it should be for the next iteration. This makes sense if Python is treating the range as a set of elements (it is), and it assigns the next one to **i** at the beginning of each iteration. Unlike a **while** loop, there is not a test for continuation. In any case, changing **i** here does not alter the number of iterations and can't be used in place of a **break**.

2.4.2 Else

The idea that the loop can be exited explicitly makes the normal termination of the loop something that should be detectable too. When a while or for loop exits normally by exhausting the iterations or having the expression become **False,** it is said to have *fallen through*. When the **for** loop in the prime number program detects a factor, it now executes a **break** statement, thus exiting the loop.

What if it never does that? In that case no factor exists, and the number is prime. The program as it stands has a flag that indicates this, but it could be done with an **else** clause on the loop.

The **else** part of a **while** or **for** loop is executed only if the loop falls through; that is, when it is not exited through a **break**. This can be quite useful, especially when the loop is involved in a search, as will be discussed later. In the case of the prime number program, an else could be used when the number is in fact prime, as follows:

```
for n in range (1, int(k/2))  # Divide K by all numbers < K/2
    if k%n == 0:               # If the remainder is 0 then n
        isprime = "no"         # divides evenly into K: not
                               # prime
        break
else:
    isprime = "yes"            # Loop not exited: it is prime
```

An **else** in a **while** loop occurs when the condition becomes false. Consider a loop that reads from input until the user types "end" and is searching for the name "Smith":

```
inp = input()
while (inp != "Smith"):
    s = input()
    if s == "end":
        break
else:
    print ("Smith was found")
# When the program reaches this point it is no
# longer known whether Smith was found.
```

Of course, the **else** is not required, and some programmers believe it is even harmful. There are always other ways to accomplish the same thing.

2.5 LOOPS THAT ARE NESTED

Just as it is possible to have if statements nested within other if statements, it is possible, and even likely, to have a loop nested within another loop. An example of nested **for** loops would be:

```
for i in range(0, 10)
```

```
for j in range (0, 10)
    print (i,j)
```

The **print** in this example would execute 100 times. Each time the outer loop executes once the inner one is executed 10 times, for a total of 10 * 10 or 100 iterations. Loops can be nested to a greater depth if necessary, and **while** and **for** loops can be nested interchangeably. Is it ever useful to do this? Yes, very often.

Since there has been a recent discussion of prime numbers and factoring, consider the problem of find the number within a given range that has the greatest number of different factors. Leaving out 1 and the number itself, 2 has no factors, nor does 3; 4 has one (=2), 5 has none, and 6 has two (2 and 3). Which number between 0 and 1000 has the most?

From the prime number game it is clear that the factors can be found using a loop. If the loop is not exited when one is found, all of them can be identified and, more importantly for this problem, counted. For a given number **k**, the factors can be identified using the following loop:

```
count = 0;
for n in range (1, int(k/2)): # Divide K by all numbers < K/2
    if k%n == 0:              # If the remainder is 0 then n
        count = count + 1
# The number k has count numbers that divide evenly into it.
```

The statement **count = count + 1** has replaced the **isprime = "no"** statement from the prime number game. When the loop ends the value of **count** will be the number of divisors it has. If this number is 0, then the number **k** is prime, by the way. Okay, the problem has been solved for any number **k**. Now solve it for all numbers between 1 and 1000 and identify the number with the largest value of **count** (i.e., the largest number of divisors). This involves another loop enclosing this one that counts from 1 to 1000.

Define a variable **maxv** which is at any given moment the number that has the greatest number of divisors, and another variable **maxcount** which is the number of divisors that **maxv** has. Initially **maxv** is 1 and **maxcount** is 0 (i.e., the number 1 has no divisors). Now loop between 1 and 1000 and replace **maxv** and **maxcount** whenever a new number is found for which the number of divisors is greater than **maxcount**. Specifically:

```
maxv = 1
maxcount = 0
```

```
for k in range(1, 1000):    # Count the divisors for a range
    count = 0;
    for n in range (2, int(k/2)): # Divide K by all numbers
                                  # < K/2

        if k%n == 0:              # If the remainder is 0
                                  # then n
            count = count + 1     # Count this divisor
    if count > maxcount:          # A new maximum
        maxcount = count          # Save the count
        maxv = k                  # and the value itself
print ("The most divisors is ",maxv," with ",maxcount)
```

The result for 1 to 1000 is:

```
The most divisors is  840  with  30
```

The result for 1 to 10000:

```
The most divisors is  7560  with  62
```

By the way, this last version needed 10 seconds to execute.

2.6 DRAW A HISTOGRAM

A histogram is a kind of graph. It usually represents the frequency of occurrence of certain discrete values. Common examples include temperature as a function of month of the year, or histograms of income as a function of year, age, race, or gender. Drawing one involves knowing how many categories there are and what the numerical values are for each category. Then the numbers are scaled so they fit in a particular area, and the rectangles are drawn so that the heights reflect the relative numerical values. Figure 2.3 shows some typical examples.

A company wishes to plot a histogram of their income for each quarter of 2016. The numerical values are stored in variables Q1,Q2,Q3, and Q4 and range between 0 and 1 million. Using fancy graphics is not possible yet, so how can simple histograms be drawn? By using text. If the histogram is drawn so that the bars are horizontal instead of vertical, then the number of characters drawn in a row can be used to represent the "height" of the histogram bar. Using the "#" character, a value of 20 could be drawn as:

```
Q1: ####################  20
```

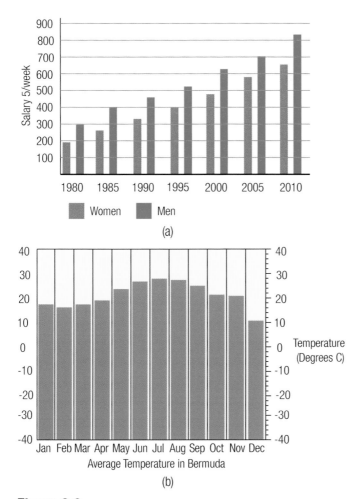

Figure 2.3
Examples of histograms.

This is another situation where a loop is necessary.

There are three parts to the histogram bar above: the label, the bar, and the data value. The label is easy to print, and in the example there are four possibilities; these are simply printed at the beginning of each line being drawn. The data value is not necessary, but it is useful for people looking at the graph to know what the exact number is. Each "#" character drawn could represent a range of values. The histogram bar is the trick. If numbers up to a million must be represented, then the bar must be scaled so that it fits on a line. If 50 characters fit on a line, then each "#" printed needs to represent 1000000/50, or 20000 dollars. Another way to say this is that every $20000 of income results in one "#" character being printed. How many "#" are printed for the first quarter? **Q1/20000** of them.

A problem: the **print** function prints out a line every time it is called. How can multiple things be printed on a line? Happily, **print** has a special parameter to allow that. The call:

```
print(i, end='!')
```

will print the variable **i** and then print the "!" string following that, every time. Normally the **print** will place an end of line character (represented as "\n") at the end of every line, but the **end=** clause allows the programmer to change this to whatever they like. If the string provided is empty (contains no characters) then the print will not print anything extra after each call, meaning specifically that no end of line will be printed. Thus, the statement:

```
print ("#", end="")
```

prints one "#" character but no end of line. If another "#" is printed, then it will come right after the one just printed. This is exactly what is needed for the histogram program. A loop that would print ten "#" characters on one line can now be written as:

```
for i in range(0,10):
 print ("#", end="")
```

Given that the value of the variable Q1 is between 0 and 1000000 and each 20000 should result in a single "#" character being printed, the first quarter histogram bar could be drawn by the following:

```
print ("Q1: ", end="")
for k in range(0, int(Q1/20000)):
    print ('#', end='')
print ("      ", q1)
```

This includes all of the labels, and the output would look like this:

Q1: ########   190000

A complete solution to the problem would draw the histogram for all four quarters along with a heading for the graph. The output might look like this:

Earnings for WidgetCorp for 2016
  Dollars for each quarter

```
================================
```
Q1: #########   **190000**

Q2: ################   **340000**

Q3: ###   **873000**

Q4: ###################   **439833**

Exercise 5 at the end of the chapter involves finishing this program.

2.7 LOOPS IN GENERAL

The concept of a loop in a programming language has been discussed for many years and has a large degree of both theory and practice underlying it. The original "loop" was a *branch* or *goto*, where the top of the loop was identified with an address or label and at the bottom there was a statement that said to "go to" or transfer control to that location. Examples of this are:

```
label1:   add 1 to x                    12    x = x + 1
          subtract 2 from min                 min = min - 2
          branch to label1                    go to 12
```

Branches were typical of assembly language programming, where each line of code was one actual computer instruction. The *goto* statement was introduced in the first real programming language FORTRAN, but was quickly supplemented by a more structured loop construct, the **do** statement. Both branch and goto statements can be conditional.

Various kinds of loop have been developed over the years, and the most commonly used variation is the **while** loop. Theory says that the only kind that is needed, and probably the most general, is the **loop** statement as defined in the *Ada* language. It is essentially an infinite loop that allows escapes at multiple and various points on specified conditions. The basic syntax is:

```
loop
      exit when condition1;
      Statements …
      …
      exit when condition2;
end loop;
```

An **exit** at the top of the loop is a **while** loop. An exit at the end could be a **repeat … until** as in *Pascal* or *C++*, and it is a simple matter to declare and initialize a control variable and test the condition to implement a **for** loop. Everything is possible with this loop syntax.

When specifically using Python, a **while** loop is all that is needed. If the range is an integer one, then the loop:

```
for i in range (a .. b):
```

is the same as the loop:

```
i = a
while i < b:
    ...
    i= i + 1
```

This loop has an initialization, a condition, and an increment. As individual entities these are somewhat hidden in Python, being masked by the syntax, but the loop control variable takes on the first value the first time the loop is executed (initialization), iterates through the selections (increment), and terminates after it selects the final one (condition). The loop control variable is not really what gets incremented; what is incremented is a count that indicates which of the items in the tuple is currently being used. In the loop:

```
for i in ("red", "yellow", "green"):
```

the variable **i** takes on the values "red," "yellow," and "green," but what gets incremented each time through the loop is an indication of which position in the tuple is represented by **i**. The value "red" is 0, "yellow" is 1, and "green" is 2 and a count implicitly starts at 0 and steps until 2 assigning values to **i**. This kind of loop is similar to that found in the language PHP, and is a level of abstraction above those in Java and C++.

2.8 EXCEPTIONS AND ERRORS

Computers do not, as a general rule, make mistakes. Like other human-designed and -constructed devices such as cars and stoves, computers can be awkward to use, can have design features that don't turn out as expected, and can even break down too quickly. But they do not make mistakes. A computer program, on the other hand, almost certainly has mistakes or *bugs* coded within it. Consumers don't usually make a distinction between the computer and the software that runs on it, but programmers and engineers must. When a computer program does not work properly, a programmer must exhaust all ways the program could be wrong before looking at an error in the computer itself.

Creating a correct program is difficult for many reasons. First of all, before any code is written, the problem to be solved must be clearly understood, and it must be the correct problem. Solving the wrong problem is a pretty common error, but can't be detected or corrected by the computer. Common examples of this sort of error come from stating the problem in English (or a human language of any description) where errors in understanding occur. "Find the average of the first ten integers," for example, is a little ambiguous. Is the first integer 0 or 1? What is meant by "average"—the mean or the median? Computer programmers tend to be quite literal, and so what they think is the answer will be written into the code, and then they will argue for that answer as being correct. It is very important to realize that, whatever the literally correct answer is, the real correct answer is based on the correct understanding of the problem. Sometimes it is stated badly, but no matter whose fault the problem is, the job of fixing it will lie with the programmer. Sometimes a little time at the beginning clarifying the question can save more time later, and sticking with an overly pedantic interpretation will cause problems in the long run.

A correct program also depends on the programmer being able to identify all possible circumstances that can occur and knowing how to deal with each of them. Failing to handle one possible situation is an error, and the program will behave unpredictably if that situation occurs in practice. Statements that handle errors appear all though real (in the field or commercial) code. In fact, it is common that there are more statements that detect and deal with errors than code that actually computes an answer. One thing that should be remembered: all lines of the code need to be tested. In very large programs this may be impossible, but every line of code that has never been executed is a potential error. Test as many as possible, including the error detection code.

User input is a frequent cause of mistakes in programs. It's not that the user is the problem; the programmer must anticipate all possible ways that a user can enter data. There is usually one correct way but many erroneous ones, and it is impossible to predict what a user will enter from a keyboard in response to any request. Similarly, the contents of a file may not be what the programmer expects. File formats are standards, but sometimes there are variations and at other times a user may have entered the data improperly. While the mistake is on the part of the user, it is also a programming mistake if the error is not detected and is allowed to have an impact on the execution of the program.

Programmers tend to make assumptions about the problem. It is a common mistake to think "this situation can never happen" and then ignore it, however unlikely the situation seems. Testing every statement for everything that could possibly go wrong may be impossible, but testing for the general situation may be possible. It would be great to be able to say "if any statement in this section of code divides by zero," or "if any variables in this code have the wrong type," then do some particular thing.

Since it is impossible to write a program of any length without there being coding errors of some kind included, a step towards a solution may be to check all data before it is operated on to ensure the pending operation is going to succeed. For instance, before performing the division **a/b**, test to make sure that **b** is not zero. This depends on the error being at least in principle predictable. Most modern languages, Python included, have implemented a way to catch errors and permit the programmer to handle them without having tests before each statement or expression. This facility is called the *exception*.

The word *exception* communicates a way to think about how errors will be handled. Some code is legal and calculates a desired value *except* under certain circumstances, or *unless* some particular thing happens. The way it works is that the program tries to perform some operation and errors are allowed to occur. If one does, the computer hardware or operating system detects it and tells Python. The program cannot continue in the way that was planned, which is why this is called an exception. The programmer can tell Python what to do if specific errors occur by writing some code that deals with the problem. If the programmer did not do this, then the default is for Python to print an error message that describes the error and then stop executing the program. Error messages can be seen as a failure on the part of the programmer to handle errors correctly.

A simple example is the divide by zero error mentioned previously. If the expression **a/b** is to be evaluated, the value of **b** can be checked to make sure it is not zero before the division is done:

```
if b != 0:
    c = a/b
```

This can be tedious for the programmer if a lot of calculations are being done, and can be error prone. The programmer may forget to test one or two expressions, especially if engaged in modifications or testing. Using exceptions is a matter of allowing the error to happen and letting the system test for the problem. The syntax is as follows:

```
try:
      c = a/b
except:
      c = 1000000
```

The **try** statement begins a section of code within which certain errors are being handled by the programmer's code. After that statement, code is indented to show that it is part of the **try** region. Nearly any code can appear here, but the **try** statement must be ended before the program ends.

The **except** statement consists of the key word **except** and, optionally, the name of an error. The errors are named by the Python system, and the correct name has to be used, but if no error name is given as in this example, then any error will cause the code in the **except** statement to be executed. Not specifying a name here is an implicit assumption that either only one kind of error could possibly occur or that no matter what error happens, the same code will be used to deal with it. Specifying an unrecognized name is itself an error. The name can be a variable, but that variable must have been assigned a recognized error name before the error occurs. The code following the **except** keyword is indented too, to show that it is part of the **except** statement. This is referred to by programmers as an *error handler*, and is executed only if the specified error occurs.

This appears to be even more verbose than testing **b**, but any number of statements can appear between the **try** and the **except**. This section of code is now protected from divide by zero errors. If any occur, then code following the **except** statement will be executed, otherwise that code will not execute. If other errors occur, then the default action will take place—an error message will be printed.

Testing specifically for the divide by zero error can be done by specifying the correct error name in the **except** statement:

```
try:
      c = a/b
except ZeroDivisionError:
      c = 1000000
```

More than one specific error can be caught in one except statement:

```
try:
      c = a/b
except (ValueError, ZeroDivisionError):
      c = 1000000
```

Clearly **(ValueError, ZeroDivisionError)** is a tuple, and could be made longer and could be assigned to a variable.

Also, there can be many **except** statements associated with a single **try**:

```
try:
      c = a/b
except ValueError:
      c = 0
exceptZeroDivisionError:
      c = 1000000
```

And, as was mentioned, a variable can hold the value of the error to be caught:

```
k = ZeroDivisionError
try:
      c = a/b
except k:
      c = 1000000
```

Finally, the exception name can be left out altogether. In that case any exception that occurs will be caught and the exception code will be executed:

```
try:
      c = a/b
except:
      c = 0
```

2.8.1 Problem: A Final Look at Guess a Number

The final version of the program involving guessing a number looks like this:

```
choice = 7
print ("Please guess a number between 1 and 10: ")
playerchoice = int(input())
if choice == playerchoice:
    print ("You win!")
else:
    print ("Sorry, you lose.")
```

Using exceptions and what has been discussed about error checking, this program can be improved. First, if the user enters something that is not an integer, it is an error. This should be caught using an exception. Also, rather than forcing the player to run the program again, a loop can be used to ask for another guess. The **input** should be within the **try** statement. The **except** statement should print an error message, and the entire collection should be within a loop that continues to ask the user to guess a number. Here is a better version:

```
choice = 7
guessed = False     # Has the user guessed a reasonable
                       number?
while not guessed: # Keep trying until they have
    print ("Please guess a number between 1 and 10: ")
    try:              # Catch potential input errors
        playerchoice = int(input())
        guessed = True  # Success so far
    except:           # An error occurred.
        print ("Sorry, your guess must be an integer.")
if choice == playerchoice:  # Correct guess?
    print ("You win!")
else:
    print ("Sorry, you lose.")
```

The variable **guessed** is set to **True** when a successful guess is made, and this stops the loop from repeating. If the user enters a real number or a string, the exception is caught before that happens, the error message is printed, and the user is asked to enter another guess.

What else is wrong with this code? Well, the user is asked to enter a number between 1 and 10, but that value is never checked to see if it is OK. True, if it falls outside the range, then it will always be an incorrect guess and the player will lose. It's a penalty for not paying attention to the rules. A program should whenever possible give the user as much information as is reasonable, so it would be better to check the value of the variable **playerchoice** and give an error message if it is out of range. The best way to do this is to place the check after the **except** statement at the bottom of the loop, and set the variable guessed to **False** if the guess is an improper one. Then the loop will repeat and the player will get another guess.

This version of the program is:

```
choice = 7
```

```
guessed = False
while not guessed:
    print ("Please guess a number between 1 and 10: ")
    try:
        playerchoice = int(input())
        guessed = True
    except:
        print ("Sorry, your guess must be an integer.")
    if playerchoice<10 or playerchoice>10: # Is the guess
                                           # in 1..10?
        print ("Your guess was",playerchoice,"which is out
                                                of range.")
        guessed = False                     # Nope. Guess again
if choice == playerchoice:
    print ("You win!")
else:
    print ("Sorry, you lose.")
```

2.9 SUMMARY

The ability to repeat a collection of operations is an essential part of any programming language. The **while** loop has a condition at the beginning, and so long as that condition is true, the statements comprising the loop will be executed repeatedly. The **for** loop has an explicit list of items for which the loop will be executed, or a range of numerical values that define how many times the code will be repeated.

Most problems that are solved using a computer program have some degree of repetition implicit in the implementation, and some computer algorithms are quite explicit about how the iterations are to be set up and how many are needed to solve the problem (*See*: Exercises 3 and 4).

Certain errors that can occur in program can be detected automatically by Python. If the programmer does not specify otherwise, then these errors cause a message and premature program termination. The **try-except** statement allows the programmer to handle errors without ending the program, and permits better communication of the kind of error that occurred, in the context of the program, to the programmer or user.

Exercises

1. Given the following definitions:

```
var1 = 12
var2 = 100
var3 = -2
var4 = 0
```

What is printed by the following **while** loops:

a.
```
while var1 < var2:
   print (var1)
   var1 = var1 + 30
```

b.
```
while var1 < var2:
   print (var1)
   var1 = var1 * 2
```

c.
```
while var1 > 0:
   var4 = var4 + 1
   var1 = var1 - 1
   print (var1, var2)
```

d.
```
while var1 > 0:
   var4 = var4 + 1
   var1 = var1 - var4
   print (var1, var2)
```

e.
```
while var1 < var3:
   print ("*", end="")
   var3 = var3 + 2
```

f.
```
while var2 > var1*var4:
   var1 = var1 + 1
   var4 = var4 + 1
   print (var1, var2)
```

2. What would be printed by the following **for** loops:

a.
```
for i in range (1, 10):
   print (i)
```

b.
```
for i in (1, 10):
   print (i)
```

c.
```
for i in ("red", "green", "blue"):
   print (i)
```

d.
```
for i in range(0, 10):
  for j in range(1, 10):
      if i == j:
          print (i)
```
e.
```
for i in range(0, 10):
  for j in range(0, 50):
      if i*i == j:
      print (i)
```
f.
```
for i in (0, 10):
    i = i * 2
    print (i)
```
g.
```
for i in range (1, 10):
    for j in range (1, i):
        print (j, end="")
    print()
```
h.
```
or i in range(0, 10):
    i = i + 1
    for j in range (1, i):
        print (j, end="")
    print()
```

3. The Greek mathematician Zeno (c. 450 BCE) is credited with creating the paradox of the Tortoise and Achilles. A tortoise challenged the great hero and athlete Achilles to a footrace. All the tortoise asked was a ten-yard head start. The idea was that once the race began, Achilles could run the ten-yard head start in a small time; however, in that same time the tortoise would move forward a small amount, perhaps a yard. When Achilles made up that yard, the tortoise would have moved ahead again a small distance; and so on. The logic was that Achilles could never catch up. The misunderstanding here is that an infinitely long series of numbers can add up to a finite value. Write a small Python program that sums the numbers ½, ¼, ⅛, ¹⁄₁₆, and so on for 20 iterations and suggest what the sum would be if it were carried to an infinite number of iterations.

4. One way to calculate the square root of a number is to use *Newton's method*. This starts with an initial guess: if the square root of **x** is being computed, then a fair initial guess **g** would be **x/2**. Successive estimates are given by the expression:

```
newg = (g + x/g)/2
```

Successive estimates are nearer and nearer to the actual square root. Write a program to compute the square root of a number that is entered from the keyboard.

5. Complete the program that draws a histogram for the earnings of WidgetCorp for four quarters of 2016. Earnings are:

   a. 190000

   b. 340000

   d. 873000

   d. 439833

6. Modify the program in Exercise 5 so that the data for the four quarters is read from the terminal (i.e., entered by the user from the keyboard). Test it for the values:

   a. 900000

   b. 874000

   d. 200000

   d. 439000

7. Modify the solution to Exercise 6 in Chapter 1 (making change) so that it makes effective use of a **for** loop. The program should still read a number between 1 and 99, which is an amount of change to be given, and print the coin values that would be used. Modify it to not use 50-cent pieces, because nobody has those anymore.

8. Convert the following **for** loops into the equivalent **while** loop:

   a.
   ```
   for i in range (1, 10):
     print (i, i*i)
   ```

   b.
   ```
   sum = 0
   for i in (range (10, 0, -1):
     sum = sum + i
     print (i, sum)
   ```

9. A good solution to Exercise 4 above (square root) would detect negative numbers and print a message to the effect that square roots of negative numbers do not exist (not as real numbers, anyway). Modify the solution to Exercise 4 to use an exception to deal with that situation, and handle other potential errors.

Notes and Other Resources

Online tutorial on Python loops: *http://www.tutorialspoint.com/python/python_loops.htm*

Cornell University summary of **if** statements and loops: *http://www.cs.cornell.edu/courses/cs1130/2012sp/1130selfpaced/module2/module2part1/ifloop.html*

Sthurlow.com, Loops, loops, loops…, *http://sthurlow.com/python/lesson04/*

1. Henry Ford and Samuel Crowther. (1922). **My Life and Work**, Garden City Publishing, Garden City, NY, *http://www.gutenberg.org/ebooks/7213*

2. David Beazley and Brian K. Jones. **Python Cookbook, 3rd Edition: Recipes for Mastering Python 3**, *http://www.onlineprogrammingbooks.com/python-cookbook-third-edition/*

SEQUENCES: STRINGS, TUPLES, AND LISTS

In this chapter

It was mentioned in Chapter 2 that **for** loops in Python are different from those found in many other languages. In Java and C++, a **for** loop has a very explicit increment; a **for** statement looks like this in Java:

From this it can be inferred that the variable **i** will start out as 0, and so long as **i** is less than 10 the loop will continue. After each iteration the value of **i** will be increased by 1, and then the condition is tested again.

In Python the iteration is more implicit, with the loop control variable taking on one of a set of values in turn. There is an implication here, too, that there is a kind of thing, a type that a variable can have, that amounts to a list or sequence of other, simpler things. This is true, and using variables having these types is an essential part of writing useful and effective code. Python offers *strings*, *tuples*, and *lists* as objects that consist of multiple parts. They are called *sequence* types. An integer or a float is a single number, whereas a sequence type consists of a collection of items, each of which is a number or a character. Each member of a sequence is given a number based on its position: the first element in the sequence is given 0, the second is 1, and so on. This is a fundamental data structure in Python and has influenced the syntax of the language.

Strings are familiar objects and have been used in programs already, so the discussion will begin there.

3.1 ■ STRINGS

A *string* is a sequence of characters. The word *sequence* implies that the order of the characters within the string matters, and that is certainly true. Strings most often represent the way that communication between a computer and a human takes place. Human language consists of words and phrases, and each word or phrase would be a string within a program. The order of the characters within a word matters a great deal to a human because some sequences are words and others are not. The string "last" is a word, but "astl" is not. Also, the strings "salt" and "slat" are words and use exactly the same characters as "last" but in a different order.

Because order matters, the representation of a string on a computer will impose an order on the characters within, and so there will be a first character, a second, and so on, and it should be possible to access each character individually. A string will also have a *length*, which is the number of characters within it. A computer language will provide specific things that can be done to something that is a string: these are called operations, and a type is defined at least partly by what operations can be done to something of that type. Because a string represents text in the human sense, the operations on strings should represent the kinds of things that would be done to text. This would include printing and reading, accessing any character, linking strings into longer strings, searching a string for a particular word, and so on.

The examples of code written so far use only string *constants*. These are simply characters enclosed in either single or double quotes. Assigning a string constant to a variable causes that variable to have the string type and gives it a value. So the statements:

```
name = "John Doe"
address = '121 Second Street'
```

cause the variables named **name** and **address** to be strings with the assigned value. Note that either type of quote can be used, but a string that begins with a double quote must end with one.

A string behaves as if its characters are stored as consecutive characters in memory. The first character in a string is at location or index 0, and can be accessed using square brackets after the string name. Using the definitions above, name[0] is "J" and name[5] = "D." If an index is specified that is too large, it results in an error, because it amounts to an attempt to look past the end of the string.

How many characters are there in the string **name**? The built-in function **len()** will return the length of the string. The largest legal index is one less than this value: the first character of a string **name** has index 0, and the final one has index 7; the length is 8. Thus, any index between 0 and **len(name)-1** is legal. The following code prints all of the characters of **name** and can be thought of as the basic pattern for code that scans through the characters in strings:

```
for i in range(0, len(name)):
    print (name[i], end="")
```

This may be a little confusing, but remember that the **range(0,n)** does not include **n**. This loop runs through values of **i** from 0 to **len(name)-1**.

Some languages have a *character* type, but Python does not. A string of length one is what Python uses instead. A component of a string is therefore another string. The first character of the string **name**, which is **name[0]**, is "J," the string containing only one character.

3.1.1 Comparing Strings

Two strings can be compared in the same manner as are two integers or real numbers, by using one of the relational operators ==, !=, <, >, <= or >=. What it means for two strings to be equal is simple and reasonable: if each corresponding character in two strings is the same, then the strings are equal. That is, for strings **a** and **b**, if **a[0] == b[0]**, and **a[1]==b[1]** and so on to the final character **n**, and **a[n] == b[n]**, then the two strings **a** and **b** are equal and **a==b**. Otherwise, **a!=b**. By the way, this implies that equal strings have the same length.

What about inequalities? Strings in real life are often sorted in alphabetical order. Names in a telephone book, files in a doctor's office, and books in a store: these tend to appear in a logical order based on the alphabet. This is also true in Python. The string "abc" is less than the string "def," for example. Why? Because the first letter in "abc" comes before the first letter in "def"; in other words, "abc"[0] < "def"[0]. Yes, characters in string constants can be accessed using their index.

A string **s1** is less than string **s2** if all characters from 0 through **k** in the two strings are equal, and **s1[k+1]<s2[k+1]**. So the following statements are true:

```
"abcd" < "abce"
"123" < "345"
"ab " < "abc"
```

In the last example, the space character "." is smaller than (i.e., comes before) the letter "c." What if the strings are not the same length? The string "ab" < "abc", so if two strings are equal to the end of one of them, then the shorter one is considered to be smaller. These rules are consistent so far with those taught in grade school for alphabetization. Trailing spaces do not matter. *Leading* spaces can matter, because a space comes before any alphabetic character; that is, " " < "a". Thus "ab" > "z".

Digits come before lowercase letters. "1" < "a", and "1a" < "a1". **Most importantly, uppercase comes before lowercase, so "John" < "john".** All of these rules are consistent with those that secretaries understand when filing paper documents. As an example that compares strings, consider the following:

```
a = "J"
b = "j"
c = "1"
if b<c:
    print ("Lcase < numbers")
else:
    print("Lcase > numbers")
if a<c:
    print ("Ucase < numbers")
else:
    print("Ucase > numbers")
```

This results in the output:

```
Lcase > numbers
Ucase > numbers
```

Problem: Does a City Name, Entered at the Console, Come before or after the Name Denver?

This involves reading a string and comparing it against the constant string "Denver." Let the input string be read into a variable named **city**. Then the answer is:

```
city = input()
if city < "Denver":
    print ("The name given comes before Denver in an
            alphabetic list")
elif city > "Denver":
    print ("The name given comes after Denver in an
            alphabetic list")
else:
    print ("The name given was Denver")
```

If "Chicago" is typed at the console as input, the result is:

```
Chicago
The name given comes before Denver in an alphabetic list
```

However, if case is ignored and "chicago" is typed instead, then the result is:

```
chicago
The name given comes after Denver in an alphabetic list
```

because, of course, the lowercase "c" comes (as do *all* lowercase letters) after the uppercase "D" at the beginning of "Denver."

3.1.2 Slicing – Extracting Parts of Strings

To a person, a string usually contains words and phrases, which are smaller parts of a string. Identifying individual words is important. To Python this is true also. A Python program consists of statements that contain individual words and character sequences that each have a particular meaning. The words "if," "while," and "for" are good examples. Individual characters can be referenced through indexing, but can words or collections of characters be accessed? Yes, if the location (index) of the word is known.

Problem: Identify a "Print" Statement in a String

The statement:

```
print ("Lcase < numbers")
```

appears in the example program above. This can be thought of as a string, and assigned to a variable:

```
statement = 'print ("Lcase < numbers")'
```

Question: is this a **print** statement? It is if the first five characters are the word "print." Each of those characters could be tested individually using:

```
if statement[0] == 'p':
    if statement[1] == 'r':
        if statement[2] == 'i':
            if statement[3]=='n':
                if statement[4]=='t':
                    if statement[5]==' ':
                        # This is a print statement.
```

This is pretty ugly, and is something that is needed often enough that Python offers a nicer way to do it. A *slice* is a set of continuous characters within a string. This means their indices are consecutive, and they can be accessed as a sequence by specifying the range of indices within brackets. The situation above concerning the print statement could be done like this:

```
if statement[0:5] == "print":
```

The slice here does not include character 5, but is 5 characters long including characters 0 through 4 inclusive. A slice from **i** to **j** (i.e., **x[i:j]**) does not include character **j**. This means that the following statements produce the same result:

```
fname[0]
fname[0:1]
```

If the first index is omitted, then the start index is assumed, so the statement:

```
if statement[0:5] == "print":
```

is the same as:

```
if statement[:5] == "print":
```

If the second index is omitted, then the last legal index is assumed, which is to say the index of the final character. So the assignment:

```
str = statement[6:]
```

results in the value of **str** being "(**Lcase < numbers**")." Both indices can be omitted, which does sound silly, but really just means from the first to the last character, or the entire string.

3.1.3 Editing Strings

Python does not allow the modification of individual parts of a string. That is, things like:

```
str[3] = "#"
str[2:3] = ".."
```

are not allowed. So how can strings be modified? For example, consider the string variable:

```
fname = "image"
```

If this is supposed to be the name of a JPEG image file, then it must end with the suffix ".jpg."

Problem: Create a JPEG File Name from a Basic String

The string **fname** can be edited to end with ".jpg" in a few ways, but the easiest one to use is the concatenation operator "+".

To *concatenate* means "to link or join together." If the variables **a** and **b** are strings, then **a+b** is the string consisting of all characters in **a** followed by all characters in **b**; the operator "+" in this context means to concatenate, rather than to add numerically. The designers of Python and many other languages that implement this operator think of concatenation as string addition.

To use this to create the image file name, simply concatenate ".jpg" to the string **fname**:

```
fname = fname + ".jpg"
```

The result is that **fname** contains "image.jpg."

File suffixes are very often the subject of string manipulations and provide a good example of string editing. For instance, given a file name stored as a string variable **fname**, is the suffix ".jpg"? Based on the preceding discussion, the question can be answered using a simple **if** statement:

```
if fname[len(fname)-4:len(fname)] == '.jpg':
```

Using a slice it could also take the form:

```
if fname[len(fname)-4:] == ".jpg"
```

A valuable thing to know is that negative indices index from the *right*-hand side of the string; that is, from the end. So **fname[-1]** is the final character in the string, **fname[-2]** is the one previous to that, and so on. The last 4 characters, the suffix, would be captured by using **filename[-4:]**.

Problem: Change the Suffix of a File Name

Some individuals use the suffix ".jpeg" instead of ".jpg." Some programs allow this, others do not. Some code that would detect and change this suffix would be:

```
if fname[len(fname)-5:] == ".jpeg":    # identfy the jpeg
                                       # suffix
    fname = fname[0:len(fname)-5]      # remove the last five
                                       # characters
    fname = fname + ".jpg"            # append the correct
                                       # suffix
```

Problem: Reverse the Order of Characters in a String

There are things about any programming language that could be considered to be "idioms." These are things that a programmer experienced in the use of that language would consider normal use, but that others might consider odd. This problem exposes a Python idiom. Given what is known so far about Python, the logical approach to string reversal might be as follows:

```
# city has a legal value at this point
k = len(city)
for i in range(0,len(city)):
    city = city + city[k-i-1]
city = city[len(city)//2:]
```

This reverses the string named **city** that exists prior to the loop and creates the reversed string. It does so in the following way:

1. Let **i** be an index into the string **city**, starting at 0 and running to the final character.

2. Index a character from the end of the string, starting at the final character and stepping backwards to 0. Since the last character is len(city) and the current index is **i**, the character to be used in the current iteration would be **k-i-1** where k is the length of the original string.

3. Append **city[k-i-1]** to then end of the string. Alternatively, a new string **rs** could be created and this character appended to it during each iteration.

4. After all characters have been examined, the string **city** contains the original string at the beginning and the reversed string at the end. The first characters can be removed, leaving the reversed string only.

An experienced Python programmer would do this differently. The syntax for taking a slice has a variation that has not been discussed; a third parameter exists. A string slice can be expressed as:

```
myString[a:b:c]
```

where **a** is the starting index, **b** is the final index+1, and **c** is the increment. Increment? If:

```
str = "This string has 30 characters."
```

Then str[0:30:2] is "Ti tighs3 hrces," which is every second character. The increment represents the way the string is sampled, that is, every **increment** character is copied into the result. Most relevant to the current example, the increment can be negative. The idiom for reversing a string is:

```
print (str[::-1])
```

As has been explained, the value of str[:] is the whole string. Specifying an increment of -1 implies that the string is scanned from 0 to the end, but in reverse order. This is far from intuitive, but is probably the way that an experienced Python programmer would reverse a string. Any programmer should use the parts of any language that they comprehend very well, and should keep in mind the likely skill set of the people likely to read the code.

Problem: Is a Given File Name That of a Python Program?

A Python program terminates with the suffix ".py." An obvious solution to this problem is to simply look at the last 3 characters in the string **s** to see if they match that suffix:

```
if  s[len(s)-3:len(s)] == '.py':
    print ("This is a Python program.")
```

Perhaps. But is "PROGRAM.PY" a legal Python program? It happens that it is. So is "program.Py" and "program.pY." What can be done here?

3.1.4 String Methods

A good way to do the test in this case is to convert the suffix to all upper- or all lowercase before doing the comparison. Comparing against ".py" means converted to lowercase, which is done by using a built-in *method* named **lower**:

```
s1 = s[len(s)-3:len(s)]
if  s1.lower()== '.py':
    print ("This is a Python program.")
```

The variable **s1** is a string that will contain the final 3 characters of **s**. The expression **s1.lower()** creates a copy of **s1** in which all characters are lowercase. It's called a *method* to distinguish it from a function, but they are very similar things. You should recall that a method is simply a function that belongs to one type or class of objects. In this case **lower**() belongs to the type (or class) *string*. There could be another method named **lower**() that belongs to another class and that did a completely different thing. The dot notation indicates that it is a method, and what class it belongs to: the same class of things that the variable belongs to. In addition, the variable itself is really the first parameter; if **lower** were a function, then it might be called by **lower(s1)** instead of **s1.lower()**. In the latter case, the "." is preceded by the first parameter.

Strings all have many methods. In the table below the variable **s** is the *target* string, the one being operated upon. This means that the method names below will appear following "s.," as in **s.lower()**. Let the value of **s** be given by **s = "hello to you all."** These methods are intended to provide the operations needed to make the string type in Python function as a major communication device from humans to a program.

Method	Explanation (What is returned?)	Example
`capitalize()`	Returns the target string but with the first letter capitalized.	`s.capitalize() == "Hello to you all."`
`count(str,beg=0, end=len(s))`	Returns a count of how many times the string **str** occurs in the target. If values for **beg** and **end** are given, then the count is performed using only character indices between **beg** and **end**.	`s.count("ll") == 2`
`endswith(suffix, beg=0, end=len(s))`	Returns **True** if the target string ends with the given suffix and return **False** otherwise. If **beg** and **end** are given, then do the test on the substring between **beg** and **end**.	`s.endswith('ll.') ==True`
`find(str, beg=0end=len(string))`	If the string **str** appears with the target string, then return the index at which it occurs; return -1 if it does not occur. If **beg** and **end** are provided, then use the substring from **beg** to **end**.	`s.find("you") == 9`
`index(str,beg=0, end=len(string))`	**Index** is the same as **find** except that it will raise an exception if the string **str** does nor occur in the target	`s.index("you") == 9`
`isdigit()`	Returns **True** if the target string contains only digits and **False** otherwise.	`s.isdigit() == False`
`islower()`	Returns **True** if the target string has at least 1 alphabetic character and all alphabetic characters are lowercase. Returns **False** otherwise.	`s.islower() == True`
`isspace()`	Returns **True** if the target string contains only whitespace characters and returns **False** otherwise.	`s.isspace() == False`

(continued)

Method	Explanation (What is returned?)	Example
`isupper()`	Returns True if s has at least one alphabetic character and all alphabetic characters are uppercase. Returns **False** otherwise.	`s.isupper() == False`
`lower()`	Converts all uppercase letters in string to lowercase.	`s.lower() == s`
`replace(old, new [, max])`	Replaces all occurrences of the string **old** in the target with the string **new**. If **max** is specified, replace at most **max** instances.	`s.replace("you all", "y'all") == "hello to y'all."`
`split(str="", num=string. count(str))`	Returns a list of substrings obtained from the target using **str** as a delimiter. Space is the default for str. Subdivide at most num times if that is specified (*see*: Chapter 3, section 3).	`s.split(" ") == ["hello","to", "you","all"]`
`splitlines( num=string. count('\n'))`	Splits the target string at all (or **num**, if it is specified) NEW-LINES and returns a list of each line with the NEWLINEs removed.	`s.splitlines() == "hello to you all."`
`upper()`	Converts the lowercase letters in string to uppercase.	`s.upper() == "HELLO TO YOU ALL."`

3.1.5 Spanning Multiple Lines

Text as seen in human documents may contain many characters, even multiple lines and paragraphs. A special delimiter, the *triple quote*, is used when a string constant is to span many lines. This has been mentioned previously in the context of multiline comments. The regular string delimiters will terminate the string at the end of the line. The triple quote consists of either of the two existing delimiters repeated three times. For example, to assign the first stanza of Byron's poem "She Walks in Beauty" to the string variable **poem**:

```
poem = '''She walks in beauty like the night
```

```
Of cloudless climes and starry skies,
And all that's best of dark and bright
Meets in her aspect and her eyes;
Thus mellow'd to that tender light
Which Heaven to gaudy day denies.'''
```

When **poem** is printed the line endings appear where they were placed in the constant. This example is a particularly good one in that most poems require that lines end precisely where the poet intended.

Another example of a string that must be presented just as typed is a Python program. A program can be placed in a string variable using a triple quote:

```
program = """list = [1,2,4,7,12,15,21]
for i in list:
    print(i, i*2)"""
```

When printed this string has the correct form to be executed by Python. In fact, the following statement will actually execute the code in the string:

```
exec (program)
```

3.1.6 For Loops Again

Earlier in this section a for loop was written to print each character in the string. That loop was:

```
for i in range(0, len(name)):
    print (name[i], end="")
```

Obviously the string could have been printed using:

```
print(name)
```

but it was being used as an example of indexing individual components within the string. The characters do not need to be indexed explicitly in Python; the loop variable can be assigned the value of each component:

```
for i in name:
    print (i, end="")
```

In this case the value of **i** is the value of the component, not its index. Each component of the string is assigned to **i** in turn, and there is no need to test for the end of the string or to know its length. This is a better way to access components in a string and, as it happens, can be used with all sequence types. Whether an index is used or the components are pulled out one at a time depends on the problem being solved; sometimes the index is needed, other times it is not.

3.2 THE TYPE *BYTES*

A *string* is a sequence of characters, a sequence being defined as a collection within which order matters. *Strings* are commonly used for communication between computers and humans: to print headings and values on the screen, and to read objects in character string form. Humans deal with characters very well. The type *bytes* represents a sequence of integers, albeit small ones. A *bytes* object of length 1 is an 8-bit integer, or a value between 0 and 255. A *bytes* object of length greater than 1 is a sequence of small integers. To be clear, if **s** is a *string* and **b** is a *bytes* then:

s[i] is a character

b[i] is a small integer

A string constant (literal) is a sequence of characters enclosed in quotes. A bytes literal is a sequence of characters enclosed in quotes and preceded by the letter "b." Thus:

```
'this is a string'
```

is a *string*, whereas:

```
b'this is a string'
```

has type *bytes*. Any method that applies to a *string* also applies to a *bytes* object, but bytes objects have some new ones. In particular, to convert a bytes object to a string, the **decode()** method is used and a character encoding should be given as the parameter. If no parameter is given, then the decoding method is the one currently being used. There are a few possible decoding methods (e.g., "utf-8"). So to convert a bytes object **b** to a character string **s**, the following would work:

```
s = b.decode ("utf-8")
```

A question remains: "why is the bytes type needed?" What is it used for? Because (and this is a little ahead of what is needed) it implements the *buffer interface*. Certain file operations require a buffer interface to accomplish their tasks. Anything read from some specific types of file will be of the type *bytes*, for example, as it has that interface. This will be discussed further in Chapters 5 and 8, but for the moment it simply serves to explain why the type exists at all.

Other than the buffer interface, the bytes type is very much like a string, and can be converted back and forth.

3.3 TUPLES

A *tuple* is almost identical to a string in basic structure, except that it is composed of arbitrary components instead of characters. The quotes can't be used to delimit a tuple because a string can be a component, so a tuple is generally enclosed in parentheses. The following are tuples:

```
tup1 = (2, 3, 5, 7, 11, 13, 17, 19)  # Prime numbers under 20
tup2 = ("Hydrogen","Helium","Lithium","Beryllium","Boron",
        "Carbon")
tup3 = "hi", "ohio", "salut"
```

If there is only one element in a tuple, there should be a comma at the end:

```
tup4 = ("one",)
tup5 = "two",
```

That's because it would not be possible otherwise to tell the difference between a tuple and a string enclosed in parentheses. Is (1) a tuple? Or is it simply the number 1?

A tuple can be empty:

```
tup = ()
```

Because they are like strings, each element in a tuple has an index, and they begin at 0. Tuples can be indexed and sliced, just like strings. So:

```
tup1[2:4] is (5, 7)
```

Concatenation is like that of strings too:

```
tup4 = tup4 + tup5          # yields tup4 = ('one', 'two')
```

As is the case with strings, the index -1 gives the last value in the tuple, -2 gives the second last, and so on. So in the example above, **tup2[-1]** is "Carbon." Also, like strings, the tuple type is immutable; this means that elements in the tuple can't be altered. Thus, statements such as:

```
tup1[2] = 6
tup3[1:] "bonjour"
```

are not allowed and will generate an error.

Tuples are an intermediate form between strings, which have just been discussed, and lists, which will be discussed next. They are simpler to implement than *list* (are *lightweight*) and are more general than strings.

Are tuples useful? Yes, it turns out, and part of their use is that they underlie other aspects of Python.

3.3.1 Tuples in For Loops

Sequences can be used in a **for** loop to control the iteration and assign to the loop control variable. Tuples are interesting in this context because they can consist of strings, or integers or floats. The loop:

```
for i in ("Hydrogen","Helium","Lithium","Beryllium","Boron",
        "Carbon"):
```

will iterate 6 times, and the variable **i** will take on the values in the tuple in the order specified. The variable **i** is a string in this case. In cases where the types in the tuple are mixed, things are more complicated.

Problem: Print the Number of Neutrons in an Atomic Nucleus

Consider the tuple:

```
atoms=("Hydrogen",1,"Helium",2,"Lithium",3,"Beryllium",4,
        "Boron",5,"Carbon",6)
```

and the loop

```
for i in atoms:
    print (i)
```

This prints:

```
Hydrogen
1
Helium
2
Lithium
3
Beryllium
4
```

```
Boron
5
Carbon
6
```

The number following the name of the element is the atomic number of that element, the number of protons in the nucleus. In this case the type of the variable **i** alternates between string and integer. For elements with a low atomic number (less than 21), a good guess for the number of neutrons in the nucleus is twice the number of protons. The problem is that some of the components are strings and some are integers. The program should only do the calculation when it is in an iteration having an integer value for the loop variable, because a string can't be multiplied by two.

A built-in function that can be of assistance is **isinstance**. It takes a variable and a type name and returns **True** if the variable is of that type and **False** otherwise. Using this function, here is a first stab at a program that makes the neutron guess:

```
atoms=("Hydrogen",1,"Helium",2,"Lithium",3,"Beryllium",4,
      "Boron",5,"Carbon",6)
for i in atoms:
    if isinstance(i, int):
        j = i*2
        print ("has ", i, "protons and ", j, " neutrons.")
    else:
        print ("Element ", i)
```

In other words, in iterations where **i** is an integer as determined by **isinstance**, then **i** can legally be multiplied by 2 and the guess about number of neutrons can be printed.

Another way to solve the same problem would be to index the elements of the tuple. Elements 0,2,4, etc. (even indices) refer to element names, while the others refer to atomic numbers. This code would look as follows:

```
atoms=("Hydrogen",1,"Helium",2,"Lithium",3,"Beryllium",4,
      "Boron",5,"Carbon",6)
for i in range(0,len(atoms)):
    if i%2 == 1:
        j = atoms[i]*2
      print ("has ", atoms[i], "protons and ", j,
            " neutrons.")
```

```
    else:
        print ("Element ", atoms[i])
```

Note that in this case the loop variable is always an integer, and is not an element of the tuple but is an index at which to find an element. That's why the expression **atoms[i]** is used inside the loop instead of simply **i** as before.

3.3.2 Membership

Tuples are not sets in the mathematical sense, because an element can belong to a tuple more than once, and there is an order to the elements. However, some set operations could be implemented using tuples by looking at individual elements. Set union and intersection, for example. The *intersection* of two sets A and B is the set of elements that are members of A and also members of B. The membership operator for tuples is the key word **in**:

If 1 in tuple1:

The intersection of A and B, where A and B are tuples, could be found using the following code:

```
for i in A:
    if i in B:
        C = C + i
```

The tuple C will be the intersection of A and B. It works by taking each known element of A and testing to see if it is a member of B; if so, it is added to C.

Problem: What Even Numbers Less than or Equal to 100 are Also Perfect Squares?

This could be expressed as a set intersection problem. The set of even numbers less than 100 could be enumerated (this is not actual code):

```
A = (2,4,6,8,10  … and so on
```

Or could be generated within a loop:

```
A = ()                    # Start with an empty tuple
for i in range(0,51):     # for appropriate integers
    A = A + (i*2,)        # add the next even number to the
                          # tuple
```

```
# Can't simply use A+i because i is integer, not a tuple.
```
Similarly, the perfect squares could be enumerated:

```
B = (4,9,16,25,36,49,64,81,100)
```

Or, again, created in a loop:

```
B = ()
for i in range(0,11):
    B = B + ((i*i),)
```

Now the set A can be examined, element by element, to see which members also belong to B:

```
C = ()
for i in A:
    if i in B:
        C = C + (i,)
```

The result is: (0, 4, 16, 36, 64, 100).

Two important things are learned from this. First, when constructing a new tuple from components, one can begin with an empty tuple. Second, individual components can be added to a tuple using the concatenation operator "+," but the element should be made into a tuple with one component before doing the concatenation.

3.3.3 Delete

A tuple is *immutable*, meaning that it cannot be altered. Individual elements can be indexed but not changed or deleted. What can be done is to create a new tuple that has new elements; in particular, deleting an element means creating a new tuple that has all of the other elements except the one being deleted.

Problem: Delete the Element Lithium from the Tuple Atoms, along with Its Atomic Number.

Going back to the tuple **atoms**, deleting one of the components—in particular, *Lithium*—begins with determining which component *Lithium* is; that is, what is its index? So start at the first element of the tuple and look for the string "Lithium," stopping when it is found.

```
for i in range(0, len(atoms)):
    if atoms[i] == "Lithium":      # Found it at location i
        break;
else:
    i = -1                         # not found
```

Knowing the index of the element to be deleted, it is also known that all elements before that one belong to the new tuple and all elements after it do too. The elements before element **i** can be written as **atoms[0:i]**. Each element consists of a string and an integer, and assuming that both are to be deleted means that the elements following element **i** are **atoms[i+2:]**. In general to delete one element the second half would be **atoms[i+1:]**. Finishing the code that deletes "Lithium":

```
if i>=0:
    atoms = atoms[0:i] + atoms[i+2:]
```

So the tuple **atoms** has not been altered so much as it has been replaced completely with a new tuple that has no *Lithium* component.

3.3.4 Update

Again, because a tuple is *immutable*, individual elements cannot be changed. A new tuple can be created that has new elements; in particular, updating an element means creating a new tuple that has all of the other elements except the one being updated, and that includes the new value in the correct position.

Problem: Change the Entry for *Lithium* to an Entry for *Oxygen*

An update is usually a deletion followed by the insertion or addition of a new component. A deletion was done in the previous section, so what remains is to add a new component where the old one was deleted. Inserting the element *Oxygen* in place of *Lithium* would begin in the same way as the simple deletion already implemented:

```
for i in range(0, len(atoms)):
    if atoms[i] == "Lithium":      # Found it at location i
        break;
else:
    i = -1                         # not found
```

Next, a new tuple for Oxygen is created:

```
newtuple = ("Oxygen", 8)
```

And finally this new tuple is placed at location **i** while *Lithium* is removed:

```
if i>=0:
    atoms = atoms[0:i] + newtuple + atoms[i+2:]
```

However, an update may not always involve a deletion. If *Lithium* is not a component of the tuple **atoms**, then perhaps *Oxygen* should be added to **atoms** anyway. Where? How about at the end?

```
else:      # If i is -1 then the new tuple goes at the end
    atoms = atoms + newtuple
```

3.3.5 Tuple Assignment

One of the unique aspects of Python is so-called *tuple assignment*. When a tuple is assigned to a variable, the components are converted into an internal form that is the one tuples always use. This is called tuple packing, and is has already been encountered:

```
atoms=("Hydrogen",1,"Helium",2,"Lithium",3,"Beryllium",4,
       "Boron",5,"Carbon",6)
```

What is really interesting is that tuple *unpacking* can also be used. Consider the tuple:

```
srec = ('Parker', 'Jim', 1980, 'Math 550', 'C+', 'Cpsc 302','A+')
```

which is a tuple packing of a student record. It can be unpacked into individual variables in the following way:

```
(fname, lname, year, cmin, gmin, cmax, gmax) = srec
```

Which is the same as:

```
fname = srec[0]
lname = srec[1]
year  = srec[2]
cmin  = srec[4]
gmin  = srec[5]
cmax  = srec[6]
gmax  = srec[7]
```

Of course, the implication is that N variables can be assigned the value of N expressions or variables "simultaneously" if both are written as tuples. Examples would be:

```
(a, b, c, d, e) = (1,2,3,4,5)
(f, g, h, i, j) = (a, b, c, d, e)
```

The expression

```
(f, g, h, i, j) = 2 ** (a,b,c,d,e)
```

is invalid because the left side of "**" is not a tuple, and Python won't convert 2 into a tuple. Also:

```
(f, g, h, i, j) = (2,2,2,2,2) ** (a,b,c,d,e)
```

is also invalid because "**" is not defined on tuples, nor are other arithmetic operations. As with strings, "+" means concatenation, though, so (1,2,3) + (4,5,6) yields (1,2,3,4,5,6).

Exchanging values between two variables is a common thing to do. It's an essential part of a sorting program, for example. The exchange in many languages requires three statements: a temporary copy of one of the variables has to be made during the swap:

```
temp = a
a = b
b = temp
```

Because of the way that tuples are implemented, this can be performed in one tuple assignment:

```
(a,b) = (b,a)
```

This is a little obscure, not to an experienced Python programmer but certainly to a beginner, and often to experienced programmers in other languages. A Java programmer could see what was meant, but initially the rationale would not be obvious. This statement deserves a comment such as "perform an exchange of values using a tuple assignment.'

3.3.6 Built-In Functions for Tuples

As examples for the table below, use the following:

```
T1 = (1,2,3,4,5)
T2 = (-1,2,4,5,7)
```

Function	Explanation (What Is Returned?)	Example
`len(T1)`	Gives the number of components that are members of T1.	`len(T1) == 5`
`max(T1)`	Returns the largest element that is a component of T1.	`max(T1) == 5` `max(T2) == 7`
`min(T1)`	Returns the smallest element that is a component of T1.	`min(T1) == 1` `min(T2) == -1`

In addition, tuples can be compared using the same operators as for integers and strings. Comparison is done on an element-by-element basis, just as it is with strings. In the example above, **T1>T2** because at the first location where the two tuples differ (the initial component), the element in **T1** is greater than the corresponding element in **T2**. It is necessary for the corresponding elements of the tuple to be comparable; that is, they need to be of the same type. So if the tuples **t1** and **t2** are defined as:

```
t1 = (1, 2, 3, "4", "5")
t2 = (-1,2,4,5,7)
```

then the expression **t1>t2** is not allowed. A string can't be compared against an integer, and the element indexed by 3 of **t1** is a string, whereas the element indexed by 3 of **t2** is an int.

3.4 LISTS

One way to think of a Python *list* is that it is a tuple in which the components can be modified. They have many properties of an *array* of the sort one might find in Java or C, in that they can be used as a place to store things and have random access to them; any element can be read or written. They are often used as one might use an array, but have a greater natural functionality.

Initially a list looks like a tuple, but uses square brackets to delimit it.

```
list1 = [2, 3, 5, 7, 11, 13, 17, 19]  # Prime numbers under 20
list2 = ["Hydrogen","Helium","Lithium","Beryllium","Boron",
        "Carbon"]
list3 = ["hi", "ohio", "salut"]
```

A list can be empty:

```
list4 = []
```

and because they are like tuples and strings, each element in a list has an index, and they begin (as usual) at 0. Lists can be indexed and sliced, as before:

```
list1[2:4] is [5, 7]
```

Concatenation is like that of strings too:

```
list6 = list1 + [23, 31]
```

yields [2, 3, 5, 7, 11, 13, 17, 19, 23, 31]

Negative values index from the end of the string. However, unlike strings and tuples, individual elements can be modified. So:

```
list1[2] = 6
```

results in **list1** being [2, 3, 6, 7, 11, 13, 17, 19]. Also:

```
list3[1:] = "bonjour"
```

results in **list3** taking the value—*oops*, it becomes:

['hi', "b', "o', "n', "j', "o', "u', "r'].

That's because a string is a sequence too, and this string consists of seven components. Each component of the string becomes a component of the list. If the string "bonjour" is supposed to become a single component of the list, then it needs to be done this way:

```
list3[1:] = ["bonjour"]
```

The other components of **list3** are sequences, and now so is the new one. However, integers are *not* sequences, and the assignment:

```
list1[2] = [6,8,9]
```

results in the value of **list2** being:

```
[2, 3, [6, 8, 9], 7, 11, 13, 17, 19]
```

There is a list within this list; that is, the third component of **list1** is not an integer, but is a list of integers. That's legitimate, and works for tuples as well, but may not be what is intended.

Problem: Compute the Average (Mean) of a List of Numbers

The mean is the sum of all numbers in a collection divided by the number of numbers. If a set of numbers already exists as a list, calculating the mean might involve a loop that sums them followed by a division. For example, assuming that **list1** = [2, 3, 5, 7, 11, 13, 17, 19]:

```
mean = 0.0
for i in list1:
    mean = mean + i
mean = mean/len(list1)
```

It can be seen that a list can be used in a loop to define the values that the loop variable **i** will take on, a similar situation to that of a tuple. A second way to do the same thing would be:

```
mean = 0.0
for i in range(0,len(list1)):
    mean = mean + list1[i]
mean = mean/len(list1)
```

In this case the loop variable **i** is an index into the list and not a list element, but the result is the same. Python lists are more powerful than this, and making use of the extensive power of the list simplifies the calculation greatly:

```
mean = sum(list1) / len(list1)
```

The built-in function **sum** will calculate and return the sum of all of the elements in the list. That was the purpose of the loop, so the loop is not needed at all. The functions that work for tuples also work for lists (**min, max, len**), but some of the power of lists is in the methods it provides.

3.4.1 Editing Lists

Editing a list means to change the values within it, usually to reflect a new situation to be handled by the program. The most obvious way to edit a list is to simply assign a new value to one of the components. For example:

```
list2 = ["Hydrogen","Helium","Lithium","Beryllium","Boron",
        "Carbon"]
list2[0] = "Nitrogen"
print (list2)
```

results in the following output:

['Nitrogen', "Helium', "Lithium', "Beryllium', "Boron', "Carbon']

This substitution of a component is not possible with strings or tuples. It is possible to replace a single component with another list:

```
list2 = ["Hydrogen","Helium","Lithium","Beryllium","Boron"
        "Carbon"]
list2[0] = ["Hydrogen", "Nitrogen"]
```

results in:

```
list2 = [['Hydrogen','Nitrogen'],'Helium','Lithium',
        'Beryllium', 'Boron','Carbon']
```

3.4.2 Insert

This is not normally what is thought of as an insertion, though. To place new components within a list, the **insert** method is provided. This method places a component at a specified index; that is, the index of the new element will be the one given. To place "Nitrogen" at the beginning of list2, which is index 0:

```
list2.insert(0, "Nitrogen")
```

The first value given to **insert**, 0 in this case, is the index at which to place the component, and the second value is the thing to be inserted. Inserting "Nitrogen" at the end of the list would be accomplished by:

```
list2.insert(len(list2), "Nitrogen)
```

However, consider this:

```
list2.insert(-1, "Nitrogen)
```

Will this insert "Nitrogen" at the end? No. At the beginning of the statement, the value of **list2[-1]** is "Carbon." This is the value at index 5. Therefore, the insert of "Nitrogen" will be at index 5, resulting in:

```
['Hydrogen', 'Helium', 'Lithium', 'Beryllium', 'Boron',
 'Nitrogen', 'Carbon']
```

3.4.3 Append

Another way to add something to the end of a list is to use the **append** method:

```
list2.append("Nitrogen")
```

Results in:

```
['Hydrogen', 'Helium', 'Lithium', 'Beryllium', 'Boron',
 'Carbon', 'Nitrogen']
```

Remember, the "+" operation will only concatenate a list to a list, so the equivalent expression involving "+" would be:

```
list2 = list2 + ["Nitrogen"]
```

3.4.4 Extend

The **extend** method does pretty much the same things as the "+" operator. With the definitions:

```
a = [1,2,3,4,5]
b = [6,7,8,9,10]
print (a+b)
a.extend(b)
print(a)
```

the output is:

[1, 2, 3, 4, 5, 6, 7, 8, 9, 10]

[1, 2, 3, 4, 5, 6, 7, 8, 9, 10]

However, if **append** has been used instead of **extend** above:

```
a = [1,2,3,4,5]
b = [6,7,8,9,10]
print (a+b)
a.append(b)
print(a)
```

the result would have been:

[1, 2, 3, 4, 5, 6, 7, 8, 9, 10]

[1, 2, 3, 4, 5, [6, 7, 8, 9, 10]]

3.4.5 Remove

The remove method does what is expected: it removes an element from the list. But unlike insert, for example, it does not do it using an index; the value to be removed is specified. So:

```
list1 = ["Hydrogen","Helium","Lithium","Beryllium","Boron",
        "Carbon"]
list1.remove("Helium")
```

results in the **list1** being ['Hydrogen', "Lithium', "Beryllium', "Boron', "Carbon']. Unfortunately, if the component being deleted is not a member of the list, then an error occurs. There are ways to deal with that, or a test can be made for trying to delete an item:

```
if "Nitrogen" in list1:
    list1.remove("Nitrogen")
```

If there is more than a single instance of the item being removed, then only the first one will be removed.

3.4.6 Index

When discussing *tuples* it was learned that the **index** method looked through the tuple and found the index at which a specified item occurred. The **index** method for lists works in the same way. So:

```
list1 = ["Hydrogen","Helium","Lithium","Beryllium","Boron",
        "Carbon"]
print (list1.index("Boron"))
```

prints "4," because the string "Boron" appears at index 4 in this list (starting from 0, of course). If there is more than one occurrence of "Boron" in the list, then the index of the first one (i.e., smallest index) is returned. If the value is not found in the string, then an error occurs. Again, it might be appropriate to check:

```
if "Boron" in list1:
    print (list1.index("Boron"))
```

3.4.7 Pop

The **pop** method is effectively the reverse or inverse of **append**. It removes the last item (i.e., the one having the largest index) from the list. If the list is empty, then an error occurs. For an example:

```
list1 = ["Hydrogen","Helium","Lithium","Beryllium","Boron",
        "Carbon"]
list1.pop()
print (list1)
```

prints the result:

```
['Hydrogen', 'Helium', 'Lithium', 'Beryllium', 'Boron']
```

To avoid the error that can occur if the list is empty, simply check to see that the length of the list is greater than zero before using **pop**:

```
if len(list1) > 0:
    list1.pop()
```

The method is called **pop** because it represents a way to implement the operation of the same name on a data structure called a *stack*.

3.4.8 Sort

This method places the components of a list into ascending order. Using the **list1** variable that has been used so often:

```
list1 = ["Hydrogen","Helium","Lithium","Beryllium","Boron",
        "Carbon"]
list1.sort()
print(list1)
```

the result is:

```
['Beryllium', 'Boron', 'Carbon', 'Helium', 'Hydrogen',
 'Lithium']
```

which is in alphabetic order. The method will sort integers and floating point numbers as well. Strings and numbers cannot be mixed, though, because they can't be compared. So:

```
list2 = ["Hydrogen",1,"Helium",2,"Lithium",3,"Beryllium",4,
        "Boron",5]
list2.sort()
```

results in an error that will be something like:

```
    list2.sort()
  TypeError: unorderable types: int() < str()
```

The meaning of this error should be clear. Things of type **int** (*integer*) and things of type **str** (*string*) can't be compared against each other and so can't be placed in a sensible order if mixed. For sort to work properly, all of the elements of the list must be of the same type. It is always possible to convert one type of thing into another, and in Python converting an integer to a string is accomplished with the **str()** function; string to integer is converted using **int()**. So **str(3)** would result in "3," and **int("12")** is 12. An error will occur if it is not possible, so **int(12.2)** will fail.

If each element of a list is itself a list, it can still be sorted. Consider the list:

```
z = [["Hydrogen",3],["Hydrogen",2],["Lithium",3],
     ["Beryllium",4],["Boron",5]]
```

When sorted this becomes:

```
[['Beryllium',4],['Boron',5],['Hydrogen',2],['Hydrogen',3],
 ['Lithium',3]]
```

Each component of this list is compatible with the others, consisting of a string and an integer. Thus they can be compared against each other. Notice that there are two entries for hydrogen: one with a number 2 and one with a number 3. The **sort** method arranges them correctly. A list is sorted by individual elements in sequence order, so the first thing tested would be the string. If those are the same, then the next element is checked. That's an integer, so the component with the smallest integer component will come first.

3.4.9 Reverse

In any sequence the order of the components within it is important. Reversing that order is a logical operation to provide, but may not be used very often. One instance where it can be important is after a sort. The **sort** method always places components into *ascending* order. If they are supposed to be in *descending* order, then the **reverse** method becomes valuable. As an example consider sorting the list **q**:

```
q = [5, 6, 1, 5, 4, 9, 9, 1, 6, 3]
q.sort()
```

The value of **q** at this point is

[1, 1, 3, 4, 5, 5, 6, 6, 9, 9]

To place this list is descending order the reverse method is used:

```
q.reverse()
```

and the result is

[9, 9, 6, 6, 5, 5, 4, 3, 1, 1]

It is hard to say whether ascending order is needed more often than descending order. Names are often sorted smallest first (ascending), but dates are more likely to require more recent dates before later ones (descending).

3.4.10 Count

This method is used to determine how many times a potential component of a list actually occurs. It *does not return the number of elements in the list*—that job is done by the **len** function. Using the list **q** as an example:

```
q = [5, 6, 1, 5, 4, 9, 9, 1, 6, 3]
print (1,q.count(1), 2, q.count(2), 3, q.count(3), 99,
       q.count(99))
```

will result in the output:

```
      1 2      2 0      3 1      99 0
```

where the spacing is enhanced for emphasis. This says that there are 2 instances of the number 1 (1,2) in the list, zero instances of 2 (2,0), one instance of the number 3 (3,1) and none of 99 (99,0).

3.4.11 List Comprehension

When creating a list of items, two mechanisms have been discussed. The first is to use constants, as in the list **q** in the previous section. The second appends items to a list, and this could be done within a loop. Making a list of perfect squares could be done like this:

```
t = []
for i in range(0,10):
    t = t + [i*i]
```

which creates the list [0, 1, 4, 9, 16, 25, 36, 49, 64, 81]. This kind of thing is common enough that a special syntax has been created for it in Python—the *list comprehension*.

The basic idea is simple enough, although some specific cases are complicated. In the situation above involving perfect squares, the elements in the list are some function of the index. When that is true the loop, index, and function can be given within the square brackets as a definition of the list. So the list **t** could be defined as:

```
tt = [i**2 for i in range(10)]
```

The **for** loop is within the square brackets, indicating that the purpose is to define components of the list. The variable **i** here is the loop variable, and **i**2** is the function that creates the elements from the index. This is a simple example of a list comprehension.

Creating random integer values? No problem:

```
tt = [random.randint(0,100) for i in range(10)]
```

The first six elements in all uppercase?

```
list1 = ["Hydrogen","Helium","Lithium","Beryllium",
         "Boron","Carbon"]
ss = [i.upper() for i in list1]
```

This is a very effective way to create lists, but it does depend on having a known connection between the index and the element.

3.4.12 Lists and Tuples

A tuple can be converted into a list. Lists have a greater functionality than tuples; that is, they provide more operations and greater ability to represent data. On the other hand, they are more complicated and require more computer resources. If something can be represented as a tuple, then it is likely best to do so. A tuple is designed to be a collection of elements that as a whole represent some more complicated object, but that individually are perhaps of different types. This is rather like a C *struct* or Pascal *record*. A list is more often used to hold a set of elements that all have the same type, more like an array. This is a good way to think of the two types when deciding what to use to solve a specific problem.

Python provides tools for conversion. The built-in function **list** takes a tuple and converts it into a list; the function tuple does the reverse, taking a list and turning it into a tuple. For example, converting list1 into a tuple:

```
tuple1 = tuple(list1)
print(tuple1)
```

yields

```
('Hydrogen', 'Helium', 'Lithium', 'Beryllium', 'Boron',
 'Carbon')
```

This is seen to be a tuple because of the "(' and ')" delimiters. The reverse:

```
v = list(tuple1)
print(v)
```

prints the text line:

```
['Hydrogen', 'Helium', 'Lithium', 'Beryllium', 'Boron',
 'Carbon']
```

and the square brackets indicate this is a list.

3.4.13 Exceptions

Exceptions are the usual way to check for errors of indexing and membership in lists. The error is allowed to occur, bur an exception is tested and handled in the case where, for example, an item being deleted is not in the list.

Problem: Delete the Element Helium from a List

Earlier, as an example of the remove method, a program snippet was written to delete the element *Helium* from a list of elements:

```
list1 = ["Hydrogen","Helium","Lithium","Beryllium","Boron",
        "Carbon"]
if "Helium" in list1:
    list1.remove("Helium")
```

Because list1 may not have *Helium* as one of the components, a check was made before an attempt to delete it. An attempt to delete an element from a list where the element does not appear in that list results in an **AttributeError**. Rather than perform an explicit test, a Python programmer would more likely use an exception here. The error can be caught as follows:

```
list1 = ["Hydrogen","Helium","Lithium","Beryllium","Boron",
        "Carbon"]
try:
    list1.remove("Helium")
except:
    print ('Can't find Helium')
```

The advantage of this over allowing the error to occur is that the program can continue to execute.

Problem: Delete a Specified Element from a List

Given the same list, read an element from the keyboard and delete that element from the list. The basic code is the same, but now the string is entered and could be anything at all. It's easier to test a program when it can be made to fail on purpose. The name is entered using the **input** function and is used as the parameter to **remove**. Now it is possible to test all of the code in this program without changing it. First, here is the program:

```
list1 = ["Hydrogen","Helium","Lithium","Beryllium","Boron",
         "Carbon"]
s = input("Enter:")
try:
    list1.remove(s)
except:
   print ('Can't find ', s)
print (list1)
```

Properly testing a program means executing all of the statements that comprise it and ensuring that the answer given is correct. So in this case, first delete an element that is a part of the list. Try Lithium. Here is the output:

Enter: Lithium

["Hydrogen", "Helium", "Beryllium", "Boron", "Carbon"]

This is correct. These are the statements that were executed in this instance:

```
list1 = ["Hydrogen","Helium","Lithium","Beryllium","Boron",
         "Carbon"]
s = input("Enter:")
try:
    list1.remove(s)   # This was successful
print (list1)
```

Now try to delete *Oxygen.* Output is:

Enter: Oxygen

Can't find Oxygen

['Hydrogen', "Helium', "Lithium', "Beryllium', "Boron', "Carbon']

This is correct. These statements were executed:

```
list1 = ["Hydrogen","Helium","Lithium","Beryllium","Boron",
         "Carbon"]
```

```
s = input("Enter:")
try:
    list1.remove(s)      # this was not successful
except:
    print ('Can't find ', s)
print (list1)
```

All of the code in the program has been executed and the results checked for both major situations. For any major piece of software this kind of testing is exhausting, but it is really the only way to minimize the errors that remain in the final program.

3.5 SET TYPES

Something of type *set* is an unordered collection of objects. An element can only be a member of a given *set* once, so in that sense it is much like a mathematical set. In fact, that's the point. Because a set is unordered, operations such as indexing and slicing are not provided. It does support membership (**is**), size (**len()**), and looping on membership (**for i in set**).

Anyone (probably an older person) who knows the *Pascal* language has some familiarity with the set type in Python.

Mathematical sets have certain specific, well-defined operations, and those are available on a Python set also.

Subset   **set1 < set2** means **set1** is a true subset of **s2**.

Intersection **set1 & set2** creates a new set containing members in common with both.

Union   **set1 | set2** creates a new set with all elements of both.

Difference   **set1-set2** creates a new set with members that are not in both.

Equality   **set1==set2** is true if both sets contain only the same elements.

Creating a new object of type *set* is a matter of specifying either that it is a *set* or what the elements are. So, one way is to use the {} syntax:

```
set1 = {1,3,5,7,9}
```

or to use the constructor:

```
set2 = set(range(1, 10))
```

which gives the set {1, 2, 3, 4, 5, 6, 7, 8, 9}. So:

set1<set2 is True

set1 & set2 is {9, 1, 3, 5, 7}   Note: order does not matter to a set.

set1 | set2 is {1, 2, 3, 4, 5, 6, 7, 8, 9}

set2 – set1 is {8, 2, 4, 6}

A new element can be added to a set using **add()**:

```
set1.add(11)
```

and removed using **remove()**:

```
set1.remove(11)
```

or **discard()**:

```
set1.discard(11)
```

If the element being removed is not in the set, then an error will occur (*Key-Error*) when **remove()** is called, but not with **discard()**. This should be tested first or be placed in an **except** statement.

All of the examples so far involve integers belonging to a set, but other types can belong as well: floating point numbers, strings, and even tuples (not *lists*). For example, the following are legal sets:

```
{"a", "e", "i", "o", "u"}
{"cyan", "yellow", "magenta"}
{(2,4), (3,9), (4,16), (5,25), (6,36), (7,49)}
```

3.5.1 Example: Craps

Craps is a dice game, for those unfamiliar with it, and commonly involves betting on the outcome. The player (*shooter*) rolls two dice. If, on the first roll (*pass*), a total of 7 or 11 is obtained, then the shooter wins. On the other hand, an initial roll of 2, 3, or 12 loses immediately. Any other roll is called the *point*. In that case the shooter continues to roll the dice. If a 7 is obtained then the shooter loses, and if the point number is rolled then the shooter wins. The shooter continues to roll until one or the other occurs. One way to implement this game in Python is to use sets.

Elements of the sets will be values on each die, which is to say one roll. There are two dice so a total of 36 combinations exist. A single roll is a tuple, such as

(1,1) or (3,4). There are only 12 distinct sums of two dice, and multiple ways to achieve them. A sequence named **roll** will be created that contains a set for each possible value, and that set contains all of the ways that the value can be obtained. For instance, there are two ways to roll a 3, so:

roll[3] = {(1,2), (2,1)}

Initially a set is created for each possible roll of a pair of dice and then is initialized as described:

```
from random import *

roll = list(range(0,13))        # Create the empty list
for i in range(1,13):           # and fill with empty sets.
    roll[i] = set()
for i in range (1,7):           # Now for each possible roll
    for j in range (1,7):       # of two dice, add that roll
        k = i+j                 # to the element of roll for
        roll[k].add( (i,j) )    # that value (sum of the
                                # dice)
```

Now **roll[i]** contains all of the ways to roll a value of **i**, In particular, **roll[7]** contains all ways to roll a 7 and **roll[11]** contains all ways to roll an 11. Thus, all of the rolls that will win on the first pass can be placed in a single set, the union of **roll[7]** and **roll[11]**:

```
winner = roll[7] | roll[11]
```

Similarly, the rolls that will lose for the shooter on the first pass are:

```
loser = roll[2] | roll[3] | roll[12]
```

If any other roll is thrown, then that becomes the point. Rolling a die amounts to getting a random number between 1 and 6 inclusive, or:

```
die1 = randrange(1,7)
die2 = randrange(1,7)
```

Remember that **randrange()** produces a number *less* than the second parameter. Given this roll, the point is the set **roll[die1+die2]**. Continuing the program from the die rolls:

```
val = (die1,die2)               # A tuple, the current roll
print ("Shooter rolls ", val)
if val in winner:               # Is this tuple a winner?
```

```
    print ("The shooter wins!")
elif val in loser:                  # Is it a loser?
    print ("The shooter loses")
else:
    point = roll[die1+die2]      # Define the point set
    print (die1+die2, " is your point.")
```

Now the dice are rolled repeatedly. If the roll is in the point set, then the shooter wins. If the roll is a 7 (in the set **roll[7]**) then the player loses. Otherwise the shooter rolls again.

```
while True:                     # Repeat until a win or
                                # loss happens
    die1 = randrange(1,7)       # Roll the dice
    die2 = randrange(1,7)
    val = (die1, die2)          # val is a tuple
    print ("Rolls ", val)
    if val in roll[7]:          # Any 7 roll loses
        print ("The shooter loses!")
        break
    if val in point:            # Rolling the 'point' wins.
        print ("The shooter makes the point. A winner!")
        break
```

And that's the game. In a real craps game this entire process is repeated, and bets are placed on each individual game as to whether the player will win or lose.

3.6 SUMMARY

There is a kind type that a variable can have that amounts to a list or sequence of other, simpler, things. This is true, and using variables having these types is an essential part of writing useful and effective code. Python offers *strings*, *tuples*, and *lists* as objects that consist of multiple parts. They are called *sequence* types.

A *string* is a sequence of characters. The word *sequence* implies that the order of the characters within the string matters, and that is true of a string. Strings most often represent the way that communication between a computer and a human takes place. Strings can be indexed to see what character is in any position (e.g., **s[i]**), can be searched for a string that occurs with it, can have characters concatenated to it, and many other useful operations. If a string **s** contains an integer, then **int(s)** will yield that integer and **str(i)** will create a string from an integer **i**.

A *tuple* is almost identical to a string in basic structure, except that it is composed of arbitrary components instead of characters. Examples are **tup1 = (2, 3, 5)** and **tup2 = ("Hydrogen","Helium","Carbon")**. A tuple can contain mixed type, such as integers and strings: **tup3 = ("star", 1, "planet", 2)**. An element of a tuple cannot be altered, so it is said to be *immutable*, although concatenation is possible.

A *list* is like a tuple but is not immutable, so individual elements can be modified. A list uses square brackets as a delimiter, instead of parentheses as used for a tuple. Changing an element involves indexing it, so if **list1** is a list then **list1[2] = 6** modifies element 2 of that list.

A *set* is an unordered collection of objects. An element can be almost any type, but can only occur in a set once. This mimics a mathematical set. Elements can be added and removed, and the set operations *union*, *intersection*, and *difference* can be performed.

Exercises

For the exercises below, assume the following definitions:

```
str1 = "okra is the closest thing to nylon i've ever eaten."
str2 = "pull the string, and it will follow wherever you
        wish."
str3 = "let out a little more string on your kite."
str4 = "every string is a different color, a different voice."
vowels = 'aeiou'
atoms=("Hydrogen",1,"Helium",2,"Lithium",3,"Boron",5,"Carb
on",6, "Oxygen",8)
```

1. What is printed by the following code snippets:
   a) **for** i **in** range(0,len(str3)):
      ```
      print (str3[i], end='')
      ```
   b) **for** i **in** range(0,len(str3)):
      ```
      print (i, end='')
      ```
   c) **for** i **in** range(0,len(str3)):
      ```
      print (str2[i], end='')
      ```
   d) **for** i **in** str3:
      ```
      print (i, end='')
      ```

e) **for** i **in** str3:
    if i **in** vowels:
        print(i, end='')
f) **for** i **in** str1:
    if not(i **in** vowels):
        print(i, end='')

2. Construct a loop that prints out all characters of **str4** that correspond to a vowel in **str3**. Note: the two strings are different lengths.

3. A *Caesar cypher* is a way to transmit a secret message. When encoding a message each character is replaced by one that is a fixed distance further along the alphabet. If that distance is 6, for example, the letter "a" would be replaced by "g," which is 6 positions further along. The characters at the end will wrap around to the beginning, so "z" will become "f." Write some Python code that will encode **str1** in this way. Ensure that it works by decrypting the following string:

"varr znk yzxotm, gtj oz corr lurruc cnkxkbkx eua coyn."

Ans: uqxg oy znk iruykyz znotm zu terut o'bk kbkx kgzkt.

4. Write a Python snippet that will create two tuples from the single tuple **atoms**: one named **elements** that contains only the names, and one called **numbers** that contains the atomic numbers of the elements in the tuple **atoms**.

5. Write a Python program that reads numbers from the keyboard and appends them to a tuple. Stop the process when a negative number is entered and then print the tuple that was created.

6. A deck of playing cards consists of 52 items: each one has one of four suits (clubs, diamonds, hearts, and spades) and within each suit are values from 1–10 and "Jack," "Queen," and "King." Write a Python program that creates a deck of cards, shuffles them, and prints out the result.

7. Write a Python program that reads names (single words) one at a time from a keyboard and deletes them from a list named **names** if they are already elements of that list. If the name is not already a member of the list, then it will be added. Typing the name "quit" terminates the program.

8. Assume that a string named **temp** exists and has a value. Write Python code that will print **temp** backwards.

9. A palindrome is a phrase (a string) that reads the same forwards and backwards. The name "hannah" is a palindrome; so is "Ogopogo," the name of a monster who lives in lake Okanogan, and the word "redivider." Write a Python program that determines whether a given string is a palindrome.

10. Most examples of palindromes contain spaces and punctuation, and these characters are ignored when deciding whether or not the phrase is palindromic. So is case. Thus, the phrase "I prefer pi" is a palindrome. With these considerations in mind, write a Python program that determines whether a string is a palindrome or not.

Notes and Other Resources

Built-in types: *https://docs.python.org/3.4/library/stdtypes.html?highlight=set#set*

Python strings: *https://docs.python.org/3/library/string.html*

Rules of Craps: *http://www.bigmcasino.com/learn-more/learn-to-play-craps/ what-are-the-basic-rules-of-craps/*

1. David Mertz. (2003). **Text Processing in Python**, Addison Wesley Professional, ISBN-13: 978-0321112545.

2. David Makinson. (2012). **Sets, Logic, and Maths for Computing**, 2nd edition, Springer, ISBN-13: 978-1447124993.

3. J. D. Oldham. (2005). **What happens after Python in CS1?** *Journal of Computing Sciences in Colleges*, *20*(6), 7–13.

FUNCTIONS

■ ■ ■ ■ ■

In this chapter

There is a large and useful set of functions built into Python. These are sometimes simply there for the using, like **print** and **input**, and sometimes are part of a module that must be imported, like **random**. However, as large as this collection of functions is, it is impossible that it will include everything that every programmer needs. At some point there will be a need to create a function that does something new, and Python should permit this.

Why would a programmer want to create a function of their own? It is partly out of convenience; if some section of code can be invoked as a function instead of being repeated many times, then there will be less typing involved. It is also to support more correct programs: a small code unit like a function can be very thoroughly tested and nearly guaranteed to be correct. And it is also to support reuse of working code: once a function is tested, it can be placed in a collection of code (module) and used again and again instead of being rewritten many times.

A function is really just some code that has a name, and can be executed simply by invoking that name. It usually represents some task that has to be done fairly frequently, but that's not a requirement. Some functions are invoked (or *called*) only once. In this context a function is a way to break up a long piece of code into many shorter pieces which, as has been pointed out, are easier to test and maintain.

A function should also have one single task, or at least one main task. That task should be represented in the function name. A function named *maximum* should have the task of locating the maximum of something; a function named *cosine* should calculate the cosine of an angle. If a function is named *wilma* it tells another programmer who is reading the code nothing about the what the program is doing, and if a function named *cosine* computes the square root of a number then it is not just uninformative but misleading. Never mind that the Python language does not insist that names be informative; there is a social compact between programmers that says that you should be as clear as possible about what your code is doing.

The fact that many functions return a value has been skipped over, but it is a key part of the function construct. The code within the function has a purpose, and often that purpose is concentrated in the return value. However it works, and whatever the code looks like, the purpose of the *cosine* function is to return a single value that is the mathematical cosine of a given angle. The nature of the function is encapsulated in that value. There are some functions that do not explicitly return a value; such a function might be called to print an error message or draw a graphical object in a window. Even if it is not specifically declared in the definition, all functions return *something*. If not defined, then it returns a value called **None**.

Enough exposition—how can functions be declared and used in Python?

4.1 FUNCTION DEFINITION: SYNTAX AND SEMANTICS

Unlike in the cases of **if** statements or **for** statements, a function definition does not involve the word "function." As an example of a simple definition in

Python, imagine a program that needs a function to print twenty "#" characters on a line. It could be defined as:

```
def pound20 ():
    for i in range(0,20):
        print ("#", end="")
```

The word **def** is known to Python and always begins the definition of a function. This is followed by the name of the function, in this case **pound20** because the function prints 20 *pound* characters (also known as a *hash* characters or *octothorpe*). Then comes the list of parameters, which can be thought of as a tuple of variable names. In this case the tuple is empty, meaning that nothing is passed to the function. Finally comes the ":" character that defines a new suite that comprises the code belonging to the function. From here on the code is indented one more level, and when the indentation reverts to the original level the function definition is complete.

Calling this function is a matter of using its name as a statement or in an expression, being careful to always include the tuple of parameters. Even when the tuple is empty, it helps distinguish a function from a variable. A call to this function would be:

```
pound20 ()
```

and the result would be that 20 "#" characters would be printed on one line of the output console.

A function can be given or *passed* one or more values that will determine the result of the function. A function **cosine**, for example, would be passed an angle, and that angle would be used

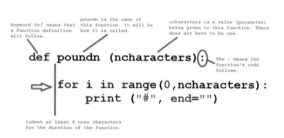

Figure 4.1
The syntax of a function definition.

to compute the cosine. Each call to **cosine** passing a different value can yield a different result. In the case of the function that prints pound characters, it might be useful to pass it the number of pound characters to print. It should not be called **pound20** anymore because it does not always print 20 characters. It will be called **poundn** this time:

```
def poundn (ncharacters):
```

```
for i in range(0,ncharacters):

    print ("#", end="")
```

The variable **ncharacters** that is given in parentheses after the function name is called a *parameter* or an *argument*, and indicates the name by which the function will refer to the value passed to it. This name is known only inside of the function, and while it can be modified within the function, this modification will not have any bearing on anything outside. The call to **poundn** must now include a value to be passed to the function:

```
poundn (3)
```

When this call is performed, the code within **poundn** begins executing, and the value of **ncharacters** is 3, the value that was passed. It prints 3 characters and returns. A subsequent call to **poundn** could be passed a different number, perhaps 8, and then **ncharacters** would take on the value 8 and the function would print 8 characters. It will print as many characters as requested through the parameter.

4.1.1 Problem: Use *poundn* to Draw a Histogram

In Chapter 2, a simple histogram was created from some print statements and loops. The same code was repeated many times, one for each histogram bar. As it happens the character used to draw the histogram bars was the pound character, so the function **poundn** could be used as a basis for a histogram program. As a reminder, here is the output that is desired:

Earnings for WidgetCorp for 2016

   Dollars for each quarter

   ==============================

Q1: ########   190000

Q2: ###############   340000

Q3: ##   873000

Q4: ###################   439833

Each pound character represents $20000, and there are four variables that hold the profit for each of the four quarters: q1, q2, q3, and q4. Given these criteria, a solution using **poundn** would call the function four times, once for each quarter:

```
print ("Earnings for WidgetCorp for 2016")
print ("   Dollars for each quarter      ")
print (" ================================")
q1 = 190000  # The dollar amounts for profits
q2 = 340000  # in each of the four quarters of 2016
q3 = 873000
q4 = 439833

print ("Q1: ", end="")
poundn(int(q1/20000))   # Raw dollar amount is divided by
                        # 20000
                        # to yield the number of characters.
print ("      ", q1)

print ("Q2: ", end="")
poundn (int(q2/20000))
print ("      ", q2)

print ("Q3: ", end="")
poundn (int(q3/20000))
print ("      ", q3)


print ("Q4: ", end="")

poundn (int(q4/20000))

print ("      ", q4)
```

Each profit value must be scaled by dividing by 20000, just as happened before. In this case the resulting value is passed to **poundn** indicating the number of "#"'s to draw.

4.1.2 Problem: Generalize the Histogram Code for Other Years

Any company will need to do financial reports every year at least. Hiring a programmer to do this task on a computer is not a reasonable thing to do, because computers can be made to do this job in a very general way. For example, given that each year will have four quarters and each quarter will have a profit, why not store these data as a list? Each year will have one list containing four items, and the name of the variable could initially be related to the year:

```
profit2016 = [190000, 340000, 873000, 439833]
```

The profit for the first quarter is **profit2016[0]**, the second quarter is **profit2016[1]**, and so on. Using this variable means passing one of the elements of the list to **poundn** instead of a simple variable, but that is fine, it's a legal expression. So drawing the characters for the first quarter would be done with the following code:

```
poundn(int(profit2016[0]/20000))
```

Now consider what else gets printed. To print everything for the first quarter the code was:

```
print ("Q1: ", end="")
poundn(int(profit2016[0]/20000))
print ("      ", q1)
```

This means that the label on the left, "Q1," the parameters to **poundn**, and the actual value of the profit are needed. All of these are available, and can be provided within a simple loop. Assuming that the loop variable **i** runs from 0 to 3, the code within that loop that duplicates the previous example can be constructed one line at a time. In each iteration the quarter is **i+1** because **i** starts at 0; convert that to a string and build the label "Q1 : " from it:

```
print (Q1: ", end="")
print ("Q"+str(i+1)+": ", end="")
```

This is probably the trickiest part. The label string is constructed from the letter "Q," a number between 1 and 4 indicating the quarter, and ":" for the terminal string. They are simply concatenated together in the **print** statement.

Now call **poundn** as before:

```
poundn(int(profit2016[i]/20000))
  poundn(int(profit2016[i]/20000))
```

finally, print the raw dollar value on the right:

```
print ("      ", q1)
print ("      ", profit2016[i])
```

So, using this plan the entire histogram can be drawn using only four statements:

```
for i in range(0,4):
    print ("Q"+str(i+1)+": ", end="")
    poundn(int(profit2016[i]/20000))
    print ("      ", profit2016[i])
```

That's pretty brief, readable, and general. Still, there's another step. Since this will be done every year, why not create a function that takes the data and the year as parameters, and do the whole job? It shall be called **pqhistogram**:

```
def pqhistogram (profit, year):
    print ("Earnings for WidgetCorp for "+str(year))
    print ("    Dollars for each quarter    ")
    print (" ==============================")
    for i in range(0,4):
        print ("Q"+str(i+1)+": ", end="")
        poundn(int(profit[i]/20000))
        print ("      ", profit[i])
```

The function **pqhistogram** produces the same output as did the original program, and does so more generally and concisely. This function also brings to light two new ideas. One is that it is possible to pass more than one parameter to a function. The second is that it is possible to call a function from within another function; in this case **poundn** is called from inside of **pqhistogram**. The call is made after defining the list that contains the profit values:

```
profit2016 = [190000, 340000, 873000, 439833]

pqhistogram (profit2016, 2016)
```

It is important to note that the parameters are positional; that is, the first value passed will correspond to the first name in the parameter list, and the second to the second. This is the default for functions with any number of parameters.

| NOTE | *A **def** statement is not a declaration. Such things are foreign to Python. A **def** statement executes, and it "creates" a new function each time it is executed. This is an advanced topic, and will be handled later.* |

4.2 ■ FUNCTION EXECUTION

When a function is called, the first statement of that function starts to execute, and it continues statement by statement through the code until the last statement of that function or until it returns prematurely. When that last

statement executes, then execution will continue from the place where it was *called*. As a function can be called from many places, Python has to remember where the function was called so that it can return. Parameters can be expressions or variables, and normally differ each time the function is called. Functions can also access variables defined elsewhere.

Most importantly, and a factor that has not been dealt with yet, is that functions return values.

4.2.1 Returning a Value

All functions return a value, and as such can be treated within expressions as if they were variables having that value. So, assuming the existence of a cosine function, it could be used in an expression in the usual ways. For example:

```
x = cosine(x)*r
if cosine(x) < 0.5:
print (cosine(x)*cosine(x))
```

In these cases the value returned by the function is used by the code to calculate a further value or to create output. The expression "cosine(x)" resolves to a value of some Python type. The most common purpose of a function is to calculate a value, which is then returned to the calling part of the program and can possibly be used in a further calculation. But how does a function get its value? In a **return** statement.

The return statement assigns a value and a type to the object returned by the function. It also stops executing the function and resumes execution at the location where the function was called. A simple example would be to return a single value, such as an integer or floating point number:

```
return 0
```

returns the value 0 from a function. The return value could be an expression:

```
return x*x + y*y
```

A function has only one return value, but it can be of any type, so it could be a list or tuple that contains multiple components:

```
return (2,3,5,7,11)
```

```
return ["fluorine","chlorine","bromine","iodine","astatine"]
```

Expressions can include function calls, so a return value can be defined in this way as well; for example:

```
return cosine(x)
```

One of the simplest functions that can be used as an example is one that calculates the square of its parameter. It nonetheless illustrates some interesting things:

```
def square (x):
    return x*x
```

The print statement:

```
print (square(12))
```

will print:

```
144
```

Interestingly, the statement:

```
print(square(12.0))
```

results in:

```
144.0
```

The same function returns an integer in one case and a float in the other. Why? Because the function returns the result of an expression involving its parameter, which in one case was an integer and in the other was real. This implies that a function has no fixed type, and can return any type at all. Indeed, the same function can have return statements that return an integer, a float, a string, and a list independent of type of the parameter passed:

```
def test (x):   # Return one of four types depending on x
    if x<1:
        return 1
    if x<2:
        return 2.0
    if x<3:
        return "3"
    return [1,2,3,4]

print (test(0))
print (test(1))
```

```
print (test(2))
print (test(3))
```

The output:

```
1
2.0
3
[1, 2, 3, 4]
```

Problem: Write a Function to Calculate the Square Root of its Parameter

Two thousand years ago the Babylonians had a way to calculate the square root of a number. They understood the definition of a square root: that if $y*y = x$ then y is the square root of x. They figured out that if y was an overestimate to the true value of the square root of x, then x/y would be an underestimate. In that case, a better guess would be to average those two values: the next guess would be $y_1 = (y + x/y)/2$. The guess after that would be $y_2 = (y_1 + x/y_1)/2$, and so on. At any point in the calculation the error (difference between the correct answer and the estimate) can be found by squaring the guess y_i and subtracting x from it, knowing that y_i*y_i is supposed to equal **x**.

The function will therefore start by guessing what the square root might be. It cannot be 0 because then x/y would be undefined. x is a good guess. Then construct a loop based on the expression $y_2 = (y_1 + x/y_1)/2$, or more generally $y_{i+1} = (y_i + x/y_i)/2$ for iteration **i**. At first, run this loop a fixed number of times, perhaps 20. Here is the function that results:

```
def root (x):        # Compute the square root of x
    y = x            # First guess: too big, probably
    for i in range(1, 20): # Iterate20 times
        y = (y + x/y)/2.0  # Average the prior guess and
                           # x/y
    return y         # Return the last guess
```

This correctly computes the square root of 2 to 15 decimal places. This is probably more than is necessary, meaning that the loop is executing more times than it needs to. In fact, changing the 20 iterations to only 6 still gives 15 correct places. This is exceptional accuracy: if the distance between the Earth and the Sun were known this accurately it would be within 0.006 inches of the correct value. The Babylonians seem to have been very clever.

What's the square root of 10000? If the number of iterations is kept at 6, then the answer is a very poor one indeed: 323.1. Why? Some numbers (large ones) need more iterations than others. To guarantee that a good estimate of the square root is returned, an estimate of the error should be used. When the error is small enough, then the value will be good enough. The error will be $x - y_i * y_i$. The function should not loop a fixed number of times, but instead should repeat until the error is less than, say, 0.0000001. This function will be named **roote**, where the "e" is for "error."

```
# Computer the square root of X to 7 decimal places
def roote (x):
y = x                   # y is supposed to be the square root
                        # of x, so
e = abs(x-y*y)          # the error is x - y*y
while e > 0.0000001:    # repeat while the error is bigger
                        # than 0.0000001
    y = (y + x/y)/2.0       # New estimate for square root

    e = abs(x-y*y)          New error value
return y
```

This function will return the square root of any positive value of **x** to within 7 decimal places. It should check for negative values, though.

4.2.2 Parameters

A parameter can be either a name, meaning that it is a Python *variable* (object) of some kind, or an *expression*, meaning it has a value but no permanence in that it can't be accessed later on—it has no name. Both are passed to a function as an *object reference*. The expression is evaluated before being given to the function, and its type does not matter in so far as Python will always know what it is; its value is assigned a name when it is passed. Consider, for example, the function **square** in the following context:

```
...
pi = 3.14159
r = 2.54
c = square (2*pi*r)
print ("Circumference is ", c)
```

The assignments to **pi** and **r** are performed, and when the call to **square** occurs, the expression **2*pi*r** is evaluated first. Its value is assigned to a temporary variable, which is passed as the parameter to square. Inside the function this parameter is named **x**, and the function calculates x squared and returns it as a value. It is as if the following code executes:

```
pi = 3.14159
r = 2.54
# call square(2*pi*r)
 parameter1 = 2*pi*r    # set the parameter value
 x = parameter1         # First parameter is named x inside
                        # SQUARE
 returnvalue = x*x      # Code within SQUARE, return x*x
c = returnvalue         # assign result of function
                        # call to c
print ("Circumference is ", c)
```

This is not how a function is implemented, but it shows how the parameter is effectively passed; a copy is made of the parameters and those are passed. If the expression **2*pi*r** was changed to a simple variable, then the internal location of that variable would be passed.

Passing more structured objects works the same way but can behave differently. If a list is passed to a function then the list itself cannot be modified, but the contents of the list can be. The list is assigned another name, but it is the same list. To be clear, consider a simple function that edits a list by adding a new

element to the end:

```
def addend  (arg):
    arg.append("End")

z = ["Start", "Add", "Multiply"]
print (1, z)
addend(z)
print (1, z)
```

The list associated with the variable z is changed by this function call. It now ends with the string "End." Output from this is:

```
1 ['Start', 'Add', 'Multiply']
2 ['Start', 'Add', 'Multiply', 'End']
```

Why is this? Because the name **z** refers to a thing that consists of many other parts. The name **z** is used to access them, and the function can't modify the value of z itself. It *can* modify what **z** indicates; that is, the components. Think of it, if it makes it simpler, as a level of indirection. A book can be exchanged between two people. The receiver writes a note in it and gives it back. It's the same book, but the contents are now different.

A small modification to **addend()** illustrates some confusing behavior. Instead of using **append** to add "End" to the list, use the concatenation operator "+":

```
def addend (arg):
    arg = arg + ["End"]

z = ["Start", "Add", "Multiply"]
print (1, z)
addend(z)
print (2, z)
```

Now the output is:

```
1 ['Start', 'Add', 'Multiply']
2 ['Start', 'Add', 'Multiply']
```

The component "End" is not a part of the list **z** anymore. It was made a component inside of the function, but it's not present after the function returns. This is because the statement:

```
arg = arg + ["End"]
```

actually creates a new list with "End" as the final component, and then assigns that new list as a value to **arg**. This represents an attempt to change the value that was passed, which can't happen: changing the value of **arg** will not change the value of the passed variable **z**. So, within the function **arg** is a new list with "End" as the final component. Outside, the list **z** has not changed.

The way that Python passes parameters is the subject of a lot of discussion on Internet blogs and lists. There are many names given for the method used, and while the technique is understood, it does differ from the way parameters are passed in other languages and is confusing to people who learned another language like Java or C before Python. The thing to remember is that the actual value of the thing (an *object reference*) being passed can't be assigned a new value inside the function, but the things that it *references* or *points to* can be modified.

Multiple parameters are passed by position; the first parameter passed is given to the first one listed in the function declaration, the second one passed is given to the second one listed in the declaration, and so on. They are all passed in the same manner, though, as object references.

4.2.3 Default Parameters

It is possible to specify a value for a parameter in the instance that it is not given one by the caller. That may not seem to make sense, but the implication is that it will sometimes be passed explicitly and sometimes not. When debugging code it is common to embed **print** statements in specific places to show that the program has reached that point. Sometimes it is important to print out a variable or value there, other times it is just to show that the program got to that statement safely. Consider a function named **gothere**:

```
def gothere (count, value):

    print ("Got Here: ",count, " value is ", value)
```

then throughout the program, calls to **gothere** would be sprinkled with a different value for **count** every time; the value of **count** indicates the statement that has been reached. This is a way of *instrumenting* the program, and can be very useful for finding errors. So the code being debugged may look like:

```
year = 2015          # The code below is not especially
                     # meaningful
a = year % 19        # and is an example only.
gothere(1, 0)
b = year // 100
c = year % 100
gothere (2, 0)
d = (19 * a + b - b // 4 - ((b - (b + 8) // 25 + 1)
     // 3) + 15) % 30
e = (32 + 2 * (b % 4) + 2 * (c // 4) - d - (c % 4)) % 7
f = d + e - 7 * ((a + 11 * d + 22 * e) // 451) + 114
gothere (3, f)
month = f // 31
day = f % 31 + 1
gothere(4, day)
return date(year, month, day)
```

Output is:

Got Here: 1 value is 0

Got Here: 2 value is 0

Got Here: 3 value is 128

Got Here: 4 value is 5

2015 4 5

The program reaches each of the four checkpoints and prints a proper message. The first two calls to **gothere** did not need to print a value, only the count number. The second parameter could be given a default value, perhaps **None**, and then it would not have to be passed. The definition of the function would now be:

```
def gothere (count, value=None):
    if value:
        print ("Got Here: ",count, " value is ", value)
    else:
        print (Got Here: ", count)
```

and the output this time is:

Got Here: 1

Got Here: 2

Got Here: 3 value is 128

Got Here: 4 value is 5

2015 4 5

The assignment within the parameter list gives the name value a special property. It has a *default value*. If the parameter is not passed, then it takes that value; otherwise, it behaves normally. This also means that **gothere** can be called with one or two parameters, which can be very handy. It is important to note that the parameters that are given a default value must be defined after the ones that are not. That's because otherwise it would not be clear what was being passed. Consider the (illegal) definition:

```
def wrong (a=1, b, c=12):
```

    ...

Now call **wrong** with two parameters:

```
wrong (2,5)
```

What parameters are being passed? Is it **a** and **b**? Is it **a** and **c**? It is impossible to tell. A legal definition would be:

```
def right (b, a=1, c=12)
```

This function can be called as:

```
right (19)
```

in which case b=19, a=1, and c=12. It can be called as:

```
right (19, 20)
```

in which case b=19, a=19, and c=12. It can be called as:

```
right (19, 19, 19)
```

in which case b=19, a=19, and c=19. But how can it be called passing **b** and **c** but not **a**? Like this:

```
right (19, c=19)
```

In this case **a** has been allowed to default. The only way to pass **c** without also passing **a** is to give its name explicitly so that the call is not ambiguous.

4.2.4 None

Mistakes happen when writing code. They are unavoidable, and much time is spent getting rid of them. One common kind of mistake is to forget to assign a return value when one is needed. This is especially likely when there are multiple points in the function where a return can occur. In many programming languages this will be caught as an error, but in Python it is not. Instead, a function that is not explicitly assigned a return value will return a special value called **None**.

None has its own type (*NoneType*), and is used to indicate something that has no defined value or the absence of a value. It can be explicitly assigned to variables, printed, returned from a function, and tested. Testing for this value can be done using:

```
if x == None:
```

or by:

```
if x is None:
```

4.2.5 Example: The Game of Sticks

This is a relatively simple combinatorial game that involves removing sticks or chips from a pile. There are two players, and the game begins with a pile of 21 sticks. The first player begins by removing 1, 2, or 3 sticks from the pile.

Then the next player removes some sticks, again 1, 2, or 3 of them. Players alternate in this way. The player who removes the last stick wins the game; in other words, if you can't move, you lose.

Functions are useful in the implementation of this game because both players do similar things. The action connected with making a move, displaying the current position, and so on are the same for the human player and the computer opponent. The current status or state of the game is simply a number, the number of sticks remaining in the pile. When that number is zero, then the game is over, and the loser is whatever player is supposed to move next. The code for a pair of moves, one from the human and one from the computer, might be coded in Python as follows:

```
displayState(val)                # Show the game board
userMove = getMove()             # Ask user for their move
val = val - userMove             # Make the move
print ("You took ", userMove, " sticks leaving ", val)
if gameOver(val):
    print("You win!")
else:
    move = makeComputerMove (val) # Calculate the
                                  # computer's move
    print ("Computer took ", move, " sticks leaving ", val)
    if gameOver(val):
        print("Computer wins!")
```

The current state of the game is displayed first, and then the human player is asked for their move. The move is simply the number of sticks to remove. When the move has been made, if there are no sticks left then the human wins. Otherwise, the computer calculates and makes a move; again, if no sticks remain then the game is over, in this case the computer being the winner. This entire section of code needs to be repeated until the game is over, of course.

There are four functions that must be written for this version: **displayState()**, **getMove()**, **gameOver()**, and **makeComputerMove()**.

The function **displayState()** prints the current situation in the game. Specifically, it prints one "O" character for each stick still in the pile, and does so in rows of 6. At the beginning of the game this function would print:

```
o o o o o o
o o o o o o
```

o o o o o o
o o o

which is 21 sticks. The code is:

```
def displayState(val):
    k = val          # K represents the number of sticks not
                     # printed
    while k > 0:  # So long as some are not printed …
        if k >=6: # If there is a whole row, print it.
            print ("O O O O O O ", end="")
            k = k - 6  # Six fewer sticks are unprinted
        else:
            for j in range(0,k):  # Print the remainder
                print ("O ", end="")
            k = 0                 # None remain
    print ("")
```

This should be obvious. Also note that the function is named for what it does. It does only one thing; it modifies no values outside of the function, and it serves a purpose that is needed multiple times. These are all good properties of a function.

The function **getMove()** will print a prompt to the user/player asking for the number of sticks they wish to remove and reads that value from the keyboard, returning it as the function value. Again, this function is named for what it does and performs a single, simple task. One possibility for the code is:

```
def getMove ():
    n = int(input ("Your move: Take away how many?  "))
    while n<=0 or n>3:
        print ("Sorry, you must take 1, 2, or 3 sticks.")
        n = int(input ("Your move: Take away how many?  "))
    return n
```

The function **gameOver()** is trivial, but lends structure to the program. All it does is test to see whether the value of **val**, the game state variable, is zero. It leaves open the idea that there may be other end of game indicators that could be tested here.

```
def gameOver (state):
    if state == 0:
        return True
    return False
```

Finally, the most complicated function, **getComputerMove()**, can be attempted. Naturally a good game presents a challenge to the player, and so the computer should win the game it if can. It should not play randomly if that is possible. In the case of this particular game, the winning strategy is easy to code. The player to make the final move wins, so if there are 1, 2, or 3 sticks left at the end, the computer would take them all and win. Forcing the human player to have 4 sticks makes this happen. The same is true if the computer can give the human player (i.e., leave the game in the state of having) 8, 12, or 16 sticks. This can be demonstrated by playing the game with actual sticks. So, if the human moves first (as it does in this implementation) the computer tries to leave the game in a state where there are 16, 12, 8, or 4 sticks left after its move. The code could be:

```
def getComputerMove (val):
    n = val % 4
    if n<=0:
        return 1
    else:
        return n
```

There are a couple of details needed to finish this game properly that are left as an exercise.

4.2.6 Scope

A variable that is defined (first used) in the main program is called a *global* variable, and can be accessed by all functions if they ask for it. A variable that is used in a function can be accessed by that function, and is not available in the main program. It's called a *local* variable. This scheme is called *scoping*: the locations in a program where a variable can be accessed is called its *scope*. It's all pretty clear unless a global variable has the same name as a local one, in which case the question is: "what value is represented by this name?" If a variable named "x" is global and a function also declares a variable having the same name, this is called *aliasing*, and it can be a problem.

In Python, a variable is assumed to be local unless the programmer specifically says it is global. This is done in a statement; for example:

```
global a, b, c
```

tells Python that the variables named **a**, **b**, and **c** are global variables, and are defined outside of the function. This means that after the function has completed execution, those variables can still be accessed by the main program and by any other functions that declare them to be global.

Global variables are thought by some programmers to be a bad thing, but in fact they can be quite useful and can assist in the generality of the functions that are a part of the program. A global variable should represent something that is, in fact, global, something that should be known to the whole program. For instance, if the program is one that plays checkers or chess, then the board can be global. There is only one board, and it is essential to the whole program. The same applies to any program that has a central set of data that many of the functions need to modify.

An example of central data is game state in a video game. In the Sticks game program for example, the function **getComputerMove**() takes a parameter—the game state. There is only one game state, and although for some games it can involve many values, in this case there is only one value: the number of sticks remaining. The function can be rewritten to use the game state variable **val** as a global in the following way:

```
def getComputerMove ():
    global val
    n = val % 4
    if n<=0:
        return 1
    else:
        return n
```

Similarly, the function that determines whether the game is over could use **val** as a global variable. On the other hand it would be poor stylistic form to have **getMove**() use a global for the user's move. The name does imply that the function will get a move, and so that value should be returned as an explicit function return value.

If a variable is named as global, then that name cannot be used in the function as a local variable as well. It would be impossible to access it, and it would be confusing. It is a common programming error to forget to declare a variable as global. When this happens the variable is a new one local to the function, and starts out with a value of 0. Thus no syntax error is detected, but the calculation will almost certainly be incorrect. It might be a good idea to identify global variables in their name. For example, place the string "_g" at the end of the names of all globals. The game state above would be named **val_g**, for example. This would be a reminder to declare them properly within functions.

Other kinds of data that could be kept globally would include lists of names, environment or configuration variables, complex data structures that represent a single underlying process, and other programming objects that are referred to as *singletons* in software engineering. In Python, because they have to be explicitly named in a declaration, there is a constant reminder of the variable's scope.

4.2.7 Variable Parameter Lists

The **print()** function is interesting because it seems to be able to accept any number of parameters and deal with them. The statement:

```
print(i)
```

prints the value of the variable **i**, and

```
print (i,j,k)
```

prints the value of all three variables **i**, **j**, and **k**. Is this some sort of special thing reserved for **print()** because Python knows about it? Nope. Any function can do this. Consider a function:

```
fprint ( "format string", variable list)
```

where the format string can contain the characters "f" or "i" in any combination. Each instance of a letter should correspond to a variable passed to the function in the variable list, and it will be printed as a floating point if the corresponding character in the format string is "f" and as an integer if it is "i." The call:

```
fprint("fi", 12, 13)
```

will print the values 12 and 13 as a float and an integer respectively. How can this be written as a Python function?

The function would start out with the following definition:

```
def fprint (fstring, *vlist)
```

The expression ***vlist** represents a set of positional parameters, any number of them. This is preceded by a specific parameter **fstring**, which will be the format string. A simple test of this would be to just print the variables in the list to see if it works:

```
def fprint (fstring, *vlist)
    for v in vlist:
        print v
```

When called as fprint("", 12, 13, 14, 15) this prints:

```
12
13
14
15
```

It removes some of the magic to point out that what is going on is that the list of variables after the * character is turned into a tuple, which is passed as the parameter, so the ***vlist** actually counts as a single parameter with many components. No magic.

To finish the original function, what has to be done is to peel characters off of the front of the format string, match them against a variable, and print the result as the format character dictates. So it is the same loop as above, but also an index into the format string increases each time through and is used to indicate the format. It is also important that the number of format items equals the number of variables:

```
def fprint (s, *vlist):
    i = 0
    if len(s) != len(vlist):     # Format string and
                                 # variable list agree?
        print ("There must be the same number of variables
                as format items.")
        return
    for v in vlist:                 # For each variable
        if s[i] == "f":             # Is the corresponding
                                    # format 'f'?
            fv = float(v)           # Yes. Make it a float
            print (fv, " ", end="") # … and print it
        elif s[i] == "i":           # Is the corresponding
                                    # format 'i'?
            iv = int(v)             # Yes. Make it an
                                    # integer
            print(iv, " ", end="")  # … and print it
```

```
else:
    print ("?", end="")      # Don't know what this
                             # is. Print it
i = i + 1
```

All of the known positional parameters must come before the variable list; otherwise the end of the variable list can't be determined. There is a second complication, that being the existence of *named* parameters. Those are indicated by a parameter such as **nlist. The two "*" characters indicate a list of named variables. This is properly a more advanced topic.

4.2.8 Variables as Functions

Because Python is effectively untyped and variables can represent any kind of thing at all, a variable can be made to refer to a function; not the function name itself, which always refers to a specific function, but a variable that can be made to refer to *any* function. Consider the following functions, each of which does one trivial thing:

```
def print0():
    print ("Zero")
def print1():
    print ("One")
def print2():
    print ("Two")
def print3():
    print("Three")
```

Now make a variable reference one of these functions by means of an

assignment statement:

```
printNum = print1    # Note that there is no parameter list
                     # given
```

The variable **printNum** now represents a function, and when invoked, the function it represents will be invoked. So:

```
printNum()
```

will result in the output:

```
One
```

Why did the statement **printNum = print1** not result in the function **print1** being called? Because the parameter list was absent. The statement:

```
printNum = print1()
```

results in a call to **print1** at that moment, and the value of the variable **printNum** will be the return value of the function. This is the essential syntactic difference: **print1** is a function value, and **print1()** is a call to the function. To emphasize this point, here is some code that would allow the English name of a number between 1 and 3 to be printed:

```
if a == 1:
    printNum = print1   # Assign the function print1 to
                        # printNum
elif a == 2:
    printNum = print2   # Assign the function print2 to
                        # printNum
else:
    printNum = print3   # Assign the function print3 to
                        # printNum

    . . .
printNum()              # Call the function represented by
                        # printNum
```

There are more subtle uses in this case. Consider this use of a list:

```
a = 1
printList = [print0, print1, print2, print3]
printNum = printList[a]
printNum()
```

will result in the output:

```
One
```

The final iteration of this is to call the function directly from the list:

```
printList[1]()
```

This works because **printList[1]** is a function, and a function call is a function followed by (). Seems overly complicated, doesn't it? It is rarely used.

For those with an interest or need for mathematics, consider a function that computes the derivative or integral of another function. Passing the function to be differentiated or integrated as a parameter may be the best way to proceed in these cases.

Example: Find the Maximum Value of a Function

Maximizing a function can have important consequences in real life. The function may represent how much money will be made by manufacturing various objects, how many patients can get through an emergency ward in an hour, or how much food will be grown with particular crops. If the function is well behaved then there are many mathematically sound ways to find a maximum or minimum value, but if a function is harder to deal with, then less analytical methods may have to be used. This problem proposes a search for the best pair of parameters to a problem that could be solved using a method called *linear programming*.

The problem goes like this:

A calculator company produces a scientific calculator and a graphing calculator. Long-term projections indicate an expected demand of at least 100 scientific and 80 graphing calculators each day. Because of limitations on production capacity, no more than 200 scientific and 170 graphing calculators can be made daily. To satisfy a shipping contract, a total of at least 200 calculators much be shipped each day.

If each scientific calculator sold results in a $2 loss, but each graphing calculator produces a $5 profit, how many of each type should be made daily to maximize net profits?

Let **s** be the number of scientific calculators manufactured and **g** be the number of graphing calculators. From the problem statement:

$100 <= s <= 200$

$80 <= g <= 170$

Also:

$s + g > 200,$ or $g > 200 - s$

Finally, the profit, which is to be maximized, is:

$P = -2s + 5g$

First, code the profit as a function:

```
def profit (s, g):
    return -2*s + 5*g
```

A search through the range of possibilities will run through all possible values of s and all possible values of g; that is, s from 100 to 200 and g from 80 to 170. The function will be evaluated at each point and the maximum will be remembered:

```
# Range for s is x0 .. x1
# Range for g is y0 .. y1
# s+g must be >= sum
def searchmax (f, x0, y0, x1, y1, sum):
    pmax = -1.0e12
    ps = -100
    pg = -100
    for s in range (x0, x1+1):        # For all possible s
        for g in range (y0, y1+1):    # For all possible g
            if s+g >= sum:            # Condition is ok?
                p = f (s, g)          # Calculate the profit.
                if p>=pmax:           # Best so far?
                    pmax = p          # Yes.
                    ps = s            # Save it and
                    pg = g            # the parameters
    return ( (ps, pg) )
```

Finally, the call that does the optimization calls the search function passing the profit function as a parameter:

```
c = searchmax (profit, 100, 80, 200, 170, 200)

print (c)
```

The answer found is the tuple (100, 170), or s=100 and g = 170, which agrees with the correct answer as found by other methods. This is only one example of the value of being able to pass functions as parameters. Most of the code that does this is mathematical, but may accomplish practical tasks like optimizing performance, drawing graphs and charts, and simulating real-world events.

4.2.9 Functions as Return Values

Just as any value, including a function, can be stored in a variable, any value, including a function, can be returned by a function. If a function that prints an English name of a number is desired, it could be returned by a function:

```
def print0():
    print ("Zero")
```

```
def print1():
    print ("One")
def print2():
    print ("Two")
def print3():
    print("Three")

def getPrintFun (a):        # Return a function to print a
                            # numeric value 0..3
    if a == 0:
        return print0       # Return the function print0 as
                            # the result
    elif a == 1:
        return print1       # Return the function print1 as
                            # the result
    elif a == 2:
        return print2       # Return the function print2 as
                            # the result
    else:
        return print3       # Return the function print3 as
                            # the result
```

Calling this function and assigning it to a variable means returning a function that can print a numerical value:

```
printNum = getPrintFun(2) # Assign a function to printNum
```

and then:

```
printNum()    # Call the function represented by printNum
```

results in the output:

```
Two
```

The function **printFun** returns, as a value, the function to be called to print that particular number. Returning the name of the function returns something that can be called.

Why would any of these seemingly odd aspects of Python be useful? Allowing a general case, permitting the most liberal interpretation of the language, would permit unanticipated applications, of course. And the ability to use a function as a variable value and a return result are a natural consequence of Python having no specific type connected with a variable at compilation time. There are many specific reasons to use functions in this way, on the other hand. Imagine a function that plots a graph. Being able to pass this function another function to be plotted is surely the most general way to accomplish its task.

4.3 RECURSION

Recursion refers to a way of defining things and a programming technique, not a language feature. Something that is recursive is defined at least partly in terms of itself. This seems impossible at first, but consider the case of a grocery list (not a Python *list*) of items such as:

milk, bread, coffee, sugar, peanut butter, cheese, jam

Each element in the list can be called an *item*, and represents something to be purchased at a grocery store. The smallest list is one having only a single element:

milk

Thus, a list can be simply an item. What else can it be? It appears to be a bunch of items separated by commas. One way to describe this is to say it can be an *item followed by a comma followed by a list*. The complete definition is, presuming that the symbol -> means "can be defined as":

list -> item   # **list** can be defined as an item

list -> item, list   # **list** can be defined as an item, a comma, and a list

In this way the list **milk** is defined as a list by the first rule. The list **milk, bread** is a list because it is an item (**milk**) followed by a comma followed by a list (**bread**). It is plain that a list is defined here in terms of itself, or at least in terms of a previous partial definition of itself.

When talking about functions, a function is recursive if it contains within it a call to itself. This is normally done only when the thing that it is attempting to accomplish has a definition that is recursive. Recursion as a programming technique is an attempt to make the solution simpler. If it does not, then it is inappropriate to use recursion. A problem some beginning programmers have with the ideas of a recursive function is that it appears that it does not terminate. Of course, it is essential that a function does return, and a program that never ends is almost always in error. The problem really is how to make certain that a chain of function calls terminates eventually.

The following function will never return once called:

```
def recur1 (i):
    recur1(i+1)
    print (i)
```

It will not result in any output, either. Why not? Because the first thing it does is call itself, and always does so. When it does, the next thing is does is call itself again, and then again, and so on. The following function, on the other hand, will terminate:

```
def recur2 (i):
    if i>0:
        recur2(i-1)
    print (i)
```

When called it checks its parameter **i**. If that parameter is greater than zero, then it calls itself with a smaller value of **i**, meaning that eventually **i** will become smaller than 0 and the chain of calls will stop. What will be printed? The first call to **recur2** that does not end up calling itself is when i==0, so the first thing printed will be 0. Then the function returns to the previous recursive call, which had to be where i == 1. The second thing printed will be 1. And so on until it returns to the original call to the function with the original value of **i**, at which point it prints **i**. This is a trivial example of a recursive function, but illustrates how to exit from the chain of calls: there must be a condition that defines the recursion. When that condition fails, the recursion ceases.

Each call to the function can be thought of as an instance of that function, and it will create all of the local variables that are declared within it. Each instance has its own copy of these, including its parameters, and each call returns to the caller as occurs with any other function call. So, when the recursive call to **recur2()** returns, the next thing to be done will be (in this case) to print the parameter value. A call to **recur2()** passing the parameter 4 will result in the following instances of that function being created:

```
recur2(4) i = 4   # This is the function state, with parameter i
                given for this instance
  i>0 so call recur2(i-1) = recur2(3)       # This is the code
                                            # executed
    recur2(3) i = 3                         # State
    i>0 so call recur2(i-1) = recur2(2)     # Code executed
      recur2(2) i = 2                       # State
```

```
    i>0 so call recur2(i-1) = recur2(1)    # Code executed
      recur2(1) i = 1                       # State
      i>0 so call recur2(i-1) = recur2(0)   # Code executed
        recur2(0) i = 0                     # State
        i== 0 so recur2 is NOT called       # Code executed
        print(i) -> print(0)                # Code executed ,
                                            # prints 0
        return                              # Code executed
      print(i) -> print(1)                  # Code executed ,
                                            # prints  1
      return                                # Code executed
    print(i) -> print(2)                    # Code executed ,
                                            # prints   2
    return                                  # Code executed
  print(i) -> print(3)                      # Code executed ,
                                            # prints     3
  return                                    # Code executed
print(i) -> print(4)                        # Code executed ,
                                            # prints       4
return                                      # Code executed
```

By tracing through the statements that are executed in this way, it can be seen that the recursion does end, and the output or result can be verified.

One important use of recursion is in reducing a problem into smaller parts, each of which has a simpler solution than does the whole problem. An example of this is searching a list for an item. If **names = [Adams, Alira, Attenbourough, ...]** is a Python list of names in alphabetical order, answer the question: "Does the name *Parker* appear in this list?" Of course there is a built-in function that will do this, but this example is a pedagogical moment, and anyway perhaps the built-in function is slower than the solution that will be devised here.

The function will return **True** or **False** when passed a list and a name. The obvious way to solve the problem is to iterate through the list, looking at all of the elements until the name being searched for is either found or it is not possible to find it anymore (i.e., the current name in the list is larger than the target name). Another, less obvious way to conduct the search is to divide the list in half, and only search the half that has the target name in it. Consider the following names in the list:

... Broadbent   Butterworth Cait Cara Carling Devers Dillan Eberly Foxworthy ...

The name in the middle of this list is *Carling*. If the name being searched for is lexicographically smaller than *Carling*, then it must appear in the first half; otherwise it must appear in the second half. That is, if it is there at all. A recursive example of an implementation of this is:

```
# Search the list for the given name, recursively.
def searchr (name, nameList):
    n = len(nameList)           # How many elements in this
                                # list?
    m = n/2
    if name < nameList[m]:      # target name is in the first
                                # half
        return searchr (name, nameList[0:m])  # Search the
                                              # first half
    elif name > nameList[m]:    # target must be in the
                                # second half
        return searchr (name, nameList[m:n]  # Search the
                                             # second half
    else:

        return True
```

If the name is in the list, this works fine. One way to think of this is that the function **searchr()** will take a string and a list as parameters and find the name in the list if it's there. The way it works is not clear from outside the function (without being able to see the source) and should not matter. SO: if the target is to be found in the first half of the list, for example, then call **searchr()** with the first half of the list.

```
    searchr (name, nameList[0:m])
```

The fact that the call is recursive is not really the concern of the programmer, but is the concern of the person who created the Python system. Now, how can the problem of a name not being in the list be solved?

When the name is not in the list, the program will continue until there is but one item in the list. If that item is not the target, then it is not to be found. So, if n=1 (only one item in the list) and **nameList[0]** is not equal to the target, then the target is not to be found in the list and the return value should be **False**. The final program will therefore be:

```
def searchr (name, nameList):
    n = len(nameList)       # How many elements in this list?
```

```
    m = int(n/2)
    if n==1 and nameList[0]!=name:  # End of the recursive
                                    # calls
        return False                # It's not in this
                                    # list.
    if name < nameList[m]:      # target name is in the first
                                # half
        return searchr (name, nameList[0:m])   # Search the
                                               # first half
    elif name > nameList[m]:    # target must be in the
                                # second half
        return searchr (name, nameList[m:n])   # Search the
                                               # second half
    else:
        return True
```

Many algorithms have fundamentally recursive implementations, meaning that the effective solution in code involves a recursive function call. Many standard examples in beginning programming are not properly implemented recursively. Commonly encountered samples with a recursive solution include the *factorial*, which has a recursive definition but is not best implemented in that manner, and any other basically linear technique (linear search, counting, min/max finding) that does not do a reasonable subdivision. Testing the first component, for example, and then recursively looking at the remaining elements is a poor way to use recursion. It would be much better to use a loop. Here's an example: find the maximum value in a given list. The non-recursive method

(reasonable) would be:

```
def max (myList):
    max = myList [0]
    for i in range(1, len(myList)):
        if myList[i] > max:
            max = myList[i]
    return max
```

This is an effective way to find the largest value in a list, and is pretty easily understood by a programmer reading the code. Now here is a recursive solution:

```
def maxr (myList):
    m1 = myList[0]
    if len(myList)>1:
```

```
        m2 = maxr (myList[1:])
    else:
        return m1
    if m1 > m2:
        return m1
    else:
        return m2
```

This function works by subdividing the list into two parts, as is often done with a recursive solution. The idea is to compare the first element in the list with the maximum of the remainder of the list to see which is bigger. For this particular problem this is not an obvious approach. It is less efficient and less obvious than the iterative version that preceded it. The use of recursion simplifies some problems, but it is not a universally applicable technique and should never be used to show off. Examples of very useful recursive functions will be examined in later chapters.

4.3.1 Avoiding Infinite Recursion

There is a limit to how many times a function can call itself without returning, because each call uses up some amount of memory, and memory is a finite resource. Usually when this happens a programming error has occurred and the function has slipped into an *infinite recursion*, in which it will continue to call itself without end. Recursion can be confusing to visualize and this sort of problem occurs frequently. How can it be avoided?

Programming the function correctly eliminates the problem, of course, but there are some basic rules that will avoid the problem at early stages. Assuming that *global variables are* not *being referenced*:

1. A function that begins with a call to itself is always infinitely recursive. The first thing the function does is call itself, and no matter what the parameters are it can never end.

2. Every recursive call within a function must have a condition upon which that call will be avoided. The function may return sometime before the call is made, or perhaps the call happens within an *if* statement, but there must be such a condition. If it exists it is expressible as a Boolean expression, and this should be placed in a comment near the recursive call. The call is suspect until this happens.

3. Avoid passing a function to itself. The call to a parameter hides the fact that recursion is taking place.

4. It is possible to have a global variable that is a count of the depth of recursion. The function will increment this count whenever a recursive call is made and decrease it just before returning. If the count ever gets larger than a reasonable estimate of the maximum depth, then the function could stop any more calls and back out, or an error message could be printed.

4.4 CREATING PYTHON MODULES

In some of the examples given so far there is a statement at the beginning that looks like "import name." The implication is that there are some functions that are needed by the program that are provided elsewhere, possibly by the Python system itself or perhaps by some other software developer. The idea of writing functions that can be reused in a straightforward way is very important to the software development process. It means that no programmer is really alone; that code is available for doing things like generating random numbers or interfacing with the operating system or the Internet, and that it does not to be created each time. In addition, there is an assumption that a module *works correctly*. When a programmer builds a collection of code for their own use, it needs to be tested as thoroughly as possible, and from that time on it can be used in a package with confidence. If a program has errors in it, then look in the code for that program first and not in the modules. This makes debugging code faster.

What is a module? It is simply a function or collection of functions that reside in a file whose name ends in ".py." Technically, all of the code developed so far qualifies as modules. Consider as an example the function from the previous section that finds the maximum value in a list. Save the functions **max()** and **maxr()** in a file named max.py. Now create a new Python program named usemax.py and place it in the same directory as max.py. If the two files are in the same directory, they can "see" each other in some sense.

Here is some code to place in the file usemax.py:

```
import max
d = [12,32,76,45,9,26,84,25,61, 66, 1,2]
print ("MAX is ", max.max(d), " MAXR is ", max.maxr(d))
```

```
if max.maxr(d) != max.max(d):
    print ("*** NOT EQUAL ****")
```

This program is just a test of the two functions to make certain that they return the same value for the same list, the variable **d**. Note two things:

1. The statement **import max** occurs at the beginning of the program, meaning that the code inside this file is available to this program. Python will look inside of this file for function and variable names.

2. When the function **max()** or **maxr()** is called, the function name is preceded by the module name (**max**) and a period. This syntax informs the Python system that the name **maxr()** (for example) is found in the module **max** and not elsewhere.

The first time that the module is loaded into the Python program the code in the module is executed. This allows any variable initializations to be performed. Henceforth that code is not executed again, and functions within the module can be called knowing that the initializations have been performed.

The module could reside in the same directory as the program that uses it, but does not have to. The Python system recognizes a set of directories and paths and modules can be placed in some of those locations as well, making it easier for other programs on the same computer to take advantage of them. On the computer used to create the examples in this book, the directory C:\ Python34\Lib can be used to store modules, and they will be recognized by **import** statements.

Finally, if the syntax **max.maxr(list)** seems a bit cumbersome, then it is possible to import specific names from the module into the program. Consider the following rewrite of **usemax.py**:

```
from max import max, maxr
d = [12,32,76,45,9,26,84,25,61, 66, 1,2]
print ("MAX is ", max(d), " MAXR is ", maxr(d))
if maxr(d) != max(d):
    print ("*** NOT EQUAL ****")
```

The statement **from max import max, maxr** instructs Python to recognize the names **max** and **maxr** as belonging to the module named max (i.e., as residing in the file named max.py). In that case the function can be called by simply referencing its name.

There would appear to be a name conflict with the package named **max** and the function named **max**, but in fact there is not. Indeed, it's not uncommon to find this sort of naming relationship (example: **random.random()**). The module name **max** refers to a file name, max.py. The function name **max** refers to a function within that file.

4.5 PROGRAM DESIGN USING FUNCTIONS – EXAMPLE: THE GAME OF NIM

Nim is a game so old that its origins have been lost. It was likely invented in China, and is one of the oldest games known. It was also one of the first games to have a computer or electronic implementation and has been the frequent subject of assignments in computer programming classes. This program will implement the game and will play one side. It will serve as an example of how to design a computer program using functions and modularity—it is an example of a

top-down design.

The game starts with three rows of objects, such as sticks or coins, and there are a different number of objects in each row. In this version there are 9, 7, and 5 "sticks," which are represented by "|" characters. A player may remove as many objects from one row as they choose, but they must remove at least one and must take them only from one row. Players take turns removing objects, and the player taking that final one is the winner.

Playing this game involves asking the user for two numbers: the row from which to remove sticks, and how many to remove. The human player will be prompted for the row, then the number. Then the computer will remove some sticks (take its turn) and print the new state.

A list named **val** contains the number of sticks in each row. Initially:

```
val = [5, 7, 9]
```

This is the game state, and is critical to the game as it defines what moves are possible. Also, when the state is [0,0,0] then the game is over.

When the user choses to remove N sticks from row M the action is:

```
val[M] = val[M] - N
```

Of course **N** and **M** must be tested to make certain that **M** is between 0 and 2, and M is as large as **val[M]**. M defines the row chosen to remove sticks from, and N is the number of sticks to remove. A move can therefore be defined as a list **[row, sticks]**.

A program that uses functions should be built from the highest level of abstraction downwards. That is, the main program should be developed first, and should be expressed in terms of functions that do logical things, but that may not be designed or coded yet. So, the main program could look something like this:

```
val = [5, 7, 9]      # the game state: 5, 7, and 9 sticks
done = False          # Is the game over?
userMove = [-1, -1] # A move is a row and a number of
                      # sticks.
print ("The game of Nim.")
rules()                       # Print the rules for the game
while not done:               # Run until the game is over
    displayState(val)         # Show the game board
    prompt(userMove)          # Ask user for their move
    ok = legalMove (userMove, val)  # Was the player's move
                                    # OK?
    while not ok:
        print ("This move is not legal.")
        displayState(val)
        prompt(userMove)       # Ask user for their move
        ok = legalMove (userMove, val)
    makeMove (userMove)        # Make it
    if gameOver(val):
        print("You win!")
        break;
    print ("State after your move is ")   # display it.
    displayState(val)
```

This program is built using components (modules) that are not written yet, but that have a purpose that is defined by what the program needs. Those modules/functions are:

rules()	- Print out the rules of the game
displayState(v)	- Print the game state (how many sticks in each row)
prompt()	- Ask the user for their move
legalMove(r, n)	- is the move legal?
makeMove(r, n)	- make this move

Using functions, the first thing that is needed is to display the game state. It prints the number of sticks in each of the three rows, and does so in a graphical way (i.e., rather than just displaying the numbers). Given the situation as described so far, the non-trivial such function is **displayState()**, which prints the current state of the game—how many sticks in each row. It will be passed a list representing the current state.

```python
def displayState(val):                  # val is the list with
                                         # the state
    for j in range(0,3):                 # there are 3 rows;
                                         # print each one
        print (j+1, ": ", end="")        # Print the row number
        for i in range(0,val[j]):        # val[j] is the current
                                         # row
            print ("| ",end="")          # print a '|' for each
                                         # stick
        print("")                        # print an end of line
```

When called at the beginning of the game, here's what the result of a call to this function would be:

```
1 : | | | | |
2 : | | | | | | |
3 : | | | | | | | | |
```

This function does a single task, uses a parameter to guide it and make it more general, and is named for what it does. These are signs of a good function. Note that the first row is labeled "1," but is in fact element 0 of the list. It is common in user interfaces to adapt to the standard human numbering scheme that begins with 1 instead of 0. When the user enters a row number care must be taken to subtract 1 from it before using it as an index.

There is no required order for writing these functions, but the next one used in the program is **prompt()**. This will ask the user to input a row and then read a row number, then prompt the user to enter a number of sticks to remove and then read that value too. The two numbers will be placed into a list that was passed so that the values can be returned to the caller.

```python
def prompt (move):
    row =    input ("Your move: which row? ")   # Prompt for row &
                                                 # read it
    sticks = input ("           how many sticks?") # Prompt for
                                                 # sticks & read
```

```
# Convert row to integer and decrement to be from 0 to 2.
  move[0] = int(row)-1            # Assign to the list[0]
  move[1] = int(sticks)          # Assign value to list[1]
```

This function again does a simple task, uses a parameter, and is named pretty appropriately.

Next is the question "Is this move legal"? A move is legal if the row is between 0 and 2 inclusive, and if the number of sticks in that row is greater than or equal to the number of sticks to be removed. The function returns **True** or **False**.

```
def legalMove(move, state):
    row = move[0]          # Which row was requested?
    sticks = move[1]       # How many sticks
    if row<0 or row>2:     # Legal number of rows?
        return False       # No
    if sticks<=0 or sticks>val[row]: # Legal number of
                                     # sticks?
        return False       # No
    return True            # Both were ok, so the move is OK.
```

Making a move involves decreasing the specified row by the specified number of sticks. This could have been done in **legalMove()** if it were thought to be OK to do multiple things in a function. Eventually that will be necessary, but for now a new function will be written, named **makeMove()**, that will actually implement a specified play in the game.

```
def makeMove(move, state):
    row = move[0]          # Subtract move[1] sticks from
    sticks = move[1]       # those that are in row move[0].
# Place the new number of sticks in the state list
    state[row] = state[row]-sticks
```

There is a strategy that will permit a player to always win. It involves computing what amounts to a *parity* value and making a move to ensure that parity is maintained. Consider the initial state and the state after taking two sticks from row 1:

Row 1 = 5 = 0 1 0 1	row 1 = 3 = 0 0 1 1
Row 2 = 7 = 0 1 1 1	row 2 = 7 = 0 1 1 1
Row 3 = 9 = 1 0 0 1	row 3 = 9 = 1 0 0 1
Parity 1 0 1 1	1 1 0 1

The parity is determined by looking at each digit in the binary representation of the values. In each column (digit position) the parity bit for that column is 1 if the number of 1 bits in the column is odd and 0 if it is even. This can be calculated using the exclusive-OR operator, which is "^" in processing. The strategy in *Nim* is to make a move that makes the parity value 0. It turns out that this is always possible if parity is not 0; in the situation above, the computer might remove 5 sticks from row 3 giving the state:

row 1 = 3 = 0 0 1 1

row 2 = 7 = 0 1 1 1

row 3 = 4 = 0 1 0 0

Parity   0 0 0 0

This is what the sketch does after every move the player makes: it makes all possible moves, computing the parity after each one. When the one with zero parity is found it makes that move. The function **eval()** calculates the current parity value as **val[0]^val[1]^val[2]**.

NOTE *The computer always wins because the user always makes the first move. Alternating who moves first would make the gameplay fairer.*

4.5.1 The Development Process Exposed

In the introduction to the Nim program it was said that this was an example of *top-down* design. This means that the larger program, or the main program, is designed first. The question should be *what are the steps involved in solving this problem?* The answer to that question is written down in terms of functions that have not been written yet, but that have a known and required purpose within the solution. In the Nim game it is known that the user's move will have to be read from the keyboard and that the current state of the game will have to be displayed, so those two functions can be presumed to be important to the solution when sketching the main program.

Once the high-level part of the program has been devised, it can be typed in and tested. The functions that are needed but are not yet written can be coded as *stubs*: functions that do not implement their task but that are present and prevent syntax errors. The first try at a solution of this sort does not, of course, solve the problem, but is simply a step towards the solution. In the case of Nim, the very first step could be something like:

```
Repeat
  Display the game
  Ask user for their move
  Make user's move
  Generate computer's move
  Make computer's move
Until someone wins
Display the winner
```

None of these steps are written as proper Python code, and that's OK for a first step. Translating this into Python would be a good idea:

```
Done = false
while not done:           # Run until the game is over
    displayState()        # Show the game board
    prompt()              # Ask user for their move
    makeMove ()           # Make it
    if not gameOver():    # Computer move?
          makeComputerMove()# Determine computer's move
    done = gameOver()     # Is the game over?
printWinner()
```

At this point in the design the data structures to be used in the solution have not been devised, nor have the algorithms needed. This is merely a sequence of steps that could lead to a program that works. The functions can now be written as stubs:

```
def displayState():          def prompt():
    print("Display state")       print("Enter move")
def makeMove():              def gameOver():
    print ("Make move")          if random.random()<0.2:
                                     return False
                                 return True
def makeComputerMove():      def printWinner():
    print ("compute a move")     print("The winner is:")
```

The output from this program might be:

```
Display state
Enter move
Make move
```

```
Display state
Enter move
Make move
compute a move
The winner is:
```

The exact output will be random, depending on what the return value of **gameOver()** is. This code can be thought of as one *iteration* of the solution, or as a *prototype*. The next step will be to refine the solution by implementing one of the stubs. Each time that happens a set of decisions will likely be made concerning the nature of the data structures used to implement the solution: the use of a list for the game state, for instance. Three integers could have been used instead, but once the decision is made one way or the other it should be stuck with unless it becomes infeasible.

Repeatedly implementing the stubs creates new prototypes, each one more functional than the one before. Some of the functions may require an application of this same process. Complex functions can be coded in terms of other stubs, and so on. The simpler functions, such as those that calculate based only on their parameter, should be completed first and should not involve permanent design choices.

A programming process of this kind can be thought of as *iterative refinement*. At all times after the first step, a complete program that compiles and runs will exist to be demonstrated and refined. This can be very useful, especially when dealing with graphical user interfaces and games. The interface might well be complete before any real functionality is present, and this permits a demonstration of the concept before the program is done.

4.6 SUMMARY

Python allows a programmer to create a function that does something new. A function is really just some code that has a name, and can be executed simply by invoking that name. It usually represents some task that has to be done fairly frequently. A function should also have one main task, and that task should be represented in the function name: *maximum*, *square*, *search*, and so on. Many functions return a value, and finding that value is frequently the purpose of the function (e.g., *sine*, *cosine*).

The name of a function can be used to call that function, but it can also be assigned to a variable, passed as a parameter to another function, or returned as a value. A function can have variables that belong to it; they are called local variables and vanish after the function returns. They can also use variables defined outside of the function if they appear in a *global* statement.

A special value named **None** is used to represent *no value*, and is returned by a function that does not explicitly return some other value. A *module* is a function or collection of functions that reside in a file whose name ends in ".py."

The use of functions can organize a computer program in a logical way. A program can be defined in terms of functions that are desired but not yet written, and then those functions can be defined as code or in terms of other functions. Functions are often named but are incomplete, and are called *stubs*—they permit the program to be compiled while still under development.

A function that calls itself is said to be *recursive*. Such functions can be very valuable in simplifying the code for some algorithms, especially ones in which something is actually defined in terms of itself, but care must be taken when programming to ensure that a recursive function always ultimately returns.

Exercises

1. Write a Python function that takes a tuple of numbers as a parameter and returns the location (index) of the maximum value found in that tuple.

2. A word processing system sometimes needs to shorten a word to make it fit on a line. Write a function that takes a string containing a single word and decides where to hyphenate it. A hyphen can occur before the endings: "ing," "ed," "ate," "tion," or "ment." It could also occur after a prefix: "pre," "post," "para," "pro," "con," or "com." Otherwise, place a hyphen somewhere in the middle of the word. The function should return a tuple containing the first and second half of the word split at the hyphen.

3. Pascal's triangle is an arrangement of numbers in rows and columns such that each number in a row is the sum of the two numbers above it. An example is:

Write a function **triangle(n)** that prints the first n rows of such a triangle. Use extra marks for proper indentation so it looks like a triangle.

4. Write a function that returns the value of a quadratic function at a particular x value. A quadratic is a polynomial of the form:

$$ax^2 + bx + c$$

The function **quad()** is passed values for **a, b, c,** and **x** and returns the value of the polynomial.

5. A quadratic polynomial has a root at any value **x** for which the value of the polynomial is zero; that is, any x such that

$$ax^2 + bx + c = 0$$

There can only be at most two such values (a tuple), and the expression for finding these values of x is:

$$x = \frac{-b \pm \sqrt{b^2 - 4ac}}{2a}$$

Write a function (**root(a,b,c)**)that returns the two roots of a quadratic equation having been passed a, b, and c. The result is a tuple, or if there is no solution (i.e., square root of a negative number, or a=0) then it returns **None**.

6. Write a function (**inputfloat(s)**) that takes a single parameter, a string to be used as a prompt, and returns a number read from the console. The function must prompt the user for the number using the given string, read the input, and return the result as a floating point number. If an error occurs return **None**.

7. The game of table tennis is sometimes called *ping-pong*. Write functions **ping()** and **pong()** that each take, as a parameter, a probability of hitting the ball. A probability is between 0.0 and 1.0. The function returns **True** if the ball is returns and **False** otherwise. There are two sides to the game, and each side serves (plays first) twice, then the other side serves twice. It will be assumed here that the server always succeeds. If ping is serving then **pong()** gets called first, then if pong succeeded then **ping()** gets called, and so on. The side that made the last successful hit wins a point. The game goes to 11 points, but must be won by a 2-point margin. Write a program that simulates *ping-pong* using two functions named **ping()** and **pong()**.

8. In *mutual recursion* two functions call each other, usually repeatedly to some depth. So: **A** calls **B**, which calls **A** again, which calls **B** again, and so on. Recode the *ping-pong* exercise (Number 7 above) so that **ping()** calls **pong()** and **pong()** calls **ping()**. The functions return a string, that of the winner of the exchange.

9. Write a function **prime(n)** that returns **True** if the number **n** is prime, and **False** otherwise. How many prime numbers are there between 1 and 1000?

Notes and Other Resources

Tutorial on Python Functions: *http://www.tutorialspoint.com/python/python_functions.htm*

Also: *http://anh.cs.luc.edu/python/hands-on/3.1/handsonHtml/functions.html*

1. Thomas S. Ferguson. **Game Theory**, *https://www.math.ucla.edu/~tom/Game_Theory/comb.pdf*

2. D. G. Luenberger. (1973). **Introduction to Linear and Nonlinear Programming (Vol. 28)**, Reading, MA: Addison-Wesley.

3. Mitchell Wand. (1980). **Induction, Recursion, and Programming**, North Holland, NY, *http://tocs.ulb.tu-darmstadt.de/82570701.pdf*

FILES: INPUT AND OUTPUT

■ ■ ■ ■ ■

In this chapter

In the early days of computing, when a respectable machine would fill a room, the *file* was invented. It was an obvious thing, really: a package in which to place data on a tape or disk drive. Storage that was not memory, which was pretty fast, was called secondary storage, and was terribly slow compared to how fast a computer could execute instructions (which is terribly slow compared to how fast a modern computer can execute instructions).

Files still exist, and a typical PC has hundreds of thousands of them. The details of how files are implemented is interesting, but unimportant to the discussion of how to use them in Python. The focus will be on how and why to use them effectively.

The first thing to know about a file is that it is a collection of bytes stored on a disk or similar device. One set of bytes can look very much like another, and unless the format of the file (i.e., the way the bytes are ordered) and its basic contents (i.e., what kind of thing the bytes represent) is known ahead of time, the information stored there is unusable. Computer programs are written assuming that the files they will read have a particular nature; if given a file that does not have that nature, the program will not function properly.

What kinds of files are there? Here is a short list:

1. *Text files.* These contain characters that a person can read, and can be thought of as documents.

2. *Executable files.* These hold instructions that a computer can execute. Such a file is a program or an "app."

3. *Data files.* It could also be a text file if it is stored as characters, but it could be a set of bytes that represent integers or real numbers.

4. *Image files.* There are many types of image files, and they contain pictures in digital format. Many digital cameras use a format called JPEG, but GIF or PNG are two of many others. Not only are images stored in such a file, but also data about how large the image is, when it was taken, and other details.

5. *Sound files.* The more common sound file is the MP3, but there are many others.

6. *Video.* MPEG and AVI are standard formats for video, and there are a great many files of this sort available on the Internet.

7. *Web pages.* These are a special kind of text file. They can be examined and modified using basic text editors, but can't be viewed properly (i.e., as a web page) except through a browser, which is really a special kind of display utility that can both draw images and connect to the Internet to download more information.

All of these files, and indeed all files, have certain things in common. Some of these things can be ignored when writing Python programs, but others cannot.

Files have names. The first way to access a file is usually by specifying its name. In human folklore, knowledge of a true name allows one to affect another person or being; knowing something's true name gives the person power over that thing. So it is with files. Knowing the name of a file is the way to access the information within.

Files have a size. It is usually expressed in bytes, which is to say simple characters. One byte is one traditional alphabetic character, although there are now many standards for characters in German and Swedish and Chinese that break that rule. Knowing how large a file is helps when using it as input, and when writing a file its size grows.

Basic operations on a file are *read* and *write*. To read from a file means to examine a byte (at least); usually bytes are read in large blocks for efficiency. This means moving a copy of the bytes from the disk into memory, because a program can only examine data that is in memory. Writing is the reverse process: a byte or bytes are copied from memory onto disk.

Files must be *open* before they can be used. To open a file a program must know its name, and then invoke the *open* function or program. If the true name of the file gives you power over it, then *open* is the spell used to wield that power. Whether a file will be read or written is normally decided at the time the file is opened. The *open* function and many other file-related operations belong to the operating system of the computer, and not normally to the language. It's one reason why so much software is not portable.

Only one program at a time can write to a file. Many programs can read a file simultaneously, but only one can write to it, and not while anyone else is reading it. Many computers can have more than one user accessing a file at a time, and the Internet certainly allows many users to access a web page at one time, and a web page is a file. However, chaos ensues if more than one user can change a file at the same moment.

Another thing to consider is that text, and therefore text files, are a principal means for communication between humans and computers. It is critical that any scheme for writing text to a file takes into account the human aspects of text: sentences, lines, paragraphs, special characters, numbers, and so on. This chapter will be concerned with the way in which Python can use files, with files as a concept in general, and with how humans think of data and files.

▌5.1▐ WHAT IS A FILE? A LITTLE "THEORY"

The claim in the previous section was that a file is "*a collection of bytes stored on a disk or similar device.*" This is correct, but it does not have enough detail to enable a programmer to take advantage of the way a file is implemented to create a good program. What is needed is an understanding of the devices that contain files and their advantages and limitations. This information will begin to explain the traditional mechanisms that have evolved for using files from programming languages generally and Python in particular.

The file as a data structure was devised for storing information on tapes and disks. Together with some other devices that are used rarely (e.g., cram files) these are referred to as *secondary storage*, where primary storage would be computer memory. Memory was (and still is) too expensive to store everything that is needed on a computer, so secondary storage has the advantages of being cheaper than memory and can contain a much larger amount of data. Modern disks can contain Terabytes of data, where one Terabyte (Tb) is 10^{12} bytes. It has been estimated that a human being's functional memory is about 1.25 Tb. A Terabyte is a lot of storage.

Most secondary storage devices store data magnetically. Since tapes are rarely seen anymore, the example presented here will be that of a disk. A disk is a circular platter made of glass or ceramic material and coated with a thin layer of magnetic material, often a compound of iron. That's why they look brown: iron oxide or *rust* is that color. The disk is mounted on a spindle that is connected to a motor, which spins it at a high rate of speed.

A device called a read/write head is made to sit above the moving disk but very near to it. This device is basically a small piece of magnetizable metal wrapped in a fine wire, not unlike the read/write heads in an old video tape recorder (VCR) or cassette machine. It is a property of magnets and coils that a moving magnet will create (induce) an electric current in a nearby coil, and a coil with a current flowing through it can create a magnetic field.

So, to write data to the moving disk, a current is sent to the read/write head, which creates a small magnetic mark on the disk below the head. Magnets have two orientations; they have a North Pole and a South Pole. Current flowing one way will create a magnet in the disk that has a North Pole appearing before the South Pole, or an N-S mark. Current flowing the other direction through the head will create a magnet on the disk that has the South Pole appearing before the North Pole, or an S-N mark. One orientation, say N-S, will represent a binary number "1," and the other (S-N) will represent a "0." In this way, binary numbers can be written to the surface of the moving disk.

Reading numbers involved the magnetic regions of the disk passing quickly past the read/write head and inducing small currents in the coil. These are amplified and classified by a simple electronic circuit that will detect current flow one way as N-S and another way as S-N, thus allowing binary numbers to be read from the disk.

Figure 5.1
The hard drive from a typical desktop computer. The disk spins at a high rate of speed and the disk head can be positioned over and portion so that data can be read or written.

There are some very complicated physics involved in a disk drive. The read/write head must be very close to the surface of a rapidly rotating disk, as close as 3 nanometers. To accomplish this, the head is actually aerodynamically *flying* above the disk. If it ever actually touches the disk surface the result is catastrophic. At the speeds involved a large section of the magnetic material on the disk's surface will be scraped away, and all data there will be lost. In addition, the read/write head will almost certainly be damaged. This event is called a head crash, and normally results in the entire disk drive being ruined. It's one reason that frequent backup copies of all data should be made.

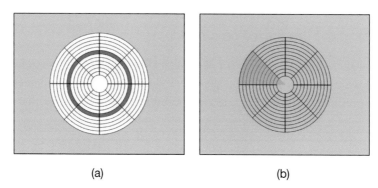

(a)   (b)

Figure 5.2
(a) A track is the set of data from one entire circle on the disk. Inner tracks are smaller but contain the same amount of data. (b) A sector is a wedge-shaped portion of the disk. The combination (track, sector) gives an address for a block of data.

The picture that is developing is that of a device that returns data as a stream of bits. To make best use of the area of the disk, the read/write head can move from the outer edge of the disk to nearly the center. Imagine a set of concentric circles on the disk's surface: the moving read head can position itself over any of them and read the data that had been written there.

The disk is divided into a set of concentric circles called *tracks*, each of which corresponds to one position of the read/write head (Figure 5.2a). The head can move across the disk surface, but for obvious reasons the positions are quantized: position 0-N$_{tracks}$ can be reached through commands to a controller that change the head position. The outermost track is numbered 0, and numbers increase as the head moves inward to the center. The disk is also divided into sectors, each of which is a wedge-shaped portion of the disk (Figure 5.2b). These are again numbered 0 to N$_{sectors}$, and create an address for a set of bits. Data can be read from sector 3 track 12 by positioning the read head over track 12 and waiting for sector 3 to rotate into position under the head. The data takes as long to read as the sector takes to pass under the read head.

This description answers two important questions. First, data can be accessed by using the <track, sector> address. The data in a single track and sector is a *block*, and all blocks are the same size in terms of bits for the sake of convenience, traditionally 512 bytes (4096 bytes for AF drives). Second, it explains why accessing data takes so long when reading from a disk. Disks rotate at 7200 RPM or 120 revolutions per second; this is one rotation every 8.3 milliseconds.

5.1.1 How Are Files Stored on a Disk?

A file can be thought of as a set of blocks. If blocks are 512 bytes in size and some data to be stored in a file consists of N bytes, then that file will need blocks, the next larger integer than N/512; it's not possible to have two files share a single block.

It gets more complicated, though, because it will not always be possible to have all of the blocks that belong to a file lie next to each other. A file might consist of many blocks, all of which are some distance apart in terms of their track and sector. There is a need for a data structure to connect these blocks in the correct order to make a file. It's not very hard to do but is another step. This data structure is written to the disk also. The result is that reading a file means finding the location of this data structure on the disk, getting the track and sector values, and then reading the data from those and copying it into memory. The data structure containing the sectors is usually found through a *file name* that the user has provided. There is a list of file names and the track/sector address of their *index sectors* in a special file someplace on the drive, or in many places. File systems tend to be organized hierarchically, so that one main name is accessed to find the files within that part of the disk (*directory*), and within that directory are names of more files and directories. It is a significant part of the function of an operating system like *Linux* or *Windows* to provide a convenient way to access files.

5.1.2 File Access is Slow

How long does it take to access a block of data on the disk? It depends on where the disk head is and where the disk rotation has placed the target block at the time the request is made. There will be only a statistical answer, but for a random block it could take an average of 10 mS to move the head to the correct track (*seek time*), and will take half of a rotation (4.15 mS). Add to this the time needed to read the block, which is $8.3*1/N_{sectors}$ mS, or about 0.008 mS for a disk with 1024 sectors. This can be ignored, and the time to access a random block can be estimated as 14.15 *milliseconds*.

As a comparison, fast computer memory can access data within 8 *nanoseconds*. If a person could write the word "Gigabyte" on a whiteboard in 8 nanoseconds, then what could they do in 14 milliseconds? They could copy the entire Bible onto the board over 16 times. Disk is vastly slower than memory, and in order to use the data it must be copied into memory. This is a bottleneck in many computer systems.

5.2 KEYBOARD INPUT

Reading data from the keyboard is very different from reading data from a file. Files exist before being read, and normally have a fixed size that is known in advance. It is common to know the format of a file, so that the fact that the next datum is an integer and the one following that is a float is often known. When a user is entering data at a keyboard there is no such information available.

In fact, the user may be making up the data as they go along. Before getting too far into file input it is important to understand the kind of errors that can happen interactively.

These are using type errors, where the user enters data that is the wrong type for the programmer to use: a string instead of an integer, for example. This kind of error can arise in file input also if the format is not known in advance.

5.2.1 Problem: Read a Number from the Keyboard and Divide It by 2

In this instance the problem is one of type: how to treat integers like integers and floats like floats. When the string s is read in it's just a string, and it is supposed to contain an integer. However, users will be users, and some may type in a float by mistake. The program should not crash just because of a simple input mistake. How is this situation handled?

The problem is that when the string is converted into an integer, if there is a decimal point or other non-digit character that does not belong, then an error will occur. It seems that an answer would be to put the conversion into a **try** statement block and if the string has a decimal point then convert the string to float within the **except** part. Something like this:

```
s = input("Input an integer: ")
try:
    k = int(s)
    ks = k//2
except:
    z = float(s)
    k = int(z/2)
print (k)
```

If the user types "12" in response to the prompt "Input an integer:" then the program prints "6." If the user types "12.5" then the program catches a **ValueError**, because 12.5 is not a legal integer. The except part is executed, converting the number to floating point, dividing by 2, then finally converting to an integer.

One problem is that the **except** part is not part of the **try**, so errors that happen there will not be caught. Imagine that the user types "one" in response to the prompt. The call to **int(s)** results in a **ValueError**, and the **except** part is executed.

The statement:

```
z = float(s)
```

will result in another **ValueError**. This one will not be caught and the program will stop executing, giving a message like:

```
ValueError: could not convert string to float: 'one'
s = input("Input an integer: ")
try:
    k = int(s)
    k = k//2
except ValueError:
    try:
        z = float(s)
        k = int(z/2)
    except ValueError:
        k = 0
print (s, k)
```

5.3 USING FILES IN PYTHON: LESS THEORY, MORE PRACTICE

The general paradigm for reading and writing files is the same in Python as it is in most other languages. The steps for reading or writing a file are these:

1. **Open the file.** This involves calling a function, usually named **open**, and passing the name of the file to be used. Sometimes the *mode* for opening is passed; that is, a file can be opened for input, output, update (both input and output) and in binary modes. The function locates the file using the name and returns a variable that keeps track of the current state of input from the file. A special case exists if there is no file having the given name.

2. **Read data from the file.** Using the variable returned by **open**, a function is called to read data. The function might read a character, or a number, or a line, or the whole file. The function is often called **read**, and can be called multiple times. The next call to **read** will read from where the last call ended. A special case exists when all of the data has been read from the file (called the *end of file* condition).

OR

3. **Write data to the file.** Using the variable returned by **open**, a function is called to write data to the file. The function might write a character, or a number, or a line, or many lines. The function is often called **write**, and can be called multiple times. The next call to **write** will continue writing data from where the last call ended. Writing data most frequently appends data to the end of the file.

4. **Close the file.** Closing a file is also accomplished using a call to a function (yes, it is usually named **close**). This function frees storage associated with the input process and in some cases unlocks the file so it can be used by other programs. A variable returned by **open** is passed to **close**, and afterwards that variable can't be used for input anymore. The file is no longer open.

5.3.1 Open a File

Python provides a function named **open** that will open a file and return a value that can be used to read from or write to the file. That value actually refers to a complex collection of values that refers to the file status and is called a *handle* or a *file descriptor* in the computing literature, although knowledge of the details is not needed to use it. It can be thought of as something of type *file*, and must be assigned to a variable or the file can't be accessed. The **open** function is given the name of the file to be opened and a flag that indicates whether the file is to be read from or written to. Both of these are strings. A simple example of a call to open is:

```
infile = open ("datafile.txt", "r")
```

This will open a file named "datafile.txt" that resides in the same directory as does the Python program, and opens it for input: the "r" flag means *read*. It returns the handle to the variable **infile**, which can now be used to read data from the file.

There are some details that are crucial. The name of the file on most computer systems can be a path name, which is to say the name including all directory names that are used to find it on your computer. For example, on some computers the name "datafile.txt" might have the complete path name "*C:/parker/introProgramming/chapter05/datafile.txt*." If path names are used, the file can be opened from any directory on the computer. This is handy for large data sets that are used by multiple programs, such as names of customers or suppliers.

The read flag "r" that is the second parameter is what was called the mode in the previous discussion. The "r" flag means that the file will be open for reading only, and starts reading at the beginning of the file. The default is to read characters from the file, which is presumed to be a text file. Opening with the mode "rb" opens the file in binary format, and allows reading non-text files, such as MP3 and video files.

Passing the mode "w" means that the file is to be written to. If the file exists, then it will be overwritten; if not, the file will be created. Using "wb" means that a binary file is to be written.

Append mode is indicated by the mode parameter "a," and it means that the file will be opened for writing; if the file exists, then writing will begin at the end of the existing file. In other words, the file will not start over as being empty but will be added to, at the end of the file. The mode "ab" appends data to a binary file. There are a few other modes that will be discussed when they are needed.

If the file does not exist and it is being opened for input, there is a problem. It's an error, of course; a nonexistent file can't be read from. There are ways to tell whether a file exists, and the error caused by a nonexistent file can be caught and handled from within Python. This involves an **exception**. It is always a bad idea to assume that everything works properly, and when dealing with files it is especially important to check for all likely problems.

File Not Found Exceptions

The proper way to open a file is within a **try-except** pair of statements. This will ensure that nonexistent files or permission errors are caught rather than causing the program to terminate. The basic scheme is simple:

```
try:
    infile = open ("datafile.txt", "r")
except FileNotFoundError:
        print ("There is no file named 'datafile.
            txt'. Please try again")
    return              # end program or abort this
                        # section of code
```

The exception **FileNotFoundError** will be thrown if the file name can't be found. What to do in that case depends on the program: if the file name was typed in by the user, then perhaps they should get another chance. In any case the file is not open and data can't be read.

There are multiple versions of Python on computers around the world, and some versions have different names for things. The examples here all use Python 3.4. In other versions the **FileNotFoundError** exception has another name; it may be **IOError** or even **OSError**. The documentation for the version being used should be consulted if a compilation error occurs when using exceptions and some built-in functions. For the 3.4 compiler version, all three seem to work with a missing file.

All attempts to open a file should take place while catching the **FileNot-FoundError** exception.

5.3.2 Reading from Files

After a file is opened with a read mode, the file descriptor returned can be used to read data from the file. Using the variable **infile** returned from the call to **open ()** above, a call to the method **read()** can get a character from the file:

```
s = infile.read(1)
```

Reading one character at a time is always good enough, but is inefficient. If a block on disk is 512 characters (bytes) then that should be a good number of bytes to read at one time, or a multiple of that. Reading more data than you need and saving it is called *buffering*, and buffers are used in many instances: live video and audio streaming, audio players, and even in programming language compilers. The idea is to read a larger block of data than is needed at the moment and to hand it out as needed. Reading a buffer could be done as:

```
s = infile.read(512)
```

and then dealing characters from the strings one at a time as needed. A buffer is a collection of memory locations that is temporary storage for data that was recently on secondary store.

Text files, those that contain printable characters that humans can read, are normally arranged as lines separated by a carriage return or a linefeed character, something usually called a *newline*. An entire line can be read using the **readline()** function:

```
s = infile.readline()
```

A line is not usually a sentence, so many lines might be needed to read one sentence, or perhaps only half of a line. Computer text files are structured so that humans can read them, but the structure of human language and convention is not understood by the computer, nor it is built into the file structure. However, it is normal for people to make data files that contain data for a particular item or event on one line, followed by data for the next item. If this is true then one call to **readline()** will return all of the information for a particular thing.

End of File

When there are no more characters in the file, **read()** will return the empty string: "". This is called the *end of file condition*, and it is important that it be detected. There are many ways to open and read files, but for reading characters in this way the end of file is checked as follows:

```
infile = open("data.txt", "r")
while True:
  c = infile.read(1)
  if c == '':
    print ("End of file")
    exit()
  else:
    c = infile.read(1)
```

When reading a file in a **for** statement, the end of file is handled automatically. In this case the loop runs from the first line to the final line and then stops.

```
for c in f:
    print ("'", c, "'")
```

Oddly an exception can't be used in an obvious way for handling the end of file on file input. However, when reading from the console using the input() function the exception **EOFError** can be caught:

```
while True:
  try:
      c = input()
      print (c)
  except EOFError:
      print ("Endfile")
      break
```

There are many errors that could occur for any set of statements. It is possible to determine what specific exception has been thrown in the following manner:

```
while True:
  try:
     c = input()
     print (c)
  except Exception as x:
     print (x)
     break
```

This code prints "EOF when reading a line" when the end of file is encountered.

Common File Input Operations

There are a few common ways to use files that should be mentioned as *patterns*. Although one should never use a pattern if it is not understood, it's sometimes handy to have a few simple snippets of code that are known to perform basic tasks correctly. For example, one common operation to use with files is to **read each line from a file**, followed by some processing step. This looks like:

```
f = open ("data.txt", "r")
for c in f:
     print ("'", c, "'")
f.close()
```

The expression **c in f** results in consecutive lines being read from the files into a string variable **c**, and this stops when no more data can be read from the file.

Another way to do the same thing would be to use the **readline**() function:

```
f = open ("data.txt", "r")
c = f.readline()
while c != '':
     print ("'", c, "'")
     c = f.readline()
f.close()
```

In this case the end of file has to be determined explicitly, by checking the string value that was read to see if it is null.

Another common file operation is to **copy a file to another**, character by character. A file is opened for input and another for output. The basic "read a file" pattern is used, with the addition of a file output after each character is read:

```
f = open ("data.txt", "r")
g = open ("copy.txt", "w")
c = f.read(1)
```

```
while c != '':
    g.write(c)
    c = f.readline(1)
f.close()
g.close()
```

A **filter** is a program that reads data from a file and converts it to some other form, then writes it out. This is often done from standard input and output, but can be done in the middle of a file copy. For example, to convert a text file to all lowercase, the pattern above is used with a small modification:

```
f = open ("data.txt", "r")
g = open ("copy.txt", "w")
c = f.read(1)
while c != '':
    g.write(c.lower())
    c = f.readline(1)
f.close()
g.close()
```

This filter can be done in less code if the entire file can be read in at once. The **read**() function can read all data into a string.

```
f = open ("data.txt", "r")
g = open ("copy.txt", "w")
c = f.read()
g.write(c.lower())
f.close()
g.close()
```

Two files can be merged into a single file in many ways: one file after another, a line from one file followed by a line from another, character by character, and so on. A simple merging of two files where one is copied first followed by the other is:

```
f = open ("data1.txt", "r")
outfile = open ("copy.txt", "w")
c = f.read()
outfile.write(c)
f.close()
g = open ("data2.txt", "r")
c = g.read()
outfile.write(c)
g.close()
outfile.close()
```

A more complex problem occurs when both files are sorted and are to **remain sorted after the merge**. If each line is in alphabetical order in each file then merging them means reading a line from each and writing the one that is smallest. When one file is complete, the remainder of the second file is written and all files are closed.

```python
f = open ("data1.txt", "r")
g = open ("data2.txt", "r")
outfile = open ("copy.txt", "w")
cf = f.readline()
cg = g.readline()
while cf!="" and cg!="":
    if cf<cg:
        outfile.write(cf)
        cf = f.readline()
    else:
        outfile.write(cg)
        cg = g.readline()
if cf == "":
    outfile.write(cg)
    cg = g.read()
    outfile.write(cg)
else:
    outfile.write(cf)
    cf = f.read()
    outfile.write (cf)
f.close()
g.close()
outfile.close()
```

Copying the input from console to a file means reading each line using **input()** and writing it to the file. This code assumes that an empty input line implies that the copying is complete.

```python
outfile = open ("copy.txt", "w")
line = input ("! ")
while len(line)>1 or line[0]!="!":
    outfile.write(line)
    outfile.write ("\n")
    line = input("! ")
outfile.close()
```

The end of the line is indicated by a character, which is represented by the string "\n." Reading characters from a file will read the end of line character also, and detecting it can be very important.

```
f = open ("data.txt", "r")
c = f.read(1)
while c != '':
    print ("'", c, "'")
    c = f.read(1)
    if c == '\n':
        print ("Newline")
```

CSV Files

A very common format for storing data is called Comma Separated Variable (CSV) format, named for the fact that each pair of data items have a comma between them. CSV files can be used directly by spreadsheets such as Excel and by a large collection of data analysis tools, so it is important to be able to read them correctly.

A simple CSV file named *planets.txt* is provided for experimenting with reading CSV files. It contains some basic data for the planets in Earth's solar system, and while there is no actual standard for how CSV files must look, this one is typical of what is usually seen. The first line in the file contains headings for each of the variables or columns, separated by commas. This is followed by nine lines of data, one for each planet. It's a small data file as these things are counted, but illustrative for the purpose. Here it is:

Name,	Mass,	Diam,	Density,	Grav,	Escape,	Rotation,	Day,	Dis-tance,	Period,	Moons,	Temp
Mercury,	0.364,	3032,	339,	12.1,	2.7,	1407.6,	4222.6,	36.0,	88.0,	0,	333
Venus,	5.37,	7521,	327,	29.1,	6.4,	-5832.5,	2802.0,	67.2,	224.7,	0,	867
Earth,	6.58,	7926,	344,	32.1,	7.0,	23.9,	24.0,	93.0,	365.2,	1,	59
Mars,	0.708,	4221,	246,	12.1,	3.1,	24.6,	24.7,	141.6,	687.0,	2,	-85
Jupiter,	2093,	88846,	83,	75.9,	37.0,	9.9,	9.9,	483.8,	4331.0,	67,	-166
Saturn,	627,	31783,	43,	29.4,	22.1,	10.7,	10.7,	890.8,	10747,	62,	-220
Uranus,	95.7,	31763,	79,	28.5,	13.2,	-17.2,	17.2,	1784.8,	30589,	27,	-320
Neptune,	113.0,	30775,	102,	36.0,	14.6,	16.1,	16.1,	2793.1,	59800,	14,	-330
Pluto,	0.0161,	1464,	131,	2.3,	0.8,	-153.3,	153.3,	3670.0,	90560,	5,	-375

Problem: Print the Names of Planets Having Fewer Than Ten Moons

This is not a very profound problem, and uses the raw data as it appears on the file. The file must be opened and then each line of data is read, the value of the 11th data element (i.e., index 10) retrieved and compared against 10. If larger, the name of the planet (index 0) is printed. The plan is:

Open the file

Read (skip over) the header line

For each planet

    Read a line as string **s**

    Break **s** into components based on commas giving list **P**

    If **P[10] < 10** print the planet name, which is **P[0]**

It is all something that has been done before except for breaking the string into parts based on the comma. Fortunately, the designers of Python anticipated this kind of problem and have provided a very useful function: **split()**. This function breaks up a string into parts using a specified delimiter character or string and returns a list in which each component is one section of the fractured string. For example:

```
s = "This is a string"
z = s.split(" ")
```

yields the list z = ["This", "is", "a", "string"]. It splits the string **s** into substrings at each space character. A call like **s.split(",")** should give substrings that are separated by a comma. Given the above sketch and the split() function, the code now pretty much writes itself.

```
try:
# Open the file
    infile = open ("planets.txt", "r")
# Read (skip over) the header line
    s =infile.readline()
# For each planet
    for i in range (0, 8):
# Read a line as string s
        s = infile.readline()
# Break s into components based on commas giving list P
        P = s.split (",")
# If P[10] < 10 print the planet name, which is P[0]
        if int(P[10])<10:
            print (P[0], " has fewer than 10 moons.")
except FileNotFoundError:
        print ("There is no file named 'planets.txt'.
Please try again")
```

Things to notice: almost the entire program resides within a try statement, so that if the file does not exist, then a message will be printed and the program will end normally. Also note that P[10] has to be converted into an integer, because all components of the list P are strings. Strings are what has been read from the file.

CSV files are common enough so that Python provides a module for manipulating them. The module contains quite a large collection of material, and for the purposes of the *planets.py* program only the basics are needed. To avoid the details of a general package, a simpler version is included with this book: *simpleCSV* has the essentials needed to read most CSV files while being written in such a way that a beginning programmer should be able to read and understand it.

To use it, the **simpleCSV** module is first imported. This makes two important functions available: **nextRecord()** and **getData()**. The **nextRecord()** function reads one entire line of CSV data. It allows skipping lines without examining them in detail (like headers). The function **getData()** will parse one line of data, the last one read, into a tuple, each element of which is one of the comma-separated fields.

The *simpleCSV* library needs to be in the same directory as the program that uses it, or be in the standard Python directory for installed modules. The source code resides on the accompanying disc and is called *simpleCSV.py*. The program above can be rewritten to use the *simpleCSV* module as follows:

```
import simpleCSV
try:  # Read (skip over) the header line
    infile = open ("planets.txt", "r") # Open the file
    simpleCSV.nextRecord(infile)        # Read the header
    for i in range (0, 8):              # For each planet
        simpleCSV.nextRecord(infile)    # Read a line and
                                        # collect substrings
                                        # in a list
        p = simpleCSV.getData(infile)
        if int(P[10])<10:       # If number of moons less
                                # than 10
            print (P[0], " has fewer than 10 moons.")
                                        # print the planet name
except FileNotFoundError:
    print ("There is no file named 'planets.txt'.
        Please try again")
```

Problem: Play Jeopardy Using a CSV Data Set

The television game show *Jeopardy* has been on the air for 35 years in one of its two incarnations, and is perhaps the best known such program on television. Players select a topic and a point value and are asked a trivia question that they must answer in the form of a question. There are sets of questions that have been used in Jeopardy over the years, some in CSV form, so it should be possible to stage a simulated game using Python as the moderator.

A simple version of the game could work like this: read a bunch of questions and answers, and select questions at random to ask. Questions that have single word unambiguous answers would be best. The player types in an answer and wins if they answer ten correctly before getting three wrong.

A single line of data from the file might look like this:

```
5957,2010-07-06,Jeopardy!,"LET'S  BOUNCE","$600","In  this
kid's game, you bounce a small rubber ball while picking up
6-pronged metal objects","jacks"
```

There are 7 different data fields here separated by commas. They are: Show Number, Air Date, Round, Category, Value, Question, and Answer; all are strings, but some questions may contain commas. The CSV module can deal with that.

There are many ways that a random question can be chosen. One would be to read all of the data into a list, but that would require a lot of memory. One way would be to randomly read a question from the file, but that would be hard to do because each line has a different length. What could be done relatively easily would be to pick a random number of questions to skip over before reading one to use. So, select a random number K between N and M, read K questions, and the read the next one and ask the user that question. When the end of the file is reached, it can be read again from the beginning. If the file is large enough it would be unlikely to ask the same question twice in a short time period.

Here is a sketch of how this might work:

```
Open infile as the file of questions to be used
While game continues:
    Select a random number K between N and M
    For I = N to M:
        Read a line from the file
        If no more lines:
```

```
          Close infile and reopen
  Read a question and print it, ask the user for an answer
  Read the user's answer from the keyboard
  If the user's answer is correct:
              Count right answers
  Else:
              Count wrong answers
```

If the CSV module is used, the parsing of the input file is dealt with. What is new about this? When all of the data in the file has been used, the program may not be complete. What is done then is new: close the file, reopen it, and start again from the beginning. This is an unusual action for a Python program, but illustrates the flexibility of the file system. There is a nested try-except pair, the outer one that checks the existence of the file of questions and the inner one that checks for the end of the file. When the file is reopened a new **reader** has to be created, because the old one is connected to a closed file. The file on the disk is the same, but when it is opened again a new handle is built; the old CSV **reader** is linked to the old handle.

The program counts the number of right answers (**CORRECT**) and the number of wrong ones (**INCORRECT**). When there are 10 correct answers or 3 incorrect ones, the game is over; a variable **again** is set to **False** and the main **while** loop exits. A **break** could have been used, but having the condition become **False** is the polite way to exit from a **while** loop.

The entire program looks like this:

```
# Jeopardy!
import simpleCSV, random

try:
    infile = open ("q.txt", "r")   # Open the file
    simpleCSV.nextRecord(infile)    # Read (skip over) the
                                    # header line

    CORRECT = 0
    INCORRECT = 0
    again = True
    while again:
        k = random.randint (5, 10) # How many questions to
                                   # skip?
```

```
    for i in range (0, k):
        if not simpleCSV.nextRecord(infile):
                                      # Skip this question
            infile.close()
            print ("Reopening")
            infile = open ("JEOPARDY_small.txt", "r")
            simpleCSV.nextRecord(infile)
    s = simpleCSV.getData(infile)   # Read the question
                                    # to be asked.
    print (s[5])                    # Print the question
    a = input ()                    # Read the answer
    if a.lower() == s[6].lower():   # Does player answer
                                    # agree?
        CORRECT = CORRECT + 1       # Yes. count to 10.
        if CORRECT >= 10:
            print ("You win!")
            again = False
    else:
        INCORRECT = INCORRECT + 1   # No. Count to 3
        print ("Sorry. The answer is ", s[6])
        if INCORRECT > 12:
            print ("You lose.")
            again = False
except FileNotFoundError:
    print ("There is no question file.  We can't play.")
```

The With Statement

A difficulty with the code presented so far is that it does not clean up after itself. A file should be closed after input from it or output to it is finished; none of the programs written so far do that, at least not after the file operations are complete. There has been no significant discussion of the **close()** operation, but what it does has been described. Normally when a program terminates, its resources are returned to the system, including the closing of any open files. Intentionally closing a file is important for three reasons: first, if the program aborts for some reason, open files *should* be closed by the system but may not be, and file problems can be the result. Second, as in the *Jeopardy* program, closing a file can be used as a step in re-using it. Opening it again starts reading it at the beginning. Third, closing a file frees its resources. Programs that use many files and/or many resources will profit from freeing them when they are no longer needed.

The Python *with* statement, in its simplest form, takes care of many of the details surrounding file access. An example of its use is:

```
try:
    with open ("planets.txt") as infile:    # Open the file
        simpleCSV.nextRecord(infile)         # Read the header
        for i in range (0, 9):               # For each planet
            simpleCSV.nextRecord(infile)     # Read a line,
                                             # make a list
            P = simpleCSV.getData(infile)
            if int(P[10])<10:                   # If number of moons
                                                # less than 10
                print (P[0], " has fewer than 10 moons.")
                                                # print the name
except FileNotFoundError:
    print ("There is no file named 'planets.txt'.
        Please try again")
```

Once the file is open, the *with* statement guarantees that certain errors will be dealt with and the file will be closed. The problem is that the file has to be open first, so the **FileNotFound** error should still be caught as an exception.

5.4 WRITING TO FILES

The first step in writing to a file is opening it, but this time for output:

```
outfile = open ("out.txt", "w")
```

The "w" as the second parameter to **open()** means to open the file for writing. When writing to a file it is important to note that opening it will create a new file by default. If a file with the given name already exists it will be rewritten, and the previous contents will be gone.

The basic file output function is **write()**; it takes a parameter, a string to be written to the file. It only writes strings, so numbers and other types have to be converted into strings before being written. Also, there is no concept of a line. This function simply moves characters to a file, one at a time, in the order given. In order to write a line, an end of line character has to be written. This is usually specified in a string as "\n," spoken as "backslash n." The "n" stands for newline.

Example: Write a Table of Squares to a File

This will illustrate the typical code involved in writing to a file. The file must be opened, then a loop from 0 to 25 is constructed. Each number in that range is written to the file, as is that number multiplied by itself. Each output string represents a line, and so must have a newline character added to the end.

```
outfile = open ("out.txt", "w")
outfile.write ("     X                 X squared \n")
for i in range (0, 25):
    sout = "     "+str(i)+"          "+str(i*i)+"\n"
    outfile.write (sout)
outfile.close()
```

Note that the integers are explicitly converted into strings and concatenated into a line to be written. The elements of the line could be written in separate calls to write:

```
outfile = open ("out.txt", "w")
outfile.write ("     X                 X squared \n")
for i in range (0, 25):
    outfile.write ("     ")
    outfile.write (str(i))
    outfile.write ("               ")
    outfile.write (str(i*i))
    outfile.write ("\n")
outfile.close()
```

The output file is closed after all data has been written.

5.4.1 Appending Data to a File

Opening the file in "w" mode starts writing at the beginning of the file, and will result in existing data being lost. This is not always desirable. For example, what if a log file is being created? The log should contain a record of everything that has happened, not just the most recent thing.

Opening the file in *append* mode, signified by the parameter "a," opens the file for output and starts writing at the end of the file if it already exists. This means that data can be added to the end of an existing file.

Example: Append Another 20 Squares to the Table of Squares File

The previous example created a file named "out.txt" and wrote 26 lines to it. It was a table of squares, and the final one was 24. This example will therefore begin at 25 and add 20 more values to the table.

The main difference is the opening of the output file in append mode, and starting the loop at 25 instead of at 0:

```
outfile = open ("out.txt", "a")
for i in range (25, 45):
    sout = "     "+str(i)+"         "+str(i*i)+"\n"
    outfile.write (sout)
outfile.close()
```

The file "out.txt" will contain the squares of the integer between 0 and 44 inclusive after this program runs.

5.5 SUMMARY

Files are computer structures within which data are stored, and almost always reside on disk devices, tape devices, or other secondary storage. Files have some common properties: files have names; files have a size; basic operations on a file are *read* and *write*; files must be *open* before they can be used; only one program at a time can write to a file. Access to data on a file is much slower than access to data in memory, but file data has to be moved into memory before it can be manipulated.

Exceptions are events that occur while a program is executing, such as dividing by zero. Rather than check for all possible exceptions every time a statement is executed, Python provides a **try-except** statement that allows the programmer to provide code to run when an error occurs. Specific named exceptions exist in Python that can be specifically caught, like *ValueError*, or all exceptions can be caught by not specifying a particular one.

Files are opened using a call to open passing a file name and a mode. If the mode is "r" then the file will be read from; if it is "w" it will be written to. Example: **x = open("input.txt", "r")**. Reading from a file x is accomplished by a **read** call: **x.read(n)** will return a string of **n** characters; **x.readline()** will return one line from the file **x**. When there are no more characters in the file **read()**

will return the empty string: "". This is called the *end of file condition,* and it is important that it be detected.

A CSV (*comma separated values*) file is a specific format that is common for some kinds of data, including spreadsheets. The *simpleCSV* package provided on the accompanying disc can be helpful in reading these files.

Output to a file **x** is done with a call to write: **x.write(s)** writes the string **s** to the file represented by x. The string "\n" represents the end of a line.

> **NOTE** *This chapter will be extended in Chapter 8 to expand the kind of file operations and data that can be read from and written to a file.*

Exercises

1. Write a program that reads a file name from the user (console) and prints out how many characters belong to that file.

2. Write a program that opens a file containing a list of file names. For each one print the file name followed by YES if that file exists in the current directory and NO if it does not.

3. Create a file copy facility. The program to be written reads the name of a file from the user console and creates another file with the same contents. If the original file is named "xx.txt" then the new file will be named "xx-copy.txt." The original file will always have a name ending in ".txt," and so will the copy.

4. The CSV file "avatardata.csv" contains saved information concerning the preferred avatars for players of a video game. The fields are: player code (integer), avatar type (string, no quotes), number of times this avatar was played at this level (integer), a game level reached (integer, out of 12), and the highest score achieved on this level (integer); there is no header. Read this file and determine and print which player/avatar has the highest score on each level.

5. Using a Python program, create a CSV file from "avatardata.csv" that contains only information for level 10.

6. In an HTML file (i.e., a web page) an image to be displayed is usually identified in a source tag of the form: **src="name.jpg."** The quotes are a part of the tag, and the text between them is an image file name. Write a program

that reads an HTML file and prints the names of all of the image files that it references.

7. A user will specify the name of an image file (i.e., a file name that ends in ".jpg," ".gif," or ".png") from the console. Your program will read this name and create "disp.html," an html file that, when opened by a browser, will display this image (requires a knowledge of basic HTML).

8. Two files, named *sorted1.txt* and *sorted2.txt*, contain numeric data that appear in the file in sorted ascending order (when looked at as a string). Merge these two files to create a single file having the data of both, also in sorted order.

Notes and Other Resources

Python CSV Library: *https://docs.python.org/3/library/csv.html*

1. Remzi Arpaci-Dusseau and Andrea Arpaci-Dusseau. (2015). **Operating Systems: Three Easy Pieces**, Amazon Digital Services, Inc.

2. Daniel P. Bovet and Marco Cesati. (2005). **Understanding the Linux Kernel**, O'Reilly Media.

3. Dominic Giampaolo. (1999). **Practical Filesystem Design**, Morgan Kaufmann Publishers, Inc., *http://www.nobius.org/~dbg/practical-file-system-design.pdf, www.nobius.org/~dbg/practical-file-system-design.pdf*

4. Robert Stetson. (2013). **How Disk Drives Work**, CreateSpace Independent Publishing Platform.

5. Jeopardy questions may be found at *https://docs.google.com/uc?id=0BwT5wj_P7BKXUl9tOUJWYzVvUjA&export=download*

Classes

In this chapter

How many jokes begin with a phrase like "A man walks into a bar"?
So many that when someone hears that phrase, it is likely that they will
assume it is a joke. So, to ruin the joke and speak philosophically, what is
a *man*, what is a *bar*, and what does *walking* entail? *Walking* seems to be
something that a man can do, an action they can perform. And a *bar* is a
place where a *man* can *walk*. Can a *man* do anything else but *walk*? Is a
bar the only place a man can *walk* to?

   It seems silly to examine a sentence in that way, but in the context of a computer program it may be more meaningful. Imagine that this discussion involves
a computer game or simulation. A *man* now represents some kind of thing or
object that is manipulated by the program. A *man* has properties and things it can
do, which is to say operations it can perform. What properties does a *man* have?
Well, as a small subset of the possibilities:

Property	Type
Name	String
Sex	Boolean
Phone number	Integer
Height	Float
Weight	Float
Job	String?
Home (location, address)	String?
Interests	Array of String
Income	Float
Possessions (other objects)	Array of object
Spouse	*person*
Children	Array of *person*

So a *man* would appear to be a complex data type having a number of properties. Note especially that a man can have a property or characteristic called **spouse**. A **spouse** is something called a *person*; so is a *man*, really. This is pretty abstract, but stay with it: a *man* is a *person*, and perhaps some of the characteristics of a *man* are really those of (i.e., inherited from) a *person*. In fact, it would appear that most of them are. The only thing that distinguishes a *man* from other persons would (from the list above) be *sex*, which would be (perhaps) **false** for a man and **true** for a *woman*, another kind of *person*.

Imagine that there is a whole class of things called *person* that have most of these properties. A *man* could be derived from this, since *man* has many of these properties in common. A *woman* could be another class, perhaps having a few different properties. A *man* could have, for example, a "date of last prostate exam" as a property, but a *woman* could not. A *woman* could have a "date of last pap smear," but a *man* could not. At some point, person has many common characteristics, but *man* has some that *woman* does not and vice versa.

So, considering the original proposition: what is a *bar*? It is clearly something (object) that can hold (contain) a *man*. Perhaps it can contain many *men*. *Women*? Why not? If a *person* has to be either a *man* or a *woman*, then a bar can contain some number of *person*s. A *bar* is a class of objects that can hold or contain some number of *person*s. It would be a container class, one supposes, or a holder of some kind.

So, the phrase "A man walks into a bar" might be expressed as:

aMan.walksInto (aBar)

where aMan is a particular man (a specific instance of a man class) and aBar is a specific instance of a class of objects known as bar. This man has a Name, which is to say that one of the properties that a man has is a Name, and this is really just a variable. Since each individual *man* has a **Name**, there has to be a way of getting at (accessing) each one. It is done through each instance, like so:

```
print (aMan.Name)       # Accessing /printing the name.
aMan.Name = "Ted Smith" # Assigning to the name.
```

Using this syntax, the dot (".") is placed after the name of the instance. The syntax "**aMan.Name**" means "look at the variable **aMan**, which is an instance of *man*, for a property called **Name**."

Okay, so what is **walksInto** in the above expression **aMan.walksInto(aBar)**? Considering the syntax just described, it would appear to be a function that was a part of the definition of *man*. It takes one parameter, which is something having the type *bar*.

This may all seem very abstract still, but this way of looking at things seems sensible in that it appears to organize information and provide a clear and formal way to access it and manipulate it. This discussion has been a metaphor for the concept of a *class* and the ideas behind *object orientation*, two key elements of modern programming structures. Python permits the programmer to define classes like the *man* or *bar* objects previously described and to use them to encapsulate variables and functions and create convenient modular constructions.

6.1 CLASSES AND TYPES

A **class**, in the general sense, *is a template for something that involves data and operations (functions).* An **object** is *an instance of a class, a specific instantiation of the template.* Defining a class in Python involves specifying a class name and a collection of variables and functions that will belong to that class. The man class that has been referred to so far has only a few characteristics that we know about for certain. It does have a function called **walksInto**, as one example. A first draft of the man class could be as follows:

```
class man:
    def walksInto (aBar):
        # code goes here
```

A function that belongs to a class is generally referred to as a *method*. This terminology likely refers back to a language devised in the 1970s named *Smalltalk*. According to the standard for that language, "*A method consists of a sequence of expressions. Program execution proceeds by sequentially evaluating the expressions in one or more methods.*" In the above example, **walksInto** is a method; essentially, a method is any function that is part of a class.

Classes can have their own data too, which would be variables that 'belong' to the class in that they exist inside it. Such variables can be used inside the class but can't be seen from outside.

Looking closely at the simple class **man** above, notice that it is actually still a rather abstract thing. In the narrative about a man walking into a bar it was a specific *man*, as indicated by a variable **aMan**. So it would seem that a class is really a description of something, and that examples or instances should be created in order to make use of that description. This is correct. In fact, many individual instances of any class can be created (instantiated) and assigned to variables. To create a new instance of the class **man**, the following syntax could be used:

```
aMan = man ()
```

When this is done all of the variables used in the definition of man are allocated. In fact, whenever a new man class is created, a special method that is local to man is called to initialize variables. This method is the *constructor*, and can take parameters that help in the initialization. Creating a man might involve giving him a name, so the instantiation may be:

```
aMan = man ("Jim Parker")
```

In this case the constructor accepts a parameter, a string, and probably assigns it to a variable local to the class (**Name**, most likely). The constructor is always named __init__:

```
def __init__ (self, parameter1, parameter2, …):
```

The initial parameter named **self** is a reference to the class being defined. Any variable that is a part of this class is referred to by prefixing the variable name with "self." To make a constructor for **man** that accepted a name, it would look like this:

```
def __init__ (self, name):
    self.Name = name
```

When a man is created, the statement would be:

```
aMan = man ("Jim Parker")
```

This metaphor has fulfilled its purpose for the moment. There are some exercises concerning it at the end of the chapter, but another more practical example might be better now.

6.1.1 The Python Class – Syntax and Semantics

The *man walks into a bar* example illustrates many aspects of the Python class structure but obviously omits many details, especially formal ones that can be so important to a programmer. A **class** looks like a function in that there is a keyword, **class**, and a name and a colon, followed by an indented region of code. Everything in that indented region "belongs" to the class, and cannot be used from outside without using the class name or the name of a variable that is an instance of the class.

The method **__init__** is used to initialize any variables that belong to the class. Java would call this method a *constructor*, and that's how it will be referenced here too. Any variables that belong to the class must be accessed through either an instance (from outside of the class) or by using the name **self** (from within the class). So, **self.name** would refer to a variable that was defined inside of the class, whereas simply using **name** would refer to a variable local to a method. When **__init__** is called, a set of parameters can be passed and used to initialize variables in the class. If the first parameter is **self**, it means that the method can access class-local variables; otherwise it cannot. Normally self is passed to **__init__** or it can't initialize things. Any variable initialized within **__init__** and prefixed by **self** is a class-local variable. Any method that is passed **self** as a parameter can define a new class-local variable, but it makes sense to initialize all of them in one place if that's possible.

A simple example of a class, initialization, and method is:

```
class person:
    def __init__ (self, name):
        self.name = name

    def introduce (self):
        print ("Hi, my name is ", self.name)

me = person("Jim")
me.introduce()
```

This class has two methods, __init__() and **introduce()**. After the class is defined, a variable named **me** is defined and is given a new instance of the **person** class having the name "Jim." Then this variable is used to access the introduce method, which prints the introduction message "Hi, my name is Jim." A second instance could be created and assigned to a second variable named **you** using:

```
you = person ("Mike")
```

and the method call

```
you.introduce()
```

would result in the message "Hi, my name is Mike." Any number of instances can be created, and some have the same name as others—they are still distinct instances.

A new class-local variable can be created by any method. In **introduce()**, for example, a new local named **introductions** can be created simply by assigning a value to it.

```
def introduce (self):
    print ("Hi, my name is ", self.name)
    self.introductions = True
```

This variable is **True** if the method introductions has been called. The main program can access this variable directly. If the main program becomes:

```
me = person("Jim")
me.introduce()
print (me.introductions)
```

then the program will generate the output:

```
Hi, my name is   Jim
True
```

This is the essential information needed to define and use a class in Python. A more complex example would be useful in seeing how these features can be used in practice.

6.1.2 A Really Simple Class

A common example of a basic class is a point, a place on a plane specified by x and y coordinates. The beginning of this class is:

```
class point:
    def __init__ (self, x, y):
        self.x = x
        self.y = y
```

This simply represents the data associated with a mathematical point. What more does it need? Well, two points have a distance between them. A distance method could be added to the point:

```
def distance (self, p):
    d = (self.x-p.x)*(self.x-p.x) + (self.y-p.y)*
        (self.y-p.y)
    return sqrt(d)
```

If a traditional function were to be used to compute distance, it would be written similarly but not identically. It would take two points as parameters:

```
def distance (p1, p2):
    d = (p1.x-p2.x)*(p1.x-p2.x) + (p1.y-p2.y)* (p1.y-p2.y)
    return sqrt(d)
```

The distance method uses one of the points as a preferred parameter, in a sense. The distance between points p1 and p2 would be calculated as:

```
d = p1.distance(p2)  or  d = p2.distance(p1)
```

using the distance method, but as:

```
d = distance (p1, p2)
```

if the function was used. To a degree the difference is a philosophical one. Is *distance* some property that a point has from another point (the method), or is it something that is a thing that is calculated for two things (the function)? A programmer begins, after a while, to see the methods and data of a class as belonging to the object, and as somehow being properties of it. That's what makes a class a type definition.

Many object-oriented languages offer the concept of *accessor* methods. Some languages do not allow variables that belong to a class to be used directly, or allow specific controls on access to them. The truth is that having the ability to find the value of variables and to modify them is generally a bad idea. If the only place that a class local variable can be modified is within the class, then that limits the places where that can occur, and allows more control over what is possible. Preventing errors in programs is partly a matter of restricting actions to a small region, of knowing exactly what is going on at all times.

Similarly, if some object outside of a class has access to the local variables of that class, then it promotes a dependency on a specific implementation, and one of the advantages of an object-oriented implementation is that the interface to the class is fixed and independent of the way that class is implemented. It may seem obvious that a point object has an x, y position and that those would be real numbers, but the point class is the simplest class, and taking advantage of how a class is coded it not always healthy.

All that an *accessor* method does is return a value important to a user of a class. The x and y positions are variables local to the class, and many would agree that they should have an *accessor* method:

```
def getx (self):
    return self.x
def gety (self):
    return self.y
```

Rewriting the **distance()** method to use accessor methods changes it only slightly:

```
def distance (self, p):
    d = (self.x-p.getx())*(self.x-p.getx()) +
        (self.y-p.gety())* (self.y-p.gety())
    return sqrt(d)
```

Methods called *mutators* or *setters* are used to modify the value of a variable in a class. They may do more than that, such as checking ranges and types, and tracking modifications.

```
def setx (self, x):
    self.x = x
def sety (self, y):
    self.y = y
```

There are other methods that could be added to even this simple class just in case they were needed, such as to draw the point, to return a string that describes the object, to rotate about the origin or some other point, to use a *destructor* method that is called when the object is no longer needed, and so on. Until it is known what the class will be used for, there may not be any value for this effort, but if a class is being provided for general utility, like the Python *string*, as much functionality would be provided as the programmer's imagination could invent. A draw method could simply print the coordinates, and could be useful for debugging:

```
def draw (self):
    print ("(", self.x, ",", self.y, ") ")
```

Using this class involves creating instances and using the provided methods, and that should be all. A triangle consists of three points. A triangle *class* could be defined as:

```
class triangle:
    def __init__ (self, p0, p1, p2):
        self.v0 = p0
        self.v1 = p1
        self.v2 = p2
        self.x = (p0.getx()+p1.getx()+p2.getx())/3
        self.y = (p0.gety()+p1.gety()+p2.gety())/3

    def set_vertices (self, p0, p1, p2):
        self.v0 = p0
        self.v1 = p1
        self.v2 = p2

    def get_vertices (self):
        return ( (self.v0, self.v1, self.v2) )

    def getx (self):
        return self.x

    def gety (self):
        return self.y
```

The (x, y) value of a triangle is its center, or the average value of the x and the y coordinates of the vertices. These are the basic methods. A triangle is likely to be drawn somehow, and the next chapter will explain how to do that specifically.

However, without knowing the details, a triangle is a set of lines drawn between the vertices and so might be done that way. As it is, using text only, it will print its vertices:

```
def draw (self):
    print ("Triangle:")
    self.v0.draw()
    self.v1.draw()
    self.v2.draw()
```

The triangle can be moved to a new position. A change in the x and y location specifies the change, and it is done by changing the coordinates of each of the vertices:

```
def move (self, dx, dy)
    coord = p0.getx()
    p0.setx(coord+dx)
    coord = p0.gety()
    p0.sety(coord+dy)
    coord = p1.getx()
    p1.setx(coord+dx)
    coord = p0.gety()
    p1.sety(coord+dy)
    coord = p2.getx()
    p2.setx(coord+dx)
    coord = p2.gety()
    p2.sety(coord+dy)
    self.x = self.x + dx
    self.y = self.y + dy
```

In this way of expressing things, it is clear that moving the triangle is a matter of changing the coordinates of the vertices. If each point had a **move()** method, then it would be clearer: moving a triangle is a matter of moving each of the vertices:

```
def move (self, dx, dy):
    p0.move(dx, dy)
    p1.move(dx, dy)
    p2.move(dx, dy)
    self.x = self.x + dx
    self.y = self.y + dy
```

Which of these two **move()** methods seems the best description of what is happening? The more complex are the classes, the more value there is in making an effort to design them to effectively communicate their behaviors and to make things easier to expand and modify. It is also plain that the **move()** method for a point is simpler than that for a triangle. That fact is invisible from outside the class, and it actually not relevant.

6.1.3 Encapsulation

In the example of the *point* class there is no actual need for an accessor method, because the variables can be accessed from outside the class, in spite of the arguments that have been given for more controlled use of these variables. A careful programmer would want to ensure the integrity of classes by forcing the variables to remain protected in some way, and Python allows this while not requiring it.

The variables x and y are accessible and modifiable from outside because of how they are named. Any variable name in a class that begins with an underscore character ("_") cannot be modified by code that does not belong to the class. Such a variable is said to be *protected*. A variable name that begins with two under-score characters can't be modified or even examined from outside of the class, and is said to be *private*. All other variables are *public*. This applies to method names too, so the method __init__() that is the usually constructor is private.

Rewriting the point class to make the internal variables private would be done like this:

```
class point:
    def __init__ (self, x, y):
        self.__x = x
        self.__y = y

def getx (self):
    return self.__x

def gety (self):
    return self.__y

det setx (self, x):
        self.__x = x

def sety (self, y):
        self.__yy = y
```

```
def distance (self, p):
    d = (self.__x-p.getx())*(self.__x-p.getx()) +
        (self.__y-p.gety())* (self.__y-p.gety())
    return sqrt(d)

def move(self, dx, dy):
    self.__x = self.__x + dx
    self.__y = self.__y + dy

def draw (self):
    print ("(", self.__x, ",", self.__y, ") ")
```

Now the internal variables x and y can't be modified or even have their values examined unless explicitly allowed by a method.

6.2 CLASSES AND DATA TYPES

Consider an *integer*. How can it be described so that a person who has not used one before can implement something that looks and acts like an *integer*? This is a specific case of the general problem faced when using computers—to describe a problem in enough detail so that a machine can solve it. The definition could start with the idea that *integers* can be used for counting things. They are numbers that have no fractional part, and that have been extended so that they can be positive or negative.

What can be done with them? Integers can be added and subtracted, multiplied and divided. When dividing two *integers* there can be an *integer* remainder left over. They can be displayed in many forms: as base 10 numbers, in any other base, as Roman numerals, and so on. There are other operations on integers, but these are the most commonly used ones.

What has been done here is to define a *type*. Python types, the ones built into the language, include the *integer type*, as well as floating point numbers, strings, and so on. Each is characterized by an underlying implementation, which is often hidden from the programmer, and a set of operations that are defined on things of that type. This is a fair definition of a type in general. A class can be used to implement a type—not one of the types that the language already efficiently provides, but new types that programmers find useful for their purposes. The **man** and **person** classes described earlier can be thought of as types.

When designing programs that use classes, it is likely that the classes represent types, although they may not be completely implemented. The design scheme would be to sketch a high-level solution and observe what components of that solution look and behave like types. Those components can be implemented as classes. The remainder of the solution will have structure imposed on it by virtue of the fact that these other types exist and are defined to be used in specific ways. Types can hide their implementation, for example. The underlying nature of an integer probably does not matter much to a programmer most times, and so can be hidden behind the class boundary. This has the added feature that it encourages portability: if the implementation has to change, the class can be rewritten while providing the same interface to the programmer.

The operations on the type are implemented as methods. The methods can access the internal structure of the class while providing the desired view of the data and ways of manipulating it. If a class named **integer** existed, for example, then **add()**, **subtract()**, and so on would be methods. Then instances of this class could be implemented:

```
a = integer(5)
b = integer(21)
```

and computing a sum would be:

```
c = a.add(b)
```

The underlying representation of an integer is unknown to a user of this class. All that is known is the interface, described as methods. If the interface is well-documented, then that's all a programmer needs to know. In fact, exposing too much of the class to a programmer can compromise it.

6.2.1 Example: A Deck of Cards

Traditional playing cards these days have red and black colors, four suits, and a total of 52 cards, 13 in each suit. Individual cards are components of a deck, and can be sorted: a 2 is less than a 3, a Jack less than a King, and so on. The Ace is a problem: sometimes it is the high card, sometimes the low card. A card would possess the characteristics of suit and value. When playing card games, cards are dealt from the deck into hands of some number of cards: 13 cards for bridge, 5 for most poker games, and so on. The value of a card usually matters. Sometimes cards are compared against each other (poker), sometimes the sum of values is key (blackjack, cribbage), and sometimes the suit matters. These uses of a deck of cards can be used to define how classes will be created to implement card games on a computer.

Operations on a card could include to *view* it (it could be face up or face down) and to *compare* it against another card. Comparison operations could include a set of complex specifications to allow for aces being high or low and for some cards having special values (spades, baccarat) so a definition step might be very important.

A deck is a collection of cards. There are usually one of each card in a deck, but in some places (e.g., Las Vegas) there could be four or more complete decks used when playing blackjack. Operations on a deck would include to *shuffle*, to *replace* the entire deck, and to *deal* a card or a hand. With these things in mind, a draft of some Python classes for implementing a card deck can be created:

```
class card:                         class deck:
    def __init__ (self, face,           def __init__ (self):
                     suit):             def deal_card ():
    def value():                        def deal_hand (ncards):
    def suit():                         def shuffle():
    def facevalue():                    def replace():
    def view ():
    def compare():
    def initialize()
```

The way that the methods are implemented depends on the underlying representation. When the programmer calls **deal()** they expect the method to return a **card**, which is an instance of the card class. How that happens is not relevant to them, but it is relevant to the person who implements the class. In addition, how it happens may be different on different computers, and as long as the result is the same it does not matter.

For example, a card could be a constant value **r** that represented one of the 52 cards in the deck. The class could contain a set of values for these cards and provide them to programmers as a reference:

```
class card:
    CLUBS_1 = 1
```

```
DIAMONDS_1 = 2
        . . .
HEARTS_ACE = 51
SPADES_ACE = 52

Def __init__ (self, face, suit):
        . . .
```

The variables CLUBS_1, DIAMONDS_1, and so on are accessible in all instances of the card class and have the appropriate value. Variables defined in this way have one instance only, and are shared by all instances.

A second implementation could be as a tuple. The ace of clubs would be (Clubs, 1), for instance. Each has advantages, but these will not be apparent to the user of the class. For example, the tuple implementation makes it easier to determine the suit of a card. This matters to games that have trump suits. The integer value implementation makes it easier to determine values and do specific comparisons. The value of a card could be stored in a tuple named **ranks**, for example, and **ranks[r]** would be a numerical value associated with the specific card.

6.2.2 A Bouncing Ball

Animations and computer simulations see the world as a set of samples captured at discrete times. An animation, for example, is a set of images of some scene taken at fixed time intervals, generally 1/24th of a second or 1/30th of a second. Simulations use time intervals that are appropriate to the thing being simulated. This example is a simulation and animation of a bouncing ball, first in one dimension and then in two dimensions.

A ball dropped from a height **h** falls to the ground when released. Its speed increases as it falls, because it is being pulled downwards by gravity. The basic equation governing its movement is:

$$s = 1/2at^2 + v_0t \qquad (6.1)$$

where **s** is the distance fallen at time **t**, v_0 is the velocity the object had at time **t=0**, and **a** is the value of the acceleration. For an object at the earth's surface, the value of **a** is 32 feet/second^2 = 9.8 meters/second^2. For a ball being dropped, v_0 is

0, since it is stationary initially. So, the distances at successive time intervals of 0.5 seconds would be:

Time	S (feet) = 16*t*t	S (meters) = 4.9*t*t
0	0	0
0.5	4	1.225
1	16	4.9
1.5	36	11.025
2	64	19.6
2.5	100	30.625
3	144	44.1

A *class* could be made that would represent a ball. It would have a position and a speed at any given time, and could even be drawn on a computer screen. Making it bounce would be a matter of giving the ball a value that indicated how much of its energy would be lost each time it bounced, meaning that it would eventually stop moving. Writing the code for the class **Ball** could begin with the initialization (the *constructor*):

```
class Ball:
    def __init__(self, height, elasticity):
        self.height = height
        self.e = e
        self.speed = 0.0
        self.a = 32.0
```

This creates and initializes four variables named **height**, **e**, **a**, and **speed** that are local to the class. Remember, the parameter **self** *refers to the class itself*, and any variable that begins with 'self.' is a part of the class. A variable within the function **__init__** that did not begin with 'self.' and was not **global** would belong to the function, and would be created and destroyed each time that function was called.

A method (function) that calculates the height of the ball at a specific time is something else that the **Ball** class should provide. This is simply the value of the class local variable height, so:

```
def height(self):
    return self.height
```

The **self** parameter has to be passed, otherwise the function can't access the local variable **height**. The simulation will need values of height as a function of time, and time will increase in discrete chunks. This could be implemented in a couple of ways: the class could keep track of the time since it was dropped, or it could use the time increment to determine the next speed and position. If the former then a new class variable must be used to store the time; if the latter then a means has to be found to increment the speed rather than using total duration. This second idea is simpler than it sounds. The equation of motion $s = 1/2at^2 + v_0t$ can use a time increment in place of **t**, and v_0 would be the velocity at the start of the time interval; this yields the new position. The new velocity can be found from a related equation of motion, which is:

$$v = at + v_0 \qquad\qquad (6.2)$$

where **t** is again the time increment and v_0 is the speed at the beginning of the interval.

The function that updates the speed and position in this manner will be called **delta**:

```
def delta (self, dt):
    s = 0.5*self.a*dt*dt + self.speed*dt
    height = height - s
    self.speed = self.speed + self.a*dt
```

Here the parameter **dt** is the time interval, and so that can be varied by the programmer to get position values at various resolutions.

For now this will be the Ball class. Some code is needed to test this class and show how well (or whether) it works, and this will be the main part of the program. An instance of Ball has to be created and then the delta method will be called repeatedly at time increments of, for an example, 0.1 seconds. A table of height and time can be constructed in this way, and it is a simple matter to see whether the numbers are correct. The main program is:

```
b = Ball (12.0,  0.5)
for i in range (0, 20):
    b.delta (0.1)
    print ("At time ", i*0.1, " the ball has fallen to",
b.height(),  " Feet")
```

The results are what should be expected, showing that this class functions correctly:

```
At time 0.0  the ball has fallen to 12.0  Feet
...
At time 0.5  the ball has fallen to 7.999999999999997 Feet
...
At time 1.0  the ball has fallen to -4.0000000000000036 Feet
...
At time 1.5  the ball has fallen to -24.000000000000004 Feet
...
At time 2.0  the ball has fallen to -52.000000000000014 Feet
...
At time 2.5  the ball has fallen to -88.00000000000003 Feet
...
```

Because the initial height was 12 feet, the distance fallen is 12 minus the value given above, so: 4, 16, 36, 64, and 100 feet, which is in agreement with the initial table for the times listed. It appears to work correctly.

This code does not yet do the bounce, though. When the height reaches 0 the ball is at ground level. It should then *bounce*, which is to say begin moving in the reverse direction, with a speed equal to its former downward speed multiplied by the elasticity value. This does not seem hard to do until it is realized that the ball is not likely to reach a height of 0 exactly at a time increment boundary. At one point the ball will be above 0 and then after the next time unit the ball will be below 0. When does it actually hit the ground, and where will be the ball actually be at the end of the time increment? This is not a programming issue so much as an algorithmic or mathematical one, but is a detail that is important to the correctness of the results.

It seems clear that the bounce computation should be performed in the method **delta()**. The height value in the class begins at a positive value and decreases towards 0 as the ball falls. During some specific call to **delta()**, the ball will have a positive height at the beginning of the call and a negative one at the end; this means a bounce should happen. At that time the height of the ball will be negative. The height of the bounced ball at the end of the time interval will be the negated value of the height (i.e., so it is positive again) multiplied by the elasticity.

The speed that should be used in the bounce is based not the final speed but the speed the ball was traveling at the time when the height was 0. This happens when **self.height-s** is zero, or when:

```
self.height = s = 0.5*self.a*dt*dt + self.speed*dt
```

Solve this for the time **xt** that makes the equation work out, which would be the standard solution to a quadratic equation that is taught in high school:

$$xt = \frac{-\text{self.speed} \pm \sqrt{\text{self.speed}^2 + 2a * \text{self.height}}}{a} \qquad (6.3)$$

The value of **xt** will be between 0 and **dt**, and is the time within the increment at which the ball struck the ground. At this time the ball will be moving with speed **(self.speed + self.a*xt)** instead of **(self.speed + self.a*dt)** for a normal time interval. The ball will reverse direction and reduce speed by the value of elasticity. Now the ball is moving upwards.

The ball will be slowed by gravity until it stops on its upward path and drops down again. At the top of the path its speed will be 0; at the beginning of the time interval the speed will be negative and at the end it will be positive, and that's how the peak is detected. This situation is much simpler than the bounce.

The annotated program is as follows:

```
# Ball.py
import math
class Ball:
# Constructor/initializer
    def __init__(self, height, elasticity):
        self.height = height # Current height of the ball
  self.e = elasticity  # How much energy is retained each bounce
        self.speed = 0.0     # Current speed of the ball,
                             # initially 0, down +
        self.a = 32.0        # Acceleration: G= 32 ft/sec^2

# What Java would call an accessor: not really needed.
    def getHeight(self):
        return self.height

# Calculate the new height and speed for a change in time of dt
    seconds.
    def delta (self, dt):
        startHeight = self.height        # Remember the state
                                         # before dt
        startSpeed = self.speed
        s = 0.5*self.a*dt*dt + self.speed*dt # Equation 1:
                                             # position update
        self.height = self.height - s
        self.speed = self.speed + self.a*dt  # Equation 2: Speed
                                             # update
```

```
        if self.height < 0:    # The sign changed; bounce, when?

    # Equation 3: Solve the quadratic equation to find the time
    # of bounce
            xt = (-startSpeed - math.sqrt(startSpeed*startSpeed
                   +2*self.a*startHeight))/self.a
            if xt < 0:
                xt = (-startSpeed + math.
sqrt(startSpeed*startSpeed +2*self.a*startHeight))/self.a
            print ("Bounces at time ", xt)

# Equation 2 with elasticity
            self.speed = -(self.speed + self.a*xt)*self.e
            self.height = -self.height * self.e      # Correct the
                                                     # height

            if self.e <0.03: self.e = 0.0
            else: self.e = self.e - 0.03

# Peak of the upward bounce, velocity changes sign from + to -
        elif startSpeed*self.speed < 0:   # If sign differs then
                                          # the product is -ve
            self.speed = 0                # Speed is 0 at the top
                                          # of the bounce
        print("Peak")
        print("New speed is ",self.speed," and height starts
                                 at ", self.height)
        if self.height<0.:
            self.height = 0.


b = Ball (12.0,  0.5)  # Initial height 12 feet, elasticity is 0.5
s = Screen (20, 40)

for i in range (0, 50):
    b.delta (0.1)   # Time increment is 0.1 seconds
```

How can this program be effectively tested? The computed values could be compared against hand calculations, but this is time-consuming. It was done for a few cases and the simulation was accurate. For this example, another program was written in a different programming language to calculate the same values, and the result from the two programs was compared—they were nearly exactly the same. This is not definitive, but is certainly a good indication that this simulation is working properly. In both programs similar approximations were made, and the numbers agreed to seven decimal places.

This class will be expanded later to include an animation of the bouncing ball.

6.2.3 Cat-A-Pult

Early in the development of personal computers, a simple game was created that involved shooting cannons. The player would set an angle and a power level and a cannonball would be fired towards the opposing cannon. If the ball struck the cannon then it would be destroyed, but if not then the opposing player (or the computer) would fire back at the player's cannon. This process would continue until one or the other cannon was destroyed. This game evolved with time, having more complex graphics, mountainous terrain, and more complex aspects. Its influence can be seen in modern games like *Angry Birds*.

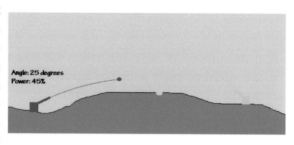

Figure 6.1
Typical configuration of a dueling cannons game.

A variation of this game is proposed as an example of how classes can be used. The basic idea is to eliminate a mouse that is eating your garden by firing cats at it; hence the name **cat-a-pult**. The game will use text as input and output, because no graphics facility is available yet. A player types the angle and the power level and the computer will fire a cat at the mouse. The location where the cat lands will be marked on a simple character display, and the player can try again. The goal is to hit the mouse with as few tries as possible.

Basic Design

Before writing any code, one needs to consider the items in this game and the actions they can take. The items will be *classes*, the actions will be *methods*. There seem to be two items: a *cannonball* (a cat) and a *cannon*. The target (the mouse) could be a class too. The cannon has a location, an angle, and a power or force with which the cannonball will be ejected. Both of the last two factors affect the distance the ball travels. The cannon is given a target as a parameter—in this example the target will be another cannon, basically to avoid making yet another class definition.

The action a cannon can perform is to be *fired*. This involves releasing a cannonball with a particular speed and direction from the location of the cannon. In this implementation an instance of the cannonball class will be created when the cannon is fired and will be given the angle and velocity as initial parameters; the ball will, from then on, be independent. As a class, the ball has a position (x, y) and a speed (dx, dy). The action that it can perform is to move, which will be accomplished using a method named **step()**, and to collide with something, accomplished by the method **testCollision()**.

Detailed Design

In the metaphor of this game, the cannonball is actually a cat and the target is a mouse, but to the program these details are not important. Here's what *is* important:

	Class Cannon	**Class Ball**
Has:	position x, y	position x, y
	angle (when fired)	speed dx, dy
	power (when fired)	name (text)
	target (another cannon)	target (a Cannon class instance)
	ball	gravity (force changing the height)
Does:	fire	step
	step	test for collision

All of the *Has* aspects are class local variables, and in this design they will be initialized within the **__init__** method of each class. This would entail the following:

```
self.x = x                  self.x = x
self.y = y                  self.y = y
self.power = 0              self.dx = dx
self.angle = 0             self.dy = dy
self.target = target       self.target = target
self.ball = None           self.gravity = 1.0
                           self.name = ""
```

The game is essentially one-dimensional. The cannonball will land at a specific x coordinate, and if that is near enough to the x coordinate of the target, then the target is destroyed and the game is over. Without a way to draw proper graphics, this can be imagined as a simple text display with the cannon on one side of the screen and the target on the other, something like that seen in Figure 6.1.

The slash character ("/") on the left represents the cannon, and the "Y" represents the mouse, which is the target. The cannon is at horizontal coordinate 12, and the mouse is at 60; both vertical coordinates are 0.

All of the *Does* aspects represent actions, or things the class object can *do*. When the cannon is fired the ball is created at the cannon coordinates (12, 0) and is given a speed that is related to the angle and power level using the usual trigonometric calculations learned in high school (Figure 6.2):

```
9 :
8 :
7 :
6 :
5 :
4 :
3 :
2 :
1 :
0 :          /                                              Y
   --------------------------------------------------------------------
   01234567890123456789012345678901234567890123456789012345678901234567890
```

Figure 6.2
ASCII (text) video of the game at the beginning.

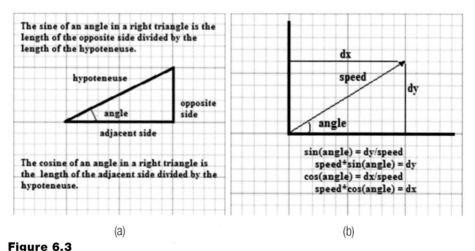

(a)   (b)

Figure 6.3
(a) A review of how sines and cosines are computed. (b) using the definition of sine and cosine to calculate the speed of the ball (or any object) in the x and y direction.

dy = sin(angle * 3.1415/180.0)

dx = cos(angle * 3.1415/180.0)

The angles passed to **sin** and **cos** must be in radians, so the value PI/180 is used to convert degrees into radians. The coordinates in this case have **y** increasing as the ball moves upwards. So, when the cannon is fired a ball is created that has the x and y coordinates of the cannon and the **dx** and **dy** values determined as above. This is accomplished by a method named **fire()**:

Fire: takes an angle and a power.
    Angle is in degrees, between 0 and 360
    Power is between 0 and 100 (a percentage)

1. Compute values for dx and dy from angle and power, where max power is 0.1

2. Create an instance of Ball giving it x, y, dx, dy, a name ("cat"), and a target (the mouse)

The simulation makes time steps of a fixed duration and calculates positions of objects at the end of that step. Each object should have a method that updates the time by one interval, and it will be named **step()**. The cannon does not move, but sometimes has a cannonball that it has fired, so updating the status of the cannon should update the status of the ball as well:

Step: make one-time step for this object in the simulation. No parameter.

1. If a ball has been fired, then update its position. This is done by calling the **step()** method of the ball.

This defines the cannon.

The ball must also possess a **step()** method, and it will update the ball's position based on its current speed and location. The **x** position is increased by **dx**, and the **y** is increased by **dy**. Gravity pulls down on the ball, effectively decreasing the vertical speed of the ball during each interval. After some trials it was determined that the value of **dy** should be decreased by the value of **gravity** during each interval. If the ball strikes the ground, it should stop moving. When does this happen? When **y** becomes smaller than 0. When this occurs, set **dx** and **dy** to 0, and check to see if the impact location is near to the target.

Step: make a one-time step for this object in the simulation. No parameter.

1. Let x = x + dx, changing the x position
2. Let y = y + dy, changing the y position
3. Decrease dy by gravity (dy = dy - gravity)
4. If the ball has struck the ground
5. Let dx = dy = gravity = 0
6. Check for collision with target

Checking to see if the ball hit the target is a matter of looking at the x value of the ball and the x value of the target. If the difference is smaller than some predefined value, say 1.0, then the target was hit. This is determined by a method that will be called **testCollision()**. If the collision occurred then success has been achieved by the player, so set a flag that will end the game.

testCollision: check to see if the ball has hit the target and, if so, set a flag:

1. Subtract the x position of the ball from the x position of the target. Call this **d**.
2. If **d** <= 1.0 then set a flag **done** to **True**.

This defines the class **Ball** and completes the two major classes.

The main program that uses these classes could look something like this:

```
mouse = Cannon (60, 0, None)      # Create the target
player = Cannon (12, 0, mouse)    # create the cannon
player.fire (42, 65)             # Example: fire cannon at
                                 # 42 degrees 65% power
done = False                     # initialize variable
                                 # 'done'
while not done:                  # so long as the simulation
                                 # is not over

    player.step()               # Update the position of
                                 # the ball.
```

Actual code for most of this example is shown in Figure 6.4, and the entire program is on the accompanying disc. Included in the disc version is an extra class that draws each state of the game as character graphics that can be displayed in the Python output window; the example in the figure does not include any output, and is unsatisfying to execute. The program on the disc will generate a numeric and graphical representation of the state, showing the axes, the cannon, the ball, and the target after each step. These can be made into distinct text files and can be made into an animation using *MovieMaker* on a Windows computer or *Final Cut* on a Mac. Such an animation is also included on the disc, and is named *catapult.mp4*.

The process by which Cat-a-pult was designed and coded loosely defines a way to design and code almost any program that uses classes.

```python
from math import *
class Ball:
    def _ _init_ _ (self, x,
                    y, dx, dy,
                    name,
                    other):
        self.xPos = x
        self.yPos = y
        self.xSpeed = dx
        self.ySpeed = dy
        self.gravity = 1.0
        self.name = name
        self.other = other

    def step (self): # One time
                     # step
        self.xPos = self.xPos +
                    self.xSpeed
        self.yPos = self.yPos +
                    self.ySpeed
        self.ySpeed = self.ySpeed
                    - self.
                      gravity
        if self.yPos < 0:
            self.xSpeed = 0
            self.xSpeed = 0
            self.gravity = 0
            self.yPos = 0
            self.testCollision()
```

```python
    def testCollision (self):
        global done
        d = self.xPos-self.
                       other.x
        if d<0: d = -d
        if d < 1.0:
            done = True

class Cannon:
    def __init__ (self, x, y,
                    other):
        self.x = x
        self.y = y
        self.other = other
        self.ball = None

    def fire (self, angle,
                power):
        dy = sin(angle *
                 3.1415/180.0)
        dx = cos(angle *
                 3.1415/180.0)
        self.ball = Ball(self.x,
                   self.y,
                   dx*power/10.0,
                   dy*power/10.0,
                   "Cat", self.other)

    def step (self):
        if self.ball != None:
            (self.ball).step()
```

Figure 6.4
The **Ball** and the **Cannon** classes from the Cat-a-pult simulation

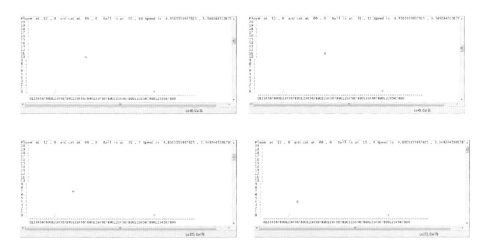

Figure 6.5
Frames from the text animation of the game.

6.3 SUBCLASSES AND INHERITANCE

Classes are designed as language features that can represent a hierarchy of information or structure. A class can be used to define another, and properties from the first class will be passed on (inherited) by the other. A class that is based on another in this way is called a *subclass*, and explanatory examples suffuse the Internet: a pet class with dogs and cats as special cases; a polygon having triangles and rectangles as subclasses; a *dessert* class, having subclasses *pie*, *cake*, and *cookie*; even the initial example in this chapter of a man and a woman class and the person class that they can be derived from. A *subclass* is a more specific case of the *superclass* (or *parent* class) on which it is based.

The examples above are for explanation, and are not really useful as software components, which begs a question about whether subclasses are really useful things. They are, but it requires non-trivial examples to really demonstrate this.

6.3.1 Non-Trivial Example: Objects in a Video Game

To some degree all objects in a game have some things in common. They are things that can interact with other game objects; they have a position within the volume of space defined by the game, and they have a visual appearance. Thus, a description of a class that could implement a game object would include:

```
class gobject:
    position = (0, 0, 0)        # Object position in 3D
    visual = None               # Graphics that represent
                                # the object
    def __init__ (self, pos, vis)
    def getPosition (self):
    def setPosition(self, p):
    def setVisual(self, v):
    def draw (self):
```

Anyone who has played a video game knows that some of the objects can move while others cannot. Objects that move can have their position change, and the position has to be updated regularly. An object that can move can have a speed and a method that updates their position; otherwise it is like a **gobject**. This is a good case for a subclass:

```
class mobject (gobject):
    speed = (0, 0, 0)   # Speed in pixels per frame the
                        # x,y,z directions
    def __init__ (self, s)
    def getSpeed(self):
    def setSpeed(self, s):
    def move(self):
    def collision(self, gobject):
```

The syntax of this has the superclass **gobject** as a parameter (apparently) of the subclass **mobject** being defined. If an instance of a **gobject** is created, its __**init**__ method is called and the resulting reference has access to all of the methods in the **gobject** definition, just as one would expect. If an instance of **mobject** is created, the __**init**__ method of **mobject** is called, but not that of **gobject**. Nonetheless, all properties and methods of both classes are available through the **mobject** reference; that is, the following is legal:

```
m = mobject ( (12, 0, 0))     # Create mboject with speed
                              # (12,0,0)
m.draw()                      # Draw this object
```

even though an **mobject** does not possess a method **draw()**; the method defined in the parent class is accessible and will be used. When the **mobject** is created it is also a **gobject,** and all of the variables and methods belonging to a **gobject** are defined also. However, the __init__() method for **gobject** is not called unless the **mobject** __init__() method does so. This means that, for the **mobject**, the values of **position** and **visual** are not specified by the constructor and will take the default values they were given in the **gobject** class. If no such value was given, they will be undefined and an error will occur if they are referenced.

Calling the __init__() method of the parent class can be done as follows:

```
super().__init__((10,10,10), None)
```

In this instance the constructor for **gobject** is called, passing a position and a visual. This would normally be done only in the __init__() of the subclass.

Now consider the following code. The methods are mainly stubs that print a message, but the output of the program is instructive:

```
class gobject:                          class mobject (gobject):
# Object position in 3D                 # Speed in pixels per frame the
   position = (0, 0, 0)                 #  x,y,z directions
# Graphics that represent the              speed = (0, 0, 0)
# object                                   def __init__ (self, s):
   visual = None                              self.speed = s
   def __init__ (self,pos,vis):            super().__init__
       self.position = pos                        ((10,10,10), None)
       self.visual = vis                      print ("mobject init")
       print ("gobject init")          def getSpeed(self):
   def getPosition (self):                     print ("getSpeed")
       return self.position                    return self.speed
       print ("getPosition")           def setSpeed(self, s):
   def setPosition(self, p):                   print ("setSpeed")
       self.position = p                       self.speed = s
       print ("setPosition")           def move(self):
   def setVisual(self, v):                     print ("Move")
       self.visual = v                 def collision(self,
       print ("setVisual")                            gobject):
   def draw (self):                            print ("collision")
       print("Draw")
                                        g = gobject ((12, 12,12), None)
                                        m = mobject((13,13,13))
                                        print (m.getPosition())
                                        m.move()
                                        m.draw()
```

Output from this is:

```
gobject init  from the creation of the gobject instance g
```

```
gobject init    when m is created it calls the parent __
                init__
mobject init    from the mobject __init__ when m is created
(10, 10, 10)    m.getPosition, showing access to parent
                methods
Move            m.move call
Draw            m.draw call, again showing access to parent
                method
```

Attempting to call **g.move()** would fail because there is no **move()** method within the **gobject** class. Hence, if an object was passed to a function that would attempt to move it, it would be critical to know whether the parameter passed was a **gobject** or an **mobject**. Consider a method that moves an object **x** out of the path of an **mobject** instance if it can, or changes the path of the **mobject** if it cannot. This method, named **dodge()**, might do the following:

```
def dodge self, (x):
    c = x.getPosition()
    c = c +  (dx, dy, 0)
    x.setPosition (c)
```

However, if the parameter is an instance of a **gobject**, then it should not be moved. The function **isinstance()** can be used to determine this. The result of:

```
isinstance (x, gobject)
```

will be **True** if x is a **gobject** and **False** otherwise. If **False**, then it can't be moved and the **dodge()** method will have to move the current **mobject** out of the way instead:

```
def dodge self, (x):
    if isinstance(x, gobject):
        self.position = self.position + (dx, dy, 0)
    else:
        c = x.getPosition()
        c = c +  (dx, dy, 0)
        x.setPosition (c)
```

6.4 DUCK TYPING

In many programming languages, types are immutable and compatibility is enforced. This is not generally true in Python, but still there are operations that require specific types. Indexing into a string or tuple must be done using something much like an integer, and not by using a float. Now that classes can be used to build what amounts to new types, more attention should be paid to the things a type should offer and the requirements this puts on a programmer. A Python philosophy could be that the fewer restrictions the better, and this is a principle of *duck typing* as well.

It should not really matter what the exact type of the object is that is being manipulated, only that it possesses the properties that are needed. In a very simple case, consider the classes point and triangle that were discussed at the beginning of this chapter. It was proposed that both could have a **draw()** method that would create a graphical representation of these on the screen, and both have a **move()** method as well. A function could be written that would move a *triangle* away from a *point* and draw them both:

```
def moveaway (a, b)
    dx = a.getx()-b.getx()
    dy = a.gety()-d.gety()
    a.move (dx/10, dy/10)
    b.move (-dx/10, -dy/10)
```

Question: which of the parameters, **a** or **b**, is the *triangle*, and which is the *point*? Answer: it does not matter. Both classes have the methods needed by this function, namely **getx()**, **gety()**, and **move()**. Because of this the calls are symmetrical, and both of the following are the same:

```
moveaway (a, b)
moveaway (b, a)
```

In fact, a class that possesses these three methods can be passed to **moveaway()** and a result will be calculated without error. The essence of duck typing is that, so long as an object offers the service needed (i.e., a method of the correct name and parameter set) to another function or method, then the call is acceptable. There is a way to tell whether the class instance **a** has a **getx()** method. The built-in function **hasattr()**:

```
if hasattr (v1, "getx"):
    x = v1.getx()
```

The first argument is a class instance, and the second is the name of the method that is needed, as a string. It returns **True** if the method exists.

The name comes from the old saying that "if something walks like a duck and quacks like a duck, then it *is* a duck." As long as a class offers the things asked for, then it can be used in that context.

6.5 SUMMARY

A **class**, in the general sense, is a template for something that involves data and operations (functions). An **object** is an instance of a class, a specific instantiation of the template. Defining a class in Python involves specifying a class name and a collection of variables and functions that will belong to that class. A **method** is a function that belongs to a class, and so can have easy access to its internal data. As a first parameter, a method can be passed the **self** variable by default, which can be thought of as a reference to the object currently executing. Thus, within a method, the expression **self.x** refers to a variable **x** defined in the class. An object is created using the name of the class: for a class named **thing**, an instance **x** is created using **x = thing()**. When this occurs, if there is a method in **thing** named **__init__**, then that method is called. This is referred to as an initializer or a constructor.

Accessing methods in an object is done using a "dot" notation: **obj.method()**. Variables can be accessed in this way too.

A *subclass* is a class that possesses all of the properties of some other class, the *parent* class or *superclass*, plus some new ones. The data and methods of the parent class can be accessed from the subclass (or *child* class). A subclass of **thing** named **something** would be defined using the syntax:

class something(thing):

A class can represent a new type, where methods represent operations.

Public variables can be accessed and modified from outside of a class; *protected* variables can be accessed but not modified from outside of a class, and must begin with an underscore character (e.g., "_variable"); *private* variables can neither be accessed nor modified from outside of the class, and must begin with two underscore characters (e.g., "__variable").

The principle of *duck typing* is that it should not really matter what the exact type of the object is that is being manipulated, only that it possesses the properties that are needed.

Exercises

1. Define a class named *square* in which the construct takes the length of the side as a parameter. This class should have a method **area()** that computes and returns the area of the square.

2. Define a subclass of *square* named *button* that also has a location, passed as X and Y parameters to the constructor. A button always has a width of 10. The button class has the following methods:

   center()   Return the coordinates of the center of the button

   label(s)   Set the value of a text label to be drawn to s

3. Create a class *client*. A client is a data-only class that has no methods other than __init__(), but that holds data. In this case the client class holds a **name**, a **category** (retail or commercial), a **time** value (integer), and a **service** value (integer). All values are established when the instance is created by passing parameters to __init__(). Now create two subclasses of client, one for each category, *retail* and *commercial*.

4. Define a class named fraction that implements fractional numbers. The constructor takes the numerator and denominator as parameters, and the class provides methods to add, multiply, negate (make negative), print, and find the reciprocal of a fraction. Test this class by calculating:

$$14/16 * 3/4$$
$$1/2 - 1/4$$

   Bonus: results are reduced to smallest possible denominator.

5. Given the following class:
   class value:

```
def __init__ (self)
    self.val = randrange(0,100)
```

   and the initialization:

```
t = ()
for i in range(0,100):
    v = value()
    t = t + (v,)
```

write the code that scans the tuple **t** and locates the smallest integer saved in any of the class instances.

6. Create a class that simulates a NAND logic gate with three inputs. The output will be 1 unless all three inputs are 1, in which case the output is 0. Every time an input is changed, the output is changed to reflect the new state; thus, methods to set each input and to calculate the result will be needed, in addition to a method that returns the output.

Input 1	Input 2	Input 3	Output
0	0	0	1
0	0	1	1
0	1	0	1
0	1	1	1
1	0	0	1
1	0	1	1
1	1	0	1
1	1	1	0

Table 6.1
Truth table for the 3-input NAND gate.

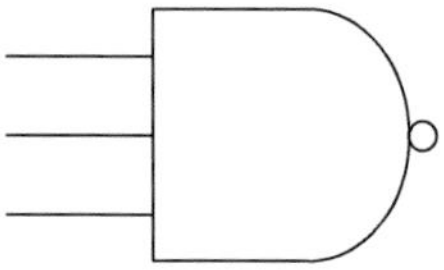

Figure 6.6
The symbolic representation used in a circuit.

7. A queue is a data structure that accepts new (incoming) data at one end (the back) and stores it in the order of arrival, giving the data at the front of the queue when requested. It's like a line at a cashier in a store: customers wait for the cashier in order of arrival. Implement a queue as a class; it has operations **into()** and **out()** to add things and remove things from the queue, and **empty()**, which returns **True** if the queue has no data in it. What is added to the queue are objects of a class *client*, as seen in Exercise 6.3 above.

8. Simulation: The gestation period for a rabbit is 28–32 days, and they will breed a week after having a litter. A female rabbit (a doe) will breed for the first time at about 100 days old. Create a class that represents a rabbit and simulate the growth of a rabbit population that starts with three does at day 0. Assume a litter size of between 3 and 8, and that half of the offspring will be male. Increase time by 1 day at a time and answer the question: "How many rabbits will there be after 1 year?" if the initial population is three does and one male (buck).

Notes and Other Resources

Notes on Python Classes:
http://www.jesshamrick.com/2011/05/18/an-introduction-to-classes-and-inheritance-in-python/
August 12, 2015. *http://componentsprogramming.com/using-the-right-terms-method/*
Duck typing in Python: *http://www.voidspace.org.uk/python/articles/duck_typing.shtml*

1. R. Chugh, P. Rondon, and R. Jhala. (2012, January). **Nested refinements: A logic for duck typing**, *ACM SIGPLAN Notices, 47*(1), 231–244.

2. Ole-Johan Dahl. (2002). **The birth of object orientation: The Simula languages**, in *Software Pioneers: Contributions to Software Engineering*, edited by Manfred Broy and Ernst Denert, Programming, Software Engineering, and Operating Systems Series, Springer, 79–80.

3. O.-J. Dahl and K. Nygaard. (1968). **Class and subclass declarations,** in *Simulation Programming Languages*, edited by J. Buxton, Proceedings from the IFIP Working Conference in Oslo, May 1967, North Holland.

4. Adele Goldberg and Alan Kay. **Smalltalk-72 Instruction Manual**, 44.

5. *ANSI Smalltalk Standard v1.9 199712 NCITS X3J20 draft*, Section 3.1, 9.

6. B. Liskov, A Snyder, R. Atkinson, and C. Schaffert. (1977). **Abstraction mechanisms in CLU**, *Communications of the ACM, 20*(8), 564–576.

GRAPHICS

In this chapter

Since the advent of *Windows*, computer graphics has been assumed as a feature of a computer. Before that it was a relatively rare thing, relegated to some research, to a few expensive Hollywood movies, and to science fiction. Believe it or not, the first use of computer graphics in a commercial motion picture was in the film *The Andromeda Strain* (1971) in which it was used to show a rotating 3D map (they called it an *electronic diagram*) of the underground installation where the action mainly takes place. A few years later the film *Westworld* (1973) used 2½ minutes of digitally processed video to show the visual perspective of an android. It was a very time-consuming and expensive task at that time; it took about 8 hours to process 10 seconds of film, or about 120 hours in all.

Modern computers all possess very fast graphics cards that perform most of the rendering tasks, and added to the built-in software on current operating systems, it allows for a very sophisticated yet simple-to-use graphical/windows interface to desktop computers. The graphics software is hierarchical; the screen itself is merely an array of picture elements (*pixels*) that can be set to any color, and it is difficult to see how that can be made to display complex pictures.

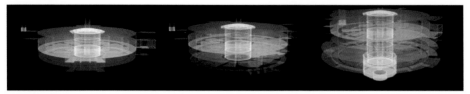

Figure 7.1
Stills from the first computer graphic sequence in a major motion picture:
The Andromeda Strain (Courtesy of Universal Studios Licensing LLC).

It has reached the point where everything seen on a computer screen is actually drawn—icons, windows, backgrounds, and even text.

What this means is that interacting with a computer is now done with graphics, not characters and text. Since that is the situation, it makes sense to permit a beginning programmer to experiment with programming graphics applications.

7.1 INTRODUCTION TO GRAPHICS PROGRAMMING

At the most primitive level of graphics software is the ability to set individual pixels. It is, as was mentioned, quite difficult to use this capability to create complex pictures. How is a dog drawn, or a building, or even just a straight line? Those things have been figured out, fortunately.

So at the bottom layer of software are functions that manipulate pixels. At the next level are lines and curves; these are the basic components of drawings and sketches. An artist with a pencil uses lines and curves to represent scenes. At the level above lines are functions that use lines to create other objects, such as rectangles, circles, and ellipses. These can be line drawings or can be filled with colors. The next higher levels can be argued about, but text is probably in the next software layer and then shading and images followed by 3D objects, which includes perspective transformation and textures.

Python does not itself have graphics tools, but various modules that are associated with Python do. The standard graphical user interface library for use with Python is *tkinter*. There are many features of this module, including the creation of windows, drawing, user interface widgets like buttons, and a host of other features. It is free and is normally included in the Python distribution but it can easily be downloaded and used with any Python version. Because there are many ways that Python can be configured on various different systems, the installation process will not be described in detail here. A graphics module will be described and is included on the DVD that accompanies this book, and it requires that *tkinter* be available. This is almost always true (remember that this book uses Python 3).

The library that allows graphics programming is called *Glib*. If the *Glib.py* file is in the same directory as the source code for the Python program that uses it, then it should work fine. *Glib* consists of a collection of functions that implement the first few levels of a graphics system and that create a window within which drawing can take place. It does not allow for interaction, animation, sound, or video, all of which are the subject of the next chapter.

7.1.1 Essentials: The Graphics Window and Colors

To start creating computer graphics, it is necessary to understand how colors and images are represented. When using a computer everything must be represented as numbers. A pixel is the color of a picture at a particular location, and so there must be a way to describe a color at that place. In physics frequency is used: each color has a specific frequency of electromagnetic radiation. Unfortunately, this does not map very well onto a computer display, because it is based on television technology. On a TV, there are three colors, red, green, and blue, that are used in various proportions to represent every color. There are red, green, and blue dots on the TV screen that are lit up to various degrees to create the colors that are seen. This is based on the way a human eye sees color; there are red, green, and blue sensors in the eye that in combination create our color perception. Another reason that frequency is not used is that there are colors that are not accurately represented as frequencies; they do not appear in the rainbow. The colors pink and brown are two examples.

So, each color in the graphics system is represented as the degree of red, green, and blue that combine to create that color. In that sense it is a bit like mixing paint. Yellow, on a computer, is a mixture of red and green. Each pixel therefore has three components: a red, green, and blue component. These could be expressed as percentages, but when using a computer it is better to select numbers between 0 and 255 (8 bits, or 1 byte) for each color. Each pixel requires 3 bytes of storage; actually 4 bytes in some cases, as will be seen shortly. If an image contains 100 rows of 100 pixels, then it has 10,000 pixels and is 10000*3=30000 bytes in size.

To humans, colors have names. Here's a list of some named colors and their RGB equivalents:

Color	Red	Green	Blue	Color	Red	Green	Blue
Black	0	0	0	Olive	128	128	0
White	255	255	255	Khaki	240	230	140
Red	255	0	0	Teal	0	128	128
Green	0	255	0	Sienna	160	83	45
Blue	0	0	255	Tan	210	180	140
Yellow	255	255	0	Indigo	75	0	130
Magenta	255	0	255	Orange	255	165	0

There are, of course, a great many more named colors, and even more colors that can be represented with RGB values in this way—16,777,202 of them in fact. Each pixel is a color value. All grey values have the special situation R=G=B, so there are 256 distinct values of grey ranging from black to white.

The graphics library provides functions for creating colors. The functions are **cvtColor()** and **cvtColor3()**:

cvtColor(g)   - Return a color value that has R=G=B = g, which is to say it specifies a grey level = g.

cvtColor3(r,g,b) - Return a color value that has the specified R,G,B values.

When using *Glib* the program must initialize the system before drawing anything. All graphics must take place between a call to **startdraw()** and a call to **enddraw()**. If **startdraw()** is not called then important items will not be initialized, most especially a drawing window will not be created and an error will occur at some time during execution. If **enddraw()** is not called then nothing will be drawn. For an abstract example, a hypothetical main program could be:

```
# start of program
   Many calculations
      . . .
```

```
    startdraw(width, height)
# Graphics calls
    . . .
    enddraw()
```

The function **startdraw()** accepts two parameters: the width and the height of the drawing region to be created. These values can be retrieved by a program using calls to the functions **Width()** and **Height()** if they are needed. **Startdraw()** creates the needed window and drawing area, initializes starting colors, fonts, and modes, but *does not open the window*. Nothing that is drawn will be visible until **enddraw()** is called.

7.1.2 Pixel Level Graphics

The only pixel level operation draws a pixel at a specified location; so, for example, the call:

```
point (x, y)
```

will set a pixel at column (horizontal position) **x** and row (vertical position) **y** to a color. What color? *Glib* has two default colors that can be set: the *fill* color, which is the color with which pixels will be drawn, polygons and ellipses will be filled, and characters will be drawn; and the *stroke* color, the color with which lines will be drawn. Setting the fill color is done using a call to the **fill()** function:

```
fill (200)          # Set the fill color to (200, 200, 200)
fill (100, 200, 100) # Set the fill color to (100, 200, 100)
```

Using one parameter sets the fill color to a grey value, whereas passing three parameters specifies the red, green, and blue values (respectively) of the fill color. Similarly the function **stroke()** can accept one or three parameters:

```
stroke (200)  # Set the stroke color to (200, 200, 200)
stroke (255, 0, 0) # Set the stroke color to
                   # (255, 0, 0) = red
```

There is one more function that could be thought to be in the pixel level category. The function **background()** is used to set the background color of the graphics window. Again, it can accept either one parameter (grey) or three (color). This leads to the first example.

Example: Create a Page of Notepaper

Notepaper has blue lines separated by enough space to write or print text between them. It often has a red vertical line indicating an indentation level, a place to begin writing. Drawing this is a matter of drawing a set of connected blue pixels in a set of rows, and then making a vertical column of red pixels. Here is one way to code this:

```
from Glib import *
y = 60                          # Height at which to start
startdraw(400, 600)             # Begin drawing things
background(255)                 # Paper should be white
fill (0, 0, 200)                # Fill color = pixel
                                # color = blue
for n in range (0, 27):         # Draw 30 horizontal blue
                                # lines
    for x in range (0,Width()): # Draw all pixels in one
                                # line
        point (x, y)            # Draw a blue pixel
    y = y + 20                  # The next line is 20
                                # pixels down
fill (200, 0, 0)                # Pixel color red
for y in range (0, Height()):   # Draw connected vertical
                                # pixels
    point (25, y)               # to form the margin line
enddraw()
```

The output of this program is shown in Figure 7.2a. When pixels are drawn immediately next to each other they appear to be connected, and so in this case they form horizontal and vertical lines. This is not easy to do for arbitrary lines; it is not obvious exactly which pixels to fill for a line between, say, (10, 20) and (99, 17). That's why the line drawing functions exist.

Example: Creating a Color Gradient

When creating a visual on a computer, the first step is to have a clear picture of what it will look like. For this example, imagine the sky on a clear day. The horizon shows a lighter blue than the sky directly above, and the color changes continuously all of the way from horizon to zenith. If a realistic sky background were needed, then it would be necessary to draw this using the tools available. What would the method be?

First, decide on what the color is at the horizon (y=ymax) and at the highest point in the scene (y=ymin). Now ask: "how many pixels between those points?" The change in pixel color will be the color difference from ymax to ymin divided by the number of pixels. Now simply draw rows of pixels beginning with the horizon and moving up the image (i.e., decreasing Y value), changing the color by this amount each time.

As an implementation, assume that the color at the horizon will be blue = (40, 40, 255) and the top of the image will be (40, 40, 128), a darker blue. The height of the image will be 400 pixels; the change in blue over that range is 127 units. Thus, the color change over each pixel is going to be 127.0/400, or about 0.32. A color can't change a fractional amount, of course, but what this means is that the blue value will decrease by 1 unit for every 3-pixel increase in height. Do not forget that the horizon is at the bottom of the image, which has the greatest Y coordinate value, so that an increase in Y means a decrease in height and vice versa.

The example program that implements this is:

```
from Glib import *
blue = 128
startdraw(400, 400)
delta = 127.0/Height()
for y in range (0, Height()):
    yy = Height()-y
    fill(40, 40, blue)
    for x in range(0, Width()):
        point (x, y)
    blue = blue + delta
enddraw()
```

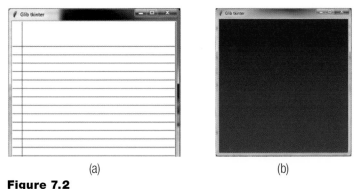

(a)   (b)

Figure 7.2
(a) A graphic of a sheet of lined paper; (b) a color gradient.

Figure 7.2b shows what the gradient image looks like (a full-color version of this and all images is on the accompanying disc).

7.1.3 Lines and Curves

Straight lines and curves are more complex objects than pixels, consisting of many pixels in an organized arrangement. A line is actually drawn by setting pixels, though. The fact that a **line()** function exists means that the programmer does not have to figure out what pixels to draw and can focus on the higher level construct, the line or curve.

A line is drawn by specifying the endpoints of the line. Using *Glib* the call is:

```
line ( x0, y0, x1, y1)
```

where one end of the line is at (x0,y0) and the other is at (x1,y1). The color of the line is specified by the stroke color. If any part of the line extends past the boundary of the window, that's OK; the line will be clipped to fit.

Example: Notepaper Again

The example of drawing a piece of notepaper can be done using lines instead of pixels, and will be a little faster. Set the stroke color to blue and draw a collection of horizontal lines (i.e., that have the same Y coordinate at the endpoints) separated by 20 pixels, as before. Then draw a vertical red line for the margin. The program is a variation on the previous version:

```
from Glib import *
y = 60                       # Height at which to start
startdraw(400, 600)          # Begin drawing things
background(255)              # Paper should be white
stroke (0, 0, 200)          # Fill color = pixel
                             # color = blue
for n in range (0, 27):      # Draw 30 horizontal blue lines
    line (0, y, Width(), y)  # Draw a blue horizontal line
    y = y + 20               # The next line is 20 pixels
                             # down
stroke (200, 0, 0)          # Pixel color red
line (25, 0, 25, Height())   # Draw a vertical red line
enddraw()
```

The output from this program is the same as that for the version that drew pixels, which is shown in Figure 7.2a.

A *curve* is trickier than a line, in that it is harder to specify. The method used in Glib is based on that in *tkinter*: a curve (arc) is defined as a portion of an ellipse from a starting angle for a specified number of degrees, as referenced from the center of the ellipse. The angle 0 degrees is horizontal and to the right; 90 degrees is upwards (decreasing Y value). The ellipse is defined by a bounding rectangle, specifying the upper left and lower right coordinates of a box that just holds the ellipse. So, looking at Figure 7.3, the rectangle defined by the upper left corner at (100, 50) and the lower right at (300, 200) has a center at (200, 125) and contains an ellipse slightly longer than it is high (upper left of the figure). The function that draws a curve is named **arc()**, and takes the upper left and lower right coordinates, a starting angle, and the size of the arc also expressed as an angle.

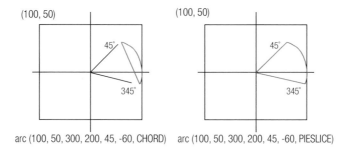

arc (100, 50, 300, 200, 45, -60, CHORD)   arc (100, 50, 300, 200, 45, -60, PIESLICE)

Figure 7.3
The result of calls to the arc function with various parameters.
This illustrates how the function can be used.

In the upper right of the figure is the arc drawn by the call **arc(100,50, 300, 200, 0, 90)**, which means that the part of the ellipse from the 0 degree point *counterclockwise* for 90 degrees will be drawn. The example at the lower left of the figure draws the curve from the 45-degree point for 90 degrees, resulting in the upper section of the ellipse being drawn. The final arc shown, at the lower right, uses a negative angle. The call **arc(100,50,300,200,45,-60)** starts at the 45-degree point and draws the arc *clockwise*, because the angle specified was negative.

This way of specifying arcs is fine for simple examples and single curves, but makes combining many arcs into a more complex curve rather difficult. Joining the ends together smoothly is the trick.

The arc() function has another parameter that can be specified. The seventh parameter tells the system what kind of arc to draw; the possibilities are ARC,

CHORD, and PIESLICE, and the default value ARC is illustrated in the figure. The call:

arc (100, 50, 300, 200, 45, -60, CHORD)

gives the result shown in Figure 7.3a. The result of the call:

arc (100, 50, 300, 200, 45, -60, PIESLICE)

is shown in Figure 7.34b. If filling is turned on, then these shapes would be filled with the default fill color. A major example involving curves/arcs is the pie chart program later in this chapter.

7.1.4 Polygons

For the purposes of discussion, a polygon will include all closed regions, including ellipses and circles. In that context, the **arc()** function can be used to draw circles and ellipses by specifying an angle very near to 360 degrees. The call:

```
arc (100, 100, 300, 300, 0, 359.9, ARC)
```

will draw a nearly complete circle, one that looks complete. However, there is a function that draws real circles and real ellipses: it is named **ellipse()**. In the default drawing mode the **ellipse()** function is passed the coordinates of the center

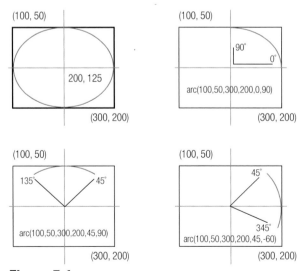

Figure 7.4
The CHORD parameter (left) and the PIESLICE parameter (Right) to the **arc** function.

of the ellipse and its width and height in pixels. If the width and height are equal, then the result is a circle. The call:

```
ellipse (100, 100, 30, 40)
```

draws the ellipse shown in Figure 7.4a. The color with which the ellipse is filled is the fill color. If no filling is desired then a call to **nofill()** turns off filling.

The default mode for drawing ellipses is referred to as CENTER mode, where the center of the ellipse is given. There are three others: RADIUS mode, in which the width and height parameters represent semi-major and semi-minor axes; CORNER mode in which the upper left corner is specified instead of the center; and CORNERS mode, in which the upper left and the lower right corner of the bounding box are specified. The mode is changed using a call to the function **ellipsemode**(), passing one of the four constants as the parameter: CENTER, RADIUS, CORNER, or CORNERS.

A rectangle is drawn using the **rect()** function. Again, there are four drawing modes. Consider the call **rect (x, y, w, h)**:

CENTER mode:	x, y are the coordinates of the center; w and h are the width and height.
RADIUS mode:	x, y are the coordinates of the center; w and r are the horizontal and vertical distances to an edge.
CORNER mode:	x, y are the coordinates of the upper left corner; w and h are the width and the height.
CORNERS mode:	x, y are the coordinates of the upper left corner; w and h are the coordinates of the lower right corner.

As with the ellipse, the rectangle drawing mode is changed by call a function, this time **rectmode()**.

The function **triangle()** draws—yes, a triangle. It is passed three points, which is to say six parameters: triangle (10,10, 20, 20, 30, 30) draws a triangle between the three points (10,10), (20,20), and (30,30).

7.1.5 Text

Drawing text is not complicated, but changing fonts is more of a problem. A font is saved on a file and has to be installed. If a font is specified by a program but does not exist, then either the finished image will look different from what was anticipated or an error will occur. Drawing text is performed by a call to text():

```
text ("Hello there.", x, y)
```

This draws the text string "Hello there!" in the graphics window so that the lower left of the text is at location x, y. The default text size is 12 pixels, but can be changed by a call to **textsize()** passing the size desired.

7.1.6 Example: A Histogram

A histogram is a way to visualize numerical data. It is especially useful for discrete data like colors or political parties or choices of some kind, but can also be used for continuous data. It displays counts of something against some other value, a category; percentage of people voting for specific parties, or the heights of grade six girls. It draws bars of various heights each representing the number of entries in each category. In this example the only problem is the plotting of the histogram, but the more general programming problem would include collecting and organizing the data. In this case the program will read a data file named "histogram.txt" that contains a few key values. The program variable names and the corresponding data file values are:

Variable	Contents
title	Title to be drawn at the top of the graph
ncategories	Number of categories
maxsize	Maximum size of any category
hlabel	Horizontal label
vlabel	Vertical label
val[1]	Value for category 1
val[2]	Value for category 2
...	
lab[1]	Label for category 1
lab[2]	Label for category 2
...	

When creating a graph, it pays to design it carefully. In this case the histogram will have the general appearance shown in Figure 7.5a. This visual layout helps with the details of the code, especially if the design has been drawn on graph paper so that the coordinates can easily be determined.

Assume that the variables needed have been read from the file (See: Exercise 2). Here's what the program must do:

Create a window about 600x600pixels in size.

Draw the horizontal and vertical axes (120, 80)

Draw the title and axis labels.

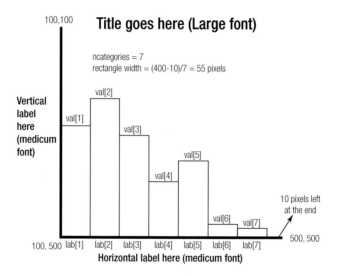

Figure 7.5
The visual design of a histogram before it is coded.

Determine the width and height of each rectangle.

For i in range (0,ncategories)

    Draw rectangle i

    Draw label i

Development can now proceed according to the plan. Create a window, set the background, and change the font to *Helvetica* (a favorite):

```
startdraw (600, 600)
background(180)
setfont("Helvetica")
```

Now draw the axes. Y-axis (vertical) from 100,100 to 100,500; X-axis (horizontal) from 100,500 to 500,500. Use a thicker line by setting the stroke weight to 3 pixels.

```
strokeweight (3)
line (100, 100, 100, 500)     # Y axis
line (100, 500, 500, 500)     # X axis
```

The title is in a large font (24 pixels) at the top part of the canvas (y=80)

```
textsize (24)              # Title uses a big font
text (title, 120, 80)      # It's at the top of the drawing
```

The horizontal axis label is in a smaller font (14 pixels) at the bottom of the canvas (y-580). It looks nicer if the text is basically centered. It's hard to do this exactly because there is no easy way to find out how long a string will be when drawn. However, a string that is 14 pixels in size and N characters long will be approximately N*14 pixels long when drawn. The axis is 400 pixels wide, so the amount of leftover space will be 400-N*14. Divide this in half to get the indentation of the left to approximately center the string!

```
textsize (14)                  # Labels use a medium sized font
cx = (400-len(hlabel)*14)/2 # How many pixels to indent
text (hlabel, 100+cx, 580)  # Centered at the bottom
```

Drawing the vertical label is more difficult, and so it will be done later. Make it a function and move on

```
verticalLabel(vlabel)
```

It is time to draw the rectangles. The width of each one will be the same, and is the width of the drawing area divided by the number of categories. The height will be the height of the drawing area divided by the maximum value to be drawn, **maxsize**. Compute those values and set the line thickness to one pixel, then set a fill color. Using the CORNER rectangle drawing mode is easiest for this application, as all that needs to be figured out is the upper left coordinate— the width and height are already known.

```
wid = (400-10)/ncategories    # Width of a box in pixels
ht = 390.0/maxsize     # Each value is this many pixels high
strokeweight (1)       # Rectangle outline 1 pixel thick
fill (200, 50, 200)    # Purple fill
rectmode (CORNER)      # Corner mode is easiest
```

Now make a loop that draws each rectangle. The X position of a rectangle is its index times the width of a rectangle—that's easy. The height of the rectangle is the value of that data element multiplied by the variable **ht** that was determined before. It's also a good idea to draw the value being represented at the top of the bar, which is just above and to the right of the rectangle's upper left.

```
for i in range(0,ncategories):
    ulx = 100 + i*wid+2         # Upper left X
    uly = 500 - val[i]*ht       # Upper left Y
    rect (ulx, uly, wid, val[i]*ht-2) # Height is val[i]*ht
    text (val[i], ulx+5, uly-2)  # Draw the value at the top
```

Finally, draw the labels for each rectangle. These are below the X axis, centered more or less within the horizontal region for each bin. The labels start at the Y axis (X=100 or so) and their location increases by the width of the bin during each iteration of the drawing loop. The Y location is fixed, at 520—the X axis is 500. Finally, an attempt to center these labels is done in the same way that it was done for the horizontal label, but the parameters are different.

```
x = 100+2    # Start at X=100 with extra for the thinck line
textsize(10)   # Use a small size font
fill (255, 255, 255)           # Text will be white
for i in range (0,ncategories): # for each rectangle
    cx = (wid-len(lab[i]*9))    # Indexnt to center the text
    if cx < 0: cx = 0           # Indent can't be negative
    text (lab[i], x+cx/2, 520)  # Draw the label
    x = x + wid                Next label is one rectangle right
enddraw()
```

Drawing the vertical label involves pulling out the individual words and drawing each one on its own pixel row. Words are separated by spaces (blanks), so one way of drawing the vertical text is to look for a space in the text, draw that word, then move down a few pixels, extract the next word, draw it, and so on until all words have been drawn. The text will be drawn starting at X=12, and the initial vertical position will be 200, moving down (increasing Y) by 40 pixels for each word. This is done by the function **verticalLabel()**, which is passed the string to be drawn:

```
def verticalLabel(v):
    lasti = 0              # Index of the next word in the string
    x = 12                 # Start drawing at X=12
    y = 200                # and Y=200
```

```
for i in range(0, len(v)): # Look at all characters in
                           # the label
    if (v[i] == " "):  # A black indicate the end of a
                       # word
        text (v[lasti:i], x, y)  #  Draw the word
        y = y + 40               # Move down 40 pxiels
        lasti = i                # end of this word is the
                                 # startof the next
    text (v[lasti:], x, y)       # Draw the last word
                                 # after exiting the loop
```

This program is available on the disk as two examples: "viperHisto.py" and "gradesHisto.py," which draw histograms of two different sets of data. The output from these two programs is shown in Figure 7.6.

This is a minimal program, and won't always create a nice image. Labels that are too long and use too many categories can cause badly formatted graphics.

7.1.7 Example: A Pie Chart

A pie chart is really just a histogram where the relative size of the categories is illustrated by an angle instead of the height of a rectangle. Each class is shown as a pie-shaped slice of a circle whose area is related to its proportion of the whole sample. Pie-shaped regions are easy, because **arc()** will draw them. So, using the same examples as before, look specifically at the grades data: there are 38 students whose grades are being displayed, and there are 360 degrees in a circle. A category of 10 students, for example (such as those receiving a "B" grade), will represent a pie slice that is 10/38 of the whole circle, or about 95 degrees. The process seems to be to determine how many degrees each category represents and draw a pie slice of that size until the whole pie (circle) is used up.

```
Create a window about 600x600 pixels in size
Draw the title label
Establish a fill color
For i in range (0,ncategories)
    Determine the angle A used for this category i
    Draw arc from previous angle for A degrees
    Draw label i for this slice
    Change the fill color
```

The labels may present a problem, as they may not fit inside the pie slice. It is probably best to display the label outside of the slice and draw a line to the slice that represents it.

The program is similar to that for the histogram. So, beginning after the label is drawn:

Find the total number of elements in all categories—in this case, the number of students in the class. This is the sum of all elements in **val.**

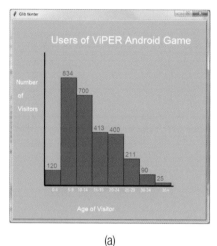

(a)

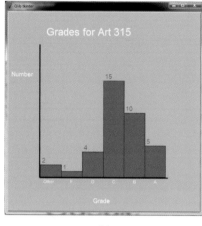

(b)

Figure 7.6
(a) Histogram of a set of data on access to a cell phone game;
(b) grades in a university art course.

```
totalSize = 0
r = 255
fill (r, 200, 200)
for i in range (0, ncategories):
    totalSize = totalSize + val[i]
```

Each count val[i] in a category represents **val[i]/totalSize** of the entire data set, or the angle **360.0*val[i]/totalSize**. The constant **360/totalSize** will be named **anglePerCount**. Now starting at angle 0 degrees, create a pie-shaped arc the size of each category:

```
angle = 0
for i in range(0,ncategories):
    span = val[i]*anglePerCount
    arc (150, 150, 450, 450, angle, span, PIESLICE)
```

Draw the label—this has been left for later, so call a function.

```
label (300, 300, 150, lab[i], angle, span)
```

The angle to start drawing must be increased so that the next arc starts where this one left off:

```
angle = angle + span
```

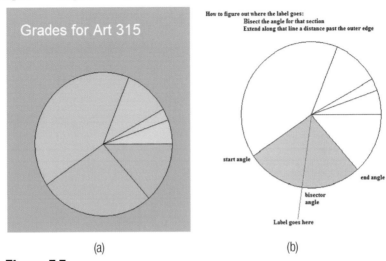

(a)   (b)

Figure 7.7
(a The pie chart drawn using Glib, (b) how to find the placement for labels on the chart.

Change the fill color so that each pie piece is a different color. The code below changes the red component just a little.

```
r = r - 20
fill (r, 200, 200)
```

Figure 7.7b shows a way to determine where a label could go; a line from the center of the circle through the outer edge points in the direction of the label. Simply find the x and y coordinates. The y coordinate is the sine of the angle * the distance from the center, and the x coordinate is the cosine of the angle * the same distance. For a distance, use the radius * 1.5. The function **label()** can now be written:

```
def label (xx, yy, r, s, a1, ap):
   angle = a1 + ap/2     # Bisector= start angle + half of
                         # span
   d = r*1.25            # Distance
   x = cos (angle*3.1415/180.) * d + xx  # Angle is radians
   y = -sin (angle*3.1415/180.) * d + yy # Y is inverted
   text (s, x, y)
```

The result is illustrated in Figure 7.8.

There's one more thing that could be added to the pie chart program. Sometimes, one of the pieces is moved out of the circle to emphasize it. It turns out that this useful feature can be implemented in a manner very similar to the way the labels were drawn. Find the bisector of the angle for that section and before it is drawn identify a new center point for that piece a few pixels down that bisector. This pulls the piece away from the original circle center.

The code is brief, and is included below to be complete:

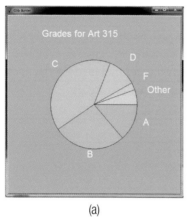 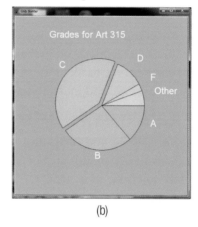

(a)   (b)

Figure 7.8
(a) The basic pie chart with labels;
(b) the chart with one of the sections separated to emphasize it.

```
def pull (x, y, a1, ap):
   angle = a1 + ap/2   # a1 is the angle, ap is the span
   d = 12              # Pull out only a small amount
                       # (12 pixels)
   y = -sin (angle*3.1415/180.) * d + y  # New center
                                         # coordinates
   x = cos (angle*3.1415/180.) * d + x
   arc (x-150, y-150, x+150, y+150, a1, ap, PIESLICE)
```

This function is called instead of the call to **arc()** for the piece that is to be pulled out. A sample output is shown in Figure 7.8b.

7.1.8 Images

Unlike the graphical components displayed so far, an *image* is fundamentally a collection of pixels. A camera captures an image and stores it digitally as pixels, and so it was never anything else. Displaying an image means drawing each pixel in the appropriate color, as captured.

Glib can load and display images in a limited fashion. Images reside in files of various formats: JPEG, GIF, BMP, PNG. The same image in each format is stored in a quite distinct way, and it can require a lot of code just to get the pixels from the image. Python, through *tkinter*, allows GIF image files to be read directly. Any image file can be converted into a GIF by using one of a hundred conversion tools, including *Photoshop*, *Paint*, and *Gimp* to name a few.

The function **loadImage()** will read a GIF image file and return an image of a sort that can be displayed in the graphics window. The file "charlie.gif" is a photo of checkpoint Charlie in Berlin, and has been included on the accompanying disc. It could be read into a Python program with the call:

```
im = loadImage ("charlie.gif")
```

The variable **im** now holds the image, and while the details are not completely relevant, it is good to know that **im.width** and **im.height** give the width and height of the image in pixels. Displaying the image is a matter of calling the function image() and passing the image and the coordinates where the upper left corner of the image is to be placed. A call such as:

```
image (im, 0, 0)
```

would display the checkpoint Charlie image.

Figure 7.9
Original test image – Checkpoint Charlie in Berlin.

The smallest Python program (using *Glib*) that can load and display an image is thus 5 lines:

```
from Glib import *
startdraw(600, 600)
im = loadImage ("charlie.gif")
image (im, 0, 0)
enddraw()
```

However, this displays the image in a window that is bigger than it is. That may be OK, but often an image is to be used as a background image, and the size of the window should be the same as the image size. If that is what is needed there is a special function to call: **imageSize()**. It must be called before **startdraw()**, of course, because it returns the size of the image, and hence the size to be passed to **startdraw()**. It returns a tuple that has the width as the first component and the height as the second.

Opening a window that is the same size as an image is accomplished as follows:

```
from Glib import *
s = imageSize("charlie.gif")
startdraw(s[0], s[1])
im = loadImage("charlie.gif")
image (im, 0, 0)
enddraw()
```

The output of this program is shown in Figure 7.9.

Pixels

An image as returned by **loadImage()** is a built-in type named *PhotoImage*. It is really not designed to be used for much except displaying in the window, but some more advanced operations are possible, if slow. For example, individual pixel values can be extracted and modified. *Glib* offers a handful of low-level functions to make pixel operations easier.

An image consists of rows and columns of pixels, and a pixel is a color. The color of the pixel at horizontal position **x** and vertical position **y** of image **pic** can be accessed using the call:

```
c = getpixel(pic, x, y)
```

The value of **c** is a color, and the components of this can be accessed using the functions:

```
r = red(c)
g = green(c)
b = blue(c)
```

Setting the value of the pixel at location (x,y) is accomplished by calling setpixel(). It requires that the image, the coordinates, and the color be passed as parameters:

```
setpixel (pic, x, y, c)
```

These functions operate on an image, not directly on the screen display. Changes to an image will only be visible if they are done before the image is displayed.

Example: Identifying a Green Car

There is a pattern here that is important to recognize when working with images at the pixel level—the raster scan. All of the pixels in the image are usually examined one at a time using a nested loop. It will look like this:

```
for i in range(0, Width()):
    for j in range(0, Height()):
        # Do something to pixel (i,j)
```

This example uses color to identify the pixels that belong to a car in an image, as seen in Figure 7.10. The problem requires identifying pixels that are "green" and somehow making them stand out in the image. What is green? All pixels have a green component. When something is green, the green component is the most significant one; it is larger than the red and blue components by some margin. In this case that margin will be arbitrarily set at 20, and if it does not work then it can be modified. If a pixel is green it will be set to black, otherwise it will become white; this will make the pixels that belong to the car stand out.

The program begins by creating a window and reading in the image:

```
startdraw(640, 480)
im = loadImage ("eclipse.gif")
```

Now look at all of the pixels, searching for a green one:

```
for i in range(0, Width()):
    for j in range(0, Height()):
        c = getpixel(im, i,j)   # Get the color of the pixel
                                # (i,j)
```

If the pixel is green, then change it to black. Otherwise, change it to white:

```
if green(c)>(red(c)+20) and green(c)>(blue(c)+20): # Green?
    setpixel (im, i, j, cvtColor3 (0,0,0))          # Black
else:
    setpixel (im, i, j, cvtColor3(255,255,255))     # White
```

An image can be saved into a file by calling the *Glib* function **save()**:

```
save (im, "out.gif")
```

(a)   (b)

Figure 7.10
(a) A green car; (b) the result of changing green pixels to black and all others to white.

The output of this program is shown in Figure 7.10b. There are some "green" pixels that do not belong to the car, but most of the car pixels have been identified.

Example: Thresholding

Image processing is a large subject all by itself, and this particular library is not the best choice for exploring it in detail. There are some basic things that can be done, and common ones include thresholding, edge enhancement, noise reduction, and count, all of which can be done using *Glib*. Thresholding in particular is an early step in many image-analysis processes. It is the creation of a bi-level image, having just black and white pixels, from a grey or color image. The previous example is different from thresholding in that a particular color was being searched for. In thresholding a simple grey value T, the *threshold*, is used to separate pixels into black and white: all pixels having a value smaller than T will be black, and the others will be white.

Glib has one more function that is useful, especially in this context. The function **grey()** will convert a color into a simple grey level, which is an integer in the range 0 to 255. It finds the mean of the three color components. The thresholding program begins in the same way as did the previous example. Look at the color of all of the pixels in the image, one at a time:

```
startdraw(640, 480)
im = loadImage ("eclipse.gif")
```

```
for i in range(0, Width()):
    for j in range(0, Height()):
        c = getpixel(im, i,j)
```

This is the standard scan of all pixels. Now convert the color c to a grey level and compare that against the threshold T=128. Pixels having a grey level below 128 will be set to black, the remainder will be white:

```
if g < T:
        setpixel (im, i, j, cvtColor3 (0,0,0))
    else:
        setpixel (im, i, j, cvtColor3(255,255,255))
image (im, 0, 0)
save (im, "out.gif")
enddraw()
```

Figure 7.11
Thresholded version of the green car image of Figure 7.10

The result, the image displayed by this program, is shown in Figure 7.11.

Transparency

A GIF image can have one color chosen to be transparent, meaning that it will not show up and any pixel drawn previously at the same location will be visible. This is very handy in games and animations. Images are rectangular, whereas most objects are not. Consider a small image of a doughnut; the pixels surrounding it and in the hole can have the pixels set to be transparent, and then when the image is drawn over another one the background will be seen through the hole.

The transparency value must be set within the image by a program. Photoshop, for example, can do this. Then when Python displays the images, the background image must be displayed first, followed by the images with transparency. As an example, Figure 7.12a shows a photo of the view through the rear and side windows of a Volvo. The window glass area, the places where transparency is desired, have been colored yellow. The color yellow was then selected in Photoshop as transparent, and the image was saved again as a GIF. A short Python program using *Glib* will display a background image and the car image over it, and the background will be seen through the window regions as in Figure 7.12b. The program is:

```
from Glib import *
s = imageSize("car.gif")        # Get size of image
startdraw(s[0], s[1])           # Open window of the right
                                # size
s  = loadImage("perseus.gif")   # Background image
t = loadImage ("car.gif")       # Car image with transparency
image (s, 0, 0)                 # Display background first
image (t, 0, 0)                 # then display the car image
enddraw()
```

7.1.9 Generative Art

In *generative art* an artwork is generated by a computer program that uses an algorithm created by the artist. The artist is the creative force, the designer of the visual display, and the computer implements it. There are many generative artists to be found on the Internet: one list can be found here:

http://blog.hvidtfeldts.net/index.php/generative-art-links/

(a)   (b)

Figure 7.12
(a) An image of a car interior. The window areas have been edited manually to be some color that does not appear in the image otherwise. This color is then set to be transparent by Photoshop or some other editing tool. (b) When the background image is drawn with the car image over it, the background can be seen through the windows.

Much generative art is dynamic, which is to say it involves motion and/or interaction, but many works are equivalent to paintings and drawings (*static*). *Glib* could be a tool for helping create these sorts of generative art works. Unlike other sorts of computer programs, those associated with art do not have a known predictable result that can be affirmed as correct or not. It is true that an artist begins with an idea of what their work should look like and what the message underlying it is, but paintings, sculptures, and generative works rarely finish the way they began.

So, either begin with an idea of what the image will look like or admit that the whole thing is an experiment and couch the idea in terms of a sentence or two. Here's one such sentence: "Imagine a collection of straight lines radiating from a set of randomly placed points within the drawing window, with each set of lines drawn in a saturated strong color."

Now an attempt would be made to create such an image using the functions that Glib offers. It is often the case that the first few tries are in error, but that one of them is interesting. An artist would pursue the interesting course instead of sticking to the original idea, of course. Here is an example: the code below was written with the idea that it would produce a collection of lines radiating from the point (400,600) from 0 degrees (horizontal right) to 180 degrees (horizontal left) with the color varying slightly:

```
r = 255
for i in range (1, 180, 2):
    stroke (r, 128, 128)
    line (400, 600, cos(i*conv)*500, sin(i*conv)*500)
    r = r - 0.5
```

The call to **line()** should have been:

```
line (400, 600, 400+cos(i*conv)*500, 600-sin(i*conv)*500)
```

so as to invert the Y coordinate. Instead, this created a much more interesting image. The code for one of the four loops in the final code is:

```
x = randrange(100, Width())
y = randrange (100, Height()-100)
r = 255
for i in range (1, 180, 2):
    stroke (128, r, 128)
    line (x, y, sin(i*conv)*500, cos(i*conv)*500)
    r = r - 0.5
```

Sometimes a small error can result in a more interesting result. This is rarely the case when writing scientific or commercial software.

 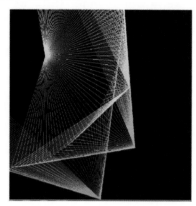

Figure 7.13
A generative artwork created partly by accident.

Generative art should be under the control of the artist, but does use random elements to add interest to the image. In the piece *Snow Boxes* by Noah Larsen a set of rectangles is drawn, but the specific size and location of these rectangles is random within constrained parameters. The overall color is also random within specified boundaries. Each rectangle is drawn as a collection of white pixels with a density that has been defined specifically for that rectangle so that the image consists of spatters of white pixels that can be identified as rectangular regions (Figure 7.14). Each time the program is executed a different image is created. The program for *Snow Boxes* was originally written in a language called *Processing*, but a Python version that uses *Glib* is:

```
# Snow boxes
# Original by Noah Larsen, @earlatron
from Glib import *
from random import *

startdraw (640, 480)
background(randrange(0,75), randrange(150,255),
randrange(0,75))

fill (255, 255, 255)
for i in range(0,10000):
    point (randrange(0,Width()), randrange(0,Height()))
for i in range(0,20):
```

```
xs = randrange (0, Width())
ys = randrange (0, Height())
xe = randrange (xs, xs+randrange(30, 300))
ye = randrange (ys, ys+randrange(30, 300))
for j in range(0,10000):
    point (randrange(xs, xe+1),randrange(ys, ye+1))
enddraw()
```

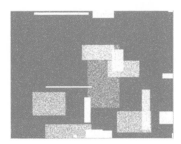 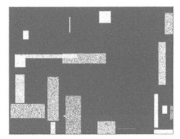

Figure 7.14
Output samples from the *Snow Boxes* program, examples of generative art.

7.2 SUMMARY

Since the advent of *Windows*, computer graphics has been assumed as a feature of a computer, but this has not always been true. Python does not have built-in features for doing graphics, but the standard user interface library *tkinter* does, and the library that accompanies this book, *Glib*, expands this and makes it more accessible. Drawing is accomplished by setting pixels within a drawing window to a desired color. Colors are specified by giving the amount of red, green, and blue that comprise the color.

Glib and most graphics libraries allow the user to draw lines, polygons, text, images, and to set pixels. These basic functions are combined by the programmer to create desired visualizations, such as histograms and pie charts.

Exercises

1. Write a Python program to create the image shown in Figure 7.15a. The image is grey, but the colors that are to be used to fill the circles are given as text. You need not include the text in your output.

2. Draw a set of 10 lines separated horizontally by 20 pixels, each parallel to the line specified by the end points (10, 20) and (200, 421). These lines may begin anywhere in the window.

3. Draw a pyramid using dark grey bricks (rectangles) as components. The base of the pyramid is to be 15 bricks horizontally, and each successive level is one brick smaller. (Figure 7.15b)

4. Draw a checkerboard. Each square should be 20x20 pixels, and the squares are red or yellow, alternating. A checkerboard is 8x8 squares.

5. Draw a triangle, a square, a regular pentagon, and a regular hexagon. Label these with their names as text above the shapes.

6. Write a program to draw a visual work in the visual style of Piet Mondrian's famous rectangular compositions, an example of which is shown in Figure 7.15d. Could triangular shapes be used instead of rectangles?

7. Modify the pie chart program so that the data is read from a file name "piein.dat."

8. Write a program that reads the file name of an image and displays the image in a window that is correctly sized.

9. The provided image named "digit.gif" contains some pixels that are pure red; that is, they have a pixel value of (255,0,0). Write a program that locates these pixels, draws a circle around them in a display of the image, and prints their x and y coordinates.

10. An *edge* in an image has the property that the pixel values on one side of the edge are significantly different (i.e., more than 40 levels) from those on the other side. Write a python program that reads an image and sets pixels at vertical edge locations to black and all other pixels to white; it then displays the result in a window. *Hints*: convert the image to grey or select one color value for the edges; make a working copy of the image.

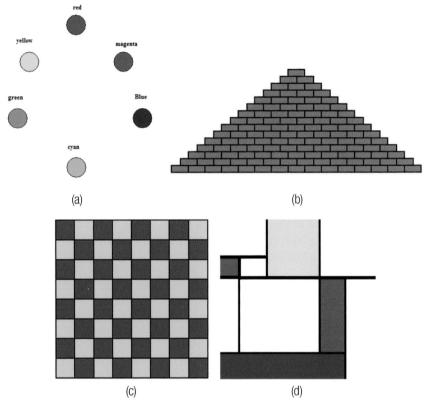

Figure 7.15
Figures to accompany the exercises.

Notes and Other Resources

Tkinter - Python interface to Tcl/Tk, *https://docs.python.org/3/library/tkinter.html*
Tkinter 8.5 reference. *http://infohost.nmt.edu/tcc/help/pubs/tkinter/web/index.html*
http://www.generativeart.com/

1. **John** F. Hughes, Andries van Dam, Morgan McGuire, David F. Sklar, James D. Foley, Steven K. Feiner, and Kurt Akeley. (2013). **Computer Graphics: Principles and Practice, 3rd Edition**, Addison-Wesley Professional.

2. Robin Landa, Rose Gonnella, and Steven Brower. (2006). **2D Visual Basics for Designers**, Delmar Cengage Learning.

3. Jeffrey McConnell. (2005). **Computer Graphics: Theory into Practice**, Jones & Bartlett Learning.

4. Matt Pearson. (2011). **Generative Art**, Manning Publications, ISBN-10: 1935182625.

Table 7.1
Glib functions and constants contained in the tkinter version.

BLACK	The color black	text (s, x, y)	Draw the string s at the point x, y
WHITE The color whit	The color white	strokeweight (s)	Draw lines that are s pixels wide
RED	The color red	cvtColor (z)	Convert integer z to a grey level
GREEN	The color green	cvtColor3(r,g,b)	Convert 3 integers to an RGB color
BLUE	The color blue	textsize(n)	Set text drawing size to n pixels
BACKSPACE	The backspace character	loadImage (s)	Read an image from a file and return it
CENTER	Center mode for ellipses and rectangles	image (im, x,y)	Display an image at (x,y) as upper left
RADIUS	Radius mode for ellipses and rectangles	copyImage(im)	Make a copy of the image and return it
CORNER	Corner mode for ellipses and rectangles	red(c)	Return the integer value of the red component of c
CORNERS	Corners mode for ellipses and rectangles	green(c)	Return the integer value of the green component of c
Width()	Returns the width of the window	blue(c)	Return the integer value of the blue component of c
Height()	Returns the height of the window	grey(c)	Convert the color c to grey

fill(r,g,b)	Set fill color	getpixel(im,i,j)	Get the pixel value (a color) at image pixel (i,j)
fill(g)	Set fill grey value	setpixel(im,i,j,c)	Set the pixel at image location (i,j) to color c
stroke (r, g, b)	Set line and outline color	save (im, s)	Save the image to a file named by the string s
stroke (g)	Set grey level for lines and outlines	background2(g)	Set the background color to grey value g
nostroke()	Turn off outline drawing	background(r,g,b)	Set the background color to (r,g,b)
ellipsemode(z)	Set ellipse drawing mode to where z is one of the following: CENTER, RADIUS, CORNER, or CORNERS	rectmode(m)	Set rectangle drawing mode to one of the following: CENTER, RADIUS, CORNER, or CORNERS
ellipse(x, y, w, h)	Draw an ellipse at x,y with specified width and height	rect (x1,y1, x2,x2)	Draw a rectangle at the given coordinates using the current mode
line(x0,y0,x1,y1)	Draw a line between the two coordinates	imageSize(s)	Examine the image file named by s and determine its size in pixels. Return a tuple (width, height)
point(x, y)	Draw a point (pixel) at x,y	arc (x0,y0,x1,y1,start, angle, s)	Draw an arc. See the description in this chapter.
triangle (x0,y0, x1,y1, x2,y2)	Draw a tringle between the three points	startdraw (width, height)	Begin drawing in an area having the specified size
		enddraw()	Stop calling Glib functions and display what was drawn

MANIPULATING DATA

■ ■ ■ ■ ■ ■

In this chapter

A fair definition of *Computer Science* would be *the discipline that concerns itself with information.* Computers are an enabling technology, but computer science is largely about how to store, retrieve, represent, compress, display, transmit, and otherwise handle information. Python happens to be pretty good at offering facilities for manipulating information or, at a lower level, data. Data becomes information when a person can interpret it, and information becomes knowledge once understood.

Repeating a theme of this book, data on a computer is stored as numbers no matter what its original form was. Computers can only operate on numbers, so an important aspect of using data is the representation of complex things as numbers. Based on many years of experience, it seems to be possible in all cases, and the manner in which the data is represented as numbers is reflected in the methods used to operate on them.

This chapter will be an examination of how certain kinds of data are represented and the consequences insofar as computer programs can use these data. Python in particular will be used for this examination, although some of the discussion is more general. Of course, the discussion will be driven by practical things and by how things can be accomplished using Python.

Most data consist of measurements of something, and as such are fundamentally numeric. Astronomers measure the brightness of stars, as an example, and note how they vary or not as a function of time. The data consists of a collection of numbers that represent brightness on some arbitrary scale; the units of measurements are always in some sense arbitrary. However, units can be converted from one kind to another quite simply, so this is not a problem. Biologists frequently count things, so again their data is fundamentally numeric. Social scientists ask questions and collect answers into groups, again a numeric result. What things are not?

Photographs are common enough in science and are not numeric values but are, instead, *visual*; they relate to a human sense that can be understood by other humans easily, rather than to an analytical approach. Of course most photographs are ultimately analyzed by a computer these days, so there must be a way to represent them digitally. Another human sense that is used to examine data is *hearing*. Birds make songs that indicate many things, including what they observe and their willingness to mate. Sounds are vibrations, and can indicate problems with machinery, the approach of a vehicle, the presence of a predator, or the current state of the weather. *Touch* is less often used, but is essential in the control of objects by humans. A person controlling a device at a great distance can profit from the ability to feel the touch of a tool across a computer network.

Then there are search engines, which can be thought of as an extension of human memory and reasoning. The ability of humans to access information has improved hugely over the past twenty years. If the phrase "python data manipulation" is entered into the Google search engine, over half a million results are returned. True, many may not directly relate to the query as it was intended, but part of the problem will be in the phrasing of the request. By the way, the first response to the query concerns the *pandas* module for data analysis, which may in fact have been the right answer.

How is all of this done? It does take some clever algorithms and good programming, but it also requires a language that offers the right facilities.

8.1 DICTIONARIES

A Python *dictionary* is an important structure for dealing with data, and is the only important language feature that has not been discussed until now. One reason is that a dictionary is more properly an advanced structure that is implemented in terms of more basic ones. A *list*, for example, is a collection of things (integers, reals, strings) that is accessed by using an index, where the index is an integer. If the integer is given, the contents of the list at that location can be retrieved or modified.

A dictionary allows a more complex, expensive, and useful indexing scheme: it is accessed by content. Well, by a *description* of content at least. A dictionary can be indexed by a string, which in general would be referred to as a *key*, and the information at that location in the dictionary is said to be *associated* with that key. An example: a dictionary that returns the value of a color given the name. A color, as described in Chapter 7, is specified by a red, green, and blue component. A tuple such as (100,200,100) can be used to represent a color. So in a dictionary named **colors** the value of **colors["red"]** might be (255,0,0) and **colors["blue"]** is (0,0,255). Naturally, it is important to know what names are possible or the index used will not be legal and will cause an error. So **colors["copper"]** may result in an index error, which is called a *KeyError* for a dictionary.

The Python syntax for setting up a dictionary differs from anything that has been seen before. The dictionary **colors** could be created in this way:

```
colors = {'red':(255, 0, 0), 'blue':(0,0,255),
          'green':(0,255,0)}
```

The braces { ... } enclose all of the things being defined as part of the dictionary. Each entry is a pair, with a key followed by a ":" followed by a data element. The pair "red":(255,0,0) means that the key "red" will be associated with the value (255,0,0) in this dictionary.

Now the name **colors** looks like a list, but is indexed by a string:

```
print (colors['blue'])
```

The index is called a *key* when referring to a dictionary. That's because it is not really an index, in that the string can't directly address a location. Instead the key is searched for, and if it is a legal key (i.e., has been defined) the corresponding data element is selected. The definition of **colors** creates a list of keys and a list of data:

Location	Keys	Data
0	"red"	(255, 0, 0)
1	"blue"	(0, 0, 255)
2	"green"	(0, 255, 0)

When the expression **colors["blue"]** is seen, the key "blue" is searched for in the list of all keys. It is found at location 1, so the result of the expression is the data element at 1, which is (0,0,255). Python does all of this work each time a dictionary is accessed, so while it looks simple it really involves quite a bit of work.

New associations can be made in assignment statements:

```
colors['khaki'] = (240,230,140)
```

Indeed, a dictionary can be created with an empty pair of braces and then have values given using assignments:

```
colors = {}
colors['red'] = (255, 0, 0)
    .   .   .
```

As with other variables, the value of an element in a dictionary can be changed. This would change the association with the key; there can only be one thing associated with a key. The assignment:

```
colors['red'] = (200.,0,0)
```

reassigns the value associated with the key "red." To delete it altogether use the **del()** function:

```
del(colors['blue'])
```

Other types can be used as keys in a dictionary. In fact, any immutable type can be used. Hence it is possible to create a dictionary that reverses the association of name to its RGB color, allowing the color to be used as the key and the name to be retrieved. For example:

```
names = {}
names[(255,0,0)] = 'red'
names[(0,255,0)] = 'green'
```

This dictionary uses tuples as keys. Lists can't be used because they are not immutable.

8.1.1 Example: A Naive Latin – English Translation

A successful language translation program is difficult to implement. Human languages are unlike computer languages in that they have nuances. Words have more than one meaning, and many words mean essentially the same thing. Some words mean one thing in a particular context and a different thing in another context. Sometimes a word can be a noun and a verb. It is very confusing. What this program will do is substitute English words for Latin ones, using a Python dictionary as the basis.

From various sites on the Internet a collection of Latin words with their English counterparts has been collected. This is a text file named "latin.txt." It has the Latin word, a space, and the English equivalent on single lines in the file. The program will accept text from the keyboard and translate it into English, word by word, assuming that it originally consisted of Latin words. The file of Latin words has 3129 items, but it should be understood that one word in any language has many forms depending on how it is used. Many words are missing in one form or another.

The way the program works is pretty simple. The file of words is read in and converted into a dictionary. The file has a Latin word, a comma, and an English word, so a line is read, converted to a tuple using **split(),** and the Latin word is used as a key to store the English word into the dictionary.

Next, the program asks the user for a phrase in Latin, and the user types it in. The phrase is split into individual words and each one is looked up in the dictionary and the English version is printed. This will not work very well in general, but is a first step in creating a translation program. The code looks like this:

```
def load_words (name, dict):    # Read the file of words
    f = open (name, "r")
    s = f.readline()            # Read one word pair
    while s != "":              # exit when the file has been
                                # read
        c = s.split (",")       # Split at the comma
        if len(c)<2:            # Possible error: no words?
```

```
            s = f.readline()    # Read next and continue
            continue
        sw = c[0].strip()       # Get the latin and English
                                # words.
        ew = c[1].strip()
        if len(ew) <=0:         # OK?
            s = f.readline()    # Nope. Just skip it.
            continue
        if ew[-1] == "\n":      # Get ride of the endline
            ew = ew[0:-2]
        dict[sw] = ew           # Place in dictionary
        s = f.readline()        # Next word pair from the file
    f.close()                   # Always close when done

dict = {}
load_words("latin.txt", dict)   # Read all of the word pairs

inp = input("Enter a latin phrase ") # Get the Latin text
while inp != "":                      # Done?
    book = inp.split(" ")             # Split at words
    for i in range(0,len(book)):      # For each word this
line
        sword = book[i].lower()           # Lower case
        try:
            enword = dict[sword]      # Look up Latin word
            print (enword, end="")    # Print English version
        except:
            print (sword, end="")     # Latin not in
                                      # dictionary
        print (" ", end="")           # Print the Latin
    print (".")
    inp = input("Enter a latin phrase ") # Do it again
```

Of course translation is more complex than just changing words, and that's all this program does. Still, sometimes it does not do too badly. A favorite Latin phrase from the TV program *The West Wing* is "Post hoc ergo propter hoc." Given this phrase the program produced:

after this therefore because of this.

which is a pretty fair translation. Trying another, "All dogs go to heaven" was sent to an online translation program and it gave

omnes canes ad caelum ire conspexerit

This program here translates it back into English as:

"all dogs to sky go conspexerit."

The word 'conspexerit' was not successfully translated, so it was left as it was (the online program translates that word as "glance"). This is still not terrible.

Sadly, it makes a complete hash of the Lord's Prayer:

Pater noster qui es in caelis sanctificetur nomen tuum.

Adveniat regnum tuum.

Fiat voluntas tua sicut in caelo et in terra.

Panem nostrum quotidianum da nobis hodie et dimitte nobis debita nostra sicut et nos dimittimus debitoribus.

Fiat voluntas tua sicut in caelo et in terra.

Amen

Is turned into:

father our that you are against heavens holy name your.

down rule your.

becomes last your as against heaven and against earth.

bread our daily da us day and dimitte us debita our as and us forgive debtors.

becomes last your as in heaven and in earth.

amen

A useful addition to the code would be to permit the user to add new words into the dictionary. In particular, it could prompt the user for words that it could not find, and perhaps even ask whether similar words were related to the unknown one, such as "dimittimus" and "dimitte." Of course, being able to have some basic understanding of the grammar would be better still.

8.1.2 Functions for Dictionaries

The power of the store-fetch scheme in the dictionary is impressive. There are some methods that apply mainly to dictionaries and that can be useful in more complex programs. The method **keys()** returns the collection of all of the keys that can be used with a dictionary. So:

```
list(dict.keys())
```

is a list of all of the keys, and this can be searched before doing any complex operations on the dictionary. The list of keys is not in any specific order, and if they need to be sorted then:

```
sorted(dict.keys())
```

will do the job. The **del()** method has been used to remove specific keys but **dict. clear()** will remove all of them.

The method **setdefault()** can establish a default value for a key that has not been defined. When an attempt is made to access a dictionary using a key, an error occurs if the key has not been defined for that dictionary. This method makes the key known so that no error will occur and a value can be returned for it; **None**, perhaps.

```
dict.setdefault(key, default=None)
```

Other useful functions include:

dict.copy()	returns a (shallow) copy of dictionary
dict.fromkeys()	creates a new dictionary setting keys and values; e.g., dict.fromkeys(("one", "two"), 3) creates {("one", 3), ("two", 3)}
dict.items()	returns a list of *dict*'s (key, value) tuple pairs.
dict.values()	returns list of dictionary *dict*'s values
dict.update(dict2)	adds the key-value pairs from dictionary dict2 to dict

The expression **key in dict** is True if the key specified exists in the dictionary dict.

8.1.3 Dictionaries and Loops

Dictionaries are intended for random access, but on occasion it is necessary to scan through parts or all of one. The trick is to create a list from the pairs in the dictionary and then loop through the list. For example:

```
for (key,value) in dict.items():
    print (key, " has the value ", value)
```

The keys are given in an internal order which is not alphabetical. It is a simple matter to sort them, though:

```
for (key,value) in sorted(dict.items()):
    print (key, " has the value ", value)
```

By converting the dictionary pairs in a list, any of the operations on lists can be applied to a dictionary as well. It is even possible to use comprehensions to initialize a dictionary. For example

```
d = {angle:sin(radians(angle)) for angle in (0,45.,90.,
    135., 180.)}
```

creates a dictionary of the sines of some angles indexed by the angle.

8.2 ARRAYS

For programmers who have used other languages, Python *lists* have many of the properties of an *array*, which in C++ or Java is a collection of consecutive memory locations that contain the same type of value. *Lists* may be designed to make operations such as concatenation efficient, which means that a *list* may not be the most efficient way to store things. A Python *array* is a class that mimics the array type of other languages and offers efficiency in storage, exchanging that for flexibility.

Only certain types can be stored in an array, and the type of the array is specified when it is created. For example:

```
data = array('f', [12.8, 5.4, 8.0, 8.0, 9.21, 3.14])
```

creates an array of 6 floating point numbers; the type is indicated by the "f" as the first parameter to the constructor. This concept is unlike the Python norm of types being dynamic and malleable. An *array* is an array of one kind of thing, and an *array* can only hold a restricted set of types.

The type code, the first parameter to the constructor, can have one of 13 values, but the most commonly used ones will be:

"b"   A C++ char type

"B"   A C++ unsigned char type

"i":   A C++ int type

"l":   A C++ long type

"f":   A C++ float type

"d":   A C++ double type

Arrays are class objects and are provided in the built-in module *array*, which must be imported:

```
from array import array
```

An *array* is a sequence type, and has the basic properties and operations that Python provides all sequence types. Array elements can be assigned to and can be used in expressions, and arrays can be searched and extended like other sequences. There are some features of arrays that are unique:

frombytes (s)   The string argument **s** is converted into byte sequences and appended to the array.

fromfile(f, num)   Read **num** items from the file object **f** and append them. An integer, for example, is one item.

fromlist (x)   Append the elements from the list x to the array.

tobytes()   Convert the array into a sequence of bytes in machine representation.

tofile(f)   Write the array as a sequence of bytes to the file **f**.

In most cases arrays are used to speed up numerical operations, but they can also be used (and will be in the next section) to access the underlying representations of numbers.

8.3 ■ FORMATTED TEXT, FORMATTED I/O

There is a generally believed theory among many users of data, including some engineers and financial analysts, that if numbers line up in nice columns then they must be correct. This is obviously not true, but appearances can matter a great deal, and numbers that do *not* line up properly for easy reading look sloppy and give people the impression that they may not be as carefully prepared as they should have been. The Python **print()** function as used so far simply prints a collection of variables and constants with no real attention to a format. Each one is printed in the order specified with a space between them. Sometimes that's good enough.

The Python versions since 2.7 have incorporated a string **format()** method that allows a programmer to specify how values should be placed within a string. The idea is to create a string that contains the formatted output, and then print the string. A simple example is:

```
s = "x={} y={}"
fs = s.format (121.2, 6)
```

The string **fs** now contains "x=121.2 y=6." The braces within the format string **s** hold the place for a value. The **format()** method lists values to be placed into the string, and with no other information given it does so in order of appearance, in this case 121.2 followed by 6. The first pair of braces is replaced by the first value, 121.2, and the second pair of braces is replaced by the second value, which is 6. Now the string **fs** can be printed.

This is not how it is usually done, though. Because this is usually part of the output process, it is often placed within the **print()** call:

```
print ("x={} y={}".format(121.2, 6) )
```

where the **format()** method is referenced from the string constant. No actual formatting is done by this particular call, merely a conversion to string and a substitution of values. The way formatting is done depends on the type of the value being formatted, the most common types being strings, integers, and floats. An example will be illuminating.

8.3.1 Example: NASA Meteorite Landing Data

NASA publishes a huge amount of data on its web sites, and one of these is a collection of meteorite landings. It covers many years and has over 4800 entries. The task assigned here is to print a nicely formatted report on selected parts of the data. The data on the file has its fields separated by commas, and there are ten of them: name, id, nametype, recclass, mass, Fall, year, reclat, reclong, and Geo-Location. The report requires that the name, recclass, mass, reclat and reclong be arranged in a nicely formatted set of columns.

Reading the data is a matter of opening the file, which is named "met.txt," and calling **readline()**, then creating a list of the fields using **split(",")**. If this is done and the fields are simply printed using **print()**, the result is messy. An abbreviated example is (simulated data):

```
infile = open ("met.txt", "r")
inline = infile.readline()

while inline !="":
    inlist = inline.split(",")
    mass = float(inlist[4])
    lat =  float(inlist[7])
    long = float(inlist[8])
    print (inlist[0], inlist[3], inlist[4], inlist[7],
           inlist[8])
    inline = infile.readline()
infile.close()
```

The result is, as predicted, messy:

```
Ashdon H5 121.13519985254874 89.85924301385958
        -126.27404435776049
Arbol Solo H6 66.94777134343516 25.567048824444797
          160.58088365396014
Baldwyn L6 47.6388587105465 -7.708508536783924
        -81.22266156597777
Ankober L6 15.265523451122064 -32.01862330869428
        102.31244557598723
Ankober LL6 57.584802700693885 -84.85880091616322
        106.31130649523368
Ash Creek L6 62.130089525516155 76.02832670618457
          -140.03422105516938
Almahata Sitta LL5 30.476879105555653 -12.906745404586
              47.411816322674
```

Nothing lines up in columns, and the numbers show an impossible degree of precision. Also there should be headings.

The first field to be printed is called *name*, and is a string; it is the name of the location where the observation was made. The print statement simply adds a space after printing it, and so the next thing is printed immediately following it. Things do not line up. Formatting a string for output involves specifying how much space to allow and whether the string should be centered or aligned to the left or right side of the area where it will be printed. Applying a left alignment to the string variable named **placename** in a field of 16 characters would be done as follows:

```
'{:16s}'.format(placename)
```

The braces, which have previously been empty, contain formatting directives. Empty braces mean *no formatting*, and simply hold the place for a value. A full format could contain a name, a conversion part, and a specification:

{ [name]   ['!' conversion]   [':' specification] }

where optional parts are in square brackets. Thus, the minimal format specification is "'{}.'" In the example "{:16s}" there is no name and no conversion parts, only a specification. After the ":" is '16s,' meaning that the data to be placed here is a string, and that 16 characters should be allowed for it. It will be left aligned by default, so if **placename** was "Atlanta," the result of the formatting would be the string "Atlanta   ," left aligned in a 16-character string. Unfortunately, if the original string is longer than 16 characters it will not be truncated, and all of the characters will be placed in the resulting string even if it makes it too long.

To right align a string, simply place a ">" character immediately following the ":". So:

"{:>16s}".format("Atlanta")

would be "   Atlanta." Placing a "<" character there does a left alignment (the default) and "^" means to center it in the available space. The alignment specifications apply to numbers as well as strings.

The first two values to be printed in the example are the city name, which is in **inlist[0]** and the meteorite class which is **inlist[3]**. Formatting these is done as follows:

```
s = '{:16s} {:10s}'.format(inlist[0], inlist[3])
```

Both strings will be left aligned.

Numeric formats are more complicated. For integers there is the total space to allow, and also how to align it and what to do with the sign and leading zeros. The formatting letter for an integer is "d", so the following are legal directives and their meaning:

Format	Explanation	Result for value 1234
'{:5d}'	An integer in a 5-character space, right aligned	" 1234"
'{:>5d}'	An integer in a 5-character space, right aligned	" 1234"
'{:<7d}'	An integer in a 7-character space, left aligned	"1234 "

(contd.)

Format	Explanation	Result for value 1234
'{:07d}'	An integer right aligned in a 7-character space filled on the left with zeros.	"0001234"
'{:,7d}'	A right aligned integer in a 7-character space with a ',' every 3 digits	" 1,234"
'{:7x}'	A right aligned integer in hexadecimal.	" 4D2"

Floating point numbers have the extra issue of the decimal place. The format character is often "f," but it can be "e" for exponential format or "g" for general format, meaning the system decides whether to use "f" or "e." Otherwise, the formatting of a floating point is like that of previous versions of Python and like that of C and C++:

Format	Explanation	Result for value 12.321
'{:.3f}'	3 digits right of the decimal	'12.321'
'{:6.2f}'	6 digits, 3 to the right of the decimal	' 12.32'
'{:>8.1}'	5 digits, 1 to the right, left adjusted	' 12.3'
'{:8e}'	8 places, exponential form	'1.232100e+01'
'{:8g}'	8 places, system decides	' 12.321'

The next three values to be printed are floating point: the mass of the meteorite and the location, as latitude and longitude. Printing each of these as 7 places, 2 to the right of the decimal, would seem to work. Or, as a format: "{:7.2f}."

The solution to the problem is now at hand. The data is read line by line, converted into a list, and then the fields are formatted and printed in two steps:

```
infile = open ("met.txt", "r")
   inline = infile.readline()
   print ("   Place    Class      Mass    Latitude
        Longitude")
   while inline !="":
      inlist = inline.split(",")
      mass = float(inlist[4])
      lat =  float(inlist[7])
      long = float(inlist[8])
      print('{:16s} {:14s} {:7.2f}'.format(inlist[0],
                         inlist[3],mass),end="")
      print ('  {:7.2f}     {:7.2f}'.format(lat, long))
```

```
    inline = infile.readline()
infile.close()
```

The result is:

```
Place            Class          Mass        Latitude      Longitude
Bloomington      L5             13.58          9.53         -150.85
Bogou            LL6            121.09        -66.28         -53.08
Alessandria      L4             106.11         63.68          10.96
Bo Xian          L5              85.92          0.33         -50.28
Ashdon           Eucrite-mmict    6.59        -88.22        -178.84
Berduc           L6             111.76        -64.20         107.10
...
```

There are many more formatting directives, and a huge number of their combinations.

8.4 ADVANCED DATA FILES

File operations were discussed Chapter 5, but the discussion was limited to files containing text. Text is crucial because it is how humans communicate with the computer; people are unhappy about having to enter binary numbers. On the other hand, text files take up more space than needed to hold the information they do. Each character requires at least one byte. The number 3.1415926535 thus takes up 12 bytes, but if stored as a floating point number it needs only 4 or 8 depending on precision.

The file system on most computers also permits a variety of operations that have not been discussed. This includes reading from any point in a file, appending data to files, and modifying data. The need for processing data effectively is a main reason for computers to exist at all, so it is important to know as much as possible about how to program a computer for these purposes.

8.4.1 Binary Files

A *binary* file is one that does not contain text, but instead holds the raw, internal representation of its data. Of course, all files on a computer disk are binary in the strict sense, because they all contain numbers in binary form, but a binary file in this discussion does not contain information that can be read by a human. Binary files can be more efficient that other kinds, both in file size (smaller) and the time it takes to read and write them (less). Many standard files types, such as MP3, exist as binary files, so it is important to understand how to manipulate them.

Example: Create a File of Integers

The *array* type holds data in a form that is more natural for most computers than a list, and also has the **tofile()** method built in. If a collection of integers is to be written as a binary file, a first step is to place them into an array. If a set of 10000 consecutive integers are to be written to a file named "ints," the first step is to import the array class and open the output file. Notice that the file is open in "wb" mode, which means "write binary":

```python
from array import array
output_file = open('ints', 'wb')
```

Now create an array to hold the elements and fill the array with the consecutive integers:

```python
arr = array('i')
for k in range (10000, 20000):
    arr.append(k)
```

Finally, write the data in the array to the file:

```python
arr.tofile(out)
out.close()
```

This file has a size listed as 40kb on a Windows PC. A file having the same integers written as text is 49kb. This is not exactly a huge saving of space, but it does add up.

Reading these values back is just as simple:

```python
inf = open ('ints', 'rb')
arrin = array('i')
for k in range (0, 10001):
    try:
        arrin.fromfile(inf, 1)
    except:
        break
    print (arrin[k])
inf.close()
```

The **try** is used to catch an end of file error in cases where the number of items on the file is not known in advance. Or just because always doing so is a good idea.

Sometimes a binary file will contain data that is all of the same type, but that situation is not very common. It is more likely that the file will have strings, integers, and floats intermixed. Imagine a file of data for bank accounts or magazine subscriptions; the information included will be names and addresses, dates, financial values, and optional data, depending on the specific situation. Some customers have multiple accounts, for example. How can binary files be created that contain more than one kind of information? By using *structs*.

8.4.2 The Struct Module

The *struct* module permits variables and objects of various types to be converted into what amounts to a sequence of bytes. It is a common claim that this is in order to convert between Python forms and C forms, because C has a *struct* type (short for *structure*). However, many files exist that consist of mixed-type data in raw (i.e., machine compatible) form that have been created by many programs in many languages. It is possible that C is singled out because the name *struct* was used.

Example: A Video Game High Score File

Video game players need little incentive to try hard to win a game, but for many years a special reward has been given to the better players. The game "remembers" the best players and lists them at the beginning and end of the game. This kind of ego boost is a part of the reward system of the game. The game program stores the information on a file in descending order of score. The data that is saved is usually the player's name or initials, the score, and the date. This mixes string with numeric data.

Consider that the player's name is held in a variable **name**, the score is an integer **score**, and the date is a set of three strings **year**, **month**, and **day**. In this situation the size of each value needs to be fixed, so allow 32 characters for the name, 4 for year, 2 for month, and 2 for day. The file was created with the name first, then the score, then the year, month, and day. The order matters because it will be read in the same order that it was written. On the file the data will look like this:

```
ccccccccccccccccccccccccccccccc iiii    cccc   cc    cc
Player's name                    Score   Year   Month Day
```

Each letter in the first string represents a byte in the data for this entry. The 'c's represent characters; the 'i's represent bytes that are part of an integer. There are 44 bytes in all, which is the size of one data *record*, which is what one set of related data is generally called. A file contains the records for all of the elements in the data set, and in this case a record is the data for one player, or at least one time that the player played the game. There can be multiple entries for a player.

One way to convert mixed data like this into a *struct* is to use the **pack()** method. It takes a format parameter first, which indicates what the *struct* will consist of in terms of bytes. Then the values are passed that will be converted into components of the final struct. For the example here the call to **pack()** would be:

```
s = pack ("32si4s2s2s", name, score, year, month, day)
```

The format string is "32si4s2s2s"; there are 5 parts to this, one for each of the values to be packed:

32s is a 32-character long string. It should be of type *bytes*.

i is one integer. However, **2i** would be two integers, and **12i** is 12 integers.

4s is a 4-character long string.

2s is a 2-character long string.

Other important format items are:

c is a character

f is a float

d is a double precision float

The value returned from **pack()** has type *bytes*, and in this case is 44 bytes long. The high score file consists of many of these records, all of which are the same size. A record can be written to a file using **write()**. So, a program that writes just one such record would be:

```
from struct import *

f = open ("hiscores", "wb")
name = bytes("Jim Parker", 'UTF-8')
score = 109800
year = b"2015"
month = b"12"
day = b"26"
```

```
s = pack ("32si4s2s2s", name, score, year, month, day)
f.write(s)
```

Reading this file involves first reading the string of bytes that represented a data record. Then it is *unpacked*, which is the reverse of what **pack()** does, and the variables are passed to the **unpack()** function to be filled with data. The **unpack()** method takes a format string as the first parameter, the same kind of format string as **pack()** uses. It will return a tuple. An example that reads the record in the above code would be:

```
from struct import *

f = open("hiscores", "rb")
s = f.read(44)
name,score,year,month,day = unpack("32si4s2s2s", s)
name = name.decode("UTF-8")
year = year.decode("UTF-8")
month = month.decode("UTF-8")
day = day.decode("UTF-8")
```

The data returned by unpack are *bytes*, and need to be converted into strings before being used in most cases. Note the input mode on the **open()** call is "rb," read binary.

A file in this format has been provided, and is named simply 'hiscore.' When a player plays the game they will enter their name; the computer knows their score and the date. A new entry must be made in the 'hiscore' file with this new score in it. How is that done?

Start with the new player data for *Karl Holter*, with a score of 100000. To update the file it is opened and records are read and written to a new temporary file (named "tmp") until one is found that has a smaller score than the 100000 that Karl achieved. Then Karl's record is written to the temporary file, and the remainder of 'hiscores' is copied there. This creates a new file named "tmp" that has Karl's data added to it, and in the correct place. Now that file can be copied to "hiscores" replacing the old file, or the file named "tmp" can be renamed as "hiscores." This is called a *sequential file update*.

Renaming the file requires access to some of the operating system functions in the module *os*; in particular:

```
os.rename ("tmp", "hiscores")
```

8.4.3 Random Access

It seems natural to begin reading a file from the beginning, but that is not always necessary. If the data that is desired is located at a known place in the file, then the location being read from can be set to that point. This is a natural consequence of the fact that disk devices can be positioned at any location at any time. Why not files too?

The function that positions the file at a specific byte location is **seek()**:

```
f.seek(44)    # Position the file at byte 44,
              # which is the second record in the hiscores
              # file.
```

It's also possible to position the file relative to the current location:

```
f.seek(44, 1)    # Position the file 44 bytes from this
                 # location,
                 # which skips over the next record in
                 # hiscores.
```

A file can be rewound so that it can be read over again by calling **f.seek(0)**, positioning the file at the beginning. It is otherwise difficult to make use of this feature unless the records on the file are of a fixed size, as they are in the file 'hiscores,' or the information on record sizes is saved in the file. Some files are intended from the outset to be used as random access files. Those files have an index that allows specific records to be read on demand. This is very much like a *dictionary*, but on a file. Assuming that the score for player *Arlen Franks* is needed, the name is searched for in the index. The result is the byte offset for Arlen's high score entry in the file.

Arlen's record starts at byte 352 (8th record * 44 bytes). He just played the game again and improved his score. Why not update his record on the file? The file needs to be open for input *and* output, so mode "rb+," meaning open a binary file for input and output, would work in this case. Then position the file to Arlen's record, create a new record, and write that one record. This is new—being able to both read and write the same file seems odd, but if the data being written is exactly the same size as the record on the file then no harm should come from it. The program is:

```
# read and print hiscore file
from struct import *
```

```
f = open ("hiscores", "r+b")   # Open binary file,input and
                               # output
pos = 44*8                     # Desired record is 8, 44
                               # bytes per
f.seek(pos)                    # Seek to that position one
                               # the file
s = f.read(44)                 # Read the target record
name = b'Arlen Franks'         # Make a new one with a new
                               # score
score = 100300
year = b'2015'
month = b'12'
day = b'26'                    # Pack the new data
ss = pack("32si4s2s2s", name,score, year,month,day)
f.seek (44*8)                  # Seek the original position
                               # again!
f.write(ss)                    # Write the new data over
                               # the old
f.close ()                     # Close the file
```

This works fine, provided that the position of Arlen's data in the file is known. It does not maintain the file in descending order, though.

Example: Maintaining the High Score File in Order

The circumstances of the new problem are that a player only appears in the high score file once and the file is maintained in descending order of score. If a player improves their score, then their entry should move closer to the beginning of the file. This is a more difficult problem than before, but one that is still practical. So, presume that a player has achieved a new score. The entire process should be:

Get the player's old score.	Read the file, get the player's record, unpack it.
Is the new score larger?	If not, close the file. Done.
Yes, so find out where the score belongs, in the file.	Look at successively preceding records until one is found that has a larger score.
Place the new record where it belongs.	Copy the records from the new position for the record ahead one position until the old position is reached.

The process is like moving a playing card closer to the top of the deck while leaving the other cards in the same order. It's probably more efficient to move the record while searching for the correct position, though. Each time the previous record is examined, if it does not have a larger score then the record being placed is copied ahead one position. This results in a pretty compact program, given the nature of the problem, but it is a bit tricky to get right. For example, what if the new score is the highest? What if the current high score gets a higher score? (See: Exercise 11)

8.5 STANDARD FILE TYPES

Everyone's computer has files on it that the owner did not create. Some have been downloaded; some merely came with the machine. It is common practice to associate specific kinds of files, as indicated initially by some letters at the end of the file name, with certain applications. A file that ends in ".doc," for example, is usually a file created by Microsoft Word, and a file ending in ".mp3" is usually a sound file, often music. Such files have a format that is understood by existing software packages, and some of them (".gif") have been around for thirty years.

Each file type has been designed to make certain operations easy, and to pass certain information to the application. Over the years a set of de facto standards have evolved for how these files are laid out, and for what data are provided for what kinds of file. And yet most users and many programmers do not understand how these files are structured or why. Many users do not care, of course, and some programmers too, but opening up these files to some scrutiny is an educational experience.

8.5.1 Image Files

Images have been processed using computers since the 1960s when NASA started processing images at the Jet Propulsion Laboratory. After some years people (scientists, mainly) decided that having standards for computer images would be useful. The first formats were ad hoc, and based essentially on raw pixel data. Raw data means knowing what the image size is in advance, so headers were introduced providing at least that information, leading to the TARGA format (.tga) and tiff (Tagged Image File Format) in the mid-1980s. When the Internet and the World Wide Web became popular, the GIF was invented, which compressed the image data. This was followed by JPEG and other formats that could be used by web designers and rendered by browsers, and each had a specific advantage. After all, reducing size meant reducing the time it took to download an image.

Once a file format has been around for a few years and has become successful it tends to stick around, so many of the image file formats created in the 1980s are still here in one form or another. There are new ones too, like PNG (Portable Network Graphics), which have been specifically designed for the Internet. Older ones (like JPEG) have found common uses in new technologies, like digital cameras. A programmer/computer scientist needs to know about the nature of the various formats, their pros and cons as it were.

8.5.2 GIF

The Graphics Interchange Format is interesting from many perspectives. First, it uses compression to reduce the size of the file, but the compression method is not *lossy*, meaning that the image does not change after being compressed and then decompressed. The compression algorithm used is called LZW, and will be discussed in Chapter 10. GIF uses a *color map* representation, so an element in the image is not a color, but instead is an index into an array that holds the color. That is, if **v = image[row][column]** then the color of that pixel is (**red[v], green[v], blue[v]**). The color itself could be a full 24 bits, but the value **v** is a byte, and so in a GIF there can only be 256 distinct colors. GIF uses a *little-endian* representation, meaning that the least significant byte of multi-byte objects comes first on the file.

One advantage of the GIF is that one of the colors can be made transparent. This means that when this color is drawn over another, the color below shows through. It is essentially a "do not draw this pixel" value. It is important for things like sprites in computer games. Another advantage of GIF is that multiple images can be stored in a single file, allowing an animation to be saved in a single file. GIF animations have been common on the Internet for many years, and while they usually represent small, brief animations such as Christmas trees with flashing lights, they can be as long and complex as television programs. Still, the fact that there can only be 256 different colors can be a problem.

A GIF is a binary file, but the first six characters are a header block containing what is called a *magic number*, or an identifying label. For a GIF file the three characters are always "GIF" and the next three represent the version; for the 1989 standard the first six characters are "GIF89a." Magic numbers are common in binary files, and are used to identify the file type. The file name suffix does not always tell the truth.

Following the header is the logical screen descriptor, which explains how much screen space the image requires. This is seven bytes:

Canvas width	2 bytes
Canvas height	2 bytes
Packed byte	1 byte

A set of flags and small values

Bit	8	7 6 5	4	3 2 1
	Global Color Table?	color resolution	sort flag	size of global color table

Background color index	1 byte
Pixel aspect ratio	1 byte

This is followed by the global color table, other descriptors, and the image data. The details can be found in manuals and online. The information in the first few bytes is critical, though, and the knowledge that LZW compression is used means that the pixels are not immediately available. Decompression is done to the image as a whole.

```
from struct import *
f = open ("test.gif", "rb")
s = f.read (13)                   # Read the header
id,  ht, wd, flags, bci,par = unpack('6shhBBB', s)
#6s  h    h    B    B   B
f.close()
id = id.decode("utf-8")
print (id)
print ("Height", ht, "Width", wd)
print("Flags:", flags)
print ("Background color index: ", bci)
print ("Pixel aspect ratio:", par)
```

8.5.3 JPEG

A JPEG image uses a lossy compression scheme, and so the image is not the same after compression as it was before compression. For this reason it should never be used for scientific or forensic purposes when measurements will be made using the image. It should never be used for astronomy, for example, although it is perfectly fine for portraits and landscape photographs.

The name JPEG is an acronym for the Joint Photographic Experts Group, and actually refers to the nature of the compression algorithm. The file format is an envelope that contains the image, and is referred to as JFIF (JPEG File Interchange Format). The file header contains 20 bytes: the magic number is the first 4 and bytes 6–10. The first 4 bytes are hex FF, D8, FF, and E0. Bytes 6–10 should be "JFIF\0," and this is followed by a revision number. A short program that decodes the header is:

```python
from struct import *

f = open ("test.jpg", "rb")
s = f.read (20)                   # Read the header
b1, b2,a1,a2,sz,id,v1, v2,unit,xd,yd, xt,yt =
unpack('BBBBh5sBBBhhBB', s)
#B   B   B   B   h  5s  B   B   B    h   h   B   B
f.close()
id = id.decode("utf-8")
print (id, "revision", v1, v2)
if b1==0xff and b2==0xd8:
    print ("SOI checks.")
else:
    print ("SOI fails.")
if a1==0xff and a2==0xe0:
    print ("Application marker checks.")
else:
    print("Application marker fails.")
print ("App 0 segment is", sz, "bytes long.")
if unit == 0:
    print ("No units given.")
elif unit == 1:
    print ("Units are dots per inch.")
elif unit == 2:
    print ("Units are dots per centimeter.")
```

```
if unit==0:
    print ("Aspect ratio is ", xd, ":", yd)
else:
    print ("Xdensity: ", xd, " Ydensity: ", yd)
if xt==0 and yt==0:
    print ("No thumbnail")
else:
    print ("Thumbnail image is ", xt, "x", yt)
```

The compression scheme used in JPEG is very involved, but is does cause certain identifiable artifacts in an image. In particular, pixels near edges and boundaries are smeared, essentially averaging values across small regions (Figure 8.1). This can cause problems if a JPEG image is to be edited, for example in Photoshop or Paint.

Figure 8.1
JPEG images tend to show artifacts at places where pixels change rapidly, like corners and edges.

8.5.4 TIFF

The *Tagged Image File Format* has a potentially huge amount of metadata associated with it, and that is all in text form in the file. It's a favorite among scientists because of that: the device used to capture the image, the focal length of the lens, time, subject, and scores of other information can accompany the image. In fact, the TIFF has been seconded for use with numeric non-image data as well. The other reason it is popular is that is can be used with uncompressed (raw) data.

The word *Tagged* comes from the fact that information is stored in the file using tags, such as might be found in an HTML file—except that the tags in a TIFF are not in text form. A tag has four components: an ID (2 bytes, what tag is this?), a data type (2 bytes, what type are the items in this tag?), a data count

(4 bytes, how many items?), and a byte offset (4 bytes, where are these items?). Tags are identified by number, and each tag has a specific meaning. Tag 257 means *Image Height* and 256 is *Image Width*; 315 is the code meaning *Artist*, 306 means *Date/Time*, and 270 is the *Image Description*. They can be in any order. In fact, the whole file structure is flexible because all components are referenced using a byte offset into the file.

A TIFF begins with an 8-byte Image File Header (IFH):

Byte order: This is 2 bytes, and is "II" if data is in little-endian form and "MM" if it is big-endian.
Version Number: Always 42.
First Image File Directory offset: 4 bytes, the offset in the file of the first image.

The other important part of a TIFF is the Image File Directory (IFD), which contains information about the specific image, including the descriptive tags and data. The IFH is always 8 bytes long and is at the beginning of the file. An IFD can be almost any size and can be anywhere in the file; there can be more than one, as well. The first IFD is found by positioning the file to the offset found in the IFH. Subsequent ones are indicated in the IFD. The IFD stricture is:

Number of tags: 2 bytes
Tags: Array of tags, size unknown
Next IFD offset: 4 bytes. File offset of the next IFD. If there are no more, then =0.

The structure of a tag was given previously, so a TIF is now defined. The image data can be, and frequently is, raw pixels, but can also be compressed in many ways as defined by the tags.

The program below reads the IFH and the first IFD, dumping the information to the screen:

```
# TIFF
from struct import *

f = open ("test.tif", "rb")
s = f.read (8)                          # Read the IFH
id,  ver, off = unpack('2shL', s)
#2s    h    L
```

```
id = id.decode("utf-8")
print ("TIFF ID is ", id, end="")
if id == "II":
    print ("which means little-endian.")
elif id == "mm":
    print ("which means big-endian")
else:
    print ("which means this is not a TIFF.")
print ("Version", ver)
print("Offset", off)

f.seek(off)                         # Get the first IFD
n = 0
b = f.read (2)                      # Number of tags
n = b[0] + b[1]*256
#n = int(s.decode("utf-8"))
for i in range(0,n):
    s = f.read (12)                 # Read a tag
    id,dt,dc,do = unpack ("hhLL", s)
    print ("Tag ", id, "type", dt, "count", dc, "Offset", do)
f.close()
```

When this program executes using "test.tif" as the input file, the first two tags in the IFD are 256 and 257 (*width* and *height*) which are correct.

8.5.5 PNG

A PNG (*Portable Network Graphics*) file consists of a magic number, which in this context is called a *signature* and consists of 8 bytes, and a collection of *chunks*, which resemble TIFF tags. There are 18 different kinds of chunk, the first of which is an image header. The Signature is always: 137 80 78 71 13 10 26 10. The bytes 80 78 71 are the letters "PNG."

A chunk has either 3 or 4 fields: a length field, a chunk type, an optional chunk data field, and a check code based on all previous bytes in the chunk that is used to detect errors (called a *cyclic redundancy check*, or CRC).

The image header chink (IHDR) has the following structure:

Image width:	4 bytes
Image height:	4 bytes
Bit depth:	1 byte. Number of bits per sample (1,2,4,8, or 16).

Color type:	1 byte. 0 (grey), 2 (RGB), 3 (color map), 4 (greyscale with transparency) or 6 (RGB with transparency)
Compression method:	1 byte. Always 0.
Filter method:	1 byte. Always 0.
Interlace method:	1 byte. 0=no interlace. 1=Adam7 interlace (See: references)

This file has compression, but it is non-lossy. It also, like GIF, allows transparency, but allows full RGB color. It does not have an option for animations, though. Reading the signature and the first (IHDR) chunk is done in the following way:

```
# PNG
from struct import *
b2 = (137, 80, 78, 71, 13, 10, 26, 10) # Correct header
types = ("Grey", "", "RGB", "Color map",
         "Grey with alpha", "", "RGBA") # Color types
f = open ("test.png", "rb")
s = f.read (8)                    # Read the header
b1 = unpack('8B', s)
if b1 == b2:
    print ("Header OK")
else:
    print ("Bad header")

s = f.read(8)   # The next chunk must be the IHDR
length, type = unpack (">I4s", s)   # Unpack the first
8 bytes print ("First chunk: Length is", length, "Type:",
type)

s = f.read (length)   # We know the length, read the chunk
wd,ht,dep,ctype,compress, filter, interlace =
unpack(">ii5B", s)
#I   I   B   B      B      B      B
print ("PNG Image width=", wd, "Height=", ht)
print ("Image has ", dep, "bytes per sample.")
print ("Color type is ", types[ctype])
if compress == 0:
    print ("Compression OK")
else:
    print ("Compression should be 0 but is", compress)
```

```
if filter==0:
    print ("Filter is OK")
else:
    print ("Filter should be 0 but is", filter)
if interlace==0:
    print ("No interlace")
elif interlace == 1:
    print ("Adam7 interlace")
else:
    print ("Bad interlace specified: ", interlace)
f.close()
```

8.5.6 Sound Files

A sound file can be a lot more complex than an image file, and substantially larger. To properly play back a sound, it is critical to know how it was sampled: how many bits per sample, how many channels, how many samples per second, compression schemes, and so on. The file must be readable in real time or the sound can't be played without a separate decoding step. All that is really needed to display an image is its size pixel format and compression.

There are, once again, many existing audio file formats. MP3 is quite complex, too much so to discuss here. The usual option on a PC would be ".wav" and, as it happens, that format is not especially complicated.

WAV

A WAV file has three parts: the initial header, used to identify the file type; the format sub-chunk, which specifies the parameters of the sound file; and the data sub-chunk, which holds the sound data.

The initial header should contain the string "RIFF" followed by the size of the file minus 8 bytes (i.e., the size from this point forward), and the string "WAVE." This is 12 bytes in size.

The next "sub-chunk" has the following form:

ID: = "fmt"

Size1:   Size of the rest of the sub-chunk

Format: 1 if PCM, another number if compressed

No. of Channels: mono=1, stereo=2, etc.

Sample rate: Sound samples per second. CD rate is 44100

Alignment: Should be No. of channels*sample rate*bits per sample/8

Bits per sample: AKA *quantization*. Bits in each sample: 8, 12 are usual.

The final section contains the following:

ID: = "data"

Size: Number of bytes in the data

Data: The actual sound data, as a large block of **Size** bytes.

A program that reads the first two sub-chunks is:

```
# WAV
from struct import *

f = open("test.wav", "rb")
s = f.read (12)
riff,sz,fmt = unpack ("4si4s", s)
riff = riff.decode("utf-8")
fmt = fmt.decode("utf-8")
print (riff, sz, "bytes ", fmt)


s = f.read (24)
id, sz1, fmt,nchan,rate,bytes,algn, bps = unpack
                                 ("4sihhiihh", s)
#4s  i   h    h    i    i    h    h
id = id.decode ("utf-8)")
print ("ID is", id, "Channels ", nchan, "Sample rate is ",
     rate)
print ("Bits per sample is ", bps)
if fmt==1:
    print ("File is PCM")
else:
    print ("File is compressed ", fmt)
print ("Byterate was ", bytes, "should be ",
rate*nchan*bps/8)
```

8.5.7 Other Files

Every type of file has a specific purpose and a format that is appropriate for that purpose. For that reason the nature of the headers and the file contents differ, but the fact that the headers and other specific fields exist should by now make some sense. When a program is asked to open a file there should be some way to confirm that the contents of the file can be read by the program. The code that has been presented so far is only sufficient to determine the file type and some of its basic parameters. The code needed to read and display a GIF, for example, would likely be over 1000 lines long. It is important, for someone who wishes to be a programmer, to see how to construct a file so that it can be used effectively by others and so that other programmers can create code that can identify that file and use it.

With that in mind, some other file types will be described briefly and considered as examples of how to organize data into a file.

HTML

An HTML (*HyperText Markup Language*) file is one that is recognized by a browser and can be displayed as a web page. It is a text file, and can be edited, saved, and redisplayed using simple tools; the fancy web editors are useful, but not necessary.

The first line of text in an HTML file should be either a variation on:

```
<!DOCTYPE html>
```

or a variation on:

```
<html>
```

The problem is that these are text files, so spaces and tabs and newlines can appear without affecting the meaning. Browsers are also supposed to be somewhat forgiving about errors, displaying the page if at all possible. A simple example that shows some of the problems while being largely correct is:

```
import webbrowser
f = open ("other.html")
html = False
while True:                     # Look at many lines
    s = f.readline()            # Read
    s = s.strip()               # Remove white space
                                # (blanks, tabs)
    s = s.lower()               # Convert to lower case for
                                # compare
    k = (s.find("doctype"))     # doctype found?
```

```
        if k>0:                       # Yes
            kk = s.find("html")       # Look also for 'html'
            if kk >= k+7:             # Found it, after DOCTYPE
                html = True           # Close enough
                break
        else:
            k = s.find("html")              # No 'doctype'. 'html'?
            if k>0 and s[k-1] == "<":       # Yes. Preceded by '<'?
                html = True                 # Yes, Close enough.
                break
        if len(s) > 0:                # is the string non-blank?
            html = False              # Yes. So it is not HTML
                                      # probably
            break

if html:
    webbrowser.open_new_tab('other.html')
else:
    print ("This is not an HTML file.")
```

This program uses the *webbrowser* module of Python to display the web page if it is one. The call webbrowser.open _ new _ tab('**other.html**') opens the page in a new tab, if the browser is open. This module is not a browser itself. It simply opens an existing installed browser to do the work of displaying the page.

EXE

This is a Microsoft executable file. The details of the format are involved, and require a knowledge of computers and formats beyond a first-year level, but detecting one is relatively simple. The first two bytes that identify an EXE file are:

Byte 0: 0x4D

Byte 1: 0x5a

It is always possible that the first two bytes of a file will be these two by accident, but it is unlikely. If the file being examined is, in fact, an EXE file, then a Python program can execute it. This uses the operating system interface module *os*:

```
import os
os.system ("program.exe")
```

8.6 SUMMARY

A fair definition of Computer Science would be the discipline that concerns itself with information. Computers can only operate on numbers, so an important aspect of using data is the representation of complex things as numbers. Most data consist of measurements of something, and as such are fundamentally numeric.

A *dictionary* allows a more complex indexing scheme: it is accessed by content. A dictionary can be indexed by a string or tuple, which in general would be referred to as a *key*, and the information at that location in the dictionary is said to be *associated* with that key.

A Python *array* is a class that mimics the array type of other languages and offers efficiency in storage, exchanging that for flexibility. The *struct* module permits variables and objects of various types to be converted into what amounts to a sequence of bytes. It has a **pack()** and an **unpack()** method for converting Python variables into sequences of bytes.

The string **format()** method allows a programmer to specify how values should be placed within a string. The idea is to create a string that contains the formatted output, and then print the string.

Python data can be written to files in raw, binary form. It is also possible to position the file at any byte in a binary file, allowing the file to be read or written at any location.

Exercises

1. Ask the user for a file name. Extract the suffix and use it to look up the type of the file in a dictionary and print a short description of it. Recognized types include *image* files (jpg, gif, tiff, png), *sound* files (wav), and others (dll, exe).

2. Modify the Latin translation program so that it asks the user for a translation of any word it cannot find and adds that word to the dictionary.

3. Write a program that reads keys and values (strings) from the console and creates a dictionary from those data. When the user types the word "done" then the input is complete. City names are good examples of values, and could represent the city where the person named in the key lives.

4. Modify the answer to Exercise 3 so that after the data entry is complete, the user can enter a value and the program will print all of the keys associated with that value.

5. Given a dictionary, write a function **writedict()** that writes that dictionary to a file, and another function **readdict()** that will read that file and recreate the dictionary. For simplicity assume that the keys are simple numbers or strings.

6. The PNM file format for images has three types of image in two forms: monochrome, grey, and color, saved as text or in binary form. A binary grey level image is called a PGM (Pixel Grey Map) and has a short header followed by pixels. The header is text and consists of the identifying code "P5" followed by the width of the image in pixels (NC), followed by the height (NR), followed by the maximum value for a grey level (NGL) followed by an end of line. Now the data follows as rows of NC bytes:

P5

nc nr ngl

Write a program that will read an image file in this format and display it on the screen as an image using Glib.

http://netpbm.sourceforge.net/doc/pgm.html

7. Assume that the following variables exist and have the obvious meanings: **year, month, day, hour, minute, second**. All are integer except **second**, which is a *float*. The ISO 8601 standard for displaying dates uses the format: YYYY-MM-DDThh:mm:ss.s
   where the letter "T" ends the date portion and begins the time. An example would be
   2015-12-27T10:38:12.3
   Write a function that takes the given variables as parameters and prints the date in this format.
   http://www.w3.org/TR/NOTE-datetime

8. Write a Python program that opens a file named by the user from the keyboard; the file has the suffix ".jpg," ".gif," or ".png." Determine whether the file contents agree with the suffix, and print a message indicating the result.

9. A concordance is a list of words found in a text. Build a concordance using a *dictionary* that keeps track of the number of times that a word is used, in addition to its mere presence. Print the resulting list in alphabetical order.

10. Write a program that prints out checks. The date and the payee are entered as strings and the amount is entered as a floating point number, the maximum amount being 1000 dollars. The FOR field is always "Books." The program formats the check according to the following image (Figure 8.2), where:

The date is line 3 starting at character 58

The pay to field is line 6 starting at character 20

The numeric amount is line 6 starting at character 57

The text amount is line 8 character 10

The FOR field is line 12 character 15

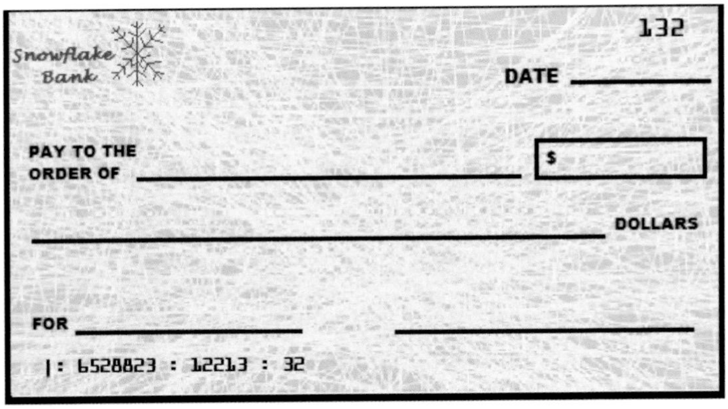

Figure 8.2
Check format.

Notes and Other Resources

List of free datasets to download: *https://r-dir.com/reference/datasets.html*

NASA Meteorite Landing Database: *https://data.nasa.gov/view/ak9y-cwf9*

String Formatting: *https://infohost.nmt.edu/tcc/help/pubs/python/web/format-spec.html*

The Array type: *https://docs.python.org/3/library/array.html*

Image file formats: *https://www.library.cornell.edu/preservation/tutorial/presentation/table7-1.html*

http://www.scantips.com/basics09.html

Home page for MPEG: *http://mpeg.chiariglione.org/*

GIF 1989 specification: *http://www.w3.org/Graphics/GIF/spec-gif89a.txt*

Byte by byte GIF: *http://www.matthewflickinger.com/lab/whatsinagif/bits_and_bytes.asp*

TIFF Description: *http://www.fileformat.info/format/tiff/egff.htm#TIFF.FO*

PNG Specification: *http://www.w3.org/TR/PNG/*

Adam7 Interlacing: *http://www.libpng.org/pub/png/pngpics.html*

EXE file format: *http://www.delorie.com/djgpp/doc/exe/*

File Signatures: *http://www.garykessler.net/library/file_sigs.html*

Sample PGM Images: *http://people.sc.fsu.edu/~jburkardt/data/pgmb/pgmb.html*

1. Gunter Born. (1995). **The File Formats Handbook**, Cengage Learning EMEA, ISBN-13: 978-1850321170.

2. David Kay. (1994). **Graphics File Formats**, Windcrest, ISBN-13: 978-0070340251.

3. Dr. Charles R. Severance. (2013). **Python for Informatics: Exploring Information**, CreateSpace Independent Publishing Platform, ISBN-13: 978-1492339243.

4. Alan Tharp. (1988). **File Organization and Processing, 1st edition**, John Wiley & Sons, ISBN-13: 978-0471605218.

5. John Watkinson. (2001). **MPEG Handbook**, Focal Press, ISBN-13: 978-0240516561.

MULTIMEDIA

▪ ▪ ▪ ▪ ▪

In this chapter

For a great many people computers have become the platform of choice for the delivery of entertainment, education, and information. Part of the reason for this is the ubiquity and speed of the Internet, but the main reason is that computers can deliver media in almost any form: text and images, sound, video, animation, and mixtures of all of these. If someone has something to say, the computer can present it to the world in full color and 5.1 channel sound. Moreover, the availability of free and inexpensive tools for content creation allows almost anyone to be a music producer or film director.

Python can be used to process and display most forms of media through packages that can be downloaded and installed. There are many of these and multiple versions in a bewildering array of combinations. It is not possible to discuss all of the ways that Python can be used to do multimedia and all of the packages and libraries that help programmers implement these things. A facility has already been described for displaying images and graphics: *Glib*. Why not simply add more media capability to *Glib*, thus building on what has already been discussed? At the same time, of course, yet another module is being added to the global mixture.

This extended version of *Glib* is built using an easily available module that must be installed first—that module is *Pygame*. For the new version of *Glib* to work properly, *Pygame* must be installed on the host computer first. This should not be difficult, but the process varies depending on the operating system and the nature of the computer (e.g., 32 bit or 64 bit) so the process will not be described here. The Resources section at the end of the chapter provides links and references that will be helpful.

It is essential to install a version of *Pygame* that works with Python 3.

There are two versions of *Glib*. The version that was used in Chapter 7 uses *tkinter* as a basis and should not require anything extra to be installed. It is referred to as *Static Glib*, whereas the new, extended version is *Dynamic Glib*. *Dynamic Glib* is upwards compatible from *Static Glib* in that all programs that run using *Static Glib* should also run using *Dynamic Glib*, and produce a very similar output. There are some differences between the two, such as font styles and such. There are also new programming idioms that will be needed when using *Dynamic Glib* on account of the dynamic nature of some of the media forms. In fact, one way to look at it is to think of *Static Glib* and *Dynamic Glib* as being two different operating modes of the same library. *Dynamic Glib* is used in dynamic mode, where interaction with the user can occur, the graphics screen can change, and sound can be played.

Dynamic mode will be explained using the example of mouse positions and button clicks, which represent a form of dynamic interaction that most people would have experienced. Following that, animation, video, and sound can be discussed and combined into interesting projects.

9.1 ■ MOUSE INTERACTION

Using mouse position and button presses is a basic form of communication with a computer. The use of the mouse position to activate some visual device on the screen like a button is familiar to everyone who uses a computer, although it is being gradually replaced by touch screens. The idea is that when the user moves the mouse, a cursor or indicator moves correspondingly. The position of this cursor indicates a point on the screen that is active in some way, and if a graphical device is there then it can be manipulated using the mouse buttons. The problem is that a mouse button press can occur at any time; it is unpredictable. This is what programmers call an *event*: something that happens at an unpredictable moment that must be dealt with. Some software someplace must be watching the mouse at all times, determining the x,y coordinates of the cursor on the screen and drawing the cursor in the correct place.

The *Glib* module keeps track of the mouse using *Pygame* and continually updates the position, which can be accessed using functions: **mouseX()** and **mouseY(),** which return the most recent x and y coordinates. However, if a user's Python program is executing, how can the *Glib* system also run and update the mouse position? It cannot. So, a dynamic mode program gives up control and lets *Glib* control most of the work.

A dynamic *Glib* program consists of two parts: an initialization part and a drawing part. Initialization takes place only once, when the program starts executing; it can take place in a function called **initialize()**, or it can be in the main program. *Glib* will call a function named **initialize()** once, if it exists.

The part of the computer that draws will be coded as a function named **draw()**. *Glib* will call this function many times each second, and the programmer is expected to redraw the graphics window each time. This scheme allows the mouse position to update very frequently and allows the programmer to access the most recent mouse coordinates from within the **draw()** function, which can take the place of the main program. A simple example of the dynamic mode and use of the mouse is a program that moves a circle around the screen. The scheme described here is something that will be familiar to programmers of the *Processing* language.

Example: Draw a Circle at the Mouse Cursor

Using *Glib* requires the use of the function **startdraw()** to initialize things, in particular to establish the size of the drawing window. In *Dynamic Glib* the call to **startdraw()** will also call the user's **initialize()** function if one exists. Other code can appear between **startdraw()** and **enddraw()**, usually calculations and initializations. Once **enddraw()** is called control passes to the user's **draw()**

function. It will be called 30 times per second by default, although this rate can be changed.

Drawing a circle at the current mouse position involves repeatedly determining the mouse position and then drawing a circle at that set of coordinates. This should be done within **draw()**. Initialization in this program is trivial so no **initialize()** function is needed.

```
Import Glib

def draw ():
    Glib.background(200)
    Glib.fill (255, 0, 0)
    Glib.ellipse (Glib.mouseX(), Glib.mouseY(),  30, 30)

Glib.startdraw(400, 400)
Glib.enddraw()
```

The result is a red circle that follows the mouse! The **draw()** function sets the background color to a grey level of 255, then sets the fill color to red, then draws the circle (ellipse). It does this 30 times per second, every time **draw()** is called. The most recent mouse position is always found using the functions **Glib. mouseX()** and **Glib.mouseY()**. It seems like it should not be necessary to set the fill color each time, so that can be put in the main program between **startdraw()** and **enddraw()** or in the **initialize()** function:

In main:
```
import Glib

def draw ():
    Glib.background(200)
    Glib.ellipse (Glib.
mouseX(), Glib.mouseY(),
30, 30)

Glib.startdraw(400, 400)
Glib.fill (255, 0, 0)
Glib.enddraw()
```

In **initialize()**:
```
import Glib

def initialize ():
    Glib.fill (255, 0, 0)

def draw ():
    Glib.background(200)
    Glib.ellipse (Glib.
mouseX, Glib.mouseY, 30, 30)

Glib.startdraw(400, 400)
Glib.enddraw()
```

Is it necessary to call the **background()** function each time draw is called? Yes. This function not only sets the background color but fills the screen with it, thus erasing what has been drawn so far. Unless a call to **background()** occurs in **draw()**, all of the circles drawn to that point will be visible (Figure 9.1).

If the statement:

```
from Glib import *
```

appears at the beginning of the program then the *Glib* functions won't have to be prefixed with the name **Glib**. *Variables* that belong to *Glib* still do. The **import** * allows all of the names from *Glib* to be used in the program, but is not always recommended because it complicates the collection of names to be remembered. Still, for the purposes of this chapter, it will be used.

Example: Change Background Color Using the Mouse

The idea here is to change the background color based on the mouse position. There are only two directions to move, horizontally or vertically, so one of the three colors will remain constant; let that color be blue. The horizontal mouse position will control the red value, with the leftmost position representing no red and the rightmost representing full red (255). Similarly, the mouse being at the bottom of the image represents no green, and at the top it represents full green. The background color will be changed in **draw()** accordingly.

Given that the position of the mouse on the screen is given by **mouseX()**, the value of the red coordinate will be **(mouseX()/width*255)**. It may require a change in x coordinate of multiple pixels to shift the color by one unit. A similar expression is used to change the green value.

Figure 9.1
Using the mouse to control elements of an image.

The program is:

```
from Glib import *
import Glib

def draw ():
    r = int((Glib.mouseX/width) *255.0)
    g = int((Glib.mouseY/height)*255.0)
    background (r, g, 128)

startdraw(400, 400)
enddraw()
```

9.1.1 Mouse Buttons

Mouse button *clicks*, as they are called, can be retrieved by writing a function that handles them. Each time a mouse button is pressed, *Glib* tries to call a function named **mousePressed()**. If there is no such function, that's OK, and nothing else happens. If the user writes a function named **mousePressed()**, then it will be executed. Similarly, when a mouse button is released, it tries to call **mouseReleased()**. If the mouse button is pressed, then the mouse is moved, and then it is released, the coordinates of the press and the release point will be different, and both can be retrieved. For example, when the mouse button is pressed, the mouse coordinates could be saved as the beginning of a line, and when released the coordinates could be the end of the line. Multiple lines could be drawn in this way.

Example: Draw Lines Using the Mouse

Using the scheme described above, the function **mousePressed()** will store the mouse position in global variables **x0** and **y0**, and **mouseReleased()** will store the release coordinates at **x1** and **y1**. **mouseReleased()** will also draw the line from (x0,y0) to (x1, y1):

```
from Glib import *
import Glib
x0 = x1 = y1 = y0 = 0

def mousePressed (b):
    global x0, y0
    x0 = Glib.mouseX()
    y0 = Glib.mouseY()
```

```
def mouseReleased (b):
    global x1, y1
    x1 = Glib.mouseX()
    y1 = Glib.mouseY()
    line (x0, y0, x1,y1)

startdraw(400, 400)
enddraw()
```

Note that there is no **draw()** function and no **initialize()** function. Drawing is performed inside of **mouseReleased()**, and no initialization is needed. This is a rare situation. These functions accept one parameter, which is the number of the button that was pressed: left is 0, middle is 1, and right is 2. Note that all buttons could be pressed before any are released. In this example it does not matter what button is pressed; the result is the same.

These functions are traditionally called *callback* functions. The occurrence of some event causes the function to be called.

Example: A Button

This example will change the background color of the drawing window when a graphical button is pressed. A button, in the user interface sense, is a rectangular region on the computer screen that responds to a mouse click with a specific action. It is a two-part process: when the mouse cursor enters the rectangular region, the button is said to be *activated*. Sometimes it will be caused to change color at this point, or some other action will be performed that indicates that it is ready to function. When a mouse button is pressed while the button is activated, then some action occurs, usually as defined by a function being called. The basic idea is simple enough to implement, although some buttons can have complex actions such as sounds, images, and irregular shapes.

The cursor is within a rectangular region when its coordinates are greater than the upper left coordinate of the rectangle and smaller than the lower right coordinates. When that occurs the button is ready to be pressed, and should change color. This does not require anything but knowledge of the mouse coordinates. It the left button is pressed in this state (activated), then the action defined by the button will occur; the background color will change, in this case. The program begins as normal, with imports and initialization. Here is a program that does this for a button at (100, 100) that is 60x20 pixels in size:

```
from Glib import *
from random import *

x0 = 100            # upper left button position
y0 = 100
w = 60              # Button size
h = 20
bc = cvtColor(200)  # Initial color
active = False      # Is the button currently active?

def draw ():
    global bc, w, h, x0, x1, y0,y1, active
    background (red(bc), green(bc), blue(bc))
                                # Set background color to bc
    x = mouseX()            # Is the mouse in the rectangle?
    y = mouseY()
    if x>x0 and x<x0+w and y>y0 and y<y0+h:
        fill (50, 200, 50)    # YES. Button is active. Green
        active = True
    else:
        fill (200, 50, 50)    # NO. Button is inactive. Red
        active = False
    rect (x0, y0, w, h)       # Draw the button

def mouseReleased (b):
    global active, bc
    if active and b==0:       # Button active? Left button
                              # released?
                              # If so generate a random
                              # background color.
        bc = (randrange (100, 200), randrange(100,200),
            randrange(100, 200))

startdraw(400, 400)
enddraw()
```

All of the software buttons everywhere work in basically this way.

9.2 THE KEYBOARD

Like mouse motions and button presses, pressing a key on the keyboard is an *event*. Like button presses, a key press is a single event with multiple options. The fact that a key has been pressed is an event, and exactly which key it was is a detail, just as it was when a mouse button was pressed. It is important to understand that using a function such as **input()** will not be successful when trying to read from the keyboard with an event-driven system, although knowing about events can be valuable in understanding how **input()** could be implemented. When **input()** is called it does not return until a line has been read; **keyPressed()** captures the key press event. It appears that a call to **input()** may involve many key press events. What software receives them? That is the important question. The situation is really too confusing to be resolved sensibly, so the rule is: *never use* input() *and related functions when handling key presses.* It is OK to call **print()** because it is printing to a console device for which no conflict exists.

Every key press will eventually correspond to a key release, so there are two callback functions again:

keyPressed(k):   Called when a key is pressed. Parameter **k** is the key that was pressed.

keyReleased(k):   Called when a key is released. Parameter **k** is the key that was released.

The parameters are not characters in the normal sense, but are numeric codes that can identify the character. These are based on the Pygame character constants, but extends them slightly. Table 9.1 gives a list of all of the constants provided by *Glib*. As an example, if a program must recognize when the up arrow key is pressed, the **keyPressed ()** function that would do this is:

```
def keyPressed (k):
    if k == K_UP:
        print ("Up arrow key pressed.")
```

In an event-driven program it is unusual for key presses to be converted into strings, as they normally would be in a typical console-style program. That's because it is expected that the interface to the event-driven program will be through mouse gestures and using single key commands from the keyboard, like "up arrow" meaning "move forward."

Example: Pressing a "+" Creates a Random Circle

This program will draw a circle at a random location when the "+" key is pressed. Old circles will remain. This illustrates the use of the keyboard in an obvious way. The initialization is to clear the screen and set the background color

Table 9.1
Glib Character Constants

Backspace	K_BACKSPACE	J	K_j	Function F10	K_F10		
tab	K_TAB	K	K_k	Function F11	K_F11		
Clear	K_CLEAR	L	K_l	Function F12	K_F12		
Return/Enter	K_RETURN	M	K_m	Function F13	K_F13		
Pause	K_PAUSE	N	K_n	Function F14	K_F14		
Esc	K_ESCAPE	O	K_o	Function F15	K_F15		
Space	K_SPACE	P	K_p	Num lock	K_NUMLOCK		
Exclamation !	K_EXCLAIM	Q	K_q	Caps lock	K_CAPSLOCK		
Quote "	K_QUOTEDBL	R	K_r	Scroll Lock	K_SCROL-LOCK		
Hash #	K_HASH	S	K_s	Right Shift	K_RSHIFT		
Dollar $	K_DOLLAR	T	K_t	Left Shift	K_LSHIFT		
Ampersand &	K_AMPERSAND	U	K_u	Right ctl	K_RCTRL		
Quote '	K_QUOTE	V	K_v	Left ctl	K_LCTRL		
Left Paren (	K_LEFTPAREN	W	K_w	Right alt	K_RALT		
Right Paren)	K_RIGHTPAREN	X	K_x	Left alt	K_LALT		
Asterisk *	K_ASTERISK	Y	K_y	Right meta	K_RMETA		
Plus +	K_PLUS	Z	K_z	Left meta	K_LMETA		
Comma ,	K_COMMA	Del	K_DELETE	Left super	K_LSUPER		
Minus -	K_MINUS	Keypad 0	K_KP0	Right super	K_RSUPER		
Period .	K_PERIOD	Keypad 1	K_KP1	Mode	K_MODE		
Slash /	K_SLASH	Keypad 2	K_KP2	Help	K_HELP		
Zero 0	K_0	Keypad 3	K_KP3	Print	K_PRINT		
One 1	K_1	Keypad 4	K_KP4	Sys Req	K_SYSREQ		
Two 2	K_2	Keypad 5	K_KP5	Break	K_BREAK		
Three 3	K_3	Keypad 6	K_KP6	Menu	K_MENU		
Four 4	K_4	Keypad 7	K_KP7	Power	K_POWER		
Five 5	K_5	Keypad 8	K_KP8	Euro	K_EURO		
Six 6	K_6	Keypad 9	K_KP9	A	K_A		
Seven 7	K_7	Keypad .	K_KP_PERIOD	B	K_B		
Eight 8	K_8	Keypad /	K_KP_DIVIDE	C	K_C		
Nine 9	K_9	Keypad *	K_KP_MULTIPLY	D	K_D		
Colon :	K_COLON	Keypad -	K_KP_MINUS	E	K_E		
Semicolon ;	K_SEMICOLON	Keypad +	K_KP_PLUS	F	K_F		

Less <	K_LESS	Keypad Enter	K_KP_ENTER	G	K_G
Equals =	K_EQUALS	Keypad =	K_KP_EQUALS	H	K_H
Greater >	K_GREATER	Up arrow	K_UP	I	K_I
Question ?	K_QUESTION	Down Arrow	K_DOWN	J	K_J
At @	K_AT	Right Arrow	K_RIGHT	K	K_K
Left Bracket [	K_LEFTBRACKET	Left Arrow	K_LEFT	L	K_L
Backslash \	K_BACKSLASH	Insert	K_INSERT	M	K_M
Right Bracket]	K_RIGHTBRACKET	Home	K_HOME	N	K_N
Caret ^	K_CARET	End	K_END	O	K_O
Underscore _	K_UNDERSCORE	PageUp	K_PAGEUP	P	K_P
Back quote `	K_BACKQUOTE	PageDown	K_PAGEDOWN	Q	K_Q
a	K_a	Function F1	K_F1	R	K_R
b	K_b	Function F2	K_F2	S	K_S
c	K_c	Function F3	K_F3	T	K_T
d	K_d	Function F4	K_F4	U	K_U
e	K_e	Function F5	K_F5	V	K_V
f	K_f	Function F6	K_F6	W	K_W
g	K_g	Function F7	K_F7	X	K_X
h	K_h	Function F8	K_F8	Y	K_Y
i	K_i	Function F9	K_F9	Z	K_Z

and fill color. The **keyPressed()** function generates random x,y coordinates and draws a circle there:

```
from Glib import *
from random import *

def keyPressed (k):
    if k == K_PLUS:
        ellipse (randrange(0,width), randrange(0,height),
                 30, 30)

startdraw(400, 400)
fill (200, 0, 0)
background (200)
enddraw()
```

The key value is passed as an integer, but the built-in function **chr()** will convert that to the proper character in many cases. What is possibly the shortest functional *Glib* program simply reads the keys and prints them on the console:

```
from Glib import *

def keyPressed(k):
```

```
        print (chr(k))
    startdraw()
    enddraw()
```

The **startdraw()** function has default parameters, and creates a 50x50 pixel window if no size is specified. This program does not draw anything, so **draw()** is not needed.

Example: Reading a Character String

There are some reasons why an event-driven program might wish to read data from the user as a string. Perhaps a name is required, or a key value to access a database, or a password. Whatever the reason, it should be possible to read a string using **keyPressed()**. The way it would normally be done is to read one character at a time, normal for **keyPressed()**, and construct a string by concatenation. That's how this program works:

```
from Glib import *

s = ""
t = ""

def keyPressed(k):       # k is the value of the key that
                         # was pressed
    global s, t
    if k == K_RETURN:    # Typing RETURN ends the string
                         # construction
        t = s
        s = ""
        return
    if k == K_BACKSPACE and len(s)>0:   # Delete the
                                        # previous character
        s = s[0:len(s)-1]  # Shorten the string by one
                           # character
    else:
        s = s + chr(k)     # Append the new character to
                           # the string

def draw ():
    global s, t
    background (200)
    text ("Enter a string: ", 10, 100)
    text (s, 20, 130)
```

```
if (t != ""):
    text ("Completed string is "+t, 20, 150)

startdraw(200, 200)
enddraw()
```

The global variable **s** holds the string being built, and the string **t** holds the final string. Characters are captured from the keyboard by **keyPressed()** and fall into one of three categories:

1. Most characters are added to the global string **s** through concatenation. The character passed to **keyPressed()** is an integer. The **chr()** function converts it to a character which is added to the end of **s**.

2. A BACKSPACE will delete the last character typed from the string. This is done using a substring from 0 to the second last character.

3. A RETURN will end the string. The current string in **s** will be assigned to **t**, and **s** will be reset to an empty string.

This kind of string data entry is especially useful when entering file names and numeric parameters. There are frequently special interface objects (*widgets*) that perform these tasks, such as *text boxes*. *Glib* could be used to implement such a widget (*see*: Exercise 6).

9.3 ANIMATION

Making graphical objects change position is simple, but making them seem to move is more difficult. Animation is something of an optical illusion; images are drawn in succession, and so quickly that the human eye can't detect that they are distinct images. Small changes in position in a sequence of these images will be seen as motion rather than as a set of still pictures. A typical animation draws a new image (*frame*) between 24 and 30 times per second to make the illusion work.

There are two kinds of animation that can be done using *Glib*. The first involves objects that consist of primitives that are drawn by the library. A circle can represent a ball, for instance, or a set of rectangles and curves could be a car. The second kind of animation uses images, where each image is one frame in the sequence. These images are displayed entirely in rapid succession to create the animation. In the first case the animation is being created as the program executes, whereas in the second the animation is complete before the program runs, and the program really just puts it on the screen.

9.3.1 Object Animation

Animating an object involves updating its position, speed, and orientation at small time intervals, so all of these aspects of the object must be kept in variables. If there are many objects being animated, then all of these variables must exist for each object, and are updated at the end of each time interval. If the animation is displaying 30 frames per second, then a new frame is drawn every 0.03 seconds. In *Glib* the function named **framerate()** can be called passing the number of times that **draw()** will be called each second, and then **draw()** can do the work needed to update the objects and draw the frame.

Example: A Ball in a Box

Imagine a ball bouncing in a square box. A box has three dimensions, of course, but for this example it will be restricted to two, so it will look like a circle within a square. The ball is moving, and when it strikes one of the sides of the square it will bounce, thus changing direction. There is one moving object: the ball. Graphically it is simply a circle, with position **x,y** and speed **dx** in the x direction and **dy** in the y direction. It will have size 30 pixels. The box will simply be the window the circle is drawn in.

During each frame the ball will move **dx** pixels in the x and **dy** pixels in the y direction, so within the **draw()** function the position is updated as:

```
x = x + dx
y = y + dy
```

This new position is where to draw the circle. However, if the ball is outside of the box after it is moved, then a bounce has to be performed. That is, if the new position of x is, for instance, less than 0, then it would have struck the left side of the square and then changed x direction (bounced). In this case, and also if x>width, the bounce is implemented by:

```
dx = -dx
```

Similarly, if the y coordinate of the ball becomes less than 0 or greater than the height, then it bounces vertically:

```
dy = -dy
```

This would all be true if the ball were very tiny, a single point, but it has a size of 30 pixels, and the coordinates of the circle are the coordinates of its center. This means that the method described above will bounce the circle only after the center coordinate passes the boundary, meaning that half of the circle is already on the other side. It's easy to fix: the ball is 30 pixels in size, so it should bounce when it gets within 15 pixels of any boundary. For example, the x bounce should occur when **x<=15 or x>=width-15**. The entire solution is:

```
# Bouncing ball animation.
from Glib import *

def draw ():
    global dx, dy, x, y
    background (200)          # Erase the prior frame
    x = x + dx                # Change ball position
    y = y + dy
    if x<=15 or x>=width-15:  # Bounce in X direction?
        dx = -dx
    if y<=15 or y>=height-15: # Bounce in Y direction?
        dy = -dy
    ellipse (x, y, 30, 30)    # Draw the ball
startdraw(200, 200)
x = 100                       # Initial x position of the
                              # ball
y = 100                       # Initial y position
dx = 3                        # Speed in x
dy = 2                        # Speed in y
fill (30, 200, 20)            # Fill with green
enddraw()
```

Eight frames from this animation showing the ball bouncing in a corner of the box are shown in Figure 9.2. An entire second's worth of frames (30) are given on the accompanying disc.

If there are many objects then all of the positions and speeds, and perhaps even shape, size, and color would have to be kept and updated during each frame. There are two usual ways to do this. In the first case the parameters are kept in arrays (lists). There would be an array of x coordinates, an array of y coordinates, of speeds, and so on. Each frame could involve an update to all elements of the arrays. Updating the position can be done like this:

```
for i in range(0,Nobjects):
```

```
x[i] = x[i] + dx[i]
y[i] = y[i] + dy[i]
```

The other usual method for handling multiple objects is to create an object *class* that contains all of the parameters needed to display the object. There is still an array, but it is an array of object instances, and if it is cleverly programmed the class can be updated by calling an **update()** method:

```
for i in range(0,Nobjects):
    ball[i].update()
```

Example: Many Balls in a Box

This example uses the same premise as the previous one, but will draw many balls in the window, all of them bouncing. Both methods for keeping track of objects, arrays, and classes will be illustrated. The *many arrays* solution has lists for x and y, for dx and dy, for color and for size. All parameters are initialized at random when the program begins.

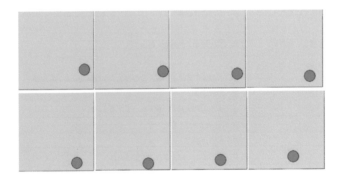

Figure 9.2
Bouncing ball in a box.

The solution that uses classes defines a class **ball** within which the position, speed, color, and size are defined. The constructor initializes the values, and the update method changes the ball's position and performs any needed bounces. The two solutions are:

Arrays	Class
from **Glib** import * from **random** import *	from **Glib** import * from **random** import *

```
def draw ():
    global dx, dy, x, y
    background (200)   # Erase the
                       # prior frame
    for i in range(0,n):
        x[i] = x[i] + dx[i] # Change
                            # position
        y[i] = y[i] + dy[i]
        if x[i]<=sizes[i]/2 or \
           x[i]>=width-sizes[i]/2:
                        # Bounce X?
            dx[i] = -dx[i]
        if y[i]<=sizes[i]/2 or \
           y[i]>=height-sizes[i]/2:
                        # Bounce Y?
            dy[i] = -dy[i]
        fill (red(colors[i]),
             green(colors[i]),
             blue(colors[i]))
        ellipse (x[i], y[i],
            sizes[i], sizes[i])
                    # Draw the ball

startdraw(400, 400)
n = 50
x = []      # Initial x position of
            # the balls
y = []      # Initial y position
dx = []     # Speed in x
dy = []     # Speed in y
colors = []
sizes = []
for i in range (0,n):
    x = x + [randrange(15,width-15)]
    y = y +
[randrange(15,height-15)]
    dx = dx + [randrange (-2, 2)]
    dy = dy + [randrange (-2, 2)]
    sizes = sizes + [randrange
                        (2,30)]
    colors = colors +[(randrange
                        (100, 200),
        randrange(100, 200),
        randrange(100, 200)),]
nostroke()
enddraw()
```

```
class Ball:
    def __init__ (self):
        self.x = randrange (15,
                            width-15)
        self.y = randrange (15,
                            height-15)
        self.dx = randrange (-2, 2)
        self.dy = randrange (-2, 2)
        self.size = randrange (2, 30)
        self.color = (randrange (100,
                            200),
        randrange (100, 200),
            randrange (100, 200))

    def draw (self):
        self.x = self.x + self.dx
                    #Change position
        self.y = self.y + self.dy
        if self.x<=self.size/2 or
        self.x>=width-self.size/2:
                        # Bounce X?
            self.dx = -self.dx
        if self.y<=self.size/2 or
           self.y>=height-self.size/2:
                        # Bounce Y?
            self.dy = -self.dy
        fill(self.color[0],
            self.color[1], self.color[2],
                    self.color[3])
        ellipse (self.x, self.y,
            self.size, self.size)
                    # Draw the ball

def draw ():
    global dx, dy, x, y
    background (200)   # Erase the
                       # prior frame
    for i in range(0,n):
        balls[i].draw()

startdraw(400, 400)
n = 50
balls = []
for i in range (0,n):
    balls = balls + [Ball()]
nostroke()
enddraw()
```

Figure 9.3
Many bouncing balls in a box.

These two solutions illustrate how classes work very neatly. The class contains individual properties of a ball and many are created; the arrays contain many instances of each property. So **x[i]** and **ball[i].x** represent the same thing. In this case the two programs are about the same size, but the class-based implementation encapsulates the details of the ball and what can be done with it. The class-based **draw()** function only says "draw each ball," but in the array implementation the **draw()** function looks at all of the details of all balls to draw them. One of the implications is that it would be possible to divide the labor between two persons, one who wrote the class and another who wrote the rest of the code. For large programs this can matter quite a lot.

9.3.2 Frame Animation

The hard work in frame animation is done before the computer program is written. An animator has created drawings of an object in various stages of movement. All the program does is display frames one after the other, often looping them to create the desired effect. A common example of this is the animation of *gait*, walking or running. An artist draws multiple stages of a single step, being careful to ensure that timing is correct: how long does it take for a normal person to stake a pair of steps (left, right)? This time should agree with the frames the artist creates. If it takes one second to make the step, then it should be drawn as 30 frames.

Other kinds of animation are performed too. A fire can be animated as a very few frames, as can smoke and water. The program that draws the animation reads all of the image files into a collection. When the animation is played, the program displays one image after another within the draw function. This can be complicated by the fact that there may be multiple animations playing at the same time, possibly of different lengths and frame sizes.

Example: Read Frames and Play Them Back as an Animation

In this example there are 10 drawn animation frames of a cartoon character walking. These frames are intended to represent a single gait cycle, and so should be repeated. The program will do the following: when the up arrow key is pressed and held down, the character drawn in the window will "walk"; otherwise a still image will be displayed.

First the images should be read in and stored in an array (list) so that they can be played repeatedly. Then the **keyPressed()** function should be written so that when the up arrow key is pressed the frames will be drawn. A flag can be set **True** when the key is pressed, and **False** when the key is released so that **draw()** can tell when to draw frames and when not.

```
def keyPressed (k):
    global keydown
    keydown = True

def keyReleased(k):
    global keydown
    keydown = False
```

A list named **frames** is initialized with all of the images in the sequence. All that **draw()** does is play the next one, using a global variable **f** to identify the current frame.

```
def draw ():
    global keydown, f
    if keydown:
        image (frames[f], 0, 0)
        f = f + 1
        if (f > 10):
            f = 1
```

It cycles through the frames and repeats when all have been displayed.

The initialization can be a simple matter of reading ten images into variables and creating a list. This code does it in a loop, using a number in the name and incrementing it:

```
startdraw(320, 240)
keydown = False
frames = []
for i in range (1, 10):
    s = "images/a00"+str(i) +".bmp"
    x = loadImage (s)
    frames = frames + [x,]
x = loadImage ("images/a010.bmp")
frames = frames + [x,]
```

```
x = loadImage ("images/a011.bmp")
frames = frames + [x,]
f = 1
image (frames[0], 0, 0)
enddraw()
```

The variable **frames** is a list holding all of the images, and **frames[i]** is the ith image in the sequence.

The building of the file name is interesting. It is common to use numbered names for animation frames; things like *frame01, frame02*, and so on. In this case the sequence is *a***.bmp* where the ***** represents a three-digit number. If the variable **i** is an integer, then **str(i)** is a string containing that integer, but leading zeros are not present. Thus, for values of i between 0 and 9 (one digit), the string will be **"a00"+str(i)+".bmp"**; for values of **i** between 10 and 99 (two digits), the string will be **"a0"+str(i)++".bmp"**; finally, for numbers between 100 and 999, the string will be **"a"+str(i)+".bmp"** (three digits). The leading zeros are manually inserted into the string.

The animation frames for the gait sequence are on the disk along with this code.

Example: Simulation of the Space Shuttle Control Console (A Class That Will Draw an Animation at a Specific Location)

Animations can sometimes be used to decorate a scene in interesting ways. A control panel showing video screens and data displays could use animations to fill the screens, giving the illusion of real things being monitored. A class that can play a frame-by-frame animation at any location on the screen could be instantiated many times, once for each display.

The class would have to read the frames it was to play and store them, play back the frames in a loop when requested, and place them within the window at any location. None of these tasks is especially hard. Code for reading frames from a file was written for the previous example, as was code for displaying the frames. Each class instance would need a frame count so that the loop could start over at the right place, and each class instance could have an animation with a different number of frames. Finally, placing at the right location is a matter of passing the correct parameters to the **image()** function. The class would be instantiated given the position as x and y coordinates of the upper left corner.

Sometimes, especially when multiple animations are playing, it will be necessary to slow down some animations so that they look right. The *Glib* code calls **draw()** a fixed number of times each second, but that may not always be the correct speed for an animation. A count can be introduced so that the frame advances to the next only when a count exceeds a fixed delay value. If the count is 2, for example, then 2 calls to **draw()** are required before a new frame is chosen, meaning that the frame rate has been decreased by 50%.

The specific example is supposed to implement a "simulation" of a space shuttle control console. This is a visual simulation, not one that allows interaction at any level, and the idea is to insert animations into a still photo of a real shuttle console and make it look more active. Figure 9.4a shows the static image that will be used. There are many video screens visible, and the program being developed will replace the still image on some of those screens with moving, animated images.

Three of the screens are selected for animation. The image was displayed using Paint and the coordinates of the upper left corner of each of these screens was determined, as were the sizes. Figure 9.4b shows the location of these regions on the image.

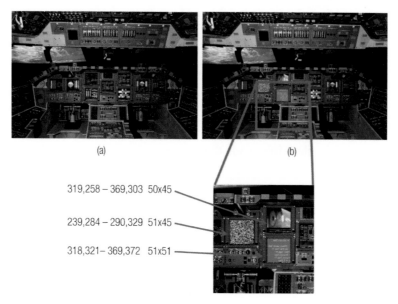

(a) (b)

319,258 – 369,303 50x45

239,284 – 290,329 51x45

318,321 – 369,372 51x51

Figure 9.4
https://commons.wikimedia.org/wiki/File:STSCPanel.jpg

The code for the class starts like this:

```
class Anim:
    def __init__ (self, x, y):   # Constructor -------------
        self.frames = []         # The actual images
        self.xpos = x            # Position of upper left
        self.ypos = y
        self.n = 0               # How many frames are there?
        self.f = 0               # Which frame is currently
                                 # being shown?
        self.active = False      # Is this animation being
                                 # played?
        self.delay = 1           # Used to slow the frame
                                 # rate
        self.count = 100000      # When count>delay a frame
                                 # is drawn

    def draw (self):
        if self.active:  # Draw the current frame at the
                         # correct location
            image (self.frames[self.f], self.xpos, self.ypos)
            self.count = self.count + 1  # Increment count.
            if self.count >= self.delay: # Change the frame
                                         # yet?
                self.f = self.f + 1      # Yes. And also
                                         # reset the count
                self.count = 0
            if (self.f >= self.n):       # Loop the frames;
                                         # start over at 0
                self.f = 0
```

The part of the class that reads the frames as images is basically taken from the previous example:

```
    def getframes (self, s1, s2):
        self.frames = []            # The list variable
                                    #'frames' contains all
                                    # images
        for i in range (0, 100):  # Up to 100images can be
                                  # read.
            if i<10:
                s = s1 + "0"+str(i) + s2
                print ("Reading ", s)
            elif i<100:
```

```
        s = s1 + str(i) + s2
    x = loadImage (s)
    if x == None:
        self.n = i
        print ("Saw ", self.n, " frames.")
        break
    self.frames = self.frames + [x,]
```

There is a flag named **active** that determines whether the animations are currently running or not. The methods **start()** and **stop()** turn the animation on and off by toggling this variable.

```
    def start(self):
        self.active = True

    def stop (self):
        self.active = False
```

Finally, for this class, the delay can be set using a call to the **setdelay()** method, which simply changes the value of a class local variable **delay**.

```
    def setdelay (self, d):
        self.delay = d
The draw() method of the program simply draws the
animations by calling their respective draw() methods:

def draw ():
    a.draw()
    b.draw()
    c.draw()
```

The main program opens the window and loads and draws the background image:

```
startdraw(800, 531)   # The size of the background image
background = loadImage ("images/800px-STSCPanel.jpg")
image (background, 0, 0)
```

The first animation, at x=239 and y=284, will show some television static, seven frames of which were created for this purpose using another program. A class instance is created to draw at (239,284) and **getFrames()** is called to load the images (the file names are "g100.gif" through "g106.gif"):

```
a = Anim(239, 284)
a.getframes ("images/g1", ".gif")
```

The second animation is at x=319 and y=258 and will display some exterior shots of the space shuttle. The process is the same as before, but the file names are "g200.jpg" through "g204.jpg." In addition, a delay of 100 is set, because these images are to be displayed for multiple seconds each to simulate a display scanning a set of cameras:

```
b = Anim (319, 258)
b.getframes ("images/g2", ".jpg")
b.setdelay(100)
```

Finally the third animation, at x=319 and y=322, consists of a computer display showing Python code (this *class*, in fact). It was created by another program and consists of nine frames named "g300.gif" through "g308.gif." This animation is delayed a little as well so that it appears as if the text is scrolling properly:

```
c = Anim (319, 322)
c.getframes ("images/g3", ".gif")
c.setdelay(10)
```

The last step in the program is to start all of the animations playing:

```
a.start()
b.start()
c.start()
enddraw()
```

The example is complete on the disk, and needs to be executed with the *images* directory, which contains the animation frames.

https://commons.wikimedia.org/wiki/File:STSCPanel.jpg

9.4 ■ RGBA COLORS – TRANSPARENCY

In Chapter 7, it was seen how it was possible to use transparency in an image to allow the visualization to 'see through' to an image in the background. As it happens, any pixel can be assigned a degree of transparency that permits the same visual character. A color can be assigned a value that dictates how opaque or transparent it is, allowing colors behind it to influence how that pixel is seen. One can think of this as a fourth color value, in addition to red, green, and blue. It is referred to as *alpha*, and a color with four color parameters is said to be in the RGBA color space, for *R*ed, *G*reen, *B*lue, and *A*lpha.

If the value of Alpha is 255, then the color is opaque; as it decreases in value the transparency increases until at Alpha=0 pixel or object cannot be seen. A program that draws three overlapping circles using colors with an Alpha value of 60 shows the visual effect of using transparency (Figure 9.5a). Transparency is specified in this case by providing the Alpha value as a fourth parameter to **fill()**:

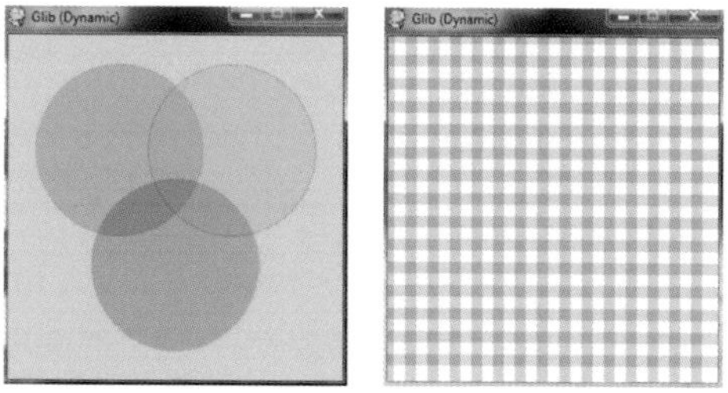

(a)   (b)

Figure 9.5

(a) Overlapping circles filled with transparent versions of red, green, and blue create new colors in the overlapping regions. (b) Stroke colors can have transparency too. Where the red and blue lines intersect, the red under the blue is seen as purple.

```
from Glib import *

startdraw(300, 300)
fill (255, 0, 0, 60)
ellipse (100, 100, 150, 150)
fill (0, 255, 0, 60)
ellipse (200, 100, 150, 150)
fill (0, 0, 255, 60)
ellipse (150, 200, 150, 150)
enddraw()
```

Transparency can be added to stroke colors also, and in the same way (Figure 9.5b). For example:

```
stroke (255, 0, 0, 65)
```

9.5 SOUND

Sound is an essential component of digital media. Proof? Almost nobody watches silent films anymore, and nobody makes them. Video games are rarely played with the sound turned off. There are a few important reasons for this.

1. Much human communication is through sound. Speech is the best example, but non-speech sounds, clapping, stamping of feet, and so on, are ways that people make their feelings and intentions known.

2. Sounds are associated with events. When an object falls to the floor a sound occurs with the impact. A button is pressed and a doorbell rings. These sounds are important indicators.

3. Sounds cause emotional reactions in people. Music can do this; it can convey a mood better than almost anything else. But sound can also indicate things unseen. A growling in the dark; a screech in the sky; the sound of an approaching vehicle around a curve in the road.

In *Glib* a sound is much like an image in terms of how it is used. A sound file is loaded and assigned to a variable, then that variable can be used to play, stop, rewind, and perform all audio operations on that sound. Each sound must be loaded into a distinct variable and has its own controls. The Glib interface to sounds files should therefore look familiar.

One problem is that the sound system does not have a large variety of sound files that it can handle: ".wav" and ".ogg" are about it. This leaves the more popular format, "mp3," out of contention for Python media software, at least for now.

The first step in playing a sound is to load the file. The function **loadSound()** is used for this, passing the name of the sound file:

```
s = loadSound ("song.wav")
```

Playing the sound is done using the **playSound()** function of *Glib*:

```
playSound (s)
```

Stopping a sound from playing is a matter of calling **stopSound()**. Setting the volume means calling **volumeSound()** passing a parameter between 0.0 and 1.0, where 0.0 is no sound and 1.0 is maximum volume. That's pretty much it for the basics.

Example: Play a Sound

The act of reading and playing a sound file will illustrate the essential operations for using sound. The file input is done as an initialization. Starting to play the file could be done that way too. Calling **playSound()** repeatedly from **draw()** will cause the file to start playing over and over again. A solution is to start some sounds in the main program; another is to set a flag when a sound starts playing and check the flag. The best way would be to record the time when the sound started playing and see if the current time exceeds the length of the sound.

If **playSound()** is called with a second parameter, an integer, then the sound will be replayed or repeated that many times. The call **playsound(s, 3)** plays the sound **s** three times. If the requested file does not exist, then **loadSound()** returns **None**.

Example: Control Volume Using the Keyboard. Pause and Unpause

This example adds volume control. The function **volumeSound**() accepts a single parameter, and it is a number between 0.0 (lowest volume) and 1.0 (highest volume). Adding a volume control is as simple as coding a **keyPressed**() function that changes the volume level by an increment each time a key is pressed. Use "+" for a volume increase and "-" for a decrease. The new program is:

```
from Glib import *

def keyPressed(k):
    global volume, s
    if k == K_PLUS:
        volume = volume+.1
    elif k == K_MINUS:
        volume = volume-.1
    if volume<0: volume = 0
    if volume>1: volume = 1
    volumeSound(s, volume)

startdraw()
s = loadSound ("sun.wav")
volume = 1.0
volumeSound (s, volume)
if s == None:
    print ("No such sound file.")
else:
    playSound(s)
enddraw()
```

Example: Play a Sound Effect at the Right Moment: Bounces

A sound effect represents some event, and needs to be played at the moment the event happens. Synchronizing the two things is as simple as playing a sound when the event is detected. This example program will play a sound representing a ball hitting something when a simulated ball hits the side of the window and bounces. The bouncing ball animation program will provide the impact event: when the ball hits the side of the window, the sound of an impact will be played.

The sound effect is a file, and was recorded using an inexpensive microphone, a computer with a sound card, and the *Audacity* software, which is free and downloadable (see the end-of-chapter resources). The sound of a glass hitting a desk was recorded, edited, and saved as a ".wav" file named "bounce.wav." The program was modified to read that file, and then play it back whenever a collision with the window was detected. The program has three new lines of code:

```
# Bouncing ball animation.
from Glib import *

def draw ():
    global dx, dy, x, y
    background (200)              # Erase the prior frame
    x = x + dx                    # Change ball position
    y = y + dy
    if x<=15 or x>=width-15:      # Bounce in X direction?
        playSound (s)
        dx = -dx
    if y<=15 or y>=height-15:     # Bounce in Y direction?
        dy = -dy
        playSound(s)
    ellipse (x, y, 30, 30)        # Draw the ball

startdraw(200, 200)
x = 100                           # Initial x position of the
                                  # ball
y = 100                           # Initial y position
dx = 3                            # Speed in x
dy = 2                            # Speed in y
s = loadSound ("bounce.wav")
fill (30, 200, 20)                # Fill with green
enddraw()
```

In many situations there can be a small delay between the event and the sound being played. A sound can rarely be played instantaneously.

9.6 VIDEO

The video facilities provided by *Glib* are limited, but the library increases the functionality of the underlying *Pygame* module. It is important to understand that video plays at a particular rate and, unlike audio, must acquire a portion of the display window within which to be drawn. This means that playing a video in the normal way takes control away from the programmer and allows the video software autonomy. This can cause some trouble, as programmers often want to draw into the display window as well.

Using the basic functionality it is possible to play an MPEG-formatted video with sound anywhere in the window, and the window can be sized to suit the purpose. Only a single video can be played in this way at one time, though. A video has characteristics of both sounds and images: the video resides in a file; it is placed in a specific location in the window, and has a two-dimensional size (a width and height), but the image displayed changes as a function of time. Also, a video can have sound as one of its properties. However, because multiple videos may have multiple sound channels, only one of them is given the sound output channel, meaning that only one can play sound.

A video is read into a variable in the same way as an image or sound: a function **loadVideo()** returns a variable that references the data on an MPEG file which is specified by file name as the parameter. A video is played by calling the function **playVideo()** and passing the value returned by **loadVideo()**. The smallest program that plays a video file would be something like this:

```
from Glib import *

startdraw(400, 400)
s = loadVideo ("ellipsis.mpg")
if s != None:
    playVideo(s)
enddraw()
```

The file being opened and played is one provided on the accompanying disc, "ellipsis.mpg," and it has no sound. The variable **s** represents the video in the program, and is returned by **loadVideo()**. It is, in fact, a reference to a *Glib* class named **Gvideo**. If it has the value **None**, then no video file was loaded for some reason: perhaps the file does not exist or is in a format that can't be processed. *Glib* only recognizes MPEG video files, and even then only MPEG I. The **playVideo()** function places the image in the upper left corner of the window and begins playing it, sound included.

There are a small collection of useful functions in *Glib* for dealing with videos. They are:

pauseVideo(m): Parameter **m** is a video. Pauses the video if it is playing or resumes it if it is paused

stopVideo (m): Parameter **m** is a video. Stops playing the video m

rewindVideo (m): Parameter **m** is a video. Returns the video to the beginning

isVideoPlaying (m): Parameter **m** is a video. Returns True if the video is playing

setVideoVolume(m, v): Parameter **m** is a video. Adjusts the audio volume on the video **m** to be the value **v**, where **v=0** is the minimum and **v=1.0** is the maximum

lengthVideo (m): Parameter **m** is a video. Returns the length of the video in seconds

whereVideo(m): Parameter **m** is a video. Returns the current location in the video, in seconds from the start

getVideoFrame(m): Parameter **m** is a video. Returns the current video frame playing

setVideoFrame(m, f): Parameter **m** is a video. Changes the playback so the next frame in the video to play is frame **f**

getVideoPixel(m, x, y): Parameter **m** is a video. Returns the value of the pixel at location **(x,y)** in the *frame currently being displayed*

sizeVideo (m): Parameter **m** is a video. Returns the dimensions of a video frame. The video must be loaded

videoSize (s): Parameter **s** is a string. Returns the dimensions a frame in the video file **s**, where **s** is a string. Use this for finding the size before loading the file

locVideo (m, x, y, w, h): Position the video **m** at position **(x,y)** in the window, and make it **w**x**h** pixels in size. Does not start it playing

Example: Carclub – Display the Video carclub2.mpg (Annotated)

When the **p** key is pressed the video will pause, and when pressed again it will resume. Display the video at location 100, 100 in the window and make it 200x200 pixels. Display the number of the current frame and the current time of the frame being played.

This program uses eight of the fifteen video functions. First the file is loaded and the location and size are set using **locVideo()**. Then the main program starts the video playing.

The **draw()** function is responsible for updating the numeric values displayed. It resets the background and then checks to see if the video is playing; it displays "Playing" if so, or "Not playing" otherwise. The current position, current time, and total time are extracted and displayed using calls to **text()**.

Finally the pause feature is implemented. In the function **keyPressed()** the function checks that the key pressed was "p," and if so it calls **pauseVideo()**. This function keeps track of whether or not the function is playing and knows whether to start or stop the video. Here is the program:

```
from Glib import *

def draw ():
    global vid
    background (0, 200, 190)         # Clear the background,
                                     # set to aqua.
    if isVideoPlaying(vid):          # Playing? Print an
                                     # indicator
        text ("playing", 10, 40)
    else:
        text ("Not playing", 10, 40)
    whr = whereVideo(vid)            # Current time of play
    text ("Frame "+str(getVideoFrame(vid)), 10, 60)
                                     # Current frame
    text ("Length "+ str(whr)+" of "+str(lengthVideo(vid)),
                                        40, 370)

def keyPressed(k):
    global vid
    if k == K_p:                     # Key pressed was a 'p'
        pauseVideo(vid)              # Pause

startdraw(500, 500)
vid = loadVideo("carclub2.mpg")      # Load the car club video
locVideo(vid, 100, 100, 200, 200) # Position it at
                                     # (100, 100)
playVideo(vid)                       # Play it.
enddraw()
```

A screen shot of this program in action is shown in Figure 9.5. Note that the current time is displayed to 16 or so digits. This can be changed to display something more reasonable (see: Exercise 8).

There are four different ways to "play" a video using Glib, and each has a distinct set of pros and cons and a process for how to manage the video. After loading the video into variable m:

1. **Using the Glib functions – loadVideo(), locVideo(), play()** and so on isolate the programmer from the actual video class *Gvideo*. These are

typically used when there are one or two videos and there is no complicated processing going on. Only one video with sound can be played; the others will play muted.

2. **AutoPlay(m)** – The video **m** will play automatically in the current display window. The user has some control: the video can be paused and can be located at a specific location and size. It will play at the internally designated rate (frames per second) with sound. Only one video with sound can be played in this way; the others will not have the sound played.

3. **PlayVideo(m)** – The video will play at its internal frame rate, but a frame will not be displayed until the **drawVid()** function is called. If **drawVid()** is called inside of the user's **draw()** function then the frames will be displayed at the *Glib*-specified frame rate, but some video frames might be missed.

4. **DrawFrame(m, f)** – The frame numbered **f** of the video **m** will be drawn. Sound will not play. This permits the best control of the video, because each frame can be played at any speed without missing any; or, every second or third frame can be played; or random frames can be played. The video can even be played backwards – simply start **f** at the largest frame value and decrease by 1 each time.

Three of these different styles are illustrated in the table below:

```
from Glib import *          from Glib import *          from Glib import *
# Use the Glib functions    # Use playVideo/drawVid     # Use the Gvideo methods

startdraw (500,500)         def draw ():                def draw ():
s = loadVideo ("vid1.           global s, t                 global s, t, frame
            mpg")               drawVid(s)                  drawFrame (s, frame)
locVideo (s, 0, 0, 200,         drawVid(t)                  drawFrame(t, frame)
          200)              startdraw (500,500)             frame = frame + 1
t = loadVideo ("vid2.       s = loadVideo ("vid1.       startdraw (500,500)
            mpg")                       mpg")           frame = 0
locVideo (t, 210, 0,        locVideo (s, 0, 0, 200,     s = loadVideo ("vid1.
          200, 200)                   200)                         mpg")
autoPlay(t)                 t = loadVideo ("vid2.       locVideo (s, 0, 0, 200,
autoPlay(s)                             mpg")                     200)
                            locVideo (t, 210, 0,        t = loadVideo ("vid2.
enddraw()                             200, 200)                    mpg")
                            playVideo(t)                locVideo (t, 210, 0,
                            playVideo (s)                         200, 200)
                            enddraw()                   enddraw()
```

Figure 9.6
Car club video. (Left) While playing. (Right) While paused.

Exercise: Threshold a Video (Processing Pixels)

In Chapter 7, a program was written that thresholded an image. It converted each pixel to a grey value and if that value was smaller than a specified threshold it would be set to black; otherwise it would be set to white. Each frame of a video is an image, and it should be possible to threshold each frame and then display it. *Glib* provides the **getVideoPixel()** function that returns the value of a specified pixel in the current frame of a video.

This example will use **draw_frame()** to display the video, and **draw_frame()** will be called from the user's draw() function. After the frame is displayed each pixel in the frame is examined (**getVideoPixel ()**), converted to a grey value (**grey(p)**), and tested against a threshold; if smaller than the threshold, it will be drawn as black by calling **fill (0)** and drawing the pixel with **point ()**. Otherwise, the pixel will be drawn as white. The original image is displayed at the top of the window, the thresholded one below. Thus the window has to be created initially with double the height of the image to make room for two copies.

```
from Glib import *

def draw ():
    global frame, v, wid, ht, x
    background (200)
    draw_frame(v, frame)
```

```
    for i in range (0,wid):
        for j in range(0,ht):
            p = getVideoPixel (v, i, j)
            g = grey(p)
            if g<t:
                fill (0)
            else:
                fill (255)
            point (i, j+ht)
    frame = frame + 1
    fill (0)
    text ("Original: Frame"+str(frame), 10, 30)
    text ("Thresholded: Frame "+str(frame), 10, ht+30)

s = videoSize("carclub2.mpg")
startdraw(s[0],s[1]*2)
v = loadVideo ("carclub2.mpg")
frame = 1
wid = s[0]
ht = s[1]
t = 100
locVideo(v, 0, 0, wid, ht)
enddraw()
```

Figure 9.7
Real-time thresholding of a video, frame by frame.

9.7 SUMMARY

A facility has already been described for displaying images and graphics: Glib, and here more media capability is added to Glib, thus building on what has already been discussed, so that sound and video can be displayed. The new library is *dynamic Glib* and offers the same functionality as previously plus sound, animation, and video.

Using mouse position and button presses is a basic form of communication with a computer. The *Glib* module keeps track of the mouse using *Pygame* and continually updates the position as two variables: **mouseX** and **mouseY** hold the most recent x and y coordinates. If the user writes a function named **mouse-Pressed()**, then it will be executed when a mouse button is pressed. Similarly, when a mouse button is released it tries to call **mousereleased()**. A software graphical *button* is a rectangle or other area which, if the mouse button is clicked while the mouse cursor is within that area, will perform a task; in other words, the click while the cursor is in that area calls a function.

The keyboard is similarly dealt with by having a user-coded function **key-Pressed()** and another named **keyReleased()**. They are passed the value of the key that was pressed as the parameter.

Animation is performed by rapidly displaying drawn images, or frames, one after the other, or by creating and drawing graphical objects and then changing their positions. A function named **draw()** can be written by the programmer to draw the frames many times each second.

Sounds are displayed by reading them from a file and calling a play() function when the sound is needed. Sounds can be music, voice, ambiance, or sound effects.

Video is the most resource-consuming of the media types. Glib allows videos to be recalled and placed in the window, and to be played automatically or frame by frame.

Exercises

1. Write a program that figures out how fast the mouse is moving (pixels per second assuming 30 frames per second) and displays that value.

2. Consider the example that prints a circle at a random position when a "+" key is pressed. Modify it so that when the "-" key is pressed, the previous circle is deleted (no longer appears on the screen).

3. Write a program that reads lines from a file as pairs of x,y coordinates on a single line and draw them all. Each line would have four integers:

   100   100   200   200

   which are the (x,y) coordinates of the start and endpoints of the line. In the example above, the line would be drawn between (100, 100) and (200, 200).

4. Implement a circular button. It is represented on the screen as a circle at (100, 100) of size 30 pixels. Normally it is red, but it turns green when activated. When a mouse button is pressed while the button is activated, a rectangle is drawn somewhere (random) in the window.

5. Implement a button that normally has the text "Yes" drawn within it, but that changes that text to "No" when the button is activated. Pressing it does nothing.

6. Use *Glib* to implement a *text box* that permits a file name or other text to be entered when the mouse cursor is within that region defined by the box. Use this to create a program that allows the user to enter a file name of an image and have the program display this image in the window.

7. Modify the program from Exercise 5 above so that a sound is made when the button is pressed. A clicking sound would be most appropriate, but whatever it is it must be of short duration.

8. Floating point values, such as the current time of the video in seconds, are often converted into strings and require ten or more digits to be displayed. Write a function that changes a floating point number so that it will display in five digits, and modify the video display program named *carclub* so that all floats are displayed with only two digits to the right of the decimal.

9. Modify the simulation of the space shuttle console so that videos are played in the simulated screens instead of frame-by-frame animations.

Notes and Other Resources

Thanks to the estate of composer and musician and friend Michael Becker **for the use of the song 'Holding On,' and for the use of the .wav file.**

Download for the *Pygame* module. *http://www.pygame.org/download.shtml*

An excellent sound editor for .wav and .mp3 files. *http://www.goldwave.ca/*

Another excellent sound file editor. *http://sourceforge.net/projects/audacity/*

Complete Pygame documentation. https://media.readthedocs.org/pdf/pygame/latest/pygame.pdf

Convert video files into MPEG-I format. *http://video.online-convert.com/convert-to-mpeg-1*

A good tutorial on video formats. *http://www.videomaker.com/article/c10/15362-video-formats-explained*

Free software that converts between video formats. *http://www.any-video-converter.com/products/for_video_free/*

1. Al Sweigart. (2012). **Making Games with Python & Pygame**, CreateSpace Independent Publishing Platform, ISBN-13: 978-1469901732.

2. Sean Riley. (2003). **Game Programming with Python**, Charles River Media.

3. Vic Costello. (2016). **Multimedia Foundations, 2nd edition**, Focal Press, ISBN-13: 978-0415740036.

4. Richard Boulanger and Victor Lazzarini (Eds.). (2010). **The Audio Programming Book**, The MIT Press, Har/DVD edition, ISBN-13: 978-0262014465.

5. Sendpoints. (2015). **GUI: Graphical User Interface Design**, ISBN-13: 978-9881383495.

6. Mahesh Venkitachalam. (2015). **Python Playground: Geeky Projects for the Curious Programme**r, No Starch Press, ISBN-13: 978-1593276041.

BASIC ALGORITHMS

■ ■ ■ ■ ■

In this chapter

An algorithm, as discussed in previous chapters, is a step-by-step description of a means to solve a problem. As someone who is learning to program, what are the most important algorithms? That rather depends on how "important" is defined. Does it reflect commercial value? Number of times it is used? Pedagogical uses? Since there are many ways an algorithm can be important, this chapter deals with the most common algorithms discussed on programming web pages and in introductory computing texts. None of these methods require a knowledge of advanced mathematics or data structures.

10.1 SORTING

Most people know what sorting is and can sort a small sequence of numbers in a few seconds. Each may have a distinct strategy for doing it, but few can explain to someone else how to sort an arbitrary set of numbers. They themselves may not know how they do it; they can simply tell when something is sorted, and have some process for sorting in mind. In short, the process of sorting is one of the simplest things that is hard to describe.

Because sorting is so important in computer science, it has been studied at great length. But what is it? Sorting involves placing things in an order defined by a function that ranks them somehow. For numbers, ranking means using the numerical value. So: the sequence 1, 3, 2 is not in proper order, but 1, 2, 3 is in ascending (getting larger) order and 3, 2, 1 is in descending (getting smaller) order. Formally, a sequence **s** is in *ascending* order if $s_i <= s_{i-1}$ for all **i**. The act of sorting means arranging the values in a sequence so that this is true. It is clear that it can be decided when a sequence is sorted.

So how can a sequence be placed in sorted order? By using a *sorting algorithm*, of course. For all of the following discussion on sorting, assume that the problem is to sort into ascending order.

10.1.1 Selection Sort

Small sequences are easier to sort than longer ones, and may provide some insight into the process. The sequence:

$$8 \quad 4$$

is not sorted in ascending order, but testing this is easy and fixing it is trivial: simply swap the two values. The longer sequence:

$$8 \quad 4 \quad 9$$

is also not sorted but is more difficult to sort because it is longer and there are more combinations of the numbers that are unsorted. How can this sequence be placed in order? Here's one idea:

1. Find the smallest element in the list.
2. Swap that element for the element at the beginning of the list.
3. Find the smallest element in the rest of the list.
4. Swap that element for the second element in the list.

    … and so on until the list is sorted.

This is called the *selection sort* algorithm, because at each stage it selects the smallest of the unsorted items in the list and places it where it belongs. Consider the following list:

[12, 18, 5, 21, 9]
  0   1 2 3   4 - index

The smallest element in this list is 5, at index 2. Swap element 2 for element 0:

[**5**, 18, 12, 21, 9]

The bold elements above are in sorted order, which here is only the one at location 0. For the remainder of the elements, repeat the process of finding the smallest element and placing it at the beginning of the unsorted list (element 1). That means swapping 9 for 18, element 4 for element 1:

[**5, 9**, 12, 21, 18]

Repeating, it turns out that element 2, value 12, is now the smallest, and is in the correct place.

[**5, 9, 12**, 21, 18]

Now the value 18 is smallest and should be placed at location 3.

[**5, 9, 12, 18, 21**]

Now the sort is complete. When only one remains it must be in the correct place.

Finding the smallest element in a list involves three things. First, begin with the initial element and assume that is it the smallest. Identify it using its index **imin**. Next, check the value of all successive elements in the list (from **imin** to the end of the list) against the value at **imin**. Finally, in the case where one of the successive values at index **k** is smaller than the one at index **imin**, set imin to **k** to indicate where a new smallest value was found. In simple, imprecise English, scan all of the elements above **imin** and remember the location of the smallest one. Presuming that the list to be sorted is named **data**, the code for finding the smallest element from **imin** to the end of the list is:

```
for i in range (imin, len(data)):
    if data[i] < data[imin]:
        imin = i
```

This code does work, but it modifies **imin**, which is used to determine the loop bounds, within the loop itself. This can be confusing to some, and is bad form generally. It is better to code this loop as:

```
imin = istart
for i in range (iend, len(data)):
    if data[i] < data[imin]:
        imin = i
```

What happens after this is to swap the smallest value found for the one at location **istart**. In most programming languages this would take three statements, which would look something like this:

```
temp = data[imin]
data[imin] = data[istart]
data[istart] = temp
```

One of the joys of Python is that this swap can be performed using a different, some would say prettier, syntax:

```
(data[istart], data[imin]) = (data[imin], data[istart])
```

This is the core of the algorithm, and needs to be done for all values of **imin**; that is from 0 to len(data)-1. This is another for loop, of course, within which this code is placed. That outer loop would be:

```
for istart in range (0, len(data)-1):
```

This is all that is needed for the sort. Writing it as a function, it looks like this:

```
def selection (data):
  for istart in range (0, len(data)-1):
      imin = istart
      for i in range(istart,len(data)):
          if data[i] < data[imin]:
              imin = i
      (data[istart], data[imin]) = (data[imin], data[istart])
```

This sorting method appears to be natural to humans. It is the one most often described by students when asked how they sort numbers. It is not the fastest in many cases, but does a small number of swaps. If the data is already sorted it does no swaps; if it is in reverse order it does **len(data)-1** swaps, the smallest that can be done and still sort the list. When looking at algorithms it is common to define a worst case and a best case, and to define performance not in seconds but in terms of one of the operations performed. In that way the nature of the computer, whether it is fast or slow, does not affect the analysis. For sorting it is common to select the operation to be used as a basis for comparison to be the compare operation: data[i]<data[imin]. How many of these are done?

The best case for the selection sort occurs when the list is already sorted. In that case it will perform close to N^2 comparisons, where N = len(data). This is the same number of comparisons needed for the worst case, in which the list is in reverse order. At least it is consistent. However, it minimizes the number of times swaps occur, and if swapping is expensive then this could be the sorting method to choose.

Selection sort is *unstable*. If there are repeated values in the data, then they will of course end up together in the final, sorted list. However, if a sort is *stable* they will remain in the same order they were originally. Selection sort, like many others, does not guarantee this. It seems as if this is a minor thing, but it does matter in some cases. Consider a list of names in a list that are given, in order of some sort of score, on a web page. Names for tie scores should always be in the same order on the page, so that if the page is refreshed or a link is followed the page looks the same.

It should be said here that generally there is no best sorting method. The properties of such a method would be:

1. Fast. Selection sort is N^2 in terms of comparisons. The best one can normally expect from any sort would be N*log(N) in the worst case.
2. Does not need extra space. This means that the array can be sorted in place, with perhaps a temporary variable for performing swaps.
3. Performs no more than N swaps in the worst case.
4. *Adaptive*. The method detects when it is finished instead of looping through unproductive iterations. If, for example, such a method is given an already sorted list, it will finish in a single pass through the data.
5. Stable.

No method has all of these characteristics.

10.1.2 Merge Sort

If there were a "best" sorting algorithm then this would be the place to describe it. As there is not, perhaps the best thing to do would be to look at an algorithm that is quite different from the selection sort, and that has properties that it does not have. The method named *merge sort* fits that description nicely: it is an N*log(N) sort, it does need extra space, and it uses more than N swaps but it is stable.

Merge sort is an example of a *divide and conquer* style of algorithm, in which a problem is repeatedly broken up into sub-problems, often using recursion, until they are small enough to solve; the solutions are combined to solve the larger problem. The idea behind merge sort is to break the data into parts that can be sorted trivially, then combine those parts knowing that they are sorted. Using the sample data from the selection sort example, the first step in the merge sort is to split the data into two parts. There are 5 elements in this list, and the middle element would be at 5//2, or 2, so the two parts are:

[12, 18]   [5, 21, 9]

Splitting again, the first set has 2 elements, the middle being at 0; the second set has 3 elements, so split at 1:

[12]   [18]   [5]   [21,1]

The final split breaks the data into individual components:

[12]   [18]   [5]   [21]   [1]

The splitting is done in such a way that the original locations are remembered. This happens in the recursive solution, but could be done in other ways. One way to visualize this is as a *tree* structure:

```
            [12, 18, 5, 21, 9]
             /             \
        [12, 18]          [5, 21, 9]
         /   \             /    \
      [12]   [18]        [5]    [21, 9]
                                 /  \
                               [21]  [9]
```

This completes the *divide* portion of the *divide and conquer*. Now that the individual elements are available, it is easy to sort them, as pairs. On the lower right the pair [21] and [9] is out of order, so they must be swapped with each other.

Now they are sorted. On the next level upwards, looking from left to right, the elements are sorted, although most are single elements:

$$[12, 18, 5, 21, 9]$$

$$[12, 18] \qquad\qquad [5, 21, 9]$$

$$[12] \qquad [18] \qquad\qquad [5] \qquad [9, 21]$$

Moving up again, [12] and [18] are combined to make [12,18], a sorted pair. On the right, the singleton [5] is merged with the pair [9,21] by looking at the beginning of each list and copying the smallest element of the pair into a new list:

Step	List 1	List 2		Merged list	
1	[5]	[9, 21]	→	[5]	5 is smaller than 9
2	[]	[9, 21]	→	[5, 9]	first list is empty, copy 9
3	[]	[21]	→	[5,9,21]	first list is empty, copy 21
4	[]	[]			Final list: [5,9,21]

The result is:

$$[12, 18, 5, 21, 9]$$

$$[12, 18] \qquad\qquad [5, 9, 21]$$

At each stage, the lists contain more elements and they are sorted internally, smallest element at the beginning. Combining a pair of these is simply a matter of looking at the element at the beginning of each and copying the smallest one to the result until the lists are empty. The next, and final, merge in this set of data would be:

Step	List 1	List 2		Merged list	
1	[**12**, 18]	[**5**, 9, 21]	→	[5]	5 is smaller than 12, copy 5
2	[**12**, 18]	[**9**, 21]	→	[5, 9]	9 is smaller than 12, copy 9
3	[**12**, 18]	[**21**]	→	[5,9,12]	12 is smaller than 21, copy 12
4	[**18**]	[**21**]	→	[5,9,12,18]	18 is smaller than 21, copy 18
5	[]	[**21**]	→	[5,9,12,18,21]	First list is empty, copy 21

The final list is [5, 9, 12, 18, 21] which is sorted, as promised.

Once the data has been split into individual components, the merge stage creates sorted pairs, the next merge creates sets of 4 sorted numbers, the next 8, and so on, doubling each time until they are all sorted. A logical way to write the program is to use recursion, where each recursive call splits the data in two more parts until there is only one element. The lowest level of recursion combines the individuals into sorted pairs, and returns to the next level where the pairs are combined into fours, then eights, and so on until at the highest level the list is completely sorted. Written as a recursive function this is:

```python
data = [12, 18, 5, 21, 9]
def mergesort (data):
    n = len(data)        # For this call there are n elements
                         # to be sorted
    if n <= 1:           # Divide the data into two parts
        return           # unless n-1, which means sorting is
                         # complete
    middle = n//2        # Index of the element in the middle
    lower = data[:middle]  # Lower indexes, or the left
                           # sublist
    upper = data[middle:]  # Larger indices, or the right
                           # sublist
    mergesort(upper)     # Sort the left sublist
    mergesort(lower)     # Sort the right sublist

# There are now two sorted sublists of length N//2.
# Merge them into one list of length N
    (i,j,k) = (0,0,0)
    while i < len(lower) and j < len(upper):  # One sublist
                                       # may be shorter ...
        if lower[i] <= upper[j]:# If the element at index i
                                # of the
            data[k]=lower[i]    # left list is smaller,
                                # copy it to the result
            i=i+1
        else:
            data[k]=upper[j]    # Otherwise copy the element
                                # at index j
            j=j+1               # of the right sublist to
                                # the result
        k=k+1                   # Result gets longer by 1 element
```

```
for i in range (i,len(lower)):  # If the left list was
                                # longer, copy
    data[k] = lower[i]          # the remaining items to
                                # the result
    k = k + 1
for j in range (j, len(upper)): # If the right list was
                                # longer, copy
    data[k] = upper[j]          # the remaining items
                                # to the result
    k = k + 1
```

The merge sort is not as obvious as was selection sort, but is faster in most cases. It has another interesting application: it can be used to sort files. If a file contains, for example, a billion data samples that need to be sorted it is unlikely that they can be read into memory and sorted with a selection sort. How then to sort them?

10.2 SEARCHING

Searching is the act of determining whether some specific data item appears in a list and, if so, at which index. It seems like an odd thing to do; what can be done knowing this information? It is especially useful when multiple lists hold different data concerning the same items. An employee, as one example, might have their various data saved as a name list, an employee ID list, phone number, office number, home address, and so on. The same index gives information of the same individual for each list. Thus, search the employee ID list for 18762; if that index is 32, then the employee's name can be found at **name[32]**.

Of course Python has built-in operations on a list that will do this:

```
if 18762 in employeeID:  # Is this ID a member of the list?
    k = employeeID.index(18762)  # What is the index of
                                 # 18762?
```

A reason to examine searching algorithms is that not all languages possess these specific features and not all programs are written in Python. Another is that someone had to implement the operations for the Python system itself, and they had to know how. Did they do a good job? Are the built-in operations as fast as ones that a programmer could code for themselves? This will be discovered using an experiment.

10.2.1 Timings

Any section of code in Python requires some amount of time to execute. The specific amount depends on many things: the computer being used, the Python compiler, the specific statements, the data, and random events such as what other programs are executing on that computer at the same time. However, if it is important to know whether a section of code is faster than another, there are timing functions that can provide a pretty good idea. The time module includes a function named **clock()** that returns (on Windows) the elapsed time expressed in seconds elapsed since the first call to this function. On Linux it behaves differently, and **time.time()** may be a better choice. Be sure to look it up.

Timing a section of code is done by calling **time.clock()** before and after the code executes and subtracting the two times. For example, timing a search of a list using the in operator could be done this way:

```python
import time

list = [19872,87656,10982,18756,56344,29765,12856,12534,
        88768,90012]
t0 = time.clock()
if 90012 in list:
    found = True
t1 = time.clock()
print ("Time was ", t1-t0)
```

This prints the message:

Time was 2.062843880463903e-05

That's a pretty small time, as is to be expected. When run again the result was 3.07232e-06; running again gets 2.194514766e-06 and again 7.9002531e-06. These numbers are all small but very different. Since that is true it is better to time many executions of the code and divide by the number of times it ran:

```python
t0 = time.clock()
for i in range (0,10000):
    if 90012 in list:
        found = True
t1 = time.clock()
print ("Time was ", (t1-t0)/10000)
```

This yields more consistent results: 5.5284e-07, 5.5951e-07, and 5.415e-07 in three different trials. Averaging the result of multiple trials gives even better results, because spurious times on any one run will be averaged out.

10.2.2 Linear Search

Consider the list that was used in the timing example:

```
list = [19872,87656,10982,18756,56344,29765,12856,12534,
        88768,90012]
```

Finding whether the target number 90012 appears in this list is a matter of looking at each element to see if it is equal to the target. If so the answer is "yes" and, by the way, the index at which it was found is also known. This can be done in a basic **for** statement:

```
index = -1
for i in range(0,len(list)):
    if  list[i] == target:
        index = i
        break
# If the value of index is >= 0 then it was found.
```

This algorithm looks at each element asking "Is this equal to the target?" When/if the target is located, the loop ends and the answer is known. If the target is not a member of the list, then the algorithm has to examine all members of the list to determine that fact. Thus, the worst case is when the element is not in the list, and it requires N comparisons to find that out. If the element is a part of the list then, on the average, it will require N/2 comparisons to find it. It could be the first element, or the last, or any of the others, which averages out to N/2.

If the list is in sorted order then the loop can be exited as soon as it is known whether the element is in the list or not. That is, as soon as the target is smaller than the element it is being compared against in the list, it is clear that it can't be a member of the list, and the loop can be exited. This normally speeds up the execution, but the penalty is that the list has to be sorted, and the time needed to do this (only once, of course) has to be taken into account.

10.2.3 Binary Search

If the list has been sorted then there is a faster way to search for an element. The list can be divided into two parts by looking at the value in the middle of the list and comparing it to the target. If the target is smaller than the middle element, then it would have to be in the lower indices (left), otherwise it would have to exist in a higher valued index (to the right). What this means for performance is that the search area is cut in half each time a comparison is done.

This idea seems simple, but is actually difficult to get right in an implementation. At conferences where many PhDs in computer science are presenting papers, it has been found that fewer than 10% of the participants can code a binary search that works the first time. The terminal conditions are tricky: in particular, how can it be determined that the target is not in the list? OK, so the details are crucial. At the beginning there is a list, and its length is known. The index of the middle element is known too, and the list is sorted. So: find the index of the middle element:

```
istart = 0
iend = len(list)
m = (iend+istart)//2
```

If the target is in the list, is it at a smaller index than m (i.e., is **list[m]>target**):

```
if list[m]>target:
```

If so, don't bother looking at any index bigger than **m**. In other words, the largest index to look at would be **m-1**:

```
iend = m-1
```

If the target is in the list, is it at a larger index (i.e., is **list[m]<target**)? If so, don't look at any locations with an index less than **m**; in other words:

```
elif list[m]<target:
  istart = m+1
```

If **target = list[m]** then it has been found and the algorithm terminates.

```
else:
    return m
```

This code has to be repeated until the target has been found, or it has been determined that it is not in the list. The loop condition is critical. The loop continues so long as **istart <= iend** so that if the final step finds the target in the list, then it will return the index. If the loop exits without finding the element, then the index value is -1. The final code, as a function, is:

```
def search (list, target):
    istart = 0
```

```
iend = len(list)
while istart<=iend:
    m = (iend+istart)//2
    if list[m]>target:
        iend = m-1
    elif list[m]<target:
        istart = m+1
    else:
        return m
return None
```

The speed of the binary search depends on the fact that it is searching a randomly accessible data set like a Python list or a Java array, and not a file. It will take on the order of log(n) probes into the list to find what it is looking for or to determine that it is not there.

Timing the binary search gave an execution time of 3.305e-06 seconds, still slower than the built-in operation.

10.3 RANDOM NUMBER GENERATION

Python offers a random number module named **random** that offers a broad collection of random number generation facilities. How is it possible to generate a random number using software? Shouldn't a computer program execute consistently and always produce the same answer each time? Yes, it should. The resolution of this apparent problem lies is the definition of random.

First, randomness is defined only for collections of events or numbers. One number, or even a small collection, can't be said to be random. Randomness reflects the *lack of a pattern*, and only one or two events don't really display a pattern. Randomness is more of a statistical property of a sequence, and is not necessarily related strictly to unpredictability. After all, if a computer program can generate random numbers, then it should be possible to predict the next one it will generate.

A random number generator (RNG) on a computer is referred to as *pseudo-random*; it is not truly random, but exhibits properties of randomness. These properties can be tested statistically. A typical RNG returns a floating point number between 0.0 and 1.0. This value can easily be transformed into a random number, either real or integer, in any desired range. A die roll is an integer between

1 and 6 inclusive. An RNG function named rand01() can be converted into a die roll as:

```
int(rand01()*6 + 1)
```

If the numbers generated by rand01() are random, then it should produce die rolls that each have a probability of 1/6. If not then there is a bias.

If a coin is flipped many times and the sequence HTHTHTHTHTHTHTHT results, the probability of H or T (heads or tails) is 0.5, or 50%, which is what would be expected. If a sequence has the correct percentages for each outcome, then it passes the *frequency test*. Yet this sequence is probably not random because of the obvious pattern in the results. The frequency test is not enough.

A second test would consider pairs in the sequence and compare the probability of occurrence of each pair against the theoretical. In the coin toss there are four possible pairs: HH, HT, TH, and TT. Each pair should appear with equal probability, and yet the string above shows only HT instances. It is not random. A standard suite of randomness tests called Diehard includes a more complex version of this test, involving groups of five elements in the sequence, each one having a theoretical probability of 1 in 120. This kind of test can be called the *serial test* or *overlapping permutations*.

A third test involves using the RNG to generate poker hands. The probability of specific hands is well-known, and any consistent variation from these probabilities would imply a flaw in the RNG. This is the *poker test*. Any complex random game could be used, and the Diehard suite uses the game of craps.

There are many other tests that could be applied, and all are based on generating complex situations and comparing the theoretical distribution of properties generated against what the RNG creates. So, now that there are ways of testing an RNG, can one be written in Python and tested?

10.3.1 Linear Congruential Method

Pseudo-random number generators basically shuffle the bits around in a number in complex and non-repeating ways; at least, they don't repeat for a large number of trials. A historically common method for doing this is to calculate a value that is bound to be larger than the place where it is to be stored and keep only the remainder each time. The value of this remainder is pseudo-random under certain conditions. A linear equation can be used and is fast to calculate:

$$X_{i+1} = (aX_i + b) \bmod m \tag{10.1}$$

where X_i is the previous random number in the sequence and X_{i+1} is the next one. The value of **m** should be quite large and it should be a prime number. Many computers have used a 32-bit integer size, and as it happens $2^{32} - 1$ is a good value for **m** (= 2147483647). Python integers can be as large as desired, so larger values could be used. Keeping then to 32 bits is accomplished using an *and* operation and masking the result with a 32-bit constant: `0xFFFFFFFF`.

Values for **a** and **b** are more flexible, but large values are a good idea, and too many factors can cause problems. One good set of values is **a=69069** and **b=362437**. This method uses a previous value to calculate the next one, so an initial value is required. This is called the *seed*, and it must be possible for a user/ programmer to be able to set this seed value to whatever they choose. If not then the RNG will generate the same set of values each time it is used. That's actually a good thing for debugging, because when tracking down a problem, it is important that the program behave consistently.

The basic RNG described above would be:

```
_xseed = 76951

def irand01 ():
   global _xseed
   _xseed = (69069*_xseed+362437) & 0xFFFFFFFF
   return _xseed
```

This function returns a number between 0 and 2147483647, and resets the seed (**_xseed**, a global) each time. It's a good start, but what is wanted is a function that returns a number between 0 and 1; so, a second function does this simply by dividing the above result by 2147483647:

```
def rand01():
   return irand01()/0xFFFFFFFF
```

A function that can set the seed is needed too:

```
def setseed (x):
    global _xseed
    _xseed = x
```

A commonly used function in the Python *random* package is **randrange(a, b)**, which returns a random integer between **a** and **b**. The code for a die has already been written, and so the math is known. Using the tools just written, this is coded as:

```
def randrange (n1, n2):
    x = (int) (rand01()*(n2-n1+1)) + n1
    return x
```

How can a random number generator be made to generate a different set of numbers every time a program starts using it? Simply by setting the seed to a number that is hard to predict. Such a number is found in the low bits (milliseconds and microseconds) of the system clock. It is impossible to predict what these will be. So randomizing the RNG can be accomplished like this:

```
def randomize ():
    global _xseed
    _xseed = int(time.time ()) & 0xFF
```

The **time.time()** function returns the number of seconds since a fixed date in the past, called the *epoch*. This date is usually January 1st, 1970, midnight.

Other methods for generating random numbers exist and are commonly used. Python's random class uses the *Mersenne Twister* algorithm, which is often seen as a default in programming languages but is a trifle slow. *Blum-Blum-Shub* resembles the linear congruential but uses the relation $x_{i+1} = x_i^2 \bmod m$ where **m** is the product of two prime numbers. Dozens more methods exist. There are also practical methods for generating true random numbers, and these are based on specific hardware that captures a truly random process such as radioactive decay, the photoelectric effect, or random electromagnetic noise.

Finally, there are web sites that will offer random numbers and sequences on request. *Random.org* will serve up true random numbers, for example, and there are dozens of other such sites. The time needed to connect to a server and upload a random number is considerable, so they should be used knowing the tradeoff of time for random number quality.

10.4 CRYPTOGRAPHY

Cryptography involves sending messages that only certain intended people can receive and understand. This involves *codes* and *ciphers*. A code substitutes one string for a longer message; there is a code book in which the code strings are associated with their relevant message. So, the string "A76" could mean "retreat 100 meters." Code books had to be changed regularly because eventually one would fall into the hands of someone who was not supposed to have one.

A cipher is an algorithm that converts one string of characters into another one of generally the same length. It can operate on bits, on characters, or on blocks of characters. A cipher does not have a code book but does have a key, which is a string of numbers or characters, that the algorithm uses to transform the original string (called the *plaintext*) into the encrypted string (called the *ciphertext*). The ciphertext can be transmitted safely because it cannot be understood without the key.

Cryptography has become much more important in the last 30 years or so. It's not just that the world is an uncertain place. It is more that people wish to share private information across the Internet. If a purchase is made with a credit card, then the card number should be encrypted before sending it to the seller. Access to certain sites that have valuable services or information requires a password. Installing new software requires an access key. These are all examples where encryption is required.

It should be mentioned that the secure transfer of information depends on *operational security* as well as on encryption. Someone with a password can access all services and data associated with that password, so keys and passwords must be protected. This aspect is beyond the ability of a programmer to control, and is often the way security systems are broken.

There is some terminology that needs to be understood. A *symmetric key* system uses one key to encode and the same key to decode. *Asymmetric* systems like *public key* systems use one key to encrypt the message, a key that anyone can know, and a second, private key that only the recipient knows and is used to decrypt. A *block cipher* applies a key to a collection (block) of data, often a size of 64, 128, or 256 bits at a time. A *stream cipher* is usually a symmetric key cipher that encrypts a plain text character with a character from the key. It's also called a *state cipher* because the encryption of the next character depends on what has happened before.

Knowing a little about encryption is important, but it is also important to understand that it is a very complex and highly mathematical subject, and requires a significant amount of study to become an expert.

10.4.1 One-Time Pad

Having just said how complex the field of cryptography is, the first algorithm to be examined is, in fact, rather old and perfectly secure, if difficult to use in practice. Suppose person A wishes to send person B the message "Meet you at nine pm at location alpha." Encoding this requires a sequence of random characters at least as long as the message. In actual use, this cipher often used pages from books as keys, books that were easily accessible by both parties. In this case the following text is used as the key: "it was the best of times it was the worst of times." The encryption process, known to both, and in fact not really a secret, is to apply the exclusive OR operation to corresponding characters in the message and the key to produce the ciphertext:

```
m   e   e   t   y   o   u   a   t   n   i   n   e   p   m   a   t   l   …   Message
i   t   w   a   s   t   h   e   b   e   s   t   o   f   t   i   m   e   …   Key
4   17  18  21  10  27  29  4   22  11  26  26  10  22  25  8   25  9   …   Encrypted
```

The exclusive OR operation is a bit-by-bit logical operator that is 0 if the two bits are equal and is 1 otherwise. It is applied to the numerical representations of the characters. This is quite handy because it is very fast and can easily be accomplished using simple hardware. Consider the first character in the message "m." The first character in the key is "i." The ASCII codes are the numbers 109 and 105 respectively, or in binary:

0 1 1 0 1 1 0 1   109 "m"

0 1 1 0 1 0 0 1   105 "i"

0 0 0 0 0 1 0 0   4 Exclusive OR

One interesting observation here is that different characters can be encrypted to the same cipher text byte, as in the above string where "s" and "t" both encrypt to 26. Anyway, now this ciphertext is transmitted to B and is decoded in exactly the same way that it was encoded: apply the exclusive OR between the ciphertext and the same key (symmetric key):

```
4    17   18   21   10   27   29   4    22   11   26   26   10   22   25   8    encrypted
i    t    w    a    s    t    h    e    b    e    s    t    o    f    t    i    Key
105  116  119  97   115  116  104  101  98   101  115  116  111  102  116  105  Key ints
109  101  101  116  121  111  117  97   116  110  105  110  101  112  109  97   XOR
M    e    e    t    y    o    u    a    t    n    i    n    e    p    m    a    Decrypted
```

The Python code that can do the basic encryption is:

```
pt = "meetyouatninepmatlocationalpha"
key = "itwasthebestoftimesitwastheworstoftimes"
ct = ""
xt = ""

for i in range(0,len(pt)):
    v = ord(pt[i])^ord(key[i])
    print(v)
    ct = ct + chr(v)
print (ct)
```

The exclusive-OR operator is "^", and the expression **ord(pt[i])^ord(key[i])** performs the XOR on the message and the key bytes, as numbers. Doing it again with the same key gets the message back.

The reason that this is called a *one-time pad* is that the key can only be used once, otherwise the cipher is not secure. The security lies in the randomness of the key, and reusing it reduces the randomness. Eventually if the same key is used often enough, an observer, someone who can intercept all of the messages, can extract the pattern and determine the key. So in practice the keys were written on pads of paper and, once used, were destroyed. Keeping the pads synchronized between the sender and receiver can be a problem, especially if there are many of each. Hence, although the system is secure, it is not used very often.

10.4.2 Public Key Encryption (RSA)

A public key system is commonly used for secure communication across computer networks, and involves one key for encryption and another for decryption. There are many variations on the basic idea, some being much too complex to discuss in a few pages, but the RSA algorithm is relatively simple, quite popular, and very secure. It is named for its inventors **R**ivest, **S**hamir, and **A**dleman.

The mathematical idea that underlies RSA is that one can find three very large integers **e**, **d**, and **n**

$$\left(m^e\right)^d \bmod n = m$$

for any **m**, and that even knowing **e** and *n* or even ***m***, it can be extremely difficult to find **d**. The values **d** and **e** are the keys, and **m** is the message.

So, encrypting a message would work as follows: A sends message m to B using B's publicly known encryption key e:

$$c = m^e \bmod n$$

The value of **c** is the ciphertext and can be transmitted to B. When B receives the message, it is decrypted using their private key d:

$$m = c^d \bmod n$$

where n > m. This works because of the original assertion that $(m^e)^d$ **mod n = m**. The success of this method depends on a few other things: can c^d **mod n** be calculated quickly enough for large numbers (i.e., 500 bits), and can the numbers **d, e**, and **n** be found to make this work?

The first step in determining the keys is to select two very large prime numbers **p** and **q**. Let **n = p*q**. A *large* number in this context has hundreds of bits, but that creates a cumbersome example, so smaller numbers will be used in this discussion.

Now calculate **φ(n) = (p-1)*(q-1)** and find an integer **e** so that **e** and **n** are co-prime; that is the greatest common divisor between **e** and **n** is 1.

Let d = (e-1) mod φ(n) so that d*e mod n = 1. This can be found using a search, which may be infeasible due to the size of the numbers:

```
for i in range (e, n):
    if (i*e)%j == 1:
        d = i
        break
```

or a mathematical process that uses Euler's theorem can give the answer faster, and code has been provided for this on the accompanying disc.

Example: Encrypt the Message "Depart at Dawn" Using RSA

The first step is to determine some keys to use and to distribute the public key. Using the prime numbers 73 and 83 (far too small for a real situation) the determination of the keys is:

n is 6059 and φ(n) is 5904

e is 17, chosen because it is prime. Now find d such that d*e mod n = 1. Searching for it is practical for numbers this size and one gets:

$$d = 3473$$

So the public key is (17 , 6059) and the private key is (3473).

The message is 14 characters long, and would be 112 bits; n is only 10 bits long, and the message has to be shorter than this. In this instance the message can be sent one character at a time, but this is generally poor practice. Normally larger blocks of data are encrypted at one time. The plaintext string is converted into integers using **ord**(), and each one is encrypted using the formula:

$$c = m^e \bmod n$$

An example would be:

```
message = "Depart at dawn"
imessage = ()
cmessage = ()
for i in range (0, len(message)):
    m = ord(message[i])
    imessage = imessage +(ord(message[i]),)
    c = (m**e) % n
    cmessage = cmessage + (c,)
```

Now the message consists of 14 blocks of 1 character each. It can be transmitted to the recipient, who is normally named B or Bob, in this form. The sender, named A or Alice, had access to the public key only, which is all that is needed to encrypt the message. It cannot be decrypted using the public key.

d given d·e ≡ 1 (mod φ(n))

Bob receives the ciphertext message, which in this case is:

(4652, 3518, 4274, 5770, 1663, 344, 2498, 5770, 344, 2498, 2144, 5770, 1725, 4601)

He takes each block and decrypts it using:

$$m = c^d \bmod n$$

The Python code for this could be:

```
dmessage = ()
for i in range (0, len(cmessage)):
    c = cmessage[i]
    m = (c ** d) % n
    dmessage = dmessage + (m, )
```

The resulting decrypted message is:

(68, 101, 112, 97, 114, 116, 32, 97, 116, 32, 100, 97, 119, 110)

Which is the original message. Notice that because only one block per character was encrypted, the effect is that of a substitution cipher, in which each letter has been replaced by another. This is very easy to decrypt by noting patterns of letters and frequencies of letters in the language; the letter "e" is usually the most commonly used letter in an English message. That is why the message is encrypted as blocks of characters. It is highly unlikely that a large block would be repeated exactly, and if it were it would be difficult to guess what it was anyway.

10.5 COMPRESSION

A little arithmetic will start this discussion. The song "Blackbird" by The Beatles is almost exactly 4 minutes long. This is 240 seconds, and if it was converted into digital form, it would be sampled at a rate of 44,100 samples each second. This means that the song has 240*44100 = 10.6 million samples. But wait—it's stereo, so double that to 21.2 million samples. A typical sample is 16 bits, so this works out to 42.4 million bytes; 42 megabytes! The MP3 file for this song is typically 1.9 megabytes. How is that possible? By using a *compression* algorithm.

Data compression is all about ways to take, for example, 100 bytes of information and turn it into 10 bytes while losing none of the essential message. Of course, compressed data is incomprehensible just to look at and must be decompressed in order for it to be used. Data is often compressed before storing it in a file to reduce its footprint on the storage device, or before transmitting it along a communications channel to take better advantage of limited bandwidth.

The question of how a string of data bytes can be made shorter while losing no important information remains, and a simple example may be in order. Consider a cartoon image. These have a relatively small number of distinct but vivid colors, usually less than 10 colors and the color variation within any region is small. The example image in Figure 10.1 is in PNG form and is 23.2 Kbytes in size at 400x456 (= 182400) pixels. As raw data it would be a little over 182Kbytes in size, 547 Kbytes if RGB color was used.

Figure 10.1
Sample image for compression.

A simple compression technique that will work in this case is called *run-length encoding*. In its simplest form data bytes are preceded by a count indicating how many repetitions of that value were encountered in the data. So if there was a section of data:

1 1 0 0 0 0 0 0 2 2 2 1 2 1 2 0 0 0 0 0 0 2 2 2 2 2

This would be encoded as

2 1	6 0	3 2	1 1	1 2	1 1	1 2	5 0	5 2
Two	six	three	a	a	a	a	five	five
ones	zeros	twos	one	two	one	two	zeros	twos

In this case the original data required 26 bytes and the compressed data required 17 bytes. The new data takes 65% of the space that the original does. This is not a huge saving, but is probably worth the effort. It does depend heavily on the nature of the data.

Consider the image of Figure 10.1. The color areas are uniform and rather large, so this image would be an ideal candidate for run-length encoding. When writing the program, it is important to use a binary file and convert the value and count into unsigned bytes before writing them to the file. This is a new data type called an *unsigned byte* that was not discussed in Chapter 8, and has the code "B." So, writing the count and value could be done like this:

```
s = pack("BB", n, v[1])
    f.write(s)
```

The entire program that will run-length encode the image will read the image file and collect identical pixels, counting them as they are collected, until a change in pixel value occurs. Then the (count, value) pair is written to the file. Also the pair will be written if 255 pixels have been collected, since that is the biggest number that can be counted in 8 bits. The result is a binary file of pairs of numbers (count, value) that represent the pixels in the image. As there are only two colors, value can be 0 or 1, 0 being white and 1 being green; in general there can be 256 distinct values. The encoding program looks like this:

```
from struct import *
import Glib
def emit(v, n, f):    # Write a pair of bytes (count, value)
    s = pack("BB", n, v[1])   #" 'B' is unsigned byte.
    f.write(s)
```

```
Green = (123, 210, 0)          # The object color
White = (255, 255, 255)        # The background color

Glib.startdraw(400, 456)
b1 = Glib.loadImage ("b1.png")  # Read the image
outf = open ("b1.txt", "wb")    # Open the output file
Glib.image (b1, 0, 0)           # Display the image
count = 0
value = Glib.getpixel (b1,0,0)  # Read a pixel value
                                # initially
for j in range (0, 456):
    for i in range (0, 400):       # For every image pixel
        if count ==255:            # Largest possible count.
            emit (value, count, outf) # Write (255, value)
            count = 0                 # Reset the count
        c = Glib.getpixel (b1, i, j)  # Get the next pixel
value
        if c == value:                # Same as before?
            count = count + 1     # Yes. Increment the count
        else:                         # No, different
            emit(value, count, outf)  # Write the count and
                                      # value
            count = 1                 # Reset the count
            value = c                 # and the value
if count>0:      # After the loop ends are there pixels to
                 # write?
    emit (value, count, outf)            # Yes, so do it.
outf.close()
Glib.enddraw()
```

The decoding program reads pairs of unsigned bytes from the binary file, and creates pixels. A pair (12, 0) would be 12 white pixels, for instance. A pair (12, 1) could be 12 pixels of some other color, and this program writes the pixels so it decides what color that will be. It will read pairs and draw pixels, into an image of 400 columns and 456 rows, until all are accounted for. A program that does this (not the only one possible) is:

```
from struct import *
import Glib

Glib.startdraw(400, 456)
inf = open ("b1.txt", "rb")  # Open the run length encoded
                             # file
```

```
i = 0
j = 0
cols = 400              # The size is known, but could be a
rows = 456              # part of the data file.

while True:
    s = inf.read(2)     # Read a (count, value) pair
(bytes)
    if len(s) <= 0:     # End of file?
        break           # Yes. Exit loop, stop drawing.

    c,v = unpack("BB", s)   # Convert to integers
    if v == 255:            # Background pixel? (White)
        Glib.fill (255, 255, 255)
    else:                   # Object pixel? (Green)
        Glib.fill (123, 210, 0)

    for k in range (0, c):  # Draw the pixels to the
                            # screen.
        if i >= cols:       # At end of column, add 1 to row
            i = 0
            j = j + 1
        Glib.point (i, j)       # Draw as a 'point'
        i = i + 1               # Next pixel (increase X)
    if j>= 456:             # Last row
        break
Glib.enddraw()
```

The more complex the data is, in this case meaning the more distinct values the data can take, the less useful this encoding method will be. In some cases it can make the file size *larger* that the raw data would have been. In the case of this particular image, the run-length encoded file is about 6K bytes, as opposed to half a million bytes that would have been needed for the raw image, saved as pixels. Still, this serves as a basic proof that it is possible to compress a data file without losing any information. There are, of course, many more algorithms that will compress data to a greater extent and with fewer constraints.

10.5.1 Huffman Encoding

If a typical text file is examined carefully, it can be found that the vast majority of the file consists of relatively few characters. As a general estimate, over

95% of the characters can be accounted for by between 25–30 distinct values. A coding scheme that took this into account would reduce the size of a text file, and perhaps it would generalize to other kinds of file. For example, in many files the value 0 is the most common, and giving it a smaller representation than, say, 9 may reduce the overall file size.

This is not really a novel idea. The international Morse code is based on this idea and has been around for a long time, beginning in 1836. The most commonly used letters in English are shown in Table 10.1. In the Morse code the letter "E" is represented by a single dot, the letter "T" is a single dash, and "A" is a dot followed by a dash. In other words the most common letters have the smallest code representation, as a general rule. This is how the Huffman code is organized too.

Table 10.1
Frequency of Letters in English Text

Letter	Frequency %	Letter	Frequency %	Letter	Frequency %	Letter	Frequency %
E	12.5	R	6.1	F	2.3	K	0.7
T	9.3	H	5.4	P	2.0	X	0.19
A	8	L	4.1	G	2.0	J	0.16
O	7.6	D	4.0	W	1.9	Q	0.11
I	7.3	C	3.1	Y	1.7	Z	0.09
N	7.1	U	2.7	B	1.5		
S	6.5	M	2.5	V	1.0		

A Huffman code is constructed from the ground up, like a wall. The lower levels of the wall represent the least frequently used symbols, and have the greatest number of bricks above them. The final code will be binary numbers, and the length of the code in bits for a symbol is related to the number of bricks above it. The wall is actually shaped like a pyramid, and is called a binary tree by computer science folks. It's a very useful structure in general, but the description will be restricted here to its use in Huffman codes.

As an example, consider the English text:

I think that at that time none of us quite believed in the Time Machine[11]

The characters occur in this particular text with the following frequencies:

t	10	a	4	q	1	k	1
e	9	m	3	c	1	s	1
i	8	o	2	d	1	l	1
n	5	u	2	v	1		
h	5	b	1	f	1		

The 'leaves' (or *nodes*) at the bottom of the tree (it is drawn upside-down) contain the lowest frequency items, and so are placed first. Each two nodes in the tree will have one node above them, straddling them, containing the sum of the frequencies of all nodes below. All characters are turned into nodes, and each also contains the number of occurrences of that letter. This collection of nodes will be called a *heap*. Initially all have only one character, but this will change.

The rule in building the tree is to pick the pair of nodes (initially characters) that sum to the smallest number and connect them using another node, one above them that has a left and right node. The first bricks, alphabetically, would be "b" and "c" both with a frequency of 1. The first two would look like this:

Figure 10.2
A step in the Huffman algorithm, lowest level

The bottom nodes have characters and counts. The one above has only a count, and it is the sum of the counts of the two nodes it is connected to. This new node, with a count of 2, is placed back in the heap and the nodes for B and C are removed. The heap will always get smaller.

Repeating this process with the others, the smallest pair we can make is with "d" and "f," then "k" and "l," and then "q" and "s." At that point the smallest node is "v" with a count of 1, but there are no more nodes with a count of 1. The smallest sum is 2, which uses "v" and 'o':

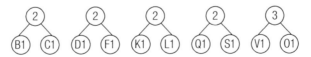

Figure 10.3
Entire Huffman bottom level complete

All of these are in the heap, and a search is done for the smallest sum of nodes. The character "u" has a count of 2 and so do any of the nodes above that link to two other characters. These are nodes too, so link "u" with the leftmost node above to get a bigger grouping—this is called a *subtree*, because it is a tree, but it is also part of a bigger tree. The 'u' node and the other gives a sum of 4:

Figure 10.4
The first 3 deep tree section: U B C

The tree that is being built has the least commonly used characters placed at a greater distance from the top of the tree than are the frequently used characters. This distance will be used to construct the codes, smaller for common characters. Now the smallest sums of two nodes in the tree is 4, the nodes connecting "d," "f," "k," and "l":

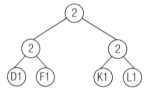

Figure 10.5
Next step in the Huffman algorithm: D F K F:

The method here takes the smallest two nodes, which are going to create the smallest sum, and connects them, removing the original nodes and replacing them with the new one. The smallest nodes now are the node connecting "q" and "2" (value 2), the node with "m" (value 3) and the node connecting "v" and "o" (value 3). The node with "m" will be selected to link to the 2-valued node. The tree is a disconnected collection of nodes, but right now looks like this:

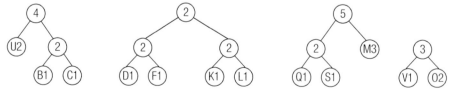

Figure 10.6
Three lower levels complete.

plus all of the unconnected nodes for individual letters. So, what's next? The smallest valued character remaining is 'a' at 4. That would make the smallest sum 7 after connecting it with the subtree on the right ('v' and 'o'). Next in the heap are the two 4-nodes above to create an 8, and linking 'h' (5) and 'n' (also 5) to get a 10:

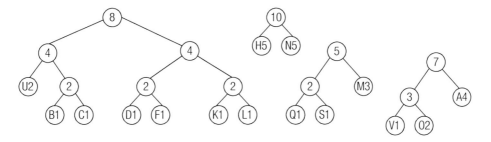

Figure 10.7
The next level of the Huffman tree complete.

The pattern should be clear by now. Notice that the nodes with nothing below them always consist of characters, and the nodes above have only numbers. But oops—the space characters were not counted, and they must be for the message to make any sense. There are 14 spaces in the message. The final sum will be 14+9 for the space. A node for a space has to be added to the heap.

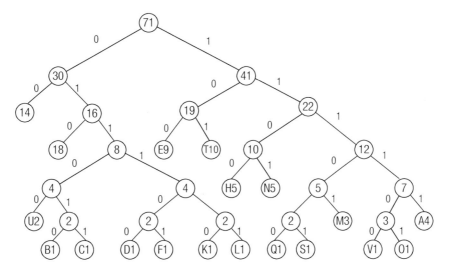

Figure 10.8
The final tree

The last two steps don't involve any new characters, but they will link all of the nodes together and make them accessible from one single node at the top. The final (top) node should have a value that is the length of the original string.

Now comes the bottom line: what was the point of all this? The tree that has been constructed will be used to construct the codes for each letter, and the length of each code will be the number of nodes between the characters and the top (*root*) of the tree. The path to each left node is labeled with a digit, in this case a 0, and the path to the right nodes is labelled with a 1, as in the tree above. The code for any character is read off of the links that were followed to get from the top of the tree to the node containing the character. So the space character, the most common one, is reached by going left two times; its code will be "00." The "t" is the second most frequent character, and is reached from the top node by going right, then left, then right; the code is "101." The complete set of codes is:

' '	00	A	11111	D	011100	V	111100
T	101	M	11101	F	011101		
E	100	U	01100	K	011110		
I	010	O	111101	L	011111		
H	1100	B	011010	Q	111000		
N	1101	C	011011	S	111001		

The coded message is the concatenation of all of the codes for the characters in the order they appear in the message. The encoded message would read:

```
 i    t   h    i    n    k     t    h   a    t    a    t
010 00 101 1100 010 1101 011110 00 101 1100 11111 101 00 11111 101 00
 t   h    a    t    t    i   m    e    n    o    n    e
101 1100 11111 101 00 101 010 11101 100 00 1101 111101 1101 100 00
  o    f    u    s     q    u    i   t    e    b
111101 011101 00 01100 111001 00 111000 01100 010 101 100 00 011010
  e    l    i    e    v    d    i    n    t    h    e
100 011111 010 100 111100 100 011100 00 010 1101 00 101 1100 100 00
  t    i   m    e    m    a    c    h    i    n    e
101 010 11101 100 00 11101 11111 011011 1100 010 1101 100
```

This amounts to 259 bits = 33 bytes. The original string is 71 bytes long, so the compressed data is 46% of the size of the original data. The Huffman coded string is broken into 8-bit bytes and transmitted that way:

```
01000101 11000101 10101111 00010111 00111111 01001111
```

11010010 11100111 11101001 01010111 01100001 10111110
11101100 00111101 01110100 01100111 00100111 00001100
01010110 00001101 01000111 11010100 11110010 00111000
00101101 00101110 01000010 10101110 11000011 10111111
01101 110 0 010 1101 100

Decoding requires the table or the tree. If a known table is used, such as the natural frequencies of English letters, then it would not have to be transmitted along with the message. The use of a Python *dictionary* type makes the program for decoding very elegant indeed. Given the table and the message, bits are removed from the beginning of the message and placed into code string until they match one of the codes in the table. The Huffman code has the property that the bit sequences are unique when appended as a long message. The first bit sequence that matches a code will be the code for the first letter in the message.

```
# Huffman decode
# This is the coded message:
bitstring = "010001011100010110101111000101110011111101001111111"+\
"01001011100111111010010101011101100001101111101111011000011110"+\
"10111010001100111001001110000110001010110000011010100011111101"+\
"01001111001000111000001011010010111001000010101011101100001111"+\
"01111101101111000101101100"
table = {}                     # This is the table of codes
table['00']    = " "
table["11111"]  = "A"
table["011100"] = "D"
table["111100"] = "V"
table["101"]    = "T"
table["11101"]  = "M"
table["011101"] = "F"
table["100"]    = "E"
table["01100"]  = "U"
table["011110"] = "K"
table["010"]    = "I"
table["111101"] = "O"
table["011111"] = "L"
table["1100"]   = "H"
table["011010"] = "B"
table["111000"] = "Q"
table["1101"]   = "N"
table["011011"] = "C"
table["111001"] = "S"
```

```
# Pull bits from the string making a substring until the
# substring is found in the dictionary. Then emit the
# character indexed.

# Loop until all bits are used
while len(bitstring) > 0:
    code = ""              # Clear the current code
                           # While code NOT in the dictionary …
    while not (code in table):
                           # Add the next bit from the message
        code = code + bitstring[0]
                           # Remove that bit from the message
        bitstring = bitstring[1:]
# When the code matches, print the character corresponding
# to the code
    print (table[code], end="")
```

10.5.2 LZW Compression

Like many algorithms, LZW compression is named after the people who devised it: A. Lempel, J. Ziv, and Terry Welch. It has been the standard for data compression for many years, it was the method used in the GIF file format, and was used in many versions of PDF. It is not the most effective method of compression, but it is lossless and efficient. Like the Huffman code, LZW creates a table from the original text and uses the codes in the table to perform the compression. Unlike the Huffman code, the decompression stage does not require that the table be known in advance; it builds the table as it decompresses the file. The LZW algorithm also replaces multiple characters with single codes, thus increasing the compression rate.

LZW compression usually begins with a known code table, most often the 256 ASCII characters, but any table known by the compressor and decompressor will work. As an example, another short section of text from *The Time Machine* will be compressed:

The Time Traveller for so it will be convenient to speak of him was expounding a recondite matter to us His grey eyes shone and twinkled and his usually pale face was flushed and animated The fire burned brightly and the soft radiance of the incandescent lights in the lilies of silver caught the bubbles that flashed and passed in our glasses.

Punctuation has been removed for simplicity. The algorithm begins with a table of characters, in this instance the ones that appear in the quote, but in general the table can contain any starting set of symbols. This is called the *code table*, and associates a numerical code with a string. The code table in this case will consist of the letters (uppercase) and their values starting with 0: "A"=0, "B"=1, and so on. The space has to be included as well. The code sequence 024 would be the string "ACE" using this scheme.

Naturally there has to be more to this if it is to be a viable compression method. When encoding, the characters are examined one at a time and appended to an input string, and looked up in the table. If the string is found in the table, then the next character is read and appended to the string and it is looked up again. This repeats until the string is not found, at which point a few things happen: the code for the last string that was found is written to the output, the new string that was encountered in the string but not found in the table is added to the tables, and the process continues using the last character read in. This means that not only characters but also short strings that occur in the text will have numeric codes, and that the table will be created from the text that was given.

Consider the text in the example: The first character seen is "T":

1. "T" exists in the table already, so a new character is read in and appended to the "T" to create the pair "TH."
2. "TH" is *not* in the table. The character "T" has the code 19, so 19 is written to the output file.
3. The string "TH" is added to the table. It will be code 27.
4. The input string is now "H."
5. The character "H" is in the table and has code 7. The next character is read in and appended to "H" creating "HE."
6. "HE" is not in the table, so the code for character "H," which is 7, is written to the output file.
7. The string "HE" is added to the table, code 28.
8. The input string is now "E."

The process repeats. If a multiple-character string is found in the table, then the steps are basically the same. Hypothetically:

1. The character "T" is next and is in the table. Read the next character "H" and append to "T" to get "TH."

2. "TH" is in the table. Read the next character "E" and append to "T" to get "THE."

3. "THE' is not in the table to emit the code for "TH," which is 27.

4. Input string is now "E."

Step 1 repeats until a string is obtained that has not been seen before. In the example here the first 27 codes are letters and the space character. The next few codes are:

TH 27	HE 28	E 29
T 30	TI 31	IM 32
ME 33	E T 34	TR 35

The first 3-character string (*trigram*) in the table is "E T."

Python's dictionary type is especially valuable for coding the LZW algorithm. The facility for looking up a string in a table is exactly what is required here. The critical part of the program could be written as follows:

```
# count is the next unassigned symbol
# ch is the last character read in
# s is the current character string
# inf is the input file (text)
s = ""                     # Initial string is empty.
ch = inf.read(1).upper()   # Read the first character, upper
                           # case.
while len(ch) > 0:         # While the file still has data …
    if s+ch in dict:       # Is string concatenated with ch
                           # in the table?
        s = s + ch         # Yes. Concatenate and repeat
    else:                          # No.
        print (dict[s]," ", end="")  # Print the code for
                           # the string s
        dict[s+ch] = count    # Put the new string into
                           # the dictionary
        count = count + 1     # New code is next integer.
        s = ch               # String is now the last
                           # character read.
    ch = inf.read(1).upper()   # Read a new character
```

When decoding the LZW file, the initial table is known. Again, this is often just the ASCII characters but can be something else, and in this case is the letters plus the space. The file contains codes, not characters, but the codes are in the table, right? No, only the starting codes are in the table. So decoding the message in the example starts easily. The first few codes in the message are:

19 7 4 26 19 8 12 29 19 17 0 21 ...

The first code is read in and is the code for the letter "T." This is followed by 7 ("H") and 4 ("E") and so on until the code 29 is reached. There is no entry for the code 29 in the table. This is where the really clever part of the LZW algorithm happens.

When decoding, *the program builds the table again*. After all, the characters are in the same order in the encoded data, so it should be possible to reproduce the process that was used to build the code table in the first place. When the first code is read in, the code is expected to be in the table, and the corresponding letter "T" is written and placed into a string. The next code is read and corresponds to 'H.' Now "TH" is added to the dictionary, and "H" is written and becomes the current string. Now "E" is seen, "HE" is added to the table, and "E" is written, and so on. Again a dictionary can be used to store the codes, but a list is more efficient. The indices are codes, which are numbers, so a list is fine here. The central part of the process is:

```
code1 = int(inf.readline())     # CODE1 is the first code
                                # on the file
print (dict[code1], end="")     # Output the string for
                                # CODE1
while True:                     # While mode codes on the
                                # file ...
    code0 = int(inf.readline()) # CODE0 is the next code
                                # on the file
    if code0 < len(dict):       # Is CODE0 in the table?
        s = dict[code0]         # YES. S is the string
                                # for CODE0
    else:
        s = dict[code1]         # NO. S is the string for
                                # CODE1
        s = s + ch              # Append CH to S.
    print (s, end="")           # IN EITHER CASE emit S
    ch = s[0]                   # CH becomes the first
                                # character of S
    dict = dict + [dict[code1]+ch,] # Add new string to the
                                    # table
```

```
count = count + 1
code1 = code0
```

A pseudo-code summary of both the encoding and decoding processes is given in Figure 10.9, and working programs are provided on the disc (lzwe.py and lzwd.py). If punctuation is to be added, then a different conversion to uppercase would have to be done. For practical applications, the entire ASCII character set would be used at the outset.

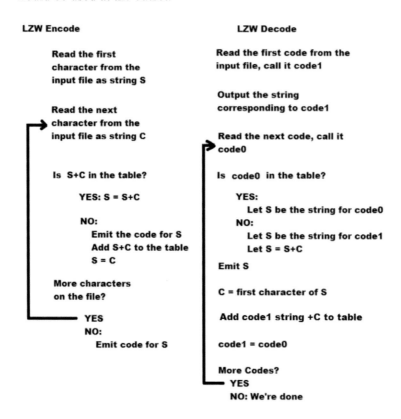

Figure 10.9
The LZW encode and decode algorithms.

10.6 HASHING

A hashing algorithm attempts to characterize a complex piece of data with something simpler, and preferably unique. The most common example would be to find a number that could represent a character string. A hashing algorithm has to be fast, because the idea very often is to convert a string into an index to a list or tuple. Consider the string "while." There are five characters (bytes) here. How can this string be used as an index into a tuple?

Any numerical operation on the codes used to represent the character might work, but some result in codes that are too large. Simply adding the codes would give a value of 537, which could work but also might be too large. Imagine the application is to look up Python key words; there are 33 of them. The value resulting from the hash should be an index between 0 and 32, so take the hash mod 33. If that is tried the result is that half of the 33 entries will be empty, and half will have two or more strings that have the same index. The result is:

4: "None"	12: "return"	21: "try"	31: "global"
6: "class"	13: "global"	22: "is"	
7: "from"	14: "as"	25: "finally"	
9: "while"	15: "lambda"	27: "or"	
10: "and"	17: "in"	29: "False"	
11: "continue"	20: "True"	30: "for"	

When two things hash to the same value it is said to be a collision. In this case the collisions are:

(class, def)	(False, nonlocal)	(return, del)	(from, not)	(lambda, with)
(True, elif)	(while, if)	(from, yield)	(global, assert)	(False, else)
(from, import)	(and, pass)	(is, break)	(is, except)	(None, raise)

Two values can't occupy the same location in a tuple, so something must be done. The simplest way to deal with collisions is to have extra space in the list or tuple. If the size of the tuple is specified as 145, then all strings hash to distinct values. Of course, now 112 tuple entries are empty, but does that really matter? The alternative to a table indexed by hashing (a hash table) would be a list that has to be searched, and hashing is very much faster.

As it happens, simply adding the characters together is not a very good hashing method. There are a few well-known ones.

djb2

This algorithm starts with a predefined seed for a hash value, multiplies it by 33 and adds the next character from the string, multiplies that by 33, adds the next character, and so on. The code is:

```
def djb2 (s, size):
    sum = 5381
    for i in range (0, len(s)):
        sum = sum*33 + ord(s[i])
    sum = sum%size
    return sum
```

Why multiply by 33? It works well, and nobody knows why. The seed of 5381 can be changed to see how different values work. With the configuration given here, there will need to be 112 elements in the tuple to avoid collisions. If the program is changed slightly so that an exclusive OR replaces the sum, the size decreases to 105. That is:

```
sum = sum*33 ^ ord(s[i])
```

10.6.1 sdbm

This is a method devised for scrambling bits, but makes for a good hashing function. The iteration is hash(i) = hash(i - 1) * 65599 + str[i]. The number 65599 is arbitrary, but happens to be prime. A function to implement this is:

```
def sdbm (s, size):
    hash = 0
    for i in range (0, len(s)):
        hash = ord(s[i]) * 65599 + hash
    return hash%size.
```

There are many other hashing methods (see: Knuth). The idea is an important one. It is, for example, a way to implement Python dictionaries: hash the key to an integer and use that to access the value.

10.7 SUMMARY

The goal of this chapter was to introduce important algorithms or general techniques used in computer science. *Sorting* is a traditional programming problem for undergraduates and is essential in many data-handling applications. The selection sort and the merge sort were discussed at length.

Searching involves finding some piece of data within a larger collection. A *linear search* starts at the beginning and looks at consecutive elements until the target is found. A *binary search* splits the data into two halves each time an element in the set is examined and so is faster, but it depends on the data being sorted.

Random number generation creates a sequence of numbers that satisfies a statistical test for randomness. Such numbers are crucial in computer simulations and games, and in some numerical algorithms.

Cryptography involves sending messages that only certain intended people can receive and understand. A *cipher* is an algorithm that converts one string of characters into another one of generally the same length. The *one-time pad* method was examined, followed by the very popular RSA algorithm.

Data compression is about ways to take many bytes of information and turn them into fewer bytes while losing none of the essential message. Of course, compressed data is incomprehensible just to look at and must be decompressed in order for it to be used. This section demonstrated *run length encoding, Huffman* codes, and the *LZW* algorithm.

The final section was a brief discussion of *hashing*, a way to convert strings or other complex data types and reduce them to simpler forms such as integers. The *djb2* and the *sdbm* methods were singled out as being typical of the way that such algorithms work.

Exercises

1. Hashing algorithms must be fast. Use the timing schemes discussed in this chapter to determine which of the three hashing algorithms presented is the fastest.

2. When a sequence of numbers is sorted into ascending order then element i-1 is always smaller than or equal to element i. Here is a description of a sorting algorithm: scan the data set S to find any pairs of adjacent locations where S[i-1] > S[i], and when any are found swap the two values. Repeat the process until the array is sorted. Does it ever get sorted? What is the best case and what is the worst case? Implement the method in Python.

3. Compare the linear congruential random number generator described in this chapter against the *random()* function in Python. Implement a die roll using each method, and roll a die 1000 times. Which method is nearest to the expected frequency distribution (equal for all values)? Repeat the process 1000 times and score Python one point when its random number generator wins by this measure, and score the book's generator one point when it wins. Which is the overall winner?

4. The quality of a hashing algorithm is measured by how random the hash codes are when given a sample set of strings. One estimate of randomness is the number of cells with more than one value hashed to it (the best here would be 0), and the average number of values hashed to occupied cells—this should be close to 1. Measure these for the three hashing methods presented for a size of 60 cells.

5. Data for registrants in a swimming competition consists of the swimmers name, number, national ranking, and time in the 200-meter freestyle competition. These data are located in four lists: **name, number, rank, t200.** In all cases the same index is used to access all of the data for the same person. Sort these data in descending order on time and identify the persons in the top three spots and their times.

6. *Steganography* works by concealing a message rather than making it unreadable, as is done when using encryption. In the ideal situation nobody will even suspect that there is a second message hidden within the first. Consider a scheme that uses the spaces in a message: a single space is a '0' and a double space is a "1." The letters are coded as 5-bit codes starting with "A" = 00000, "B" = 00001, and so on. Write programs that encode and decode such messages.

Notes and Other Resources

Random.org random number server. *https://www.random.org/*

A pretty good description of RSA: *https://en.wikipedia.org/wiki/RSA_%28cryptosystem%29*

Encode/decode stenographic messages disguised as spam. *http://www.spammimic.com/*

1. Donald Knuth. (1997). **The Art of Computer Programming, Volume 3: Sorting and Searching, 3rd Edition**, Addison-Wesley, 138–141, ISBN 0-201-89685-0.

2. Anany Levitin. **Introduction to the Design & Analysis of Algorithms, 2nd Edition**, 98–100, ISBN 0-321-35828-7.

3. Robert Sedgewick. (1998). **Algorithms in C++, Parts 1–4: Fundamentals, Data Structure, Sorting, Searching, 2nd Edition**, Addison-Wesley Longman, 273–274, ISBN 0-201-35088-2.

4. G. Marsaglia. (2003). *http://www.csis.hku.hk/~diehard*

5. Makato Matsumoto and Takuji Nishimura. (January 1998). **Mersenne twister: A 623-dimensionally equidistributed uniform pseudo-random number generator**, *ACM Trans. Model. Comput. Simul. 8*(1), 3–30, DOI = http://dx.doi.org/10.1145/272991.272995

6. Lenore Blum, Manuel Blum, and Mike Shub. (1982). **Comparison of two pseudo-random number generators**, *Advances in Cryptology: Proceedings of CRYPTO '82*, Plenum, 61–78.

7. Claude E. Shannon. (October 1949). **Communication theory of secrecy systems** (PDF), *Bell System Technical Journal, 28*(4), 656–715, retrieved 2011-12-21, doi:10.1002/j.1538-7305.1949.tb00928.x

8. **The Only Unbreakable Cryptosystem Known—The Vernam Cipher**, retrieved 2014-03-17, Pro-technix.com

9. B. Schneier. (1994). **Description of a new variable-length key, 64-bit block cipher (Blowfish)**, in *Fast Software Encryption*, edited by Ross Anderson, Cambridge Security Workshop Proceedings (December 1993), Springer-Verlag, 191–204.

10. Steven W. Smith. (2007). **Data Compression Tutorial: Part 1**, *http://www.eetimes.com/document.asp?doc_id=1275417&page_number=2*

11. H. G. Wells. (1895). **The Time Machine**, William Heinemann, *http://www.gutenberg.org/cache/epub/35/pg35.txt*

CHAPTER **11**

PROGRAMMING FOR THE SCIENCES

■ ■ ■ ■ ■

In this chapter

It is true that the earliest calculating devices were created to help with commercial concerns, like payments, credit, and inventory. The abacus is an excellent example—it does basic arithmetic and was likely an early "cash register." Much older devices do exist, such as the Lebombo bone that helped ancient African bushmen do simple calculations and keep track of time. The electronic computer, on the other hand, was designed to carry out scientific calculations, in particular those related to decrypting military messages and building the atom bomb. Computers are, of course, used for those things still, but there is now a vast array of computations in the scientific domain that could not be carried out without the help of a computer.

Scientists from different disciplines would disagree about what the most important algorithms and techniques for science were. That's because of the widely disparate things that physicists and biologists, as two examples, study. There are a few recurring problems that pop up in almost all science domains, and some important techniques that generalize to many science and some non-science areas.

11.1 FINDING ROOTS OF EQUATIONS

The root of an equation is the x coordinate corresponding to its zero value. This may not be the smallest or the largest value, but the place where a function equals zero is often important. For example, if a function for the error in a calculation can be found, then finding the place where the error is zero would be important. In one dimension the problem being solved is:

$$x: f(x) = 0 \tag{11.1}$$

Or in other words, find the value of **x** that results in **f(x)** being equal to zero. The function could be quite complicated, but for the technique to work it should have a derivative.

The basis of many root finding procedures is *Newton's method.* The procedure begins with a guess at the right answer. The guess in many cases does not have to be very accurate, but is simply a starting point. If a range of values is given within which to find the solution, the center of that range may be a good starting guess. So, here is a problem to start with:

$$f(x) = (x-1)^3 \quad \text{between} \quad x = -2 \text{ and } x = 12 \tag{11.2}$$

The center of the range is x = 5.

The initial guess is called x_0, and here $x_0 = 5$. The function value there, $f(x_0)$, is 64. The algorithm now says that the next guess for x, x_1, will be:

$$x_0 - f(x_0)/f'(x_0) \tag{11.3}$$

where $f'(x_0)$ is the derivative of **f** at the point **x= x_0**. This is a wrinkle—the derivative of f has to be calculated. It's easy to do for many functions, hard for others. A numerical method will be examined a little later in this chapter, so in the meantime it is possible to simply code a function that gives the derivative, having done the calculus on paper and then written the function based on that. The derivative of $(x-1)^3$ is $3x^2 - 6x+3$.

```
# Roots of a function
def objective (x):
    return (x-1)*(x-1)*(x-1)

def deriv (x):
    return 3*x*x - 6*x+3

# Range is -2 to +12
x = 5.
fx = 1000.
delta = 0.000001
print ("Step 0: x=", x, " obj = ", objective(x))
i = 1
while abs(fx) > delta:
    f = objective(x)
    ff = f/deriv(x)
    x = x - ff
    fx = objective(x)
    print ("Step ",i,": x=", x, " obj = ", fx)
    i = i + 1
```

Step 0: x= 5.0 obj = 64.0
Step 1 : x= 3.666666666666667 obj = 18.96296296296297
Step 2 : x= 2.7777777777777777 obj = 5.618655692729766
Step 3 : x= 2.185185185185185 obj = 1.6647868719199308

. . .

Step 14 : x= 1.0137019495631274 obj = 2.5724508967303e-06
Step 15 : x= 1.0091346330420865 obj = 7.622076731056633e-07

The correct answer in this case is x=1.0, so the method gets to within 0.009 of the correct root in 15 steps. Depending on the application, this could be fine. What if the initial guess was terrible? If the process starts at x = 500 then it takes 27 steps, but gets just a little closer to the right answer (x=1.0087). Starting at -500 also takes 27 steps.

It's possible that there is no root. What happens in that case? The program keeps looking. It overshoots, and then goes back, and forth, and back again. To present this from happening it is common to place a limit of the number of times the program will try. When this limit is exceeded an error occurs indicating that there is no solution.

This first example has illustrated some common concepts that are used in *numerical analysis*, which is the mathematical discipline encompassing the computation of mathematical functions and operations. The common concepts include:

The **initial guess**: It is relatively common to have a numerical algorithm begin at a guessed value.

The **delta**: It is also common to have an algorithm step when the change in the result or some mathematical feature becomes smaller than a specified threshold, called *delta*.

Iteration: Numerical methods frequently repeat a calculation expecting it to converge on the correct result, using the previously calculated value as the new starting point.

Maximum iterations: A user of a numerical method can assume that the method will not converge (get close enough to the right answer) if a specified number of attempts have been made.

11.2 DIFFERENTIATION

Determining the derivative of a function is something that is often thought of as a symbolic operation, and the result is valid for any value of the function. This may not always be true, and it may not be easy to do in the general case. Think about what the previous algorithm does—it needs the derivative of a function at one specific point. Can that be determined if the algebraic form of the function is not known? Yes, it can, to within some degree of accuracy.

The derivative of a function at a point **x** is the slope of the curve defined by that function at that point. The definition of the derivative of **f** at the point **x** is:

$$f'(x) = (f(x + h) - f(x - h))/(2h) \tag{11.4}$$

as **h** gets smaller and smaller, what is called a *limit* in calculus. This formula is essentially the mathematical definition of a derivative. On a computer **h** can be made quite small, but can never be zero. If the expression above is used as an estimate of the derivative, it will work in many cases. It is based on sampling two points of the function each time. An improvement can be made by using more points; for example:

$$f(x) = \frac{-f(x+2h) + 8f(x+h) - 8f(x-h) + f(x-2h)}{12h} \tag{11.5}$$

uses four points and often produces better results.

Coding this uses a function passed as a parameter. It makes sense that the function to be differentiated would be a parameter to the function that differentiates it; other parameters will be **x**, the point at which it will be evaluated, **delta**, the accuracy desired, and **niter**, the maximum number of iterations. The calculation should take place in a try-except block so that numerical errors will be caught. The two-point and the four-point versions of the function that performs numerical differentiation are:

```
def deriv1 (f, x, delta=0.0001,
niter=20):  # Two point
            # derivative
  global n0
  h = 0.001
  n = 0
  dx = f(x)
  while n<niter:
      try:
          old_dx = dx
          dx = (f(x+h)-f(x-h))/
                          (2*h)
          n = n + 1
          if abs(dx-old_dx) <
                          delta:
              n0 = n
              return dx
      except:
          print ("Exception
                      deriv1")
          return 0
```

```
def deriv2 (f, x, delta=0.0001,
niter=20):  # Four point
            # derivative
  global n1
  h = 0.001
  n = 0
  dx = f(x)
  while n<20:
      try:
          old_dx = dx
          dx = (-f(x+2*h)+
            8*f(x+h)- \8*f(x-h)+
              f(x-2*h))/(12*h)
          n = n + 1
          if abs(dx-old_dx) <
                          delta:
              n1 = n
              return dx
      except:
          print ("Exception
                      deriv2")
          return 0
```

Testing these functions is an excellent demonstration. First a function to be differentiated is written. The previous example on finding roots has a simple one (renamed as f1):

```
def f1 (x):
    return (x-1)*(x-1)*(x-1)
```

That example also has a function that represents the derivative of f1 at the point **x** (renamed df1):

```
def df1 (x):
    return 3*x*x - 6*x+3
```

The function **df1()** should return the exact derivative of **f1()**, and can be used to check the value returned by **deriv1()** or **deriv2()**. Create a loop that runs over a range of **x** values and compare the value returned from **df1()** to that returned by **deriv1()** and/or **deriv2()**:

```
for i in range (1,20):
    x = i*1.0
    f = f1(x)
    df = df1(x)
    mydf = deriv1 (f1, x)
    mydf2 = deriv2(f1, x)
    print (f, df, mydf, n0, "    ", mydf2, n1)
```

The result looks something like this:

f(x)	df(x)	result from deriv1	Niter	result from derive2	Niter
0.0	0.0	9.999999e-07	1	-2.2209799e-19	1
1.0	3.0	3.0000009999	2	2.999999999999	2
8.0	12.0	12.00000099999	2	11.999999999999	2
		. . .			
4913.0	867.0	867.0000010015	2	867.0000000024	2
5832.0	972.0	972.000001001	2	972.0000000021	2

Both functions give excellent results in a very few iterations in this case. Of course, some functions present more difficulties than do simple polynomials. [2]

11.3 INTEGRATION

An integral is most often thought of as the *area under a curve*, where the curve is a function (Figure 11.1a). Numerical integration amounts calculating that area using an algorithm. The area of a rectangle is easy to calculate, so if the region under a curve could be reasonably approximated by a bunch of rectangles, then the problem would be solved. This is the idea behind the *trapezoidal rule*. The integral from x0 to x1 of a function f(x) can be approximated by the width $(x_1 - x_0)$ multiplied by the height (the average value of the function in that range), which is just a rectangle that approximates the area under the curve (Figure 11.1b). In mathematical notation:

$$\int_{x0}^{x1} f(x) = (x_1 - x_0)\frac{(f(x_0) + f(x_1))}{2} \tag{11.6}$$

This would generally be a pretty poor approximation of a curve, and would yield correspondingly bad approximations of the integral. However, the smaller the width $x_1 - x_0$ the more accurate the approximation can be, and so using a great many small trapezoids would be much better than using only one (Figure 11.1c). How many? That is not known at the outset, but could be increased from an initial guess until a desired accuracy was achieved.

A function that performs integration using this method would accept a function, the starting x_0 and the ending x_1 for the integral. The function would break the interval between x_0 and x_1 into **n** parts, when **n** is an initial guess. The function is evaluated for all **n** parts, the area of each trapezoid is computed, and they are summed to get the final result. Now increase **n** and do it again. If the two values are close enough (**delta**) then the process is complete.

This will be done in two steps. First a function **trap0()** that computes and returns the sum of N trapezoids. The obvious but slow way to do this is:

```
f trap0 (f, x0, x1, n):    # Slow method
    dx = (x1-x0)/n         # Divide range into N parts
    xa = x0                # Start at x0
```

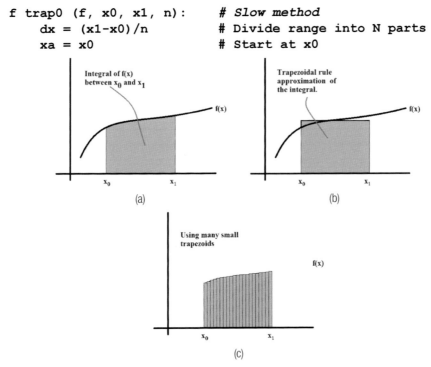

(a)

(b)

(c)

Figure 11.1
Numerical integration by summing many small areas under a curve.

```
xb = x0+dx              # Current trapezoid is xa to xb
sum = 0                 # Sum of areas starts at 0.0
for i in range(0, n):   # Add up N trapezoids
    f0 = f(xa)          # Compute function at xa and xb
    f1 = f(xb)
    sum = sum + dx*(f1+f0)/2  # Area of the trapezoid
    xa = xa + dx        # Next xa and xb are dx from
    xb = xb + dx        # the current ones
return sum              # The sum is the integral.
```

The integration function **trapezoid()** will call this function with increasing values of **n** until two consecutive results show a small enough difference (i.e., smaller than a provided delta value):

```
def trapezoid (f, x0, x1, delta=0.0001, niter=1024):
    n = 4
    resold = trap0(f, x0, x1, 2)
    resnew = trap0(f, x0, x1, 4)
    while abs(resnew-resold) > delta:
        if n>niter: break
        resold = resnew
        n = n * 2
        resnew = trap0 (f, x0, x1, n)
    return resnew
```

The function **trap0()** can be sped up significantly by not re-computing the function twice each time through the loop, but remembering the previous value instead (Exercise 2). A more popular algorithm for integration is *Simpson's Rule*, which tries to minimize the error even more by using a quadratic approximation to the curve at the top of the trapezoid, instead of a straight line.

11.4 OPTIMIZATION: FINDING MAXIMA AND MINIMA

Finding extreme values, either the maximum or minimum, is a very common problem in computing, not just in science but in many disciplines. It is sometimes referred to as *optimization*. Naturally finding a *best* (in some sense) value would be appealing. What is the least amount of fuel needed to travel from Chicago to Atlanta? What route between those two cities requires the least amount of driving time? What route is shortest in terms of distance? There are many reasons to want an optimum and many ways to define what an optimum is.

In the following discussion the function to be optimized will be provided, so there will no guesswork on that subject. The question concerns how to find location (parameters) where the minimum or maximum occurs.

11.4.1 Newton Again

Figure 11.2 shows an example of a function to be optimized. There is a minimum of 7 at the point x= 1. How can this be found? If the nature of the function is known, for instance that it is a quadratic polynomial, then the optimum can be found immediately. It will be at the point where the derivative is zero. The problem of optimization is that one does not know much, if anything, about the function. It can only be evaluated, and perhaps the derivatives can be found numerically. Given that, how can the min or max be found?

If the derivative can be found, then it may be possible to search for an optimum point. At a value **x**, if the derivative is negative, then the slope of the curve is negative at that point; if the derivative is positive then the slope is positive. If an x value can be found where the slope is negative (call this point x_0) and another where it is positive (call this x_1), then the optimum (slope = 0) must be between these two points. Finding that point can be done as follows:

1. Select the point between these two ($x = (x_0 + x_1)/2$).
2. If the derivative is negative at this point, let $x_0 = x$. If positive let $x_1 = x$.
3. Repeat from step 1 until the derivative is close enough to 0.

This process is pretty much random. Finding the two starting points is a matter of guessing until they are found. The search range gets smaller by a factor of 2

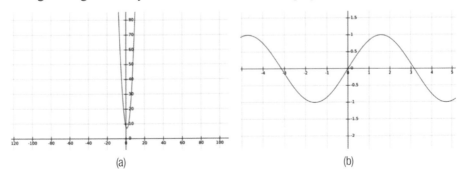

(a) (b)

Figure 11.2
(a) Analytical function with a minimum. (b) A sine function has many minima and maxima.

each iteration. The fact that the function can be evaluated at any point means that it is possible to make better guesses. In particular, it's possible to assume that the function is approximately quadratic at each step. Quadratics have an optimum at a predictable place. The method called *Newton's Method* fits a quadratic at each point and moves towards its optimal point.

The method is iterative, and without doing the math the iteration is:

$$x_n = x_{n-1} - \frac{f'(x)}{f''(x)} \tag{11.7}$$

A function to calculate the first *and* second derivative is needed. The formula for the second derivative is based on the definition of differentiation, as was the formula for the first. It is:

$$f''(x) = \frac{f(x+h) - 2f(x) + f(x-h)}{h^2} \tag{11.8}$$

The program should therefore be straightforward. Repeat the calculation of $x_{n-1} - f'(x)/f''(x)$ until it converges to the answer. This will be the location of the optimum. An example function would be:

```
def newtonopt (f, x0, x1, delta=0.0001, niter=20):
    x = (x0+x1)/2
    fa = 1000.0
    fb = f(x)
    i = 0
    print ("Iteration 0: x=", x, " f=", fb)
    while (abs(fa-fb) > delta):
        fa = fb
        x = x - deriv(f, x)/derivsecond(f, x)
        fb = f(x)
        i = i + 1
        print ("Iteration ", i, ": x=", x, " f=", fb)
        if i>niter:
            return 0
```

This finds a local optimum between the values of x0 and x1. A local optimum may not be the largest or smallest function value that the function can produce, but may be the optimum in a local range of values.

Figure 11.2a shows a typical quadratic function. It is $f(x) = x^2 - 2x + 8$, and has an optimum at $x = 1$. Because it is quadratic the Newton optimization function above finds the result in a single step. Figure 11.2b is a sine function, and can be seen to have many minima and maxima. Any one of them might be found by the Newton method, which is why a range of values is provided to the function.

The **newtonopt()** function successfully finds the optimum in Figure 11.2a at x=1, and finds one in Figure 11.2b at x = 90 degrees (π/2 radians). If there is no optimum the iteration limit will be reached. If either derivative does not exist, then an exception will occur.

11.4.2 Fitting Data to Curves – Regression

Scientists collect data on nearly everything. Data are really numerical values that represent some process, whether it be physical, chemical, biological, or sociological. The numbers are measurements, and scientists model processes using these measurements in order to further understand them. One of the first things that is usually done is to try to find a pattern in the data that may give some insight into the underlying process, or at least allow predictions for situations not measured. One of the common methods in data analysis is to *fit a curve* to the data; that is, to determine whether a strong mathematical relationship exists between the measurements.

As an example, a set of measurements of tree heights will be used. The height of a set of a specific variety of trees is made over a period of ten years and the data resides in a file named "treedata.txt." The question: is there a linear relationship (i.e., does a tree grow generally the same amount each year)? Specifically, what is that relationship (i.e., how much can we expect a tree to grow)? Figure z shows a visualization of these data in the form of a *scattergram* or *scatter plot*, in which the data are displayed as points in their (x,y) position on a grid.

The "curve" to be fit in this case will be a line. What is the equation of the line that best represents the data in the figure? If that were known then it would be possible to predict the height of a tree with some degree of confidence, or to estimate a tree's age from its height.

One form of the equation of a line is the point-slope form:

y = mx+b

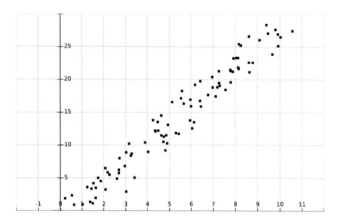

Figure 11.3
A scattergram of a typical set of measurements.

where **m** is the *slope* (angle) of the line and **b** is the *intercept*, the place where the line crosses the Y axis. The goal of the *regression* process, in which the best line is found, is to identify the values of **m** and **b**. A simple observation is needed first: the equation of a line can be written as:

$$mx + b - y = 0$$

If a point actually sits on this line, then plugging its **x** and **y** values into the equation will result in a 0 value. If a point is not on the line, then **mx+b-y** will result in a number that amounts to an error; its magnitude indicates how far away the point is from the line. Fitting a line to the data can be expressed as an optimization problem: find a line that minimizes the total error over all sample data points. If **(x$_i$,y$_i$)** is data point **i** then the goal is to minimize:

$$\sum_{i=0}^{n}(mx_i + b - y_i)^2 \qquad (11.9)$$

by finding the best values of **m** and **b**. The expression is squared so that it will always be positive, which simplifies the math. It may be possible to do this optimization using a general optimization process such as Newton's, but fortunately for a straight line the math has been done in advance. Other situations are more complicated, depending on the function being fit and the number of dimensions.

A simple linear regression is done by looking at the data and calculating the following:

$$\text{meanX} = \text{mean value of } x = \frac{\sum x}{n}$$

$$\text{MeanY} = \text{mean value of } y = \frac{\sum y}{n}$$

$$\text{stdX} = \text{standard deviation of } x = \sqrt{\frac{\sum (x - \text{mean}x)^2}{n-1}}$$

$$\text{stdY} = \text{standard deviation of } y = \sqrt{\frac{\sum (y - \text{mean}y^2)}{n-1}}$$

$$\text{r} = \text{correlation between x and } y = \frac{\sum (x - \text{mean}x)(y - \text{mean}y)}{\sqrt{\sum x^2 \sum y^2}}$$

Each of these can be calculated using a separate function. Then the slope of the best line through the data would be:

$$m = r\frac{\text{std}y}{\text{std}x} \qquad (11.10)$$

And the intercept is:

$$b = \text{mean}y - m*\text{mean}x \qquad (11.11)$$

The function **regress()** that does the regression accepts a tuple of X values and a corresponding tuple of Y values, and returns a tuple **(m, b)** containing the parameters of the line that fits the data. It depends on other functions to calculate the mean, standard deviation, and correlation; these functions could generally be more useful in other applications. The entire collection of code is:

```
from math import *

def mean (x):
    sum = 0.0
    for i in range (0, len(x)):
        sum = sum + x[i]
    sum = sum/len(x)
    return sum

def sdev (x, meanx):
    sum = 0
    for i in range (0, len(x)):

def regress (x, y):
    mx = mean(xdata)
    my = mean(ydata)
    sdx = sdev (xdata, mx)
    sdy = sdev (ydata, my)
    if sdx == 0: return
    r = correlate
                (xdata,ydata,mx,my)
    m = r * sdy/sdx
    b = my - m * mx
    return (m, b)
```

```
        sum = sum + (x[i]-            f = open ("treedata.txt", "r")
            meanx)*(x[i]-meanx)       s = f.readline ()
    sum = sum/(len(x)-1)              xdata = ()
    return sqrt (sum)                 ydata = ()

def correlate (x, y, meanx,          # Main program: test regress
                   meany):           # Read each lines as a string
    sum1 = 0                         # and split at the comma;
    sumx2 = 0                        # 2 reals
    sumy2 = 0                        while s != "":
    for i in range(0,len(x)):            for i in range (1,len(s)):
        z = (x[i]-meanx)*(y[i]-              if s[i] == ",": break
                    meany)               x = float(s[0:i-1])
        sum1 = sum1 + z                  y = float(s[i+1:])
        sumx2 = sumx2 + \                xdata = xdata + (x,)
           (x[i]-meanx)*(x[i]-           ydata = ydata + (y,)
                    meanx)               s = f.readline()
        sumy2 = sumy2 + \
           (y[i]-meany)*(y[i]-        line = regress(x, y)
                    meany)
    return sum1/sqrt(sumx2*sumy2)
```

11.4.3 Evolutionary Methods

A *genetic algorithm* (GA) or an *evolutionary algorithm* (EA) is an optimization technique that uses natural selection as a metaphor to optimize a function or process. The idea is to create a collection of many possible solutions (a *population*), which are really just sets of parameters to the objective function. These are evaluated (by calling the function) and the best of them are kept in the population; the remainder are discarded. The population is refilled by combining the remaining parameter sets with each other in various ways in a process that mimics reproduction, and then this new population is evaluated and the process repeats.

The idea is that the population contains the best solutions that have been seen so far, and that by recombining them a new, better set of solutions can be created, just as nature selects plants and animals to suit their environment. This method does not require the calculation of a derivative, so it can be used to optimize "functions" that can't be handled in other ways. It can also deal with large dimensions; that is, functions that take a large number of parameters.

This idea may be new, and so developing it with an example may be the best way to illustrate it. Consider the problem of finding the minimum of a function of two variables. This is really an attempt to find values for x and y that result in the smallest function result. Evolutionary algorithms are often tested on quite nasty functions, having lots of local minima or large flat regions. Two such functions will be used here: the *Goldstein-Price* function:

$$(1+(x+y+1)^2 (19 - 14x+3x^2 - 14y + 6xy+3y^2)$$
$$(30+(2x+3y)^2 (18 - 32x+12x^2+48y - 36xy+27y^2))$$ (11.12)

and *Bohachevsky's* function:

$$x^2 + y^2 - 0.3\cos(3px) - 0.4\cos (4py) + 0.7$$ (11.13)

Graphs of these functions are shown in Figure 11.4.

The first step in the evolutionary algorithm is to create a population of potential solutions. This is just a collection of parameter pairs **(x,y)** created at random. The population size for this example will be 100, and is a parameter of the EA process. This is done in the obvious way:

```
def genpop (population_size):
    pop = ()
    for i in range(0, population_size):
        p = (randrange(-10, 10),  randrange(-100, 100))
        pop = pop + (p,)
    return pop
```

The population is a tuple of a hundred **(x, y)** parameter pairs. Now these need to be evaluated, and so the objective function must be written. This will differ for each optimization problem, of course. In this case it is the sum of the errors

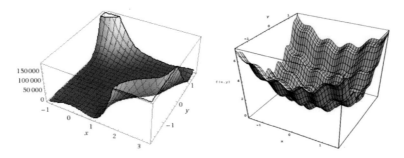

Figure11.4
Two-dimensional functions to be optimized.

between a given line (one of the parameters) and the data points. One way to calculate this is:

```
def objective (x, y):    # One of many possiblke objective
                         # functions
    return goldsteinprice (x, y)
#    return boha (x, y)
def goldsteinprice (x, y):   # Goldstein-Price function
                             # f(0, -1) = 3
    return (1+(x+y+1)**2 * (19-14*x+3*x*x - 14*y +6*x*y +
            3*y*y)) * \(30+(2*x-3*y)**2 * (18-32*x+12*x*x+
            48*y-36*x*y+27*y*y))

def boha (x, y):
    z = x*x + y*y -0.3*cos(3*pi*x) - 0.4*cos(4*pi*y) + 0.7
    return z
```

All members of the population are evaluated, and the best ones—in this case the ones having the smallest objective function value—are kept. A good way to do this is to have the values in a tuple **E** where **E[i]** is the result of evaluating parameters **P[i]**, and sorting the collection is descending order on **E**. Since there are 100 entries in **E** this will mean that **E[0:n]** will contain the best **n%** of the population. The function **eval()** will create a tuple of function evaluations for the whole population, and **sort()** will sort these and the corresponding parameters. These contain nothing new, and will not be shown here. The program here will select the best 10% and discard the remainder, replacing them with copies of the good ones.

The key issue is one of introducing variety in the population. This means changing the values of the parameters while, one would hope, improving the overall performance of the group. Using the metaphor of natural selection and genetics, there are two ways to introduce change into the population: *mutation* and *crossover*. Mutation involves making a small change in a parameter. In real DNA, a mutation would change one of the base pairs in the sequence which would usually amount to a rather small change, but which will be fatal in some cases. In the EA being written, a *mutation will be a random amount added to or subtracted from a parameter*. Mutations occur randomly and with a small probability, which will be named **pmut** in the program. Values between 0.015 and 0.2 are typical for **pmut**, but a best value can't be determined, and is problem specified. A value of 0.02 will be used here.

The function **mutate()** will examine all elements in the global population, mutating them at random (i.e., adding random values):

```
def mutate (m):
    global pmut, population
    for i in range (int(m), len(population)):
        c = population[i]
        if random () < pmut:          # Mutate the x parameter
            c[0] = c[0] + random()*10.0-5
        if random () < pmut:          # Mutate the y parameter
            c[1] = c[1] + random()*10.0-5
        population[i] = c
```

A crossover is more complex, involving two sets of parameters. It involves swapping parts of the parameters sets from two "parents." Some parameters could be swapped entirely, in this case meaning that (x0, y0) and (x1, y1) would become (x0, y1) and (x1, y0). Other times parts of one parameter would be combined with parts of another. There are implementations involving bit strings that make this easier, but when using floating point values as is being done here, a good way to do a crossover is to select two "parents" and replace one of the parameters in each with a random value that lies between the original two.

```
def crossover (m):
    global population, pcross
    for i in range (m, len(population)):   # Keep the best ones
                                           # unchanged
        if random () < pcross:             # Crossover at the
                                           # given rate
            k = randrange(m, len(population))  # Pick a random
                                               # mate
            w = randrange (0, 1)            # Change X or Y?
            c = population[i]               # Get individual 1
            g1 = c[w]                   # Get X or Y for this guy
            cc = population[k]          # get individual 2
            g2 = cc[w]                  # Get X or Y
            if (g1>g2): t = g1; g1 = g2; g2 = t
                                        # swap so g1 is smallest
            c[w] = random()*(g2-g1) + g1   # Generate new
                                           # parameter for 1
            cc[w] =random()*(g2g1) + g1    # Generate new
                                           # parameter for 2
```

Sample output from three attempts to find the optimal value of Bohachevsky's function is:

Iterations	x	y	Result
5	[0.002528698,	0.0]	at 9.158793881192118e-05
173	[5.38185770e-10,	-0.0006229]	at 1.2643415301605287e-05
4	[-0.0007491,	0.0]	at 8.0394329584621e-06

This shows that sometimes the process takes much more time to arrive at a solution than others. It depends on the initial population, as well as on the parameters of the program: the mutation and crossover probabilities, the percentage of the top individuals to retain, and the nature of the mutation and crossover operators themselves.

Figure 11.5 outlines the overall process involved in the optimization. Details on specific techniques can be found in the references.

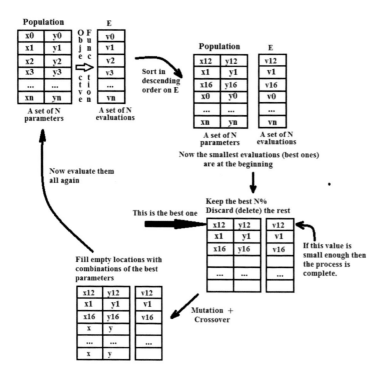

Figure 11.5
The evolutionary algorithm process.

11.5 LONGEST COMMON SUBSEQUENCE (EDIT DISTANCE)

So far in this chapter the methods being discussed are numerical ones, and given the topic being discussed that makes some sense. There are, on the other hand, many algorithms that are not numeric in nature, but may be more symbolic, involve patterns, pictures, sounds, or other more complex data forms. It is true that at some level all problems to be solved on a computer must be formulated using numbers, but in the examples so far the numbers are really the subject of the problem, and the problem would be solved numerically even if done with a pencil and paper. In other cases this is not so.

As a major example, consider the problem of comparing two sequences of DNA. A sequence in this instance consists of a string of letters, each one referred to as a *base* in the sequence. DNA consists of a long sequence of base pairs involving four molecules: Adenine (A), Guanine (G), Thymine (T), and Cytosine (C) linked together chemically. These ultimately define the structure of a protein, and it is the sequence that is important. A common problem in computational biology is to find the longest sequence in common between two DNA strands, where the samples may be from different individuals or even different species. Methods for doing this tend to involve the *edit distance* or *Levenshtein distance*.

The edit distance is a way of specifying how similar or dissimilar two strings are to one another by finding the minimum number of editing operations required to transform one string into the other. An editing operation can be a change in a character, a deletion, or an insertion. For example, what is the edit distance between the word "planning" and the word "pruning"? It is 3:

```
planning
pranning    change "l" to "r"
prunning    change "a" to "u"
pru ning    delete "n"
```

How is this used when looking at DNA? A DNA sequence is a set of the codes read from a piece of DNA, and is a string containing only the letters G, A, T, and C. Comparing two pieces of DNA is a matter of comparing the two strings. So, the two strings AGGACAT and ATTACGAT are distance 3 from each other. The longest common subsequence has 5 characters in it:

```
AGGAC AT
ATTACGAT
```

11.5.1 Determining Longest Common Subsequence (LCS)

Exhaustive searching of two S1 and S2 strings for the longest common subsequence would simply be too slow for any practical purpose. Fortunately, a lot of work has been done over the past 50 years on this problem, and the method of choice appears to be the *Smith-Waterman* method. It builds a matrix (two-dimensional array) where each character of the first string represents a column of the matrix, and each character in the other string forms a row, in order of appearance. The matrix is filled with numbers using the following relation:

$$T(i,j) = \max \begin{bmatrix} T(i-1,j-1) + \sigma(S_1(i), S_2(j)) \\ T(i-1,j) + \text{gap penalty} \\ T(i,j-1) + \text{gap penalty} \\ 0 \end{bmatrix} \quad (11.14)$$

The function $\sigma(a,b)$ gives a penalty for a match/mismatch between two characters a and b. Here it will be 2 for a match and -2 for a miss. The *gap penalty* is the value assigned to having to leave a gap in the sequence to perform a better match. Usually this would be -1. The scheme offers a degree of flexibility, so that different penalties (and rewards) can be applied in different circumstances.

The first step in the *Smith-Waterman* method is to create a matrix (a table) **T** in which there are **len(S1+1)** columns and **len(S2+1)** rows. The first index in T(i,j) refers to the column and the second index is the row. The values in the current row are a function of those in the previous one. Place a 0 in each element of the first row and the first column. For the two strings used previously this would look like the table below.

S2 \ S1		A	G	G	A	C	A	T
	0	0	0	0	0	0	0	0
A	0	*						
T	0							
T	0							
A	0							
C	0							
G	0							
A	0							
T	0							

Now, for any element T(i,j) the neighboring elements are:

$$T(i-1, j-1) \quad T(i, j-1) \quad T(i+1, j-1)$$
$$T(i-1, j) \quad T(i, j) \quad T(i+1, j)$$

The first cell to fill in the table T is $T(1,1)$, marked with a "*" character in the example to the left. The relation used to fill this cell has four parts:

1. $T(i-1, j-1) + \sigma(S_1(i), S_2(j))$ The characters in the row and column match, so $\sigma(S_1(i), S_2(j)) = \sigma(A, A) = 1 + T(0,0) = 2$

2. Gap penalty is -1, $T(i-1, j) = 0$, $T(0, 1) = 0$. Result is -1

3. Gap penalty is -1, $T(i, j-1) = T(1,1) = 0$. Result is -1

4. Result is 0

The maximum value of these four calculations is 1, so $T(1, 1) = 2$.

S2 \ S1		A	G	G	A	C	A	T
	0	0	0		0	0	0	0
A	0	2	*					
T	0							
T	0							
A	0							
C	0							
G	0							
A	0							
T	0							

The next cell to compute is $T(2,1)$. This time the two characters are not the same, so:

1. $T(i-1, j-1) + \sigma(S_1(i), S_2(j))$ where $\sigma(S_1(i), S_2(j)) = \sigma(G, A) = -1 + T(1,0) = -2$

2. Gap penalty is -1, $T(i-1, j) = T(1,1) = 2$.
   Result is $2 - 1 = 1$

3. Gap penalty is -1, $T(i, j-1) = T(2,1) = 0$. Result is -1
   Result is 0
   and so $T(2,1) = 1$

For $T(3,1)$:

1. G and A are not the same, $\sigma(G, T) = -2$:

2. $T(i-1, j) = T(2,1) = 1$ so $1 - 1 = 0$

3. $T(i, j-1) = T(3,0) = 0$ so $0 - 1 = -1$

4. 0

    Result is 0

For $T(4,1)$:

1. $\sigma(A, A) = 2$,
2. $T(i-1, j) = T(3, 1) = 0$, 0-gap $= -1$
3. $T(i, j-1) = T(4, 0) = 0$, 0-gap $= -1$
4. 0

    Result is 2

For $T(5, 1)$:

1. $\sigma(C, A) = -2$,
2. $T(i-1, j) = T(4, 1) = 2$, 2-gap $= 1$
3. $T(i, j-1) = T(5, 0) = 0$, 0-gap $= -1$
4. 0

    Result is 1

For $T(6, 1)$:

1. $\sigma(A, A) = 2$,
2. $T(i-1, j) = T(5, 1) = 1$, 1-gap $= 0$
3. $T(i, j-1) = T(6\ 0) = 0$, 0-gap $= -1$
4. 0

    Result is 2

Finally for $T(7,1)$:

1. $\sigma(T, A) = -2$,
2. $T(i-1, j) = T(6, 1) = 2$, 2-gap $= 1$
3. $T(i, j-1) = T(7\ 0) = 0$, 0-gap $= -1$
4. 0

Result is 1

    The result after row 2 is complete is:

S2 \ S1		A	G	G	A	C	A	T
	0	0	0	0	0	0	0	0
A	0	2	1	0	2	1	2	1
T	0							
T	0							

Now move to the next row. The process repeats until all cells have been examined and assigned values. For this example the final matrix is:

S2 \ S1		A	G	G	A	C	A	T
	0	0	0	0	0	0	0	0
A	0	2	1	0	2	1	2	1
T	0	1	0	0	1	0	1	4
T	0	0	0	0	0	0	0	3
A	0	2	1	0	2	1	2	2
C	0	0	1	0	0	4	3	2
G	0	0	3	2	1	3	2	1
A	0	2	2	1	4	3	5	4
T	0	1	1	0	3	2	4	7

The lower right entry is column 7 row 8, or (7,8).

This matrix indicates the degree of match at points in the string. To determine the actual match between the strings, begin with the largest value in the matrix. In this case it is in the lower right corner, but that's not always true. Wherever the maximum is, start at that point in the matrix and trace left and upwards; this is essentially moving from the end of each string back to the beginning. At each step the move is left, up, or diagonally.

The process will build two ways to match the string. One indicates how to change **s1** into **s2** (call this **M1**), and the other indicates how to turn **s2** into **s1** (call this **M2**). Both strings are constructed from, in this case, (7,9) back to (0,0).

```
def backtrack():
  global s1, s2
  mi = 0
  mj = 0
  m1 = ""
  m2 = ""
  maxv = T[mi][mj]
  for j in range (1, len(s2)+1):
      for i in range (1,
                      len(s1)+1):
          if T[i][j] >= maxv:
              maxv = T[i][j]
              mi = i
              mj = j
```

This backtracking stage is the tricky part. Begin with two empty strings **M1** and **M2**. Locate the largest value in the matrix (there may be more than one) and begin at that set of i,j coordinates: call this point (**mi,mj**).

```while mi>0 or mj>0:```
  ```t11 = T[mi-1][mj-1] # Diagonal```
  ```t01 = T[mi][mj-1]   # Up```
  ```t10 = T[mi-1][mj]   # Left```
	A step to the left from this point is to **(mi-1, mj)**; upwards is **(mi, mj-1)**; diagonally up-left would be **(mi-1,mj-1)**. The direction to be selected is the one that has the largest value of **T**, with a bias towards the diagonal if there is no specific maximum (i.e., all three are equal).

```# Diagonal is best```
```if t11>=t01 and t11 >= t10:```
  ```m1 = s1[mi-1] + m1```
  ```m2 = s2[mj-1] + m2```
  ```mi = mi - 1```
  ```mj = mj - 1```
	A movement in the diagonal direction implies a simple match or mismatch. The action should be to copy the corresponding character from **s1** into **M1** and the character from **s2** into **M2**, then set **mi = mi − 1** and **mj = mj − 1**.

```# UP is best```
 ```elif t01>t11 and t01 > t10:```
   ```m1 = s1[mi-1] + m1```
   ```m2 = "_" + m2```
   ```mj = mj - 1```
	A movement upwards implies that there is to be a gap inserted into **M2**, and so **s1** matches. Place a "_" character into **M2** and place the current **(mi)** character into **M1**. Leave **mi** alone but let **mj = mj − 1**, thus moving up in the matrix.

```# Left is best```
 ```elif t10>t11 and t10>t01:```
   ```m1 = "_"+m1```
   ```m2 = s2[mj-1]+m```
   ```mi = mi - 1```
	A movement left implies that a gap is to be inserted into **M1**, and so **M2** matches. Place a "_" character into **M1** and **s1[mj]** into **M2**, Leave **mj** alone but set **mi = mi − 1**, thus moving left.

```# End of WHILE Loop```	This process continues until either **mi** or **mj** becomes smaller than 0.

```if mi>0:```
   ```m1 = s1[0:mi] + m1```
```if mj > 0:```
   ```m2 = s2[0:mj] + m2```
	If **mi** or **mj** is not zero it means there are some characters left over in one of the two strings. Copy them into the corresponding match string **M1** or **M2**.

If there is more than one cell in T with a maximum value, then a route should be traced back from each maximum.

For the example string the result is:

M1 = AGGACCAT
M2 = ATTAC _ AT

There is a mismatch at the GG/TT pair and an inserted gap in M2.

11.6 SUMMARY

A discussion of some of the more important problem types studied by scientists was presented along with some method for their solution. The root of an equation is the place where its value is zero, and Newton's method was described as a means of finding a root. Newton's method requires that the derivative of the function be known, so means of numerically determining the derivative were also discussed.

Since derivatives could be calculated, methods for performing integration were described and functions for doing the calculation using the trapezoidal rule were written.

One of the more common calculations in science is to find an *optimum value* for a function. Another method of Newton's was used to find maxima or minima of a function.

The modeling of data is important in scientific (and other) disciplines. A method for finding the best straight line that passes through a set of data was illustrated (linear regression) and code was designed and tested for this problem.

Evolutionary algorithms can be used to find the optimum of a function, and is especially useful when dealing with multidimensional functions or functions that have many local optima, and when no derivative of the function exists.

Biologists sometimes need to match sequences of DNA. A method that does this using bases as characters and sequences as strings was presented; this is the *Smith-Waterman* algorithm for local sequence matching, and is commonly used for these problems.

Exercises

1. Modify the root finding example so that a numerical derivative is used instead of an analytical one (i.e., use derive1() or derive2()). This is a more practical situation. What is the effect?

2. Modify the trap0() function in the trapezoid rule example so that it never calls the function being evaluated more than once for any point.

3. Look up Simpson's Rule and code your own version. Compare it with the trapezoid rule for two functions of your choice. Which one is more accurate after each iteration?

4. Write a function error() that accepts X and Y data tuples, and values a and b. It returns the total error between the data points and the curve ax2+bx.

5. The (natural) logarithm of a value v is defined to be the integral of 1/x from 1 to v. Create a function that calculates the natural log using the existing integration function.

6. Run the evolutionary algorithm to optimize the Goldstein-Price twenty times. Does it ever fail to approach the minimum? How often? What can be done if an EA does not arrive at an optimum, and how can it be determined?

7. Using software developed in this chapter, find two positive numbers whose sum is 9 and so that the product of one number and the square of the other number is a maximum.

Notes and Other Resources

Online edit distance calculator: *http://planetcalc.com/1721/*

Smith-Waterman algorithm: *http://www.slideshare.net/avrilcoghlan/the-smith-waterman-algorithm*

https://www.youtube.com/watch?v=jrJ23aaByE8

1. D. Levy. Lecture Notes, (Ch 5) **Numerical Differentiation**, *http://www2.math.umd.edu/~dlevy/classes/amsc466/lecture-notes/differentiation-chap.pdf*

2. William Press, Saul Teukolsky, William Vetterling, and Brian Flannery. (2007). **Numerical Recipes: The Art of Scientific Computation, 3rd edition**, Cambridge University Press.

3. Richard Hamming. (1987). **Numerical Methods for Scientists and Engineers**, Dover Publications.

4. J. R. Parker. (2002). **Genetic Algorithms for Continuous Problems, 15th Canadian Conference on Artificial Intelligence, Calgary, Alberta**, May 27–29.

5. D. E. Goldberg. (1989). **Genetic Algorithms, Optimization, and Machine Learning**, Addison-Wesley, Reading, MA.

6. *vlab.amrita.edu.* (2012). **Global Alignment of Two Sequences - Needleman-Wunsch Algorithm**, Retrieved 9 December 2015, *vlab.amrita.edu/?sub=3&brch=274&sim=1431&cnt=1*

7. S. B. Needleman and C. D. Wunsch. (1970). **A general method applicable to the search for similarities in the amino acid sequence of two proteins**, J. Mol. Biol., 48, 443–453.

8. T. F. Smith and M. S. Waterman. (1981). **Identification of common molecular subsequences**, J. Mol. Biol., 147(1), 195-197.

## CHAPTER 12

HOW TO WRITE
GOOD PROGRAMS

■ ■ ■ ■ ■

In this chapter

There is no general agreement on how best to put together a good program. *Good*, by the way, means functionally correct, readable, modifiable, reasonably efficient, and that solves a problem that someone needs solved. This chapter will be distinct from the others in this book: we'll move into second person narrative, partly because of the more personal nature of the subject material. Writing code for some people is like telling a story or making a painting: it's not that it is art, but that it is personal. If you wish to insult a programmer, say that their code is poorly structured, or naïve, or in some way less than adequate.

There are many processes that have been described for programming, and the truth is that not only is there not one *best* one, but it is rarely certain than any of them is better than any of the others. When someone writes a program, they are trying to solve a problem. What they are doing is translating a loose collection of ideas into a form that can be represented on a computer, which is to say as numbers. The ideas are associated with algorithms, things that can be shown to work for at least a range of situations. Then that needs to be converted into a sequence of steps that leads to a solution to the original problem.

This is in part a problem in *synthesis*, the combining of separate components, elements, and ideas into a coherent whole. There is something called synthesis programming, but that's not what is being discussed. The parts of a program include decision constructs (IF statements), looping (FOR and WHILE), expressions, assignment statements, and data structures (tuples, dictionaries, strings, etc.). There is a degree of skill involved in using these units to build a sensible larger program. This skill is somewhat individual. No two programmers will create exactly the same program for a non-trivial problem.

What we're going to do in this chapter is show the development of an entire computer program, with all of the intermediate steps, flaws, errors, and flashes of genius (if any). Why? The answer is "because that is rarely done in lectures or in a book." When teaching mathematics the professor often shows the proof of a theorem on the blackboard (or as PowerPoint slides) and explains the steps. What they never do is show how the theorem was actually proved when the original person proved it—dead ends, days of no progress, good ideas, bad ideas: the whole messy process.

This is crucial. No theorem and no computer program flows fully formed and correct from someone's head. Observing the full process may be a valuable stage in the education of a programmer. They will see that the process is prone to error, even for good programmers. They'll see that not all ideas that seem good are actually good; that the process is not a linear one, but that it appears in some sense to spiral, gaining functionality at each loop. And they will see that there can be a simple and obvious method that could be agreed upon by many different programmers and yet adapted for each new situation. The method that we'll use is called *iterative refinement*, and it is nearly independent of language or philosophy. Of course, not everyone will agree.

One example program will be a computer game, and one that can't be played without a computer. It will be a breakout style game that uses circles instead of rectangles. The other will be a system that formats typed text.

12.1 PROCEDURAL PROGRAMMING – WORD PROCESSING

In the early days of desktop publishing, the programs that writers used did not display the results on the screen in "what-you-see-is-what-you-get" form. Formatting commands were embedded within the text and were implemented by the program, which would create a printable version that was properly formatted. Programs like *roff, nroff, tex*, and variations thereof are still used, but most writing tools now look like *Word* or *PageMaker* with commands being given through a graphical user interface.

There is a limit to what kind of text processing can be done using simple text files, but when you think about it that's really what a typewriter produces—simple text on paper with fixed size fonts. That worked for a very long time. It was good enough for Ernest Hemingway and Raymond Chandler.

The program that will be developed here will accept text from a file and format it according to a set of commands that have a specific format and are predefined by the system. The input will resemble that accepted by *nroff*, an old Unix utility, but will be a subset for simplicity. Since it uses standard text input and output any measurements will be made in characters, not inches or points. Commands will begin on a new line with a "." character and will be alphabetic. A line beginning with ".br", for instance, results in a forced line break. Some commands take a parameter: the command ".ll 55" sets the line length to 55 characters.

Here is a list of all of the commands that the system will recognize:

.pl n	Sets the page length to n lines
.bp n	Begin page n
.br	Break
.fi	Fill output lines (e.g., justify)
.nf	Don't fill output lines
.na	No justificaton
.ce n	Center the next n input lines
.ls n	Output n-1 line spaces after each line
.ll n	Line length is n characters

.in n	Indent n characters
.ti n	Temporarily indent n characters
.nh	Do not hyphenate
.hy	Hyphenation on
.sp n	Generate n lines

The program will read a text file and identify the words and the commands. The words will be written to an output file formatted as described by the commands. The default will be to right justify the text, and to use empty lines as paragraph breaks. The questions to be answered here are:

1. How does one begin creating such a program?
2. Can the process of program creation be described?
    a. Is the process systematic or casual?
    b. Is there only one process?

Beginning with the last question first, there is *no* single process. What is presented here is only one, but it should be understood that there are others, and that some processes probably work better than others for some kinds of program. The program to be created here will not use classes, and will involve a classical or traditional methodology generally referred to as *top-down*. Some people only use object-oriented code, but a problem with teaching that way is that a class contains traditional, procedure-oriented code. *To make a class, one must first know how to write a program.*

12.1.1 Top-Down

The idea behind top-down programming is that the higher levels of abstraction are described first. A description of what the entire program is to do is written in a kind-of English/computer hybrid language (*pseudocode*), and this description involves making calls to functions that have not yet been written but whose function is known. When the highest level description is acceptable, then the functions used are described. In this way the high-level decisions are described in terms of the lower level, whose implementation is postponed until the details are appropriate. The process repeats until all parts have been described, at which time the translation of the pseudocode into a real programming language can proceed, and should be straightforward. This can result in many distinct programs, but all should do basically the same thing, simply in somewhat different ways.

For the task at hand, the first step is to sketch the actions of the program as a whole. The program begins by opening the text file and opening an output file. The basic action is to copy from input to output, with certain additions to the output text. The data file is read in as characters or words, but output as lines and pages. So perhaps the following:

```
Open input file inf
Open output file outf
Read a word w from inf
While there is more text on inf:
    If w is a command:
        Process the command w
    Else:
        The next word is w. Process it
    Read a word from inf
Close inf
Close outf
```

This represents the entire program, although lacking a degree of detail. As Python this would look almost the same:

```
filename = input ("PYROFF: Enter the name if the input
                   file: ")
inf = open (filename, "r")
outf = open ("pyroff.txt. "w")
w = getword (inf)
while w != "":
    if iscommand(w):
        process_command (w)
    else:
        process_word (w)
    w = getword(inf)
inf.close()
outf.close()
```

In order for the program to compile the functions, they must exist. They should initially be *stubs*, relatively non-functional but resulting in output:

```
from random import *

def getword (f):
    print ("Getword ")

def iscommand(w):
```

```
    print ("ISCOMMAND given ", w)
    if random()< 0.5:
        return False
    return True

def process_command (w):
    print ("Processing command ", w)

def process_word (w):
    print ("Processing the word ", w)
```

This program will run, but never ends because it never reads the file. Still, we have a structure.

Now the functions need to be defined, and in the process further design decisions are made. Consider **getword()**: what comprises a *word* and how does it differ from a *command*? A command starts at the beginning of a line with a "." character. It is followed by two alphabetic characters that are defined by the system. If the two characters do not match any combinations in the list of commands, then it is not a command. A word, on the other hand, begins or ends with a white space (blank, tab, or end of line) and contains all of the characters between those white spaces. It may not be a word in the traditional sense, in that it may not be an English word; it could be a number or other sequence of characters. Those may cause problems, but it will be left up to the user to figure it out. Example: a long URL may extend over a line. The program has to do something, and so will probably put an end of line when the count of characters exceeds a maximum and leave the problem to the user to fix.

So, let's figure out the **getword()** function. It will construct a word as a character string from individual characters that have been read from the input file. A first try could be:

```
def getword(f):
    w = ""
    while whitespace(ch(f)):
        nextch(f)
    while not whitespace(ch(f)):
        w = w + ch(f)
        nextch(f)
    print ("Getword is ", w)
    return w
```

The function **whitespace()** returns **True** if its parameter is a white space character. The function **nextch()** reads the next character from the specified file, and the function **ch()** returns the value of the current character. To effectively test **getword()**, we need to implement these three functions. Here's a first attempt:

```
def whitespace (c):
    if c == " ": return True
    if c == "\t": return True
    if c == "\n": return True
    return False

def ch(f):
    global c
    return (c)

def nextch(f):
    global c
    c = f.read(1)
```

This way of handling input is a bit unusual, but there is a reason for it. We are anticipating a need to buffer characters or to place them back on the input stream. It is similar to the input scheme used in Pascal, or the system found in early forms of UNIX which used **getchar – putchar - ungetc**. The necessity of extracting commands from the input stream, and that commands must begin a new line, might make this particular scheme useful. The initial implementation of **nextch()** simply reads a new character from the file, but it could easily be modified to extract a character from a buffer, and refile the buffer if it is empty. Both would look the same to the programmer using them.

The program runs, but has a problem: it never terminates. After the text file has been read, the program seems to call **nextch()** repeatedly. After some thought the reason is clear—when the input request results in an empty string ("") the current character is not a white space, and the loop in **getword()** that is building a word runs forever. This is a traditional end-of-file problem and can be solved in a few different ways: a special character can be used for EOF, a flag can be set, or the empty string can be tested for in the loop explicitly. The latter solution was chosen, and fixes the infinite loop. The word construction loop in **getword()** becomes:

```
while not whitespace(ch(f)) and ch(f) !="":
```

A possible next step is to distinguish between commands and words. Because a command starts a line and begins with a "." there are two things to do: mark the beginning of a new line, and look up the input string in a table of commands. The command could be searched first, then if it matches a command name we could back up the input to see if it was preceded by a newline character ("\n"). A newline counts as a white space, and another option would be to set a flag when a newline character is seen, clearing it when another character is read in. Now a string is a command if the flag set before it was read in and it matches one of the commands. Timing is everything in this method, but white space separates words, so it could work by simply remembering (saving) the last white space character seen before any word. That sounds like a good idea.

Oops. When implemented, none of the commands are recognized. A table of names was implemented as a tuple:

```
table = (".pl",".bp",".br",".fi",".nf",".na",".ce",
         ".ls",".ll",".in",".ti",".nh",".hy",".sp")
```

The **nextch()** function was modified so:

```
def nextch(f):
    global c, lastws
    c = f.read(1)
    if whitespace(c):
        lastws = c
```

and the function **iscommand()** is implemented by checking for the newline and the match of the string in the table:

```
def iscommand(w):
    global table, lastws
    if lastws == "\n":
        if w in table:
            return True
    return False
```

To discover the problem some print statements were inserted that show the previous white space character and the match in the table for all calls to **iscommand()**. The problem, which should have been obvious, is that when the command is read in, the last white space seen will be the one that *terminated* it, not the one in front of it.

A solution: keeping the same theme of remembering white space characters, how about save the previous *two* white space characters seen. The most recent white space will be the one that terminated the word string, and the second most recent will always be the one before it. All of the others, if any, would have been skipped within **getword()**. The solution, as coded in the **nextch()** function, would be:

```
def nextch(f):
    global c, clast, c2last
    c = f.read(1)
    if whitespace(c):
        c2last = clast
        clast = c
```

There are two variables needed, **clast** being the previous white space and **c2last** being the one encountered before **clast**. Now **iscommand()** is modified slightly to look for **c2last**:

```
def iscommand(w):
    global table, c2last
    if c2last == "\n":
        if w in table:
            return True
    return False
```

Yes, this now identifies the commands in the source file, even the text that looks like a command but is not: ".xx."

Notice that the development of the program consists of an initial sketch and then filling in the code as stubs and coding the stubs to be functional code, one at a time. Sometimes a stub requires further undefined functions to be used, and those could be coded as stubs too, or completed if they are small so as to allow testing to proceed. It's a judgment call as to whether to complete the stubs down the chain for one part of the program or to proceed to the next one at the current level. For example, should we have completed the **nextch() and ch()** functions before trying to design **process_command()**? It does depend on how testing can proceed and what "level" we're at. The **nextch()** function looks like it won't call other functions that have not been implemented, and it is tough to test **getword()** without finishing **nextch()**.

This discussion speaks to what the next step will be from here, and the answer is "there could be many." Let's look at commands next, because they will dictate the output, and then deal with formatting last. It is known that a string represents a command, and the function called as a consequence is **process_command()**. This function must determine which command string was seen and what to do about it. The way commands are handled and the way the output document is specified has to be sorted out before this function can be finished, but a set of stubs can hold the place of future decisions as before.

The string that was seen to be a command is stored in a tuple. The index of the string within the tuple tells us which command was seen, although a string match could be done directly. Using a tuple is better because new commands can always be added to the end of the tuple during future modifications and it is easier to modify command names. The function, which used to be a stub, is now:

```
def process_command (w):
    global table, inf, page_length, fill, center, center_
    count, global spacing, line_length, adjust, hyphenate
    k = table.index(w)
    if k == 0:                      # .PL
        s = getword(inf)
        page_length = int(s)
    elif k == 1:                    # .BP
        genpage()
    elif k == 2:                    # .BR
        genline()
    elif k == 3:                    # .FI
        fill = True
    elif k == 4:                    # .NF
        fill == False
    elif k == 5:                    # .NA
        adjust = False
    elif k == 6:                    # .CE
        center = True
        s = getword(inf)
        center_count = int(s)
    elif k == 7:                    # .LS
        s = getword(inf)
        spacing = int(s)
    elif k == 8:                    # .LL
        s = getword(inf)
        line_length = int(s)
        print ("Line length ", line_length, "characters")
```

```
elif k == 9:                # .IN
    s = getword(inf)
    indent (int(s))
elif k == 10:               # .TI
    s = getword(inf)
    temp_indent (int(s))
elif k == 11:               # .NF
    hyphenate = False
elif k == 12:               # .HY
    hyphenate = True
elif k == 13:               # .TL
    dotl ()
elif k == 14:               # .SP
    s = getword(inf)
    space (int(k))
```

This completes iteration 5 of the system and generates quite a few new stubs and defines how some of the output functions will operate. There are some flags (**hyphenate, center, fill, adjust**) and some parameters for the output process (**line_length, spacing**, etc.) that are set, and so will be used in sending output text to the file. These parameters being known, it is time to define the output process, which will be implemented starting with the function **process_word()**.

As was mentioned earlier, the program reads data one character at a time and emits it as words. There is a specified line length, and words can be read and stored until that length is neared or exceeded. Words could be stored in a string. When the line length is reached, the string could be written to the file. If right justification is being done, spaces could be added to some other spaces in the string until the line length was met exactly, or the final word could be hyphenated to meet the line length. If right justification is not being done, then the line length only has to be approached, but not exceeded.

For text centering input lines are padded with equal numbers of spaces on both sides. The page size is met by counting lines, and then by creating a new page when the page size is met, possibly by entering a form feed or perhaps by printing empty lines until a specified count is reached. Indenting is simple: the **in** command results in a fixed number of spaces being placed at the beginning of each output line; the **ti** command results in a specified number of spaces being placed at the beginning of the current line. Hyphenation is done by table lookup. Certain suffixes and prefixes and letter combinations are possible locations for a hyphen. The final word on a line can be hyphenated if a location within it is subject to a hyphen as indicated by the table.

The process is to read and build words and copy them to a string, the next output line. No action is taken until the string nears the line length, at which point insertion of spaces, hyphenation, or other actions may be taken to make the string fit the line, either closely or precisely. After a line meets the size needed it is written, perhaps followed by others if the line spacing is larger than one. So, the basic action of the **process_word()** function will be to copy the word to a string, the output buffer, under the control of a set of variables that are defined by the user through commands:

page_length	55	Number of lines of text on a single page
fill	True	Controls whether the text is being formatted
adjust	True	Controls whether the text is right justified
center	False	Controls whether text is being centered
center_count	0	Number of lines still to be centered
spacing	1	Number of lines output per line of text
nindent	0	Number of spaces on the left
line_length	66	Number of characters on one line
hyphenate	True	Are words hyphenated by the system?

The simplest version of **process_word()** would copy words to the buffer until the line was full and then simply write that line to the output file.

```
def process_word (w):
    global buffer, line_length
    if len(buffer) + len(w) + 1 <= line_length:
        buffer = buffer + " " + w
    else:
        emit(buffer)
        buffer = w
```

The code above adds the given word plus a space to the buffer if there is room. Otherwise it calls the **emit()** function to write the buffer to the output file and places the word at the beginning of a new line. This is nearly correct. Some of the output for the sample source is:

This is sample text for testing Pyroff. The default is to right

adjust continuously, but embedded commands can change this.
Now the line width should be
30 characters, and so the left
margin will pulled back. This
line is centered .xx not a
command. Indented 4

Note that the command ".ll 30" was correctly handled, but that there is an extra space at the beginning of the first line. That's due to the fact that **process_word()** adds a space between words, and if the buffer is empty that space gets placed at the beginning. The solution is to check for an empty buffer:

```
if len(buffer) + len(w) + 1 <= line_length:
    if len(buffer) > 0:
        buffer = buffer + " " + w
    else:
        buffer = w
```

This was a successful fix, and completes iteration 6 of the system, which is now 150 lines long.

Within **process_word()** there are multiple options for how words will be written to the output. What has been done so far amounts to *filling* but no *right justification*. Other options are: *no filling, centering,* and *justification*. When the filling is turned off, an input line becomes an output line. This is true for centering as well. When justification is taking place the program will make the output lines exactly **line_length** characters long by inserting spaces in the line to extend it and by hyphenation, where permitted, to shorten it. The rule is that the line must be the correct length and must not begin or end with a space. The implementation of this part of the program is at the heart of the overall system, but would not be possible without a sensible design up to this point.

12.1.2 Centering

First, a centered line is to be written to output when an end of line is seen on input. This means that the **clast** variable will be used to identify the end of line and to emit the text. Next, the line will have spaces added to the beginning and end to center it. The buffer holds the line to be written and has **len(buffer)** characters. The number of spaces to be added totals **line_length – len(buffer)**, and half will be added to the beginning of the line and half to the end. A function that centers a given string would be:

```
def do_center (s):
    global line_length
    k = len(s)              # How long is the string?
    b1 = line_length - k    # How much shorter than the line?
    b2 = b1//2              # Split that amount in two
    b1 = line_length - k - b2
    s = " "*b1 + s + " "*b2  # Add spaces to center the text
    emit(s)                 # Write to file
```

In the **process_word()** function some code must be added to handle center-ing. This code has to detect the end of line and pass the buffer to **do_center()**. It also counts the lines, because the ".ce" command specifies a number of lines to be centered.

```
if center:                  # Text is being centered, no fill
    if len(buffer) > 0:     # Add this word to the line
        buffer = buffer + " " + w
    else:
        buffer = w
    if clast == "\n":       # An input line = an output line
        do_center(buffer)                # Emit the text
        center_count = center_count - 1  # Count lines
        if center_count <= 0:            # Done?
            center = False               # Yes. Stop centering.
```

This code is not quite enough. There are two problems observed. One prob-lem is that the buffer could be partly full when the ".ce" command is seen, and must be emptied. This problem is serious, because filling may be taking place and the line might have to be justified. For the moment a call to **emit()** will hap-pen when the ".ce" command is seen, but this will have to be expanded.

The other problem is simpler: the **do_center()** function does not empty the buffer so the line being centered occurs twice in the output. For example:

margin will pulled back.

    This line is centered   ← This is correct

This line is centered .xx not ← This is wrong. Text is repeated.

a command. Indented 4

The solution is to clear the buffer after **do_center()** is called:

```
do_center(buffer)              # Emit the text
buffer = ""                    # Clear the buffer
```

12.1.3 Right Justification

Centering text is a first step to understanding how to justify it. Right justified text has the sentences arranged so that the right margin is aligned to the line. When centering, spaces are added to the left and right ends of the string so as to place any text in the middle of the line. When justifying, any space in the line can be made into multiple spaces, thus extending the text until it reaches the right margin. Naturally it would not be acceptable to place all of the needed spaces in one spot. It looks best if they are distributed as evenly as possible. However, no matter what is done there will be some situations that cause ugly spacing. We'll have to live with that.

The number of spaces needed to fill up a line is **line_length – len(buffer)**, just as it was when centering. As words are added to the line this value becomes smaller, and when it is smaller than the length of the next word to be added, then the extra spaces must be added and a new line started. That is, when

$$k = \text{line\_length} - \text{len(buffer)}$$
$$\textbf{if k} < \textbf{len(word):}$$

then adjusting is performed. First, count the spaces in the buffer and call this **nspaces**. If **k>nspaces** then change each single space into **k//nspaces** space characters and set **k = k%nspaces**. This will rarely happen. Now we need to change *some* of the spaces in the buffer into double spaces. Which ones? In an attempt to spread them around, set **xk = k + k//2**. This will be used as an increment to find consecutive spots to put spaces. So for example, let **k = 5**, in which case **xk = 7**. The first space could be placed in the middle, or at space number 2. Now count **xk** positions from 2, starting over at zero when you hit the end. This will give 4 as the next position, followed by 1, then 3, and then 0. This process seems to spread them out. Now the buffer is written out and the new word is placed in an empty buffer.

This sounds tricky, so let's walk through it. Never enter code that is not likely to work! Inside of the **process_word()** function, check to see if adjusting is going on. If so, check to see if the current word fits in the current line. If so, put it there and move on.

```
elif adjust:
    k = line_length - len(buffer)   # Number of spaces
                                    # remaining
    if k  > len(w):                 # Does the word w fit?
        if len(buffer) == 0:        # Yes. Empty buffer?
            buffer = w              # Yes. Buffer = word.
        else:                       # No. Add word to the
                                    # buffer
            buffer = buffer + " " + w
        print ("Buffer now ", buffer, k, len(w))
    else:                           # Not enough space remains
        print (buffer, k, w, len(w))
        nspaces = buffer.count(" ") # How many spaces in
                                    # buffer?
        xk = k + k//2 +1            # Space insert increment
        while k > 0:
            i = nth_space (buffer, xk)
            buffer = buffer[0:i] + " " + buffer[i:]
            k = k - 1
            xk = xk + 1
        emit(buffer)
        buffer = w
```

The function **nth_space (buffer, xk)** locates the nth space character in the string **s** modulo the string length. The spaces were not well distributed with this code in some cases. There was a suspicion that it depended on whether the number of remaining spaces was even or odd, so the code was modified to read:

```
            .   .   .
xk = k + (k+1)//2              # Space insert increment
if k%2 == 0:
    xk = xk + 1
            .   .   .
```

which worked better. The output for the first part of the test data was:

```
This is sample text for    testing Pyroff. The default is
to right adjust continuously, but embedded commands can
change this.
Now the line width    should be
30 characters, and so the left
```

```
margin will pulled back.
     This line is centered
.xx not  a command. Indented 4
characters. The  idea  behind
top-down  programming is  that
the    higher    levels    of
abstraction are     described
          .   .   .
```

The short lines are right justified, but the distribution of the spaces could still be better.

The function **nth_space()** is important, and looks like this:

```
def nth_space (s, n):
    global nindent
    nn = 0        # nn is a count of spaces seen so far
    i = 0  # i is the index of the character being examined
    while True:
        if s[i] == " ":     # Is character i a space?
            nn = nn + 1      # Yes. Count it
        if nn >= n:          # Is this enough spaces?
            return i         # Yes, return the location
        i = (i + 1)%len(s)   # Next i, wrapping around the
end
```

12.1.4 Other Commands

The rest of the commands have to do with hyphenation, pagination, and indentation, except for the ".br" command. Dealing with indentation first, the command ".in" specifies a number of characters to indent, as does ".ti." The ".in" command begins indenting lines from the current point on, whereas ".ti" only indents the next line. Since the ".ti" command only indents the next line of text, perhaps initializing the buffer to the correct number of spaces will do the trick. The rest of the text for the line will be concatenated to the spaces, resulting in an indented line.

The ".in" command currently results in the setting of a variable named **nindent** to the number of spaces to be indented. Following the suggestion for a temporary indent, why not replace all initializations of the buffer with indented ones? There are multiple locations within the **process_word()** function where the buffer is set to the next word:

```
buffer = w
```

These could be changed to:

```
buffer = " "*nindent +w
```

This sounds clean and simple, but it fails miserably. Here is what it looks like. For the input text:

```
Indented    4    characters.
.in 2
The idea behind top-down programming is that the higher
levels of abstraction are described first. A description
of what he entire program is to do is written in a kind-
of English/computer hybrid language (pseudocode), and this
description involves making calls to functions that have
not yet been written but whose function is known.
```

We get:

```
Indented    4    characters. The
        idea    behind top-down
    programming  is that    the
  higher levels of abstraction
    are    described    first.    A
    description   of   what    he
  entire program    is to do is
        written     in   a kind-of
        English/computer   hybrid
  language  (pseudocode),    and
    this description    involves
  making calls to    functions
      that    have   not yet    been
```

Can you figure out where the problem is by looking at the output? This is a skill that develops as you read more code, write more code, and design more code. There is a place in the program that will add spaces to the text, and clearly that has been done here. It is, in fact, how the text is right adjusted. The spaces are counted and sometimes replaced with double spaces. This happened here to some of the spaces used to implement the indent.

Possible solutions include the use of special characters instead of leading blanks, to be replaced when printed; finding another way to implement indenting; modifying the way right adjusting is done. Because the number of spaces at the beginning of the line is known, the latter should be possible: when counting spaces in the adjustment process, skip the **nspaces** characters at the beginning of the line. This is a modification to the function **nth_character()** to position the count after the indent:

```
def nth_space (s, n):
    global nindent
    nn = 0
    i = 0
    while True:
        print ("nn=", nn)
        if s[i] == " ":
            nn = nn + 1
            print ('" "')
        if nn >= n:
            return i
        i = (i + 1)%len(s)
        if i < nindent+tempindent:      ←
            i = nindent+tempindent      ←
```

A second problem in the indentation code is that there should be a line break when the command is seen. This is a matter of writing the buffer and then clearing it. This should also occur when a temporary indent occurs, but before it inserts the spaces. Say, the temporary indent will have the same problem as indent with respect to right adjustment, and we have not dealt with that.

The line break can be handled with a new function:

```
def lbreak ():
    global buffer, tempindent, nindent
    if len(buffer) > 0:
        emit(buffer)
    buffer = " "*(nindent+tempindent)
    tempindent = 0
```

The break involves writing the buffer and clearing it. Clearing it also means setting the indentation. Because this sequence of operations happens elsewhere in the program, those sequences can be replaced by a call to **lbreak()**. Note that a new variable **tempindent** has been added; it holds the number of spaces for a temporary indentation, and is added to the regular **nindent** value everywhere that variable is used to obtain the total indentation for a line. Now right adjustment of a temporarily indented line should work.

The **lbreak()** function is used directly to implement the ".br" command. A stub previously named **genline()** can be removed and replaced by a call to **lbreak()**.

Line spacing can be handled in **emit()**, which is where lines are written to the output file. After the current buffer is written, a number of newline characters are written to equal the correct line spacing. The new **emit()** function is:

```
def emit (s):
    global outf, lines, tempindent, spacing, page_length
    outf.write(s+"\n")
    lines = (lines + 1)%page_length
    for i in range (1, spacing):
        outf.write ("\n")
        lines = (lines + 1)%page_length
    tempindent = 0
```

What about pages? There is a command that deals with pages directly, and that is ".bp," which starts a new page. The page length is known in terms of the number of lines, and emit counts the lines as it writes them. Implementing the ".bp" command should be a matter of emitting the number of lines needed to complete the current page. Something like this:

```
def genpage ():
    global page_length, lines
    lbreak ()
    for i in range (lines, page_length):
        emit ("")
```

At this point all that is missing is the ability to hyphenate, which will be left as one of the exercises. The system appears to do what is needed using the small test file, so the time has come to construct more thorough tests. A file "preface.txt" holds the text for the preface of a book named "Practical Computer Vision Using C." This book was written using *Nroff*, and the commands not available in pyroff were removed from the source text so that it could be used as test data. It consists of over 500 lines of text. The result of the first try was interesting.

Pyroff appeared to run using this input file but never terminated. No output file was created. The first step was to try to see where it was having trouble, so a print statement was added to show what word had been processed last. That word was "spectrograms," and it appears in the first paragraph of text, after headings and such. Now the data that caused the problem is known. What is the program doing? There must be an unterminated loop someplace. Putting prints in likely spots identifies the culprit as the loop in the **nth_space()** function. Tracing through that loop finds an odd thing: the value of **nindent** becomes negative, and that causes the loop never to terminate. The test data contained a situation that caused the program to fail, and that situation resulted from a difference between *Nroff* and pyroff: in *Nroff* the command ".in -4" subtracts 4 from the current indentation, whereas in pyroff it sets the current indent to -4.

This kind of error is very common. *All values entered by a user must be tested against the legal bounds for that variable.* This was not done here, and the fix is simple. However, it reminds us to do that for all other user input values. These are processed in the function *process_command()*, so locating those values is easy. Once this was done things worked pretty well. There was one problem observed, and that was an indentation error. Consider the input text:

```
.nf
1. Introduction
.in 3
1.1 Images as digital objects
1.2 Image storage and display
1.3 Image acquisition
1.4 Image types and applications
```

The program formats this as:

```
1. Introduction
    1.1 Images as digital objects
   1.2 Image storage and display
   1.3 Image acquisition
   1.4 Image types and applications
```

There is an extra space in the first line after the indent. This seems like it should be easy to find where the problem is, but the function that implements the command, **indent()**, looks pretty clean. However, on careful examination (and printing some buffer values) it can be seen that it should not call **lbreak()** because that function sets the buffer to the properly indented number of space characters. This means that when the later tests for an empty buffer occur, the buffer is not empty and text is appended to it rather than being simply assigned to it. That is, for an empty buffer the first word is placed into it:

```
buffer = word
```

Whereas if text is present the word is appended after adding a space:

```
buffer = buffer + " " + word
```

The indent function now looks like this:

```
def indent (n):
    global nindent, buffer
    nindent = n
    emit(buffer)
    buffer = ""
```

The preface now formats pretty well, if not up to Word standards. Other problems may well exist, and should be reported to the author and publisher when discovered. The book's wiki is the place for such discussions.

12.2 OBJECT ORIENTED PROGRAMMING – *BREAKOUT*

The original game named *Breakout* was built in 1976, conceived by Nolan Bushnell and Steve Bristow and built by Steve Wozniak (some say aided by Steve Jobs). In this game there are layers of colored rectangles in the upper part of the screen. A simulated ball moves around the game window, and if it hits a rectangle it accumulates points and bounces. The ball also bounces off of the top and sides of the window, but will pass through the bottom and be lost unless the player moves a paddle into its path. If so the ball will bounce back up and perhaps score more points; if not the ball moves out of play. After a fixed number of balls are lost the game is over.

The game being developed here will use circles, that we'll call *tiles*, rather than rectangles. There will be 5 rows of tiles, each of a different color and point value: 5, 10, 15, 10, and 5 points for each row respectively. That way the most concealed row has the most points. The player will get three balls to try to clear all of the tiles away. The paddle will move left when the left arrow key is pressed and right when the right arrow key is pressed. The speed of the ball and of the paddle will be determined when the game is tested. A sound will play when a tile is removed, when the ball hits the side or top of the window, when the ball hits the paddle, and when the ball is lost. The current score and the number of balls remaining will be displayed on the screen someplace at all times.

Figure 12.1 shows an example of a breakout game clone on the left, with rectangular bricks. On the right is a possible example of how the game that we're developing here might look.

12.3 DESCRIBING THE PROBLEM AS A PROCESS

The first step is to write down a step-by-step description of how the program might operate. This may be changed as it is expanded, but we have to start someplace. A problem occurs almost immediately: is the program to be a class? Functions? Does it use Glib?

This decision can be postponed a little while, but in most cases a program is not a class. It is more likely to be a collection of classes operated by a mail program. However, if object orientation is a logical structure, and it often is, it should evolve naturally from the way the problem is organized and not impose itself on the solution.

The game consists of multiple things that interact. Play is a consequence of the behavior of those things. For example, the ball will collide with a tile resulting in some points, the tile disappearing, and a bounce. The next event may be that the ball collides with a wall, or bounces off of the paddle. The game is a set of managed events and consequences. This makes it appear as if an object oriented design and implementation would be suitable. The ball, each time, and the paddle

Figure 12.1
Variations on the game "Breakout."

could be objects (class instances) and could interact with each other under the supervision of a main program which kept track of all objects, time, scores, and other details.

Let's just focus on the gameplay part of the game, and ignore introductory windows and high score lists and other parts of a real game. The game will start with an initial set up of the objects. Tiles will be placed in their start locations, the paddle will be placed, the locations of the walls defined; then it will be drawn. The initial setup was originally drawn on paper and then a sample rendering was made, shown in Figure 12.1. The code that draws this is:

```
# Ver 0 - Render initial play area
import Glib

Glib.startdraw(400, 800)
Glib.fill (100, 100, 240)
for i in range (0, 12):
    Glib.ellipse(i*30+15, 30, 30, 30)
Glib.fill (220, 220, 90)
for i in range (0, 12):
    Glib.ellipse(i*30+15, 60, 30, 30)
Glib.fill (220, 0, 0)
for i in range (0, 12):
    Glib.ellipse(i*30+15, 90, 30, 30)
Glib.fill (180, 120, 30)
for i in range (0, 12):
    Glib.ellipse(i*30+15, 120, 30, 30)
Glib.fill (90, 220, 80)
for i in range (0, 12):
    Glib.ellipse(i*30+15, 150, 30, 30)
Glib.fill (0)
Glib.rect (180, 350,  90, 10)
Glib.enddraw()
```

This code is just for a visual examination of the potential play area. The first one is always wrong, and this one is too, but it allows us to see why it is wrong and to define a more reasonable set of parameters. In this case the tiles don't fully occupy the horizontal region, the tile groups are too close to the top, because we want to allow a ball to bounce between the top row and the top of the play area, and the play area is too large vertically. Fixing these problems is a simple matter of modifying the coordinates of some of the objects. This code will not be a part of the final result. It's common, especially in programs involving a lot of graphics, to test the visual results periodically, and to write some testing programs to help with this.

This program already has some obvious objects: a tile will be an object. So will the paddle, and so will the ball. These objects have some obvious properties too: a tile will have a position in x,y coordinates, and it will have a color and a size. It will have a method to draw it on the screen, and a way to tell if it has been removed or if it still active. The paddle has a position and size, and so does the ball, although the ball has not been seen yet.

What will the main program look like if these are the principal objects in the design? The first sketch is very abstract and depends on many functions that have not been written. This fleshes out the way the classes and the remainder of the code will interact and partly defines the methods they will implement. The initialization step will involve creating rows of tiles that will appear much like those in the initial rendering above but actually consist of five rows of tile objects. This will be done from a function **initialize()**, but each row would be created in a for loop:

```
for i in range (0, 12):
    tiles = tiles + tile(i*30+15, y, thiscolor, npoints)
```

where the tile will be created and is passed its x,y position, color, and number of points. The entire collection of tiles is placed into a tuple named **tiles**. The ball will be created at a random location and with a random speed within the space between the paddle and the tiles, and the paddle will be created so that is initially is drawn in the horizontal center near the bottom of the window.

```
def initialize ():
    score = 0
    nballs = 2
    b = ball ()              # Create the ball
    p = paddle ()            # create the paddle
    thiscolor = (100,100,240)   # Blue
    npoints = 5              # Top row is 5 points each
    for i in range (0, 12):
        tiles = tiles + tile(i*30+15, y, thiscolor, npoints)
                    # and so on for 4 more rows
```

The main **draw()** function will call the **draw()** methods of each of the class instances, and they will draw themselves:

```
def draw():
    background (200)
    b.move()                # Move the ball
    b.draw()                # Draw the ball
    p.draw()                # Draw the paddle
    for k in tiles:
        k.draw()            # Draw each tile
    text ("Score is:"+score, scorex, scorey)
    text ("Balls remaining: "+nballs, remainx, remainy)
```

When this function is called (many times each second) the ball is placed in its new position, possibly following a bounce, and then is drawn. The paddle is drawn, and if it is to be moved it will be done through the user pressing a key. Then the active tiles are drawn, and the messages are drawn on the screen. The structure of the main part of the program is defined by the organization of the classes.

12.3.1 Initial Coding for a Tile

A tile has a graphical representation on the screen, but it is more complex than that. It can collide with a ball and has a color and a point value. All of these aspects of the tile have to be coded as a part of its class. In addition, a tile can be *active*, meaning that it appears on the screen and can collide with the ball, or *inactive*, meaning that the ball has hit it and it is out of play for all intents and purposes. Here's an initial version:

```
class tile:
    def __init__(self, x, y, color, points):
        self.x = x
        self.y = y
        self.color = color
        self.points = points
        self.active = True
        self.size = 30

    def draw(self):
    if self.active:
        Glib.fill (self.color)
        Glib.ellipse (self.x, self.y, self.size, self.size)
```

At the beginning of the game every tile must be created and initialized with its proper position, color, and point value. Then the **draw()** function for the main program will call the **draw()** method of every tile during every small time interval, or *frame*. According to the code above if the tile is not active, then it will not be drawn. Let's test this.

Rule: Never write more than 20-30 lines of code without testing at least part of it. That way you have a clearer idea where any problems you introduce may be.

A suitable test program to start with could be:

```
def draw():
    global tiles
    for k in tiles:
        k.draw()

Glib.startdraw(360, 350)
red = (250, 0, 0)
print (red)
tiles = ()
for i in range (0, 12):
    tiles = tiles + (tile(i*30, 90, red, 15),)
Glib.enddraw()
```

which simply places some tiles on the screen in a row, passing a color and point value. This almost works, but the first tile is cut in half by the left boundary. If the initialization becomes:

```
tiles = tiles + (tile(i*30+15, 90, red, 15),)
```

then a proper row of 12 red circles is drawn. Modifications will be made to this class once we see more clearly how it will be used.

12.3.2 Initial Coding for the Paddle

The paddle is represented as a rectangle on the screen, but its role in the game is much more profound: it is the only way the player has to participate in the game. The player will type keys to control the position of the paddle so as to keep the ball from falling out of the area. So the ball has to be drawn, as the tiles do, but also must be moved (i.e., change the X position) in accordance with the player's wishes. The *paddle* class initially has a few basic operations:

```
class paddle:
    def __init__(self, x, y):
        self.x = x
        self.y = y
        self.speed = 3
        self.width = 90
        self.height = 10

    def draw(self):
        Glib.fill (0)
        Glib.rect (self.x, self.y, self.width, self.height)

    def moveleft(self):
        if self.x <= self.speed:
            self.x = 0
        else:
            self.x = self.x - self.speed

    def moveright (self):
        if self.x > width-self.width-self.speed:
            self.x = width-self.width
        else:
            self.x = self.x + self.speed
```

When the right arrow key is pressed a flag is set to **True**, and the paddle moves to the right (i.e., its x coordinate increases) each time interval, or frame. When the key is released the flag is set to **False** and the movement stops as a result. Movement is accomplished by calling **moveleft()** and **moveright(),** and these functions enforce a limit on motion: the paddle cannot leave the play area. This is done within the class so that the outside code does not need to know anything about how the paddle is implemented. It is important to isolate details of the class implementation to the class only, so that modifications and debugging can be limited to the class itself.

The paddle is simply a rectangle, as far as the geometry is concerned, and presents a horizontal surface from which the ball will bounce. It is the only means by which the player can manipulate the game, so it is important to get the paddle operations and motion correct. Fortunately, moving a rectangle left and right is an easy thing to do.

Testing this initial paddle class used a draw() function that randomly moved the paddle left and right, and a main program, that creates the paddle:

```
def draw():
    global p,f
    Glib.background(200)
    p.draw()
    if f:
        p.moveright()
    else:
        p.moveleft()
    if random()< .01:
        f = not f

Glib.startdraw(360, 350)
f = True
p = paddle (130)
Glib.enddraw()
```

This code works, and sums up the functionality of the paddle.

12.3.3 Initial Coding for the Ball

The ball really does much of the actual work in the game. Yes, the bounces are controlled by the user through the paddle, but once the ball bounces off of the paddle it has to behave properly and do the works of the game: destroying tiles. According to the standard class model of this program, the ball should have a **draw()** method that places it into its proper position on the screen. But the ball is moving, so its position has to be updated each frame. It also has to bounce off of the sides and top of the playing area, and the **draw()** method can make this happen. The essential code for doing this is:

```
class ball():
    def __init__ (self, x, y):
        self.x = x
        self.y = y
        self.dx = 3
        self.dy = -4
        self.active = True
        self.color = (230, 0, 230)
        self.size = 9
```

Figure 12.2
The basic elements of the game: ball, targets, and paddle.

```python
def draw(self):
    if not self.active:
        return
    Glib.fill (self.color[0], self.color[1],
            self.color[2])
    Glib.ellipse (self.x, self.y, self.size, self.size)
    self.x = self.x + self.dx
    self.y = self.y + self.dy
    if (self.x <= self.size/2) or \
            (self.x >= Glib.width-self.size/4):
        self.dx = -self.dx
    if self.y <= self.size/2:
        self.dy = -self.dy
    elif self.dy >= Glib.height:
        self.active = False
```

This version only bounces off of the sides and top, and passes through the bottom. Testing it requires a main program that creates the ball and a **draw()** function that simply calls the ball's **draw()** method:

```python
def draw():
    global b
    Glib.background(200)
    b.draw()


Glib.startdraw(360, 350)
b = ball (300, 300)
Glib.enddraw()
```

The ball is created at coordinates (300,300) and does three bounces, disappearing through the bottom after that. A bouncing ball has been coded before, so there is nothing new here yet.

12.3.4 Collecting the Classes

A next step is to test all three classes running together. This will ensure that there are no problems with variable, method, and function names and that interactions between the classes are in fact isolated. All three should work together, creating the correct visual impression on the screen. The code for the three classes was copied to one file for this test. The main program simply creates instances of each class as appropriate, really doing what the original test program did in each case:

```
Glib.startdraw(360, 350)
red = (250, 0, 0)
print (red)
tiles = ()
for i in range (0, 12):
    tiles = tiles + (tile(i*30+15, 90, red, 15),)
f = True
p = paddle (130)
b = ball (300, 300)
Glib.enddraw()
```

The **draw()** function calls the **draw()** methods for each class instance and moves the paddle randomly as before:

```
def draw():
    global tiles,p,f,b
    Glib.background(200)
    for k in tiles:
        k.draw()
    p.draw()
    if f:
        p.moveright()
    else:
        p.moveleft()
    if random()< .01:
        f = not f
    b.draw()
```

The result was that all three classes functioned together the first time it was attempted. The game itself depends on collision, which will be implemented next, but at the very least the classes need to cooperate, or at least not interfere with each other. That's true at this point in the development.

12.3.5 Developing the Paddle

Placing the paddle under control of the user is the next step. When a key is pressed then the paddle state will change, from still to moving, and vice versa when released. This is accomplished using the **keypressed()** and **keyreleased()** functions. They will set or clear a flag, respectively, that causes the paddle to move by calling the **moveleft()** and **moveright()** methods. The flag **movingleft** will result in a decrease in the paddle's x coordinate each time **draw()** is called; **movingright** does the same for the +x direction:

```python
def keyPressed (k):
    global movingleft, movingright
    if k == Glib.K_LEFT:
        movingleft = True
    elif k == Glib.K_RIGHT:
        movingright = True

def keyReleased (k):
    global movingleft, movingright
    if k == Glib.K_LEFT:
        movingleft = False
    elif k == Glib.K_RIGHT:
        movingright = False
```

From the user perspective the paddle moves as long as the key is depressed. Inside of the global **draw()** function, the flags are tested at each iteration and the paddle is moved if necessary:

```python
def draw():       # 07-classes-01-20.py
    global   ... movingleft,movingright
       .   .   .
    if movingleft:
        p.moveleft()
    elif movingright:
        p.moveright()
    p.draw()
       .   .   .
```

The other thing the paddle has to do is serve as a bounce platform for the ball. A question surrounds the location of collision detection; is this the job of the *ball* or the *paddle*? It does make sense to perform most of this task in the *ball* class, because the ball is always in motion and is the thing that bounces. However, the *paddle* class can assist by providing necessary information. Of course, the paddle class can allow other classes to examine and modify its position and velocity and thus perform collision testing, but if those data are to be hidden, the option is to have a method that tests whether a moving object might have collided with the paddle. The **y** position of the paddle is fixed and is stored in a global variable paddle, so that is not an issue. A method in paddle that returns True if the **x** coordinate passed to it lies between the start and end of the paddle is:

```
def inpaddle(self, x):
    if x < self.x:
        return False
    if x > self.x + self.width:
        return False
    return True
```

The *ball* class can now determine whether it collides with the paddle by checking its own y coordinate against the paddle and by calling **inpaddle()** to see if the ball's **x** position lies within the paddle. If so, it should bounce. The method **hitspaddle()** in the ball class returns True if the ball hits the paddle:

```
def hitspaddle (self):           # 08classes-01-21.py
    if self.y<=paddleY+2 and self.y>=paddleY-2:
        if p.inpaddle(self.x):
            return True
    return False
```

The most basic reaction to hitting the paddle is to change the direction of **dy** from down to up (**dy = -dy**).

12.3.6 Ball and Tile Collisions

The collision between a ball and a tile is more difficult to do correctly than any of the other collisions. Yes, determining whether a collision occurs is a similar process, and then points are collected and the tile is deactivated. It is the bounce of the ball that is hard to figure out. The ball may strike the tile at nearly any angle and at nearly any location on the circumference. This is not a problem in the original game, where the tiles were rectangular, because the ball was always bouncing off of a horizontal or vertical surface. Now there's some thinking to do.

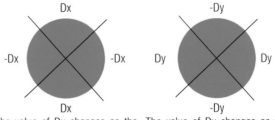

The value of Dx changes as the ball strikes one of the four parts or the circumstance.

The value of Dy changes as the ball strikes one of the four parts or the circumstance.

Figure 12.3
Different parts of the target, when colliding with the ball, generate different bounces.

The correct collision could be calculated, but would involve a certain amount of math. The specification of the problem does not say that mathematically correct bounces are required. This is a game design choice, perhaps not a programming choice. What does the game look like if a simple bounce is implemented? That could involve simply changing **dy** to **−dy**.

This version of the game turns out to be playable, even fun; but the ball always keeps the same x direction when it bounces. What would it look like if it bounced in roughly the right direction, and how difficult would that be? The direction of the bounce would be dictated by the impact location on the tile, as seen in Figure12.3. This was figured out after a few minutes with a pencil and paper, and is intuitive rather than precise.

We'll have to figure out where the ball hits the tile, determine which of the four parts of the tile this lies in, and then create the new **dx** and **dy** values for the ball. A key aspect of the solution being developed is to avoid too much math that has to be done by the program. Is this possible?

The first step is to find the impact point. We could use a little bit of analytic geometry, or we could approximate. The fact is that the ball is not moving very fast, and the exact coordinates of the impact point are not required. At the beginning of the current frame the ball was at (x,y) and at the beginning of the next is will be at (x+dx, y+dy). A good estimate of the point of impact would be the mean value of these two points, or (x+dx/2, y+dy/2). Close enough for a computer game.

Now the question is: within which of the four regions defined in Figure 12.3 is the impact point? The regions are defined by lines at 45 degrees and -45 degrees. The **atan()** function will, when using screen coordinates, have the –dx points between -45 and +45 degrees. The –dy points, where the direction of Y motion changes, involve the remaining collisions. What needs to be done is to find the angle of the line from the center of the tile to the ball and then compare that to -45 … +45.

Here is an example method named **bounce()** that does exactly this.

```
# Return the distance squared between the two points
def distance2 (self, x0,y0, x1, y1):
    return (x0-x1)*(x0-x1) + (y0-y1)*(y0-y1)

def bounce (self, t):
    dd = t.size/2 + self.size/2    # Bounce occurs when the
                                   # distance
    dd = dd * dd                   # Between ball and tile <
                                   # radii squared
    collide = False
    if self.distance2 (self.x, self.y, t.x, t.y) >= dd and \
    self.distance2 (self.x+self.dx, self.y+self.dy, t.x,
                t.y) < dd:
        self.x = self.x + self.dx/2  # Estimated impact
                                     # point on circle
        self.y = self.y + self.dy/2
        collide = True
    elif self.distance2 (self.x, self.y, t.x, t.y) < dd:
        collide = True             # Ball is completely inside
                                   # the time
    if not collide:
        return

# If the ball is inside the tile, back it out.
    while self.distance2 (self.x, self.y, t.x, t.y) < dd:
        self.x = self.x - self.dx*0.5
        self.y = self.y - self.dy*0.5
    if self.x != t.x:              # Compute the ball-tile angle
        a = atan ((self.y-t.x)/(self.x-t.y))
        a = a * 180./3.1415
    else:                          # If dx = 0 the tangent is infinite
        a = 90.0
```

```
if a >= -45.0 and a<=45.0:          # The x speed change
    self.dx = -self.dx
else:
    self.dy = -self.dy              # The y speed changes
```

After some testing the code:

```
# If the ball is inside the tile, back it out.
    while self.distance2 (self.x, self.y, t.x, t.y) < dd:
        self.x = self.x - self.dx*0.5
        self.y = self.y - self.dy*0.5
```

was added. It was found that if the ball was too far inside the tile then its motion was very odd; as it moved through the tile it constantly changed direction because the program determined that it was always colliding.

12.3.7 Ball and Paddle Collisions

Now we return to examine the collision between the ball and the paddle. The paddle seems to be flat, and colliding with any location on the paddle should have the same result. Perhaps. What if the ball hits the paddle very near to one end? There is a corner, and maybe hitting too near to the corner should yield a different bounce. This was the case in the original games. If the ball struck the near edge of the paddle on the corner it could actually bounce back in the original direction to a greater or lesser degree. This gives the player a greater degree of control, once they understand the situation. Otherwise the game is really predetermined if the player merely places the paddle in the way of the ball. It will always bounce in exactly the same manner.

The proposed idea is to bounce at a different angle depending on where the ball strikes the paddle. We need to decide how near and how intense the effect will be. If the ball hits the paddle near the center, then it will bounce so that the incoming angle is the same as the outgoing angle. When it hits the near end of the paddle it will bounce somewhat back in the incoming direction, and when it strikes the far end the bounce angle will be shallower a bounce from the center.

Let's say that if the ball hits the first pixel on the paddle it will bounce back in the original direction, meaning that **dx = -dx** and **dy = -dy**. A bounce from the center does not change **dx** but does set **dy = -dy**. If the relationship is linear across the paddle, the implication would be that striking the final pixel would set **dx = 2*dx** and **dy = -dy**. Striking any pixel in between would divide the change in dx by the number of pixels in the paddle, initially 90. If the ball hits pixel **n** the result will be:

$$\text{delta} = 2*dx/90.0$$
$$dx = -dx + n*\text{delta}$$

A problem here is that the dx value will decrease continuously until the ball is bouncing up and down. Perhaps the incoming angle should not be considered. The bounce angle of the ball could be completely dependent on where it hits the paddle and nothing else. If dx is –5 on the near end of the paddle and +5 on the far end, then:

$$dx = -5 + n*10.0/90.0$$

The code in the **draw()** method of the ball class is modified to read:

```
if self.hitspaddle():
    self.dy = -self.dy
    self.dx = -5 + (1./9.)*(self.x-p.x)
```

The user now has a lot more control. The game does appear slow, though. And there is only one ball. Once that is lost, the game is over.

12.3.8 Finishing the Game

What remains to be done is to implement multiple balls. Multiple balls are tricky because there are timing issues. When the ball disappears through the bottom of the play area it should reappear someplace, and at a random place. It should not appear immediately, though, because the player needs some time to respond; let's say three seconds. Meanwhile the screen must continue to be displayed. It's time to introduce *states*.

A state is a situation that can be described by a characteristic set of parameters. A state can be labeled with a simple number but represents something complex. In this instance specifically there will be a *play* state, in which the paddle can be moved and the ball can score points, and a *pause* state, which happens after a ball is lost. The **draw()** function is the place where each step of the program is performed at a high level, and so will be responsible for the management of states.

The current stage of the implementation has only the play state, and all of the code that manages that is in the **draw()** function already. Change the name of **draw()** to **state0()** and create a state variable **state** that can have values 0 or 1: *play* is 0, *pause* is 1. The new **draw()** function is now created:

```
def draw ():
    global playstate, pausestate
    if state == playstate:
        state0()
    elif state == pausestate:
        state1()
```

where:

```
playstate = 0
pausestate = 1
```

The program should still be playable as it was before as long as **state == playstate**. What happens in the *pause* state? The controls of the paddle should be disabled, and no ball is drawn. The goal of the *pause* state is to allow some time for the user to get ready for the next ball, so some time is allowed to pass. Perhaps the player should be permitted to start the game again with a new ball when a key is pressed. This eliminates the need for a timer, which are generally to be avoided. So, the *pause* state is entered when the ball departs the field of play. The game remains in the *pause* state until the player presses a key, at which point a new ball is created and the game enters the *play* state.

Entering the *pause* state means modifying the code in the *ball* class a little. There is a line of code at the end of the **draw()** method of the *ball* class that looks like this:

```
elif self.dy >= Glib.height:
    self.active = False
```

This is where the class detects the ball leaving the play area. We need to add to this:

```
elif self.dy >= Glib.height:
    self.active = False
```

while, of course, making certain that the variables needed are listed as global. This did not do as was expected until it was noted that the condition should have been if **self.y >= Glib.height**. The comparison with **dy** was an error in the initial coding that had not been noticed. Also, it seems like the **active** variable in the *ball* class was not useful, so it was removed.

Now in the **keyPressed()** function allow a key press to change from the pause to the play state. Any key will do:

```
if state = pausestate:
    resume()
```

The **resume()** function must do two things. First, it must change state back to *play*. Next it must reposition the ball to a new location. Easy:

```
def resume():
    global state, playstate
    b.x = randrange (30, Glib.width-30)
    b.y = 250
    state = playstate
```

This works fine. The game is to only have a specified number of balls, though, and this number was to be displayed on the screen. So, when in the play state and a ball is lost, the count of remaining balls (**balls_remaining**) will be decreased by one. If there are any balls remaining, then the pause state is entered. Otherwise the game is over. Perhaps that should be a third state: game over? Yes, probably.

The game over state is entered when the ball leaves the play area and no balls are left (in the *ball* class **draw()** method. In the global **draw()** function the third state determines if the game is won or lost and renders an appropriate screen:

```
. . .
Glib.text ("Score: "+str(score), 10, 30)
if score >= maxscore:
    Glib.background (0,230, 0)
    Glib.text ("You Win", 200, 200)
else:
    Glib.background (100, 10, 10);
    Glib.text ("You Lose", 200, 200)
    Glib.text ("Score: "+str(score), 10, 30)
```

And that's it! Screen shots from the game in various states are shown in Figure 12.4. (14playble3.py)

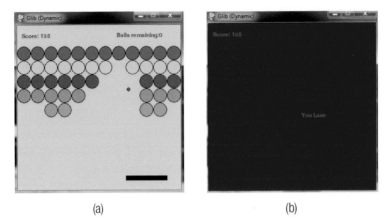

(a)   (b)

Figure 12.4
Screen shots from the game. (a) While play is going on. (b) The final screen, in this case the player has lost.

12.4 RULES FOR PROGRAMMERS

The author of this book has collected a set of rules and laws that apply to writing code, and on tens of thousands of lines written and 45 years as a programmer (he started very young). There are over 250 of them, but not all apply to Python. For example, Python enforces indenting and has no begin-end symbols. The ones that do apply are as follows:

2. Use four-space indents and not tabs.

5. Place a comment in lieu of a declaration for all variables in languages where declarations are not permitted.

6. Declare numeric constants and provide a comment explaining them.

7. Rarely use a numeric constant in an expression; name and declare them.

8. Use variable names that refer to the use or meaning of the variable.

9. Make your code clean from the beginning, not after it works.

10. A non-working program is useless, no matter how well structured.

11. Write code that is as general as possible, even if that makes it longer.

12. If the code you write is general, then keep it and reuse it when appropriate.

13. Functions longer than 12 (not including declarations) lines are suspect.

15. Avoid recursion wherever possible.

16. Every procedure and function must have comments explaining function and use.

17. Write external documentation as you code—every procedure and function must have a description in that document.

18. Some documentation is for programmers, and some is for users. Distinguish.

19. Documentation for users must never be in the code.

20. Avoid using operating system calls.

21. Avoid using machine dependent techniques.

22. Do use the programming language library functions.

23. Documentation for a procedure includes what other procedures are called.

24. Documentation for a procedure includes what procedures might call it.

26. When doing input: assume that the input file is wrong.

27. Your program should accept ANY input without crashing. Feed it an executable as a test.

28. Side effects are very bad. A proper function should return a value that depends only on its parameters. Exceptions do exist and should be documented.

29. Everything not defined is undefined.

33. Buffers and strings have fixed sizes. Know what they are and be constrained by them.

34. A handle is a pointer to a structure for an object; make certain that handles used are still valid.

35. Strings and buffers should not overlap in storage.

36. Contents of strings and buffers are undefined until written to.

40. Every variable that is declared is to be given a value before it is used.

41. Put some blank lines between method definitions.

42. Explain each declared variable in a comment.

44. Solve the problem requested, not the general case or subsets.

45. White space is one of the most effective comments.

48. Avoid global symbols where possible; use them properly where useful.

49. Avoid casts (type casting).

50. Round explicitly when rounding is needed.

51. Always check the error return codes.

52. Leave spaces around operators such as =, ==, !=, and so on.

53. A method should have a clear, single, identifiable task.

54. A class should represent a clear, single, identifiable concept.

57. Do the comments first.

58. A function should have only one exit point.

59. Read code.

60. Comments should be sentences.

61. A comment shouldn't restate the obvious.

62. Comments should align, somehow.

65. Don't confuse familiarity with readability.

67. A function should be called more than once.

68. Code used more than once should be put into a function.

69. All code should be printable.

70. Don't write very long lines. 80 Characters.

71. The function name must agree with what the function does.

72. Format programs in a consistent manner.

75. Have a log.

76. Document all the principal data structures.

77. Don't print a message for a recoverable error—log it.

78. Don't use system-dependent functions for error messages.

79. You must always correctly attribute all code in the module header.

80. Provide cross references in the code to any documents relevant to the understanding of the code.

81. All errors should be listed together with an English description of what they mean.

82. An error message should tell the user the correct way to do it.

83. Comments should be clear and concise and avoid unnecessary wordiness.

84. Spelling counts.

85. Run your code through a spelling checker.

87. Function documentation includes the domain of valid inputs to the function.

88. Function documentation includes the range of valid outputs from the function.

91. Each file must start with a short description of the module contained in the file and a brief description of all exported functions.

92. Do not comment out old code—remove it.

93. Use a source code control system.

95. Comments should never be used to explain the language.

96. Don't put more than one statement on a line.

97. Never blindly make changes to code trying to remove an error.

98. Printing variable values in key places can help you find the location of a bug.

99. One compilation error can hide scores of others.

100. If you can't seem to solve a problem, then do something else.

101. Explain it to the duck. Get an inanimate object and explain your problem to it. This often solves it. (Wyvill)

102. Don't confuse ease of learning with ease of use.

103. A program should be written at least twice—throw away the first one.

104. Haste is not speed.

105. You can't measure productivity by volume.

106. Expect to spend more time in design and less in development

107. You can't program in isolation.

108. If an **if** ends in **return**, don't use **else**.

109. Avoid operator overloading.

110. Scores of compilation errors can sometimes be fixed with one character—start at the first one.

111. Programs that compile mostly still do not work.

112. Incrementally refine your code. Start with BEGIN-SOLVE-END, then refine SOLVE.

113. Draw diagrams of data and algorithms.

114. Use a symbolic debugger wherever possible.

115. Make certain that files have the correct name (and suffix!) when opening.

116. Never assign a value in a conditional expression.

117. If you can't say it in English, you can't say it in any programming language.

118. Don't move language idioms from one language to another.

119. First, do no harm.

120. If object oriented, design the objects first.

121. Don't write deeply nested code.

122. Multiple inheritance is evil. Avoid sin.

123. Productivity can be measured in the number of keystrokes (sometimes).

125. Your code is not perfect. Not even close. Have no ego about it.

126. Variables are to be declared with the smallest possible scope.

127. The names of variables and functions are to begin with a lowercase letter.

133. Collect your best working modules into a code library.

134. Isolate dirty code (e.g., code that accesses machine dependencies) into distinct and carefully annotated modules.

135. Anything you assume about the user will eventually be wrong.

136. Every time a rule is broken, this must be clearly documented.

137. Write code for the next programmer, not for the computer.

138. Your program should always degrade gracefully.

139. Don't surprise your user.

140. Involve users in the development process.

142. Most programs should run the same way and give the same results each time they are executed.

143. Most of your code will be checking for errors and potential errors.

144. Normal code and error handling code should be distinct.

145. Don't write very large modules.

146. Put the shortest clause of an if/else on top.

149. Have a library of error-reporting code and use it (be consistent).

150. Report errors in a way that they make sense.

151. Report errors in a way that allows them to be corrected.

152. Only fools think they can optimize code better than a good compiler.

153. Change the algorithm, not the code, to make things faster. Polynomial is polynomial.

154. Copy and paste is only for prototypes.

155. It's always your fault.

156. Know what the problem is before you start coding.

157. Don't re-invent the wheel.

158. Keep things as simple as possible.

159. Data structures, not algorithms, are central to programming. (Pike)

160. Learn from your mistakes.

161. Learn from the mistakes of others.

162. First make it work; THEN make it work faster.

163. We almost never need to make it faster.

164. First make it work; then make it work better.

165. Programmers don't get to make big design decisions—do what is asked, effectively.

166. Learn new languages and techniques when you can.

167. Never start a new project in a language you don't already know.

168. You can learn a new language effectively by coding something significant in it, just don't expect to sell the result.

169. You will always know only a subset of any given language.

170. The subset you know will not be the same as the subset your coworkers know.

171. Object orientation is not the only way to do things.

172. Object orientation is not always the best way to do things.

173. To create a decent object, one first needs to be a programmer.

174. You may be smarter than the previous programmer, but leave their code alone unless it is broken.

175. You probably are not smarter than the previous programmer, so leave their code alone unless it is broken.

176. Your program will never actually be complete. Live with it.

177. All functions have preconditions for their correct use.

178. Sometimes a function cannot tell whether its preconditions are true.

180. Computers have gigabytes of memory, mostly. Optimizing it is the last thing to do.

181. Compute important values in two different ways and compare them.

182. 0.1 * 10 is not equal to 1.

183. Adding manpower to a late software project makes it later.

184. It always takes longer than you expect.

185. If it can be null, it will be null.

186. Do not use catch and throw unless you know exactly what you are doing.

187. Be clear about your intention. i=1-i is not the same as if(i==0) then i=1 else i=0.

188. Fancy algorithms are buggier than simple ones, and they're much harder to implement. (Pike)

189. The first 90% of the code takes 10% of the time. The remaining 10% takes the other 90% of the time.

190. All messages should be tagged.

191. Do not use FOR loops as time delays.

192. A user interface should not look like a computer program.

193. Decompose complex problems into smaller tasks.

194. Use the appropriate language for the job, when given a choice.

195. Know the size of the standard data types.

198. If you simultaneously hit two keys on the keyboard, the one that you do not want will appear on the screen.

199. Patterns are for the weak—it assumes you don't know what you are doing.

200. Don't assume precedence rules, especially when debugging—parenthe-size.

202. ++ and -- are evil. What's wrong with i = i + 1??

204. It's hard to see where a program spends most of its time.

205. Fancy algorithms are slow when n is small, and n is usually small. (Pike)

206. Assume that things will go wrong.

207. Computers don't know any math.

208. Expect the impossible.

209. Test everything. Test often.

210. Do the simple bits first.

211. Don't fix what is not broken.

212. If it is not broken, then try to break it.

213. Don't draw conclusions based on names.

214. A carelessly planned project takes three times longer to complete than expected; a carefully planned project takes only twice as long.

215. Any system which depends on human reliability is unreliable.

216. The effort required to correct course increases geometrically with time.

217. Complex problems have simple, easy to understand, and wrong answers.

218. An expert is that person most surprised by the latest evidence to the contrary.

219. One man's error is another man's data.

220. Noise is something in data that you don't want. Someone does want it.

12.5 SUMMARY

There is no general agreement on how best to put together a good program. A good program is one that is functionally correct, readable, modifiable, reasonably efficient, and that solves a problem that someone needs solved. No two programmers will create the same program for a non-trivial problem. The program development strategy discussed in this chapter is called *iterative refinement*, and is nearly independent of language or philosophy.

There is no single process that is best for writing programs. Some people only use object-oriented code, but a problem with teaching that way is that a class contains traditional, procedure-oriented code. To make a class, one must first know how to write a program.

The idea behind *top-down* programming is that the higher levels of abstraction are described first. A description of what he entire program is to do is written in a kind-of English/computer hybrid language (*pseudocode*), and this description involves making calls to functions that have not yet been written but whose function is known—these functions are called *stubs*. The first step is to sketch the actions of the program as a whole, then to expand each step that is not well-defined into a detailed method that has no ambiguity. Compile and test the program as frequently as possible so that errors can be identified while it is still easy to see where they are.

The key to object-oriented design is identifying the best objects to be implemented. The rest of the program will take a logical shape depending on the classes that it uses. Try to isolate the details of the class from the outside. Always be willing to rethink a choice and rewrite code as a consequence.

Exercises

1. Add sound to the game. When the ball collides with an object a sound effect should play.

2. Consider how hyphenation might be added to *Pyroff.* How would it be decided to hyphenate a word, and where would the new code be placed? In other words, sketch a solution.

3. In some versions of *Breakout*-style games, certain of the tiles or targets have special properties. For example, sometimes hitting a special target will result

in the ball speeding up or slowing down, will have an extra point value, or will change the size of the paddle. Modify the game so that some of the targets speed up the ball and some others slow it down.

4. The *Pyroff* system can turn right adjusting off, but not on. This seems like a flaw. Add a new command, ".ra," that will turn right adjusting on.

5. Most word processors allow for a *header* and a *footer*, some space and possibly some text at the beginning and end, respectively, of every page. Design a command ".he" that at the least allows for empty space at the beginning of a page, and a corresponding command ".fo" that allows for some lines at the end of a page.

6. Which three of the *Rules for Programmers* do you think make the greatest difference in the code? Which three affect code the least? Are there any that you don't understand?

Notes and Other Resources

Bouncing a ball off of a wall: *https://sinepost.wordpress.com/2012/08/19/bouncing-off-the-walls/*

1. Jon Bentley. (1999). **Programming Pearls, 2nd ed.**, Addison-Wesley Professional, ISBN-13: 978-0201657883.

2. Adrian Bowyer and John Woodwark. (1983). **A Programmer's Geometry**, Butterworth-Heinemann Ltd., ISBN-13: 978-0408012423.

3. Frederick Brooks. (1995). **The Mythical Man-Month: Essays on Software Engineering**, Anniversary Edition, Addison-Wesley Professional.

4. Jim Parker. (2015). **100 Cool Processing Sketches**, eBook, *https://leanpub.com/100coolprocessingsketches*

5. Jim Parker. (2015). **Game Development Using Processing**, Mercury Learning and Publishing.

6. R. Rhoad, G. Milauskas, and R. Whipple. (1984). **Geometry for Enjoyment and Challenge, rev. ed.**, Evanston, IL, McDougal, Littell & Company.

7. Gerald M. Weinberg. (1998). **The Psychology of Computer Programming**, Anl Sub ed., Dorset House, ISBN-13: 978-0932633422.

## CHAPTER 13

COMMUNICATING WITH THE OUTSIDE WORLD

◼ ◼ ◼ ◼ ◼

In this chapter

Python can read data from the keyboard and print on the screen, it can display graphics, audio, and video, allow mouse (and touch) interactions, and read and write data to and from files. That's a lot of communication, but it all happens on one computer—the one on which the program is running. In the age of high-speed Internet, social media, podcasts, blogs, and wikis, this is not enough. The wide world outside of the desktop beckons, and a programmer with a knowledge of Python and the relevant modules can respond.

Can a computer communicate with another one? Of course. Can a program send email? Yes, that's what a mail program like *Thunderbird* or *Outlook* does. Can a program be written that reads tweets as they are sent? Sure, but there is a price. That is: these things are done according to someone else's rules. The first email was sent in 1971 on a private network named *Arpanet*. It sent mail between distinct computers, rather than sending messages between users on a specific machine. In 1972 Unix Email was made available, and was networked in 1978; that was the start of something big.

The sender and receiver had to agree on how to encode and decode a message, and how to access it from the network. To send mail between different computers always requires a standard, a scheme that is agreed upon by implementers of the system. Otherwise mail can only be sent between UNIX systems, or Windows, or iOS. Email, to be practical, needs to be more flexible. It needs to be ubiquitous, and so all need to agree on a standard for how Email can be sent and received. A standard was eventually agreed on, and it was called the *Simple Mail Transfer Protocol* (SMTP) and was established in 1982.

This was seven years before the World Wide Web, so Email really represents the first practical way to communicate between computers over a long distance. FTP happened at about the same time. The enabling technology for the Web, TCP/IP, came next. All of these developments in networking and software combined to create the modern interconnected society, but all are based on a collection of rules that software must agree to (*protocols*) if they are to make use of the network infrastructure. This is an example of *design by contract*, in which designers create formal specifications for components and using those involves a kind-of contract or agreement between programmers developing client software and those who built the modules and designed the protocols.

There are high-level programs that provide a good user interface to the Internet and that implement these protocols beneath their visual presentation. When using Python a collection of modules are used that handle the very low-level details, but the interface to the programmer exposes the protocol. Some of these modules are provided in a standard Python installation (*smtplib*, *email*), and some are not (*MPI*, *Tweepy*), and will have to be installed before the code in this chapter will run.

When communicating with another machine a key issue is that of *authentication*. Almost all protocols require that a connection be formed between the two computers, using some kind of identification of those machines such as their IP address. Then the one initializing the connection must prove that it has permission to do what it is about to do. This resembles logging in, and involves a user identification and a password of some type. Once the user has been identified there is an exchange of messages that tell the remote computer what is desired of it, and that allow information to be returned to the caller. This process is nearly universal, but takes somewhat different forms on different systems.

13.1 EMAIL

Email is a good example of a *client-server* system, and one that gets used millions of times each minute. The Email program on a PC is the client, and allows a user to enter text messages, specify destinations, attach images, and all of the features expected by such a program. This client packages the Email message (data) according to the *Simple Message Transfer Protocol* (SMTP) and sends that to another computer on the Internet, the Email server. An Email user must have an account on the server for this to work so they can be identified and the user can receive replies; so, the process is: log into the Email server, then send the SMTP message to the Email server program on that server. Thus the client side of the contract is to create a properly formatted message, to log into the server properly, and pass the message to it.

Now the server does the work. Given the destination of the message, it searches for the server that is connected to that destination. For example, given the address xyz@gmail.com, the server for gmail.com is located. Then the email message is sent across the network to that server. The server software at that end reads the message and places it into the mailbox, which is really just a directory on a disk drive connected to the server, for the specified use **xyz**. The mail message is essentially a text file at this point.

This description is simplified but essentially accurate, and describes what has to be done by a program that is supposed to send an Email message. The Python module that permits the sending of Email implements the protocol and offers the programmer ways to specify the parameters, like the destination and the message. The interface is implemented as a set of functions. The library needed for this is *smtplib*, a part of the standard Python system.

Example: Send an Email

Sending an Email message starts with establishing a connection between the client computer and the user's mail server, the one on which they have an account (user name and password). For the purposes here a Gmail (Google) server will be used, which complicates the issue a tiny bit. The Email accounts in the example are also Gmail ones, and these can be had for free from Google.

The program must declare *smtplib* as an imported module. The sending address and the receiving address will be the same in this example, but this is just a test. Normally this will not be the situation. The Email address is the user ID for Gmail authentication and the password is defined by the user. These are all just strings.

```
import smtplib

LOGIN = yourloginID     # Login User ID for Gmail, string-
PASSWD = yourpassword   # Login password for Gmail, string
sndr = pythontextbook@gmail.com  # Sender's email address
rcvr = pythontextbook@gmail.com  # Receiver's email address
```

Part of the SMTP scheme is a syntax for Email messages. There is a header at the beginning that specifies the sender, receiver, and subject of the message. These are used to format the message, not to route it—the receiver address is specified later. A simple such message looks like this:

```
From: user_me@gmail.com
To: user_you@gmail.com
Subject: Just a message
```

A string must be constructed that contains this information:

```
msgt = "From: user_me@gmail.com\n"
msgt = msgt + "To: user_you@gmail.com\n"
msgt = msgt + "Subject: Just a message\n"
msgt = msgt + "\n"
```

Now the body of the message is attached to this string. This is the part of the Email that is important to the sender:

```
msgt = msgt + "Attention: This message was sent by Python!\n"
```

The string variable **msgt** now holds the whole message. This message is in the format defined by the Multipurpose Internet Mail Extensions (MIME) standard. The next step for the program is to try to establish a connection with the sender's email server. For this the *smtp* module is needed, specifically the **SMTP()** function. It is called passing the name of the user's Email server as a parameter, and it returns a variable that references that server. In this example that variable is named server:

```
server = smtplib.SMTP('smtp.gmail.com')
```

If it is not possible to connect to the server for some reason, then an error will occur. It is therefore a good idea to place this in a try-except block:

```
try:
    server = smtplib.SMTP('smtp.gmail.com')
except:
    print ("Error occurred. Can't connect")
else:
```

Now comes the complexity that Gmail and some other servers introduce. What has happened after the call to **smtplib.SMTP()** is that a communications session has been opened up. There is now an active connection between the client computer and the server at *smtp.gmail.com*. Some servers demand a level of security that, among other things, ensures that other parties can't modify or even read the message. This is accomplished using a protocol named *Transport Layer Security* (TLS), the details of which are not completely relevant because the modules take care of it. However, to send data to *smtp.gmail.com* the server must be told to begin using TLS:

```
server.starttls()
```

Now the user must be authenticated using their ID and password:

```
server.login(LOGIN,PASSWD)
```

Only now can a message be sent, and only if the login ID and password are correct. The sender is the string **sndr**, the recipient is **rcvr**, and the message is **msgt**:

```
server.sendmail(sndr, rcvr, msgt)
```

Now that the message has been sent, it is polite to close the session. Logging off of the server is done as follows:

```
server.quit()
```

This program will send one email, but it can be easily modified to send many emails one after the other. It can be modified to read the message from the keyboard, or perform any of the functions of a typical Email-sending program (Exercise 1).

The module email can be invoked to format the message in MIME form. The function **MIMEText(s)** converts the message string **s** into an internal form, which is a MIME message. Fields like the subject and sender can be added to the message, and then it is sent as was done before. For example:

```
import smtplib
from email.mime.text import MIMEText

LOGIN = yourloginID
PASSWD = yourpassword

fp = open ("message.txt", "r")   # Read the message from a
                                 # file
mtest = fp.read()
# Or: simply use a string
#mtest = "A message from Python: Merry Christmas."
fp.close()

msg = MIMEText (mtest)                  # Create a MIME string
sndr = pythontextbook@gmail.com         # Sender's Email
rcvr = pythontextbook@gmail.com         # Recipient's Email
msg['Subject'] = 'Mail from Python'     # Add Subject to the
                                        # message
msg['From'] = sndr                      # Add sender to the
                                        # message
msg['To'] = rcvr                        # Add recipient to the
                                        # message

# Send the message using Google's SMTP server, as before
s = smtplib.SMTP('smtp.gmail.com')   # localhost could work
s.starttls()
s.login (LOGIN, PASSWD)
s.send_message(msg)
s.quit()
```

Using **MIMEText()** to create the message avoids having to format it correctly using basic string operations.

13.1.1 Reading Email

Reading Email is more complicated than writing it. The content of an Email is often a surprise, and so a reader must be prepared to parse anything that might be sent. There can be multiple mailboxes: which mailbox will be looked at? There are usually many messages in a mailbox: how can they be distinguished? In addition, the protocol for retrieving mail from a server is different from that used to send it; in fact, there are two competing protocols: POP and IMAP.

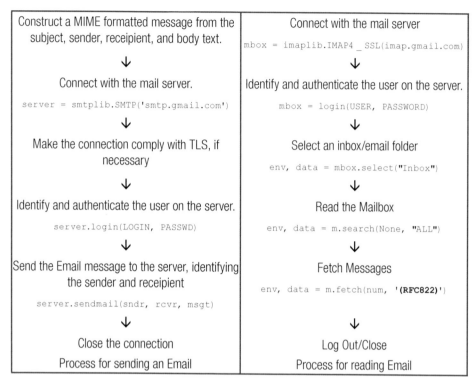

Construct a MIME formatted message from the subject, sender, receipient, and body text.	Connect with the mail server `mbox = imaplib.IMAP4 _ SSL(imap.gmail.com)`
↓	↓
Connect with the mail server. `server = smtplib.SMTP('smtp.gmail.com')`	Identify and authenticate the user on the server. `mbox = login(USER, PASSWORD)`
↓	↓
Make the connection comply with TLS, if necessary	Select an inbox/email folder `env, data = mbox.select("Inbox")`
↓	↓
Identify and authenticate the user on the server. `server.login(LOGIN, PASSWD)`	Read the Mailbox `env, data = m.search(None, "ALL")`
↓	↓
Send the Email message to the server, identifying the sender and receipient `server.sendmail(sndr, rcvr, msgt)`	Fetch Messages `env, data = m.fetch(num, '(RFC822)')`
↓	↓
Close the connection	Log Out/Close
Process for sending an Email	Process for reading Email

Figure 13.1
The procedure for sending an Email using Python.

The *Post Office Protocol* (POP) is the older of the two schemes, although it has been updated a few times. It certainly allows the basic requirements of a mail reader, which is to download and delete a message in a remote mailbox (i.e., on the server). The *Internet Message Access Protocol* (IMAP) is intended for use by many Email clients, and so messages tend not to be deleted until that is requested. When setting up an Email client one of these protocols usually has to be specified, and then it will be used from then on. The example here will use IMAP.

Example: Display the Subject Headers for Emails in Inbox

An outline for the process of reading Email is sketched on the right-hand side of Figure 13.1. Reading Email uses a different module that was used to send Email: *imaplib*, for reading from an IMAP server. The function names are different from those in *smtplib*, but the purpose of some of them is the same. The first three steps in reading Email are:

```
import imaplib
server = 'imap.gmail.com'          # Gmail's IMAP server
USER = pythontextbook@gmail.com    # User ID
PASSWORD = "password"              # Mask this password
EMAIL_FOLDER = "Inbox"

mbox = imaplib.IMAP4_SSL(server)   # Connect to the server
mbox.login(USER, PASSWORD)         # Authenticate (log in)
```

The next step is to select a mailbox to read. Each has a name, and is really just a directory someplace. The variable **mbox** is a class instance of a class named *imaplib.IMAP4_SSL*, the details of which can be found in many places, including the Internet. It has a method named **select()** that allows the examination of a mailbox, given its name (a string). The string is a variable named EMAIL_FOLDER which contains "Inbox," and the call to select() that essentially opens the inbox is:

```
z = mbox.select(EMAIL_FOLDER)
```

The return value is a tuple. The first element indicates success or failure, and if z[0] contains the string "OK" then the mailbox is open. The usual alternative is "NO." The second element of the tuple indicates how many messages there are, but it is in an odd format. If there are 2 messages, as in the example, this string is *b'2'*; if there were 3 messages it would be *b'3'*; and so on. These are called message sequence numbers.

Having opened the mailbox, the next step is to read it and extract the messages. The protocol requires that the mailbox be searched for the messages that are wanted. The *imaplib.IMAP4_SSL* class offers the **search()** method for this, the simplest form being:

```
mbox.search(None, "ALL")
```

which returns all of the messages in the mailbox. IMAP provides search functionality, and all this method does is connect to it, which is why it seems awkward to use. The first parameter specifies a character set, and None allows it to default to a general value. The second parameter specifies a search criterion as a string. There are dozens of parameters that can be used here and the documentation for IMAP should be examined in detail for solutions to specific problems. However, some of the more useful tags include:

ANSWERED: Messages that have been answered.

BCC <string>: Messages with a specific string in the BCC field.

BEFORE <date>: Messages whose date (not time) is earlier than the specified one.

HEADER <field-name> <string>: A specified field in the header contains the string.

SUBJECT <string>: Messages that contain the specified string in the SUBJECT field.

TO <string>: Messages that contain the specified string in the TO field.

UNSEEN: Messages that do not have the \Seen flag set.

So, a call to **search()** that looks for the text "Python" in the subject line would be:

```
mbox.search(None, "SUBJECT Python")
```

The search() function returns a tuple again, where the first component is a status string (i.e., "OK," "NO," "BAD") and the second is a list of messages satisfying the search criteria in the same format as before. If the second message if the only match, this string will be **b'2.'** If the first three match it will be **b'1 2 3.'**

Finally, the messages are read, or *fetched*. The *imaplib.IMAP4_SSL* class has a **fetch()** method to do this, and it again takes some odd parameters. What a programmer thinks of the interface or the API or, in other words, the *contract*, is not important. What must be done is to satisfy the requirements and accept the data as it is offered. The **fetch()** method accepts two parameters: the first is the indication of which message is desired. The first message is *b'1'*, the second is *b'2'*, and so on. The second parameter is an indicator of what it is that should be returned. The header? If so, pass "(RFC822.HEADER)" as the parameter. Why? Because they ask for it. RFC822 is the name of a protocol. If the Email body is wanted, then pass "(RFC822.TEXT)". A short list of possibilities is:

RFC822	-	Everything
RFC822.HEADER	-	No body, header only
RFC822.TEXT	-	Body only
RFC822.SIZE	-	Message size
UID	-	Message identifier

Multiple of these specifiers can be passed; for example:

```
mbox.fetch(num, '(UID RFC822.TEXT RFC822.HEADER)')
```

returns a tuple having three parts: the ID, the body, and the header. By the way, the header tends to be exceptionally long, 40 lines or so, and is mostly uninteresting to a specific application. For this example, the only part of the header that is interesting is the "Subject" part. Fields in the header are separated by the characters "\r\n" so they are easy to extract in a call to split(). Eliminating the header data for a moment, the call:

```
(env, data) = mbox.fetch(num, '(UID RFC822.TEXT)')
```

results in a tuple that has an "envelope" that should indicate "OK" (the **env** variable). The data part is a string that contains the UID and the text body of the message. For example:

```
[(b'2 (UID 22 RFC822.TEXT {718}', b"Got a collection of old
45's for sale. Contact me.\r\n\r\n-- \r\n"), b')']
```

This says that this is message 2 and shows the text of that message.

This example is supposed to print all of the subject headers in this mailbox. The call to **fetch()** should extract the header only:

```
(env, data) = mbox.fetch(num, '(RFC822.HEADER)')
```

The details of IMAP are complex enough that it is easy to forget what the original task was, which was to print the subject lines from the messages in the mailbox. All of the relevant methods have been described and completing the program is possible. The entire program is:

```
import imaplib


server = 'imap.gmail.com'                # IMAP Server
USER = "pythontextbook@gmail.com"        # USER ID
PASSWORD = ""                            # Mask this password
EMAIL_FOLDER = "Inbox"                   # Which mailbox?


mbox = imaplib.IMAP4_SSL(server)         # Connect
mbox.login(USER, PASSWORD)               # Authenticate


env, data = mbox.select(EMAIL_FOLDER)    # Select the mailbox
if env == 'OK':                          # Did it work?
```

```
        print ("Printing subject headers: ", EMAIL_FOLDER)

    env, data = mbox.search(None, "ALL")  # Select the
                                          # messages wanted.
    if env != 'OK':                       # Are there any?
        print ("No messages.", env)       # Nope.
        exit()


    for num in data[0].split():     # For each selected
                                    # message b'1 2 3 ...'
        (env, data) = mbox.fetch(num, '(RFC822.HEADER)')
                                    # Read it
        if env != 'OK':
            print ("ERROR getting message", num, ", ", env)
            break
        s = str(data[0][1])         # Look for the string
                                    # "Subject" in the header
        k = s.find("Subject")
        if (k>=0):                  # Found it?
            s =  s[k:]              # Extract the string to the
                                    # next '\r'
            k = s.find('\\r')
            s = s[:k]
            print (s)               # And print it.
    mbox.close()
else:
    print ("No such mailbox as ", EMAIL_FOLDER)
mbox.logout()
```

Typical output would be:

Printing subject headers: Inbox

Subject: Contents of Chapter 13

Subject: 45 RPM

Subject: another Email

The point of this section was to demonstrate how a Python program, or any program for that matter, must comply with external specifications when interfacing with sophisticated software systems, and to introduce the concept of a protocol, a contract between developers. Of course a program that can send Email is useful by itself.

13.2 FTP

The File Transfer Protocol is used to exchange files between computers on a network, in particular across the Internet. It provides the same sort of interface to data on a distance computer as would be expected from a file system on a desktop. It can copy a file in either direction, but can also change directories, list the directory contents, and perform other useful operations. This again presumes that the rules set up by the FTP interface are followed.

Having just seen the communication requirements for sending and receiving Email, it should be possible to predict the way that FTP will operate. A connection will have to be made to a remote computer, and some form of authentication will take place. The client (the program that established the connection) will now send a set of commands to the server, which will read and process them. Then, finally, the client will terminate the connection. This is all true.

The commands that can be processed by an FTP server include things like LIST the contents of this directory, change the working directory (CWD), retrieve a file (RETR) and send or store a file (STOR). These are sent across the network as strings and represent raw FTP commands, those that take place at a low level of abstraction in the system. Higher level commands are implemented as specific methods in the **FTP** class of *ftplib*. For example, there is a command named PWD that will display the name of the current remote directory. FTP offers a function that will send this command:

```
FTP.pwd()
```

Doing the same thing by sending the command directly would use the **sendcmd()** method of FTP, and would pass the command as a string:

```
ftp.sendcmd("PWD")
```

There is a difference to the programmer. The **pwd()** method returns the string that represents the directory, whereas when the text command is sent, the return value is the string that the FTP system returned, which is something like:

257 "/" is the current directory

An example will be used to illustrate the use of FTP.

Example: Download and Display the README File from an FTP Site

The site chosen for the example belongs to NASA, but any ftp site will work. The connection and authentication steps are:

```
from ftplib import FTP

ftp = FTP("ftp.hq.nasa.gov")   # Please don't always use
NASA
ftp.login()                    # Select a different site.
```

The login step is interesting because there are no parameters given. This is an *anonymous* FTP connection, which is common for sites that offer things for download. The default login when using the login() method is a user ID of "anonymous" and a password, if one is requested, of "anonymous." It is also possible to specify an ID and password if the user has them:

```
ftp.login("myuserid", "mypassword")
```

The **login()** function returns the site's welcome message, which is a string that can be ignored.

The example is supposed to download the file named README and display it. The method **retrlines()** can do this, because it is a text file. If it were a binary file, like an MP3 or JPG file, then the **retrbinary()** method would be used instead. The first parameter to **retrlines()** is a command. To retrieve a file the command is the keyword **RETR** followed by the file name. The simplest version is:

```
ftp.retrlines('RETR README')
```

which will display the text from the file on the screen. That's what was wanted, but the method can do more. If a function name is passed as the second parameter, then that function will be called for every line of text, and will be passed that line as a parameter. To illustrate this consider a simple function that takes a string and prints each line, looking for "\\n" characters. The function is:

```
def myprint (ss):
    s = str(ss)  # Sometimes the parameter ss is type byte.
    x = s.split("\\n")
    for i in range (0, len(x)):
        print (x[i])
```

Now a call to **retrlines()** could be as follows:

```
ftp.retrlines('RETR README', myprint)
```

or even:

```
ftp.retrlines('RETR README', print)
```

to use the standard **print()** function. Of course any function that takes a string parameter could be passed. To save the README file as a local file, for example:

```
ftp.retrlines('RETR README', open('README', 'w').write)
```

will write the file to a local one named README, but lacking the end-of-line characters.

Binary files use **retrbinary()**, and it has the same form as **retrlines()**. However, the second parameter, the function, must be passed, because binary files cannot be sent to the screen. Downloading and saving an image file might be done as follows:

```
ftp.retrbinary('RETR orion.jpg, open('orion.jpg, 'wb').write)
```

The session would end by logging out:

```
ftp.quit()
```

Uploading a file, that is moving a file from a desktop to a site on the Internet, used the method storlines() for text and storbinary() for binary files. Examples:

```
f = open ("message.txt", "rb")
ftp.storlines ("STOR message.txt", f)
```

The method copies lines from the local file to the remote one. The file to be copied is open in "rb" mode. For a binary example assume an image:

```
f = open ("image.jpg", "rb")
ftp.storbinary ("STOR image.jpg", f)
```

session.storbinary("STOR kitten.jpg," file)   # send the file

13.3 COMMUNICATION BETWEEN PROCESSES

Underneath the FTP and Email protocols, which allow interfaces to applications, lies a communications layer, the programs that actually send bytes between computers or between programs on the same computer. It is conducted very much like a conversation. One person, the client, initiates the conversation ("Hi there!"). The other (the server) responds ("Hello. Nice to see you."). Now it is the client's turn again. They take turns *sending* and *accepting* messages until one says "goodbye." These messages might contain Email, or FTP data, or TV programs. This layer does not care what the data is; none of its business, really. Its job is to deliver it.

Data are delivered in *packets*, each containing a certain amount. In order for the client to deliver the data there must be a server willing to connect to it. The client needs to know the address of a server, just as an FTP address or Email destination was required before, but now all that is needed is the host name and a *port number*. A port is really a logical construction, something akin to an element of a list. If two programs agree to share data by having one of them place it in location 50001 of a list and the other one read it from there, it gives an approximate idea of what a port is. Some port numbers are assigned and should not be used for anything else; FTP and Email have assigned ports. Others are available for use, and any two processes can agree to use one.

A module named socket, based on the interprocess communication scheme on UNIX of the same name, is used with Python to send messages back and forth. To create an example two computers should be used, one being the client and one the server, and the IP address of the server is required too.

Example: A Server That Calculates Squares

The client will open a communications link (socket) to the server, which has a known IP address. The server will engage in a short handshake (exchange of strings) and then expect to receive a number for the client. The client will send an integer, the server will receive it, square it, and send back the answer. This simple exchange is really the basis for all communications between computers: one machine sends information, the other receives it, processes it, and returns a reply based on the data it received.

The client: will begin the conversation. It creates a connection, a socket, to the server using the **socket**() function of the **socket** module. Protocols must be specified, and the most common ones will be used:

```
import socket

HOST = '19*.***.*.***'     # The remote host
PORT = 50007               # The same port as used by the server
s = socket.socket(socket.AF_INET, socket.SOCK_STREAM)
s.connect((HOST, PORT))
```

Port 50007 is used because nothing else is using it. Now the client starts the conversation, just as it appears at the beginning of this section:

```
s.send(b'Hi there!')
```

The **send()** function sends the message passed as a parameter. The string (as *bytes*) is transmitted to the server through the variable **s**, which represents the server. The client now waits for the confirmation string from the server, which should be "Hello. Nice to see you." The client calls:

```
data = s.recv(1024)
```

which waits for a response from the server. This response will be 1024 bytes long at most, and it will wait only for a short time, at which point it will give up and an error will be reported. When this client gets the response, it proceeds to send numbers to the server. They are converted into the *bytes* type before transmission. In this example it simply loops through 100 consecutive integers:

```
for i in range (0, 100):
    data = str(i).encode()
    s.send (data)
```

After sending to the server it waits for the answer. Actually that's a part of the receive function:

```
data = s.recv(1024)
```

after 100 integers the loop ends and the connection is closed:

```
s.close()
```

The Server: is always listening. It creates a socket on a particular port so that the operating system knows something is possible there, but because the server cannot predict when a client will connect or what client it will be it simply listens for a connection, by calling a function named **listen()**:

```
import socket
from random import *

HOST = ''    # A null string is correct here.
PORT = 50007
s = socket.socket(socket.AF_INET, socket.SOCK_STREAM)
s.bind ((HOST, PORT))
s.listen()
```

AF_INET and SOCK_STREAM are constants that tell the system which protocols are being used. These are the most common, but see the documentation for others. The **bind()** and the **listen()** functions are new. Associating this connection with a specific port is done using **bind().** The tuple (HOST, PORT) says to connect this host to this port. The empty string for HOST implies *this* computer. The **listen()** call starts the server process, *this* program, accepting connections when asked. A process connecting on the port that was specified in *bind()* will now result in this process, the server, being notified. When a connection request occurs, the server must accept it before doing any input or output:

```
conn, addr = s.accept()
```

In the tuple **(conn, addr)** that is returned, **conn** represents the connection, like a file descriptor returned from **open()**, and is used to send and receive data; **addr** is the address of the sender, the client, and is a string. If the **addr** were printed:

```
print ("Connected to ", addr)
```

It would look like an IP address:

```
Connected to 423.121.12.211
```

Now the server can receive data across the connection, and does so by calling **recv()**:

```
data = conn.recv(1024)
print ("Server heard '", data, "'")
```

The parameter 1024 specifies the size of the buffer, or the maximum number of bytes that can be received in one call. The variable **data** is of type *bytes*, just as the parameter to **send()** was in the client. The client was the first to send, and it sent the message "Hi there!" That should be the value of data now, if it has been received properly. The response from the server should be "Hello, nice to see you."

```
conn.send (b'Hello. Nice to see you.')
```

The same connection is used for sending and receiving.

Now the real data gets exchanged. The server will accept integers, sent as *bytes*. It will square them and transmit the answer back.

```
while True:
    data = conn.recv(1024)          # Read the incoming data
```

```
    if data:
        i = int(data)              # Convert it to integer
        print ("Received ", i)
        data = str(i*i).encode()   # Square it and convert
to bytes
        conn.send (data)           # Send to the client
```

The server can tell when the connection is closed by the client, but it is also polite to say "Goodbye" somehow, perhaps by sending a particular code. If the loop ever terminates, the server should close the connection:

conn.close()

This is a pretty good example of a data exchange and a contract, because there are specified requirements for each side of this conversation which will result in success if done correctly and failure if messed up. Failure is sometimes indicated by an error message, often a *timeout* where the client or server was expecting something that never arrived. In other cases failure is not formally indicated at all; the program simply "hangs" there and does nothing. If at any time both processes are trying to receive data, then the program will fail.

Figure 13.2 shows the communication between the client and the server as a diagram. If the client and the server are at any time both trying to accept data

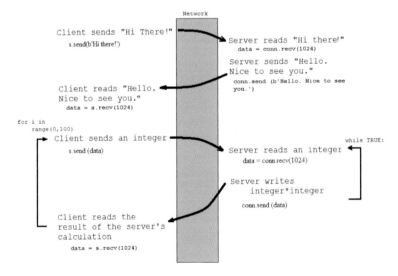

Figure 13.2
Typical communication between the client and the server processes.

from the connection, then the program will fail. In the diagram all data transfers can be seen as transmit-accept pairs between the two processes, and as read-write pairs within the server and write-read pairs within the client.

The FTP protocol can now be seen as a socket connection, wherein the client sends strings (commands) to the server, which parses them, carries out the request, and then sends an acknowledgement back.

```
# The client
import socket

# The remote host
HOST = '19*.***.*.***'
# The same port used by the server
PORT = 50007

s = socket.socket(socket.AF_INET,\
        socket.SOCK_STREAM)
s.connect((HOST, PORT))
s.send(b'Hi there!')
data = s.recv(1024)
for i in range (0, 100):
    data = str(i).encode()
    s.send (data)
    data = s.recv(1024)
s.close()
```

```
# The server
import socket

HOST = ''  # A null string is ok here.
PORT = 50007
s = socket.socket(socket.AF_INET, \
        socket.SOCK_STREAM)
s.bind ((HOST, PORT))
s.listen()
conn, addr = s.accept()
data = conn.recv(1024)
print ("Server heard '", data, "'")
conn.send (b'Hello. Nice to see you.')
while True:
# Read the incoming data
    data = conn.recv(1024)
    if data:
# Convert it to integer
        i = int(data)
        print ("Received ", i)
# Square it and convert to bytes
        data = str(i*i).encode()
# Send to the client
        conn.send (data)
    conn.close()
```

13.4 TWITTER

For the few people who may be unfamiliar with Twitter, it is a social media service that allows its users to send short (140 character) messages out to the world, or really to their subscribed listeners. From its beginning in 2006, Twitter has grown to the point where it handles hundreds of millions of messages (*tweets*) per day from their 302 million active users. It differs from Email in that it broadcasts messages, and the recipients are self-selected.

The messages are entered by Twitter users, each of whom has an account. All messages become part of a *stream*, and the ones that a particular user wants to see are pulled from that stream and placed on the user's *feed*. It is, however, possible to see the feed and examine messages as they are sent, collecting data or identifying patterns. Twitter allows access to the stream, but when using Python it requires the use of a module that must be downloaded and installed. That module is called *tweepy*.

A warning: setting up the authentication so that the Twitter stream can be accessed is not simple. A twitter account is needed, an application has to be registered, and the app must be specified as being able to read, write, and direct messages. Twitter will create a unique set of keys that must be used for the authentication: the *consumer key* and *consumer secret key*, then *the access token* and *access secret token*. Again, it does not pay to ask *why* because it simply must be done. *How* is a better question.

A tweet is limited to 140 characters, but that only considers content. The amount of data sent in a tweet is substantially larger than that, 6000 bytes or more. That's due to the large amount of metadata, or descriptive information, in a tweet. Most people never see that, but a program that reads tweets and sifts them for information will have to deal with it. The twitter interface returns tweet data in *JSON* format (JavaScript Object Notation) which is a standard for exchanging data, similar in purpose to XML. This format has to be parsed, but a second Python module named *json* will do that so no further discussion of JSON will be necessary.

Example: Connect to the Twitter Stream and Print Specific Messages

This program will examine the twitter feed and print messages that have the term "startrek" in them. It is useful to see that once again, authentication is one of the first things to do. In the case of Tweepy an object is created, passing the authentication strings. First:

```
import tweepy
import json

# Authentication details from dev.twitter.com
consumer_key = 'get your own'
consumer_secret = 'get your own'
access_token = 'get your own'
```

```
access_token_secret = ''get your own '

authentication = tweepy.OAuthHandler(consumer_key,
                consumer_secret)
authentication.set_access_token(access_token,
                access_token_secret)
```

Now something different is needed. Tweepy wants to have an object passed to it that is a subclass of one that it defines, *StreamListener*. As a part of the deal that is made with *Tweepy*, the class must have a method named **on_data()** and another named **on_error()**. The **on_data()** method is called by *Tweepy* when there is data in the stream to be read, and the data is passed as a string in JSON format; the **on-error()** method is called when an error occurs, and is passed a string with the error message. Creating this subclass will be described a little later. However, assume that it is called *tweet_listener*. The next step in the process is to create an instance of this class:

```
listener = tweet_listener()
```

Through this class instance the stream will be accessed. Now tell *Tweepy* what this instance is so it can use it. Also do the authentication:

```
stream = tweepy.Stream(authentication, listener)
```

Finally tell *Tweepy* what to extract from the Twitter stream. For this example, the call is:

```
stream.filter(track=['Star Trek'])
```

but other parts of the stream can be accessed and sent to this program: times and dates, locations, etc. In this case the track argument looks into the message text for the "Star Trek" string, case insensitive. Multiple search strings can be placed in the list: ["star trek", "casablanca"].

OK, what about the *tweet_listener* class? It is a subclass of *StreamListener*, as was said earlier. The **on_data()** method needs to parse the JSON-formatted string it is passed and print the parts of the message that are desired. Since the **filter()** call restricts the messages to those containing the string "star trek," all that has to be done in this method is to print the body of the message. Here is the class showing the method; the explanation follows:

```
class tweet_listener(tweepy.StreamListener):

    def on_data(self, data):
```

```
# Twitter returns data in JSON format - decode it first
        dict = json.loads(data)
        print (dict['user']['location'])
        print (dict['user']['screen_name'],dict['text'])
        return True

    def on_error(self, status):
        print (status)
```

The parameter data is in JSON format. To convert it into something useable, pass it to the **json.loads()** method. It returns a Python dictionary with the data available, indexed by field name. The data structure used by Twitter is complex, and is shown in small part in Table 13.1. The left side of the table shows the message field names, the right lists some of the **user** fields; **user** is a field within the message that describes the sender. The variable **dict** is the resulting dictionary.

To simply solve the problem posed, all that would have to be done is to print **dict['text']**, which is the message body. The value of **dict['user']** is the data for the sender of the message. There is a lot of that, mostly not useful to anyone but an app developer (e.g., background color of the user's window), but **dict['user']['screen_name']** is the Twitter identity of the sender, and **dict['user'] ['location']** often indicates where they are. It would be possible to collect data on where the largest number of tweets are being sent from, what kind of information is being conveyed, and in this way perhaps develop an early warning system for events happening in the world.

Table 13.1
Fields in a Twitter Message

Message fields	Fields in the user structure
Coordinates (Coordinates) Represents the geographic location of this Tweet as reported by the user or client application.	**created_at** (String) The UTC datetime that the user account was created on Twitter.
created_at (String) UTC time when this Tweet was created.	**Description** (String) The user-defined string describing their account.
favorite_count (Integer) Indicates approximately how many times this Tweet has been "liked" by Twitter users.	**geo_enabled** (Boolean) When true, indicates that the user has enabled the possibility of geotagging their Tweets.

Message fields	Fields in the user structure
Id (Int64) The integer representation of the unique identifier for this Tweet.	**Id** (64 bit int) The integer representation of the unique identifier for this User.
in_reply_to_screen_name (String) If the represented Tweet is a reply, this field will contain the screen name of the original author.	**Lang** (String) The code (BCP 47) for the user's declared user interface language.
Lang (String) When present, indicates a language identifier corresponding to the machine-detected language of the Tweet text, or "und" if no language could be detected.	**listed_count** (Int) The number of public lists that this user is a member of.
Place (Places) When present, indicates that the tweet is associated with (but not necessarily originating from) a Place.	**Location** (String) The user-defined location for this account's profile. Not necessarily a location.
retweet_count (Int) Number of times this Tweet has been retweeted.	**name** (String) The name of the user, as they've defined it. Not necessarily a real name.
Source (String) Utility used to post the Tweet, as an HTML-formatted string.	**profile_image_url_https** (String) A URL pointing to the user's avatar image.
Text (String) The actual body of the message.	**screen_name** (String) The screen name or alias that this user identifies themselves with. screen_names are unique but subject to change.
User (Users) The user who posted this Tweet. (see: structure to the right) some attributes embedded within this object are unreliable.	**status** (Tweets) If possible, the user's most recent tweet or retweet. In some circumstances, this data cannot be provided and this field will be omitted, null, or empty.
withheld_in_countries (Array of String) When present, indicates a list of uppercase two-letter country codes this content is withheld from.	**statuses_count** (Int) The number of tweets (including retweets) issued by the user.
	time_zone (String) A string describing the Time Zone this user declares themselves within.

13.5 COMMUNICATING WITH OTHER LANGUAGES

Python is terrific for many things, but it can be quite slow. It is interpreted and has a lot of overhead for many of its features; dynamic typing does not come cheap. Also, it may be hard to easily access operating system functions from Python. C, C++, and other languages do not have these problems. It's possible to write a program in Python that calls, for example, a C program to do complex calculations of system calls.

Consider the problem of finding the greatest common divisor (GCD) between two integers; that is, the largest number that divides evenly into both of them. If the GCD between N and M is 1, then these numbers are relatively prime, and they could find use in a random number generator.

Example: Find Two Large Relatively Prime Numbers

This problem will be solved using a C program to do the GCD calculation and a Python program to pass it large numbers until a relatively prime par is found. There are many C versions of the GCD program. This is a common first-year programming assignment. One such is gcd.c, provided on the accompanying disc:

```c
#include "stdafx.h"
#include <stdio.h>

int _tmain(int argc, _TCHAR* argv[])
{
    long n,m;
     scanf("%ld %ld",&n,&m);
     while(n!=m)
     {
         if(n>m)
             n-=m;
         else
             m-=n;
     }
     printf("%d",n);
     return 0;
}
```

This is written for Visual C++ 2010 Express, but very similar code will compile for other compilers and systems. The basic idea is that it reads two large numbers, named **n** and **m**, determines their largest common divisor, and prints that number to standard output. The way that Python will communicate with this C program is through the I/O system. C reads from standard input, and writes to standard output. The Python program will co-opt input and output, pushing text data containing the values of n and m to the input, and capturing standard output and copying it to a string.

This requires the use of a module named *subprocess* that permits the program to execute the gcd.exe program and connect to the standard I/O. A function named **Popen()** takes the name of the file to be executed as a parameter and runs it. It also allows the creation of *pipes*, which are data connections that can take the place of files. The Popen() call that runs the gcd program is:

```
p = subprocess.Popen('gcd.exe',
                stdin=subprocess.PIPE,
                stdout=subprocess.PIPE)
```

Connecting **stdin** and **stdout** to *subprocess* PIPEs means that now Python can perform I/O with them. When GCD starts to execute it expects two integers on input. These can now be sent from the Python program like this:

```
p.stdin.write(data)
```

The expression **p.stdin** represents the file connection to the program, and writing to it does the obvious thing. The Python program writes data to the C program, and the C program reads it from **stdin**. Data should be of type *bytes*, and should contain both large numbers in character form. Correspondingly, when the C program has found the greatest common divisor, it writes to standard output. Capturing this in Python:

```
s = str(p.stdout.readline())
```

The C program writes; the Python program reads. The value returned is of type bytes again, so it is converted into a string.

The final Python solution calls the C program repeatedly until the GCD is 1:

```
import subprocess

n = 11111122
m = 121
data = bytes (str(n)+ ' '+str(m), 'utf-8')
while True:
```

```
p = subprocess.Popen('gcd.exe',
            stdin=subprocess.PIPE,
            stdout=subprocess.PIPE)
p.stdin.write(data)
p.stdin.close()
s = str(p.stdout.readline())
print (s)
if s == "b'1'":
    print ("Numbers are ", n, m)
    break
m = m + 1
data = bytes (str(n)+ ' '+str(m), 'utf-8')
```

This method of communicating with other languages is quite universal, but slower than passing parameters to functions and methods directly. There are a lot of problems with calling functions in other languages, not the least of which concerns typing. Python, dynamically typed interpreted language that it is, would have to have the programmer perform some significant gymnastics to convert lists or dictionaries into a form that C or Java could use.

13.6 SUMMARY

Design by contract has designers create formal specifications for components, and using those involves a kind-of contract or agreement between programmers developing client software and those who built the modules and designed the protocols. For Email, as an example, sender and receiver have to agree on how to encode and decode a message, and how to access it from the network. To send mail between different computers always requires a standard, a scheme that is agreed upon by implementers of the system, a *protocol*.

The *Simple Message Transfer Protocol* is a specification of the process and data needed to send an Email message. The Python module *smtplib* provides the methods needed to interface with this system, which is to say that *smtplib* implements SMTP and provides a programmer access at various places. For reading Email there are two schemes in play: the *Post Office Protocol* (POP) and the more modern *Internet Message Access Protocol* (IMAP). An Email client must agree to satisfy one of these. They Python module for IMAP is *imaplib*.

The *File Transfer Protocol* (FTP) is used to move entire files and directories across networks. It provides the same sort of interface to data on a distance computer as would be expected from a file system on a desktop. The *ftplib* module offers methods for handling this protocol. After authentication, commands are sent as character strings, and files can be sent or received using analogs of *read* and *write* operations.

FTP is built on top of lower level communication primitives such as *sockets*, which create bidirectional data connections between two programs on different computers.

Twitter sends out a stream of data containing all of the *tweets* sent by users, and the client can scan these for tweets that are of interest (subscribed). This stream can be captured using Python and the *Tweepy* module, and automatic scanning of the feed can be done according to the user's program.

It is also possible for Python to communicate with other programs written in other languages by co-opting the input and output files for those programs and feeding data into and extracting results from the I/O channels.

Exercises

1. Write a simple Email sending program *sendmail*. It will ask for the destination from the keyboard and accept the message that way too. Multiple destination addresses can be specified by separating them with commas. The sender's Email address and the server name should be built into the program.

2. Write an application that allows a user to specify a word or words and will examine their mailbox for any Email that contains them. The corresponding Email messages will be written to a text file named "search.txt."

3. Write a Python program that will download the files named "one.txt," "two.txt," and "three.txt" from an ftp site specified by your instructor into files of the same name on a desktop computer.

4. Design and code a server program that will deal poker hands using the socket protocol. When the server is connected to by a client, the client sends a string "deal." The server will generate a random poker hand and send it as text: The spades suit in this scheme is: s1 s2 s3 s4 s5 s6 s7 s8 s9 s10 sj sq sk; hearts are "h," diamonds are "d," and clubs are "c." Write a test program that reads and prints the resulting hands.

5. **DIFFICULT**. Write a two-player pong game using sockets. The game will display a graphical version of the standard Pong screen on the local and

remote screens. The local player can move only the local paddle, and motions by the remote player are reflected on the local screen. The ball is positioned at the same place, as nearly as possible, on both screens simultaneously.

6. There are words and phrases that many governments use to indicate a potential security problem. They can examine emails and various social media outlets. Examine the Twitter stream for tweets containing the words "**assassination**," "**security**," "**weapon**," or "**hostage**." Print the tweet and location from which it claims to be sent.

7. How can the IP address of a distant site be determined? Search the Internet for that information as it can be implemented in a Python program, and implement a program that asks the user for a URL and returns an IP address for that URL.

Notes and Other Resources

Python *ftplib* documentation: *https://docs.python.org/3/library/ftplib.html*

Search criteria in IMAP: *http://tools.ietf.org/html/rfc3501#section-6.4.4*

Tweep download: *https://pypi.python.org/pypi/tweepy/3.4.0*

Tweepy intro: *http://docs.tweepy.org/en/latest/streaming_how_to.html*

How to use the Twitter API to stream tweets. *https://www.youtube.com/watch?v=pUUxmvvl2FE*

Twitter message fields: *https://dev.twitter.com/overview/api/tweets*

Twitter user fields:

JSON Tutorial: *http://www.w3schools.com/json/*

1. Todd Campbell. (2002). **The First Email Message**, *https://www.cs.umd.edu/class/spring2002/cmsc434-0101/MUIseum/applications/firstemail.html*

2. Tim Berners-Lee, Robert Cailliau, Ari Luotonen, Hendryk Nielsen, and Arthur Secret. (1994). **The World-Wide Web**, *Communications of the ACM*, *37*(8), 76–82.

3. Takeshi Sakaki, Makoto Okazaki, and Yutaka Matsuo. (2010). **Earthquake shakes Twitter users: Real-time event detection by social sensors**, in *Proceedings of the 19th International Conference on the World Wide Web (WWW '10)*, ACM, New York, NY, USA, 851–860.

## CHAPTER 14

A Brief *Glib* Reference

■ ■ ■ ■ ■

In this chapter

The reason that there are two "versions" of *Glib* is that not all schools and other institutions will permit installing new modules. The module *tkinter* is standard with Python 3, but does not by itself offer the tools for multimedia. The basic system consists of graphics operations, including image input, output, and display.

For places where it is possible to install the *pygame* module, the *dynamic Glib* module can be used. This offers the same tools as does the *tkinter* version plus has sound, mouse and keyboard interaction, and video.

What follows is documentation for both systems.

14.1 GLIB TKINTER

```
BLACK = "#000000"
WHITE = "#ffffff"
RED = "#ff0000"
```

```
GREEN = "#00ff00"
BLUE = "#0000ff"
BACKSPACE = '\b'
```

Width()

Return the width of the graphics window in pixels.

Height()

Return the height of the graphics window in pixels.

fill(r, g=1000, b=1000)

Turn on filling. Set the fill color for polygons, text color too, to (**r,g,b**) or just **r** if one parameter is given.

nofill()

Turn filling off.

stroke(r, g=1000, b=1000)

Set the line and outline color to (**r,g,b**). If one parameter is given, then it is a grey level.

nostroke()

Turn off outline drawing.

ellipsemode(z)

Set the mode for drawing ellipses. The default mode for drawing ellipses is referred to as CENTER mode, where the center of the ellipse is given. There are three others: RADIUS mode, in which the width and height parameters represent semi-major and semi-minor axes; CORNER mode in which the upper left corner is specified instead of the center; and CORNERS mode, in which the upper left and the lower right corner of the bounding box are specified.

rectmode(z)

Set the mode for drawing rectangles. The default mode for drawing ellipses is referred to as CENTER mode, in which x, y are the coordinates of the center; w and h are the width and height. In RADIUS mode x, y are the coordinates of the center; w and r are the horizontal and vertical distances to an edge. In CORNER mode x, y are the coordinates of the upper left corner; w and h are the width and the height. In CORNERS mode x, y are the coordinates of the upper left corner; w and h are the coordinates of the lower right corner.

ellipse(xpos, ypos, width, height)

Draw an ellipse. Also used for circles. Four modes as described in *ellipse-mode*.

line(x0, y0, x1, y1)

Draw a line using the current stroke color between screen coordinates (x0, y0) and (x1,y1).

point(x, y)

Draw a point (pixel) at location (**x,y**) in the current fill color.

rect(xpos, ypos, x2, y2)

Draw a rectangle. Same 4 modes as ellipse. Fill with the current fill color.

triangle (x0,y0, x1,y1, x2,y2)

Draw a triangle specified by three points.

bold()

Set font to bold.

italic()

Set font to *italic*.

normal()

Set the font weight and slant to *normal* (not bold) and *roman* (not italic).

setfont(s)

Set the font family to the name given in the string parameter **s**. Default is "Helvetica."

text(s, x, y)

Draw the text string s starting at screen coordinate (**x,y**).

quad (x0,y0, x1,y1, x2,y2, x3,y3)

Draw a quadrilateral having the four corners being (x0,y0), (x1,y1), (x2,y2) and (x3,y3).

strokeweight (n)

Set the thickness of drawn lines and strokes to **n** pixels.

arc (x0, y0, x1, y1, start, angle, s=ARC)

Draw an arc. An arc is defined as a portion of an ellipse from a starting angle for a specified number of degrees, as referenced from the center of the ellipse. The angle 0 degrees is horizontal and to the right; 90 degrees is upwards (decreasing Y value). The ellipse is defined by a bounding rectangle, specifying the upper left and lower right coordinates of a box that just holds the ellipse. The final parameter being ARC means to draw only the curve; if it is CHORD then it will draw the curve and a line joining the endpoints. PIESLICE draws the arc and lines from the endpoints of the arc to the center of the ellipse.

cvtColor (z)

Take the grey value z and return a color object that has red=z, green=z, and blue=z.

cvtColor3 (r,g,b)

Take the color component values r, g, and b (red, green, and blue) and return a color object having those values.

background(r,g=1000,b=1000)

Set the background color to the color given by components (r,g,b). This effectively clears the graphics window as well.

textsize(n)

Change the size of text to n pixels high.

14.2 IMAGES

loadImage(s)

Read the image from the file whose name is stored in the parameter s and return it as the value.

image(im, x, y)

Display the image im at window coordinate (x,y).

copyImage (x)

Return a copy of the image parameter x.

getpixel (im, i, j)

Return the color of the pixel at location (i,j) of the image im.

setpixel (im, i, j, c)

Set the pixel value (color) of the image **im** at coordinates **(i,j)** to the color **c**.

grey (c)

Return the grey level equivalent of the color c. It averages the three color components.

red (c)

Extract and return the red component of the color passed as **c**.

green (c)

Extract and return the green component of the color passed as **c**.

blue (c)

Extract and return the blue component of the color passed as **c**.

save (im, s)

Save the image im in a file named by the string s.

imageSize (s)

Acquire the size (width, height in pixels) of an image that exists as a file named **s**. Return a tuple with the (width,height). This can be executed outside of the startdraw–enddraw block so that **startdraw**() can open a window of a size appropriate to an image.

startdraw(xs=width, ys=height)

This indicates the beginning of a section of code within which drawing operations will be performed. It opens a window on the screen with a width of **xs** pixels and a height of **ys** pixels. It sets up a title on the window and does some initializations, such as setting up a font, setting drawing modes, and establishing a background color.

enddraw()

For users of *tkinter*, all this function does is to call **mainloop**(). For everyone else, this function must be called in order that control can be passed to the drawing functions and that the user's drawing can be displayed in the graphics window. It is the close to the block of code begun with the call to **startdraw**().

14.3 DYNAMIC GLIB

Symbolic names for special characters (LEFT, etc.) These are global variables that are used by the user.

```
K_BACKSPACE   = pygame.K_BACKSPACE
K_TAB         = pygame.K_TAB
K_CLEAR       = pygame.K_CLEAR
K_RETURN      = pygame.K_RETURN
K_PAUSE       = pygame.K_PAUSE
K_ESCAPE      = pygame.K_ESCAPE
K_SPACE       = pygame.K_SPACE
K_EXCLAIM     = pygame.K_EXCLAIM
K_QUOTEDBL    = pygame.K_QUOTEDBL
K_HASH        = pygame.K_HASH
K_DOLLAR      = pygame.K_DOLLAR
K_AMPERSAND   = pygame.K_AMPERSAND
K_QUOTE       = pygame.K_QUOTE
K_LEFTPAREN   = pygame.K_LEFTPAREN
K_RIGHTPAREN  = pygame.K_RIGHTPAREN
K_ASTERISK    = pygame.K_ASTERISK
K_PLUS        = pygame.K_PLUS
K_COMMA       = pygame.K_COMMA
K_MINUS       = pygame.K_MINUS
K_PERIOD      = pygame.K_PERIOD
K_SLASH       = pygame.K_SLASH
K_0           = pygame.K_0
K_1           = pygame.K_1
K_2           = pygame.K_2
K_3           = pygame.K_3
K_4           = pygame.K_4
```

```
K_5             = pygame.K_5
K_6             = pygame.K_6
K_7             = pygame.K_7
K_8             = pygame.K_8
K_9             = pygame.K_9
K_COLON         = pygame.K_COLON
K_SEMICOLON     = pygame.K_SEMICOLON
K_LESS          = pygame.K_LESS
K_EQUALS        = pygame.K_EQUALS
K_GREATER       = pygame.K_GREATER
K_QUESTION      = pygame.K_QUESTION
K_AT            = pygame.K_AT
K_LEFTBRACKET   = pygame.K_LEFTBRACKET
K_BACKSLASH     = pygame.K_BACKSLASH
K_RIGHTBRACKET  = pygame.K_RIGHTBRACKET
K_CARET         = pygame.K_CARET
K_UNDERSCORE    = pygame.K_UNDERSCORE
K_BACKQUOTE     = pygame.K_BACKQUOTE
#K_a            = pygame.K_a
K_b             = pygame.K_b
K_c             = pygame.K_c
K_d             = pygame.K_d
K_e             = pygame.K_e
K_f             = pygame.K_f
K_g             = pygame.K_g
K_h             = pygame.K_h
K_i             = pygame.K_i
K_j             = pygame.K_j
K_k             = pygame.K_k
K_l             = pygame.K_l
K_m             = pygame.K_m
K_n             = pygame.K_n
K_o             = pygame.K_o
K_p             = pygame.K_p
K_q             = pygame.K_q
K_r             = pygame.K_r
K_s             = pygame.K_s
K_t             = pygame.K_t
K_u             = pygame.K_u
K_v             = pygame.K_v
K_w             = pygame.K_w
K_x             = pygame.K_x
```

```
K_y            = pygame.K_y
K_z            = pygame.K_z
K_DELETE       = pygame.K_DELETE
K_KP0          = pygame.K_KP0
K_KP1          = pygame.K_KP1
K_KP2          = pygame.K_KP2
K_KP3          = pygame.K_KP3
K_KP4          = pygame.K_KP4
K_KP5          = pygame.K_KP5
K_KP6          = pygame.K_KP6
K_KP7          = pygame.K_KP7
K_KP8          = pygame.K_KP8
K_KP9          = pygame.K_KP9
K_KP_PERIOD    = pygame.K_KP_PERIOD
K_KP_DIVIDE    = pygame.K_KP_DIVIDE
K_KP_MULTIPLY  = pygame.K_KP_MULTIPLY
K_KP_MINUS     = pygame.K_KP_MINUS
K_KP_PLUS      = pygame.K_KP_PLUS
K_KP_ENTER     = pygame.K_KP_ENTER
K_KP_EQUALS    = pygame.K_KP_EQUALS
K_UP           = pygame.K_UP
K_DOWN         = pygame.K_DOWN
K_RIGHT        = pygame.K_RIGHT
K_LEFT         = pygame.K_LEFT
K_INSERT       = pygame.K_INSERT
K_HOME         = pygame.K_HOME
K_END          = pygame.K_END
K_PAGEUP       = pygame.K_PAGEUP
K_PAGEDOWN     = pygame.K_PAGEDOWN
K_F1           = pygame.K_F1
K_F2           = pygame.K_F2
K_F3           = pygame.K_F3
K_F4           = pygame.K_F4
K_F5           = pygame.K_F5
K_F6           = pygame.K_F6
K_F7           = pygame.K_F7
K_F8           = pygame.K_F8
K_F9           = pygame.K_F9
K_F10          = pygame.K_F10
K_F11          = pygame.K_F11
K_F12          = pygame.K_F12
K_F13          = pygame.K_F13
```

```
K_F14         = pygame.K_F14
K_F15         = pygame.K_F15
K_NUMLOCK     = pygame.K_NUMLOCK
K_CAPSLOCK    = pygame.K_CAPSLOCK
K_SCROLLOCK   = pygame.K_SCROLLOCK
K_RSHIFT      = pygame.K_RSHIFT
K_LSHIFT      = pygame.K_LSHIFT
K_RCTRL       = pygame.K_RCTRL
K_LCTRL       = pygame.K_LCTRL
K_RALT        = pygame.K_RALT
K_LALT        = pygame.K_LALT
K_RMETA       = pygame.K_RMETA
K_LMETA       = pygame.K_LMETA
K_LSUPER      = pygame.K_LSUPER
K_RSUPER      = pygame.K_RSUPER
K_MODE        = pygame.K_MODE
K_HELP        = pygame.K_HELP
K_PRINT       = pygame.K_PRINT
K_SYSREQ      = pygame.K_SYSREQ
K_BREAK       = pygame.K_BREAK
K_MENU        = pygame.K_MENU
K_POWER       = pygame.K_POWER
K_EURO        = pygame.K_EURO
K_A           = 65
K_B           = 66
K_C           = 67
K_D           = 68
K_E           = 69
K_F           = 70
K_G           = 71
K_H           = 72
K_I           = 73
K_J           = 74
K_K           = 75
K_L           = 76
K_M           = 77
K_N           = 78
K_O           = 79
K_P           = 80
K_Q           = 81
K_R           = 82
```

```
K_S          = 83
K_T          = 84
K_U          = 85
K_V          = 86
K_W          = 87
K_X          = 88
K_Y          = 89
K_Z          = 90
```

noloop()

Stop calling the draw function repeatedly. This has the effect of ceasing any dynamic activity.

```
def size (xs, ys):
    global width, height, canvas
    width = xs
    height = ys
    canvas = pygame.display.set_mode( (xs, ys),
    pygame.DOUBLEBUF, 32)    # Make the sketch window
    pygame.display.set_caption('Drawing')
```

14.4 VIDEO

loadVideo (s)

Loads a video from the file named by the string s and returns a reference to that video as a **Gvideo** class instance. This instance needs never be manipulated by the programmer, only passed to other functions.

playVideo (m)

Play the video represented by the variable m.

pauseVideo(m)

Pause (or unpause if paused) the video represented by the variable m.

stopVideo (m)

Stop playing the video represented by the variable m.

rewindVideo (m)

Place the video m back at the beginning frame.

isVideoPlaying (m)

Returns True if the video m is currently playing and False if not.

setVideoVolume(m, v)

Set the audio volume of the video m to a level between 0 (off) and 1 (maximum).

lengthVideo (m)

Return the length of the current video, in seconds.

whereVideo(m)

For the video m, return the number of seconds that the video has been playing (i.e., current position)

getVideoFrame(m)

Return the number of the current frame playing in the video m.

setVideoFrame(m, f)

Set the position of the video m so that the next frame to play will be number f.

getVideoPixel(m, x, y)

Return the pixel at location (x,y) in the video frame from m currently being displayed.

sizeVideo (m)

Return the size of a frame (width x height in pixels) of the video m.

locVideo (m, x, y, w, h)

Place the video m at position (x,y) on the graphics window, and give it size (w,h).

videoSize (s)

Return the size (width, height) of the video in the file s without loading it. For specifying the size of the graphics window.

14.5 AUDIO

loadSound (s)

Load a sound file where the file name is in string s. Return an object reference (handle) to that file.

playSound(a, loop=0)

Play the sound indicated by a.

def stopSound(a):

Stop playing the sound indicated by a.

volumeSound (a, v)

Set the volume of sound a to a value between 0 (off) and 1 (maximum).

durationSound (a)

Return the length of the sound s in seconds.

14.6 INTERACTION

mouse ()

Return the coordinates of the mouse cursor as a tuple (x,y).

14.7 OTHER

capture (s)

Save the image in the current graphics window as the image file s.

The Glib module contains two classes for internal use, an image class and a video class. They are described here only for completeness, but if you plan to use their internal code in any way please read it carefully from the source file and be certain that you understand it.

An image class:

```
class  Gimage:
    im = None      # Image
    pixels = None  # Pixels data
    w = h = 0
```

```
    def setIm (self, x):
    def get (self, x, y):
    def set (self, x, y, c):
    def save (self, s):
    def draw (self, canvas, x, y):
```

A video class:

```
class Gvideo:
    def __init__ (self, name):
    def loadVideo (self, s):
    def play(self):
    def locVideo (self, x, y, w, h):
    def draw (self):
    def copy (self, x, y, w, h):
    def stop (self):
    def rewind (self):
    def is_playing (self):
    def length (self):
    def where (self):
    def get_frame (self):
    def pause(self):
    def get_frame_number(self):
    def draw_frame(self, f, iplay=0):
    def get_pixel(self, x, y):
    def auto_play (self):
    def set_volume(self, v):
```

INDEX